Economic Development and Policy in India

UMA KAPILA, author/editor of several other books, has taught Indian Economy to undergraduate students for forty two years. She recently retired as Reader from the Department of Economics, Miranda House, University of Delhi. Presently, she is Senior Editor, Academic Foundation.

An Honours Graduate from Miranda House, University of Delhi and M.A. and Ph.D. from Delhi School of Economics, Dr. Uma Kapila has also served on the Planning Commission Study Group on "Agricultural Strategies in the Eastern Region of India for the Seventh Five Year Plan" (Perspective Planning Division).

Dr. (Mrs.) Uma Kapila is the author of the book *Oilseeds Economy of India* (1982) published by the Institute of Economic Growth. She is also the author of four other textbooks on Indian Economy, for B.A. Eco.(Hons.), B.Com.(Hons.) and for B.A.(Pass)/B.Com.(Pass). She has also co-edited along with Mr. Raj Kapila, a number of books on India's economy, banking and finance. Detailed information on these publications is readily available at the publisher's website: **www.academicfoundation.com**

Economic Development and Policy in India

Specially designed to serve the syllabus requirement of the new B.A. and B.Com (Programme) III year of the University of Delhi

UMA KAPILA

ACADEMIC FOUNDATION
NEW DELHI

Published by
ACADEMIC FOUNDATION
4772-73 / 23 Bharat Ram Road,
(23 Ansari Road), Darya Ganj,
New Delhi - 110 002. INDIA.

Phones : 23245001, 02, 03, 04.
Fax : 011-23245005
e-mail : books@academicfoundation.com
www.academicfoundation.com

Economic Development and Policy in India
by Uma Kapila

ISBN 81-7188-801-1 (Pb)

Typeset by Italics India, New Delhi.
Printed and bound in India.

New Syllabus

B.A. (P) Paper - III and B.Com. (P) Paper - XIV

Economic Development and Policy In India

(To Be offered in the 3rd Year)

(UNIVERSITY OF DELHI)

Duration: 3 hours *Max. Marks: 75*

Section A: Issues in Development and Planning with reference to India

1. Characteristics of underdeveloped countries with special reference to India.
2. Factors in development: Capital formation (physical and human), role of technology, sustainability, institutional factors.
3. Population and Economic Development, Demographic trends, urbanisation, occupational structure and population policy.
4. Employment (in the organised and unorganised sectors) and unemployment (open, under, disguised, rural, urban) in India. Employment generation schemes and their impact.
5. Issues in Indian Planning; Objectives and critical evaluation (Growth, self-reliance, employment generation, inequality reduction, poverty removal, modernisation and competitiveness, economic reforms). Saving and investment; mobilisation of internal and external finance, Centre-State financial relation.

Section B: Sectoral Aspects of the Indian Economy

1. **Agriculture**: Its importance in the Indian economy. Problems and solutions regarding low productivity, agricultural credit, agricultural labour, agricultural marketing, and agricultural pricing. The Green Revolution and its aftermath. Land reform, regional variations and choice of agrarian techniques.
2. **Industry**: Industrial Policy: pre- and post-1991. Relative roles of large and small scale. Public *vs.* private sector. The role and forms of foreign capital (foreign institutional capital, foreign direct investment).

3. **Foreign Trade**: Role and importance of foreign trade in India. The balance of trade and the balance of payments situation. India and the World Trade Organization (WTO).
4. **Prices**: Monetary and fiscal policies.

Readings:

1. M.A. Todaro, *Economic Development in the Third World*, Addison-Wesley. 6th edition Chs. 1-3.
2. Uma Kapila, *Indian Economy since Independence*, 16th edition. Academic Foundation (2004).
3. Arvind Virmani. *Accelerating Growth and Poverty Reduction: A Policy Framework for India's Development* (2004).
4. Government of India, *Economic Survey* (latest).
5. Government of India, *Five Year Plan* (latest).
6. Government of India, Finance Commission.

Note: 1. With regard to each topic listed, due emphasis should be laid on analysis and not mere description on the relevant problem.

2. Details of the relevant chapters of readings based on revised editions with selections from the current literature, will be prescribed before the course is taught.

CONTENTS

...Contd....

...Contd....

...Contd....

...Contd....

...Contd....

...Contd....

...Contd....

...Contd....

PART - II

Sectoral Analysis of Indian Economy

...Contd....

...Contd....

...Contd....

...Contd....

...Contd....

...*Contd....*

...Contd....

...Contd....

...Contd....

■.■.■.■.■

Preface

THE present book *Economic Development and Policy in India* is specially designed to meet the syllabus requirement of the restructured course on Indian economy for B.A. and B.Com (Pass) III year of the University of Delhi.

The book, in two sections, covers: (i) Issues in development and planning with reference to India and (ii) Sectoral aspects of the development of Indian economy *viz.* agriculture, industry, external sector and the important issue of prices, monetary and fiscal policies.

The book is based on the original readings recommended for the new course. An effort has been made to keep the language simple without compromising the effectiveness of the arguement or diluting the analysis.

The recent past has witnessed some disturbing developments in the global economy. The world economy is going through the worst kind of global recession often comparable with the recession of the 1930s. Almost every country around the world has been impacted by this crisis and so has been the Indian economy. We have attempted to cover the impact of global recession on various sectors of the Indian economy in the relevant chapters. Other new areas of concern like global warming and environmental issues, farmers' distress, and suicides and developments relating to WTO have also been duly covered.

In order to provide the students the latest on Indian economy with regard to development and policies, we have extensively referred to the *Eleventh Five Year Plan* documents, the latest *Economic Survey* 2008-09, the *RBI Reports* 2008-09 and also the *New Foreign Trade Policy* 2009-2014 announced on August 27, 2009.

In writing this book, I have drawn liberally from the writings of renowned economists in their specialised fields. I owe my deep sense of gratitude to them. I, therefore, take this opportunity to acknowledge my thanks and gratitude to C. Rangarajan, Jean Drèze, Amartya Sen, C.H. Hanumantha Rao, T.N. Srinivasan, S.D. Tendulkar, V.S. Vyas, K.L. Krishna, Kaushik Basu, S.K. Ray, Y.V. Reddy, Rakesh Mohan, Jagdish Bhagwati, Bimal Jalan, K. Sundaram, Pravin Visaria (late), Amaresh Bagchi, A. Vaidyanathan, Ashok Gulati, Nagesh Kumar and Arvind Virmani.

I sincerely hope, this book comes up to the expectations of the students and teachers. Suggestions for improvement are always welcome.

— *Uma Kapila*

September 2009.

PART - I

Issues in Development & Planning

Chapters :

Part-I

Trends in Development Planning

1

Economic Development, Under Development and Indian Economy

Introduction

THE world today presents a picture of sharp contrasts between developed/advanced and backward/underdeveloped/developing countries. At one extreme, there are countries like USA with per capita GNI of $ 45850 (2007) and on the other extreme are countries like Liberia with per capita GNI of $ 290.[1]

According to *World Development Report* (2009), around 16 per cent of world population lives in countries which are classified as high income developed countries like USA, Canada, Australia, countries of Western Europe, New Zealand and some of the Asian countries such as Japan, Singapore, Hong Kong. On the other hand, 84 per cent of the population lives in countries which are in the category of low income and middle income developing economies.

The Growth Report 2008[2] states that growth has accelerated in the global economy and in an even wider set of developing countries. The world population is projected to increase by 3 billion people by 2050. Unfortunately, 2 billion of this extra population will live in countries that are currently enjoying little or no growth. Thus, if these trends persist, the proportion of the world population living in low growth environments might increase.

---

1. The World Bank (2009). *World Development Report.*
2. Commission on Growth and Development (2008). *The Growth Report, Strategies for Sustained Growth and Inclusive Development.*

What Does Development Mean

The term *development* may mean different things to different people. In strictly economic terms, development has traditionally meant a sustained annual increase in GNP (or GDP) at rates varying from 5 per cent to 7 per cent or more.[3]

A common alternative economic index of development has been the rates of growth of per capita GNP i.e., the ability of a nation to expand its output at a rate faster than the growth of population. Thus, per capita GNP is equal to GNP divided by population. However, it is the real per capita GNP which measures the overall economic well-being of a population i.e., monetary growth of GNP per capita minus the rate of inflation. If the rate of growth of GNP per capita is, let us say, 4 per cent and the rate of inflation is say 5 or 6 per cent, there cannot be any improvement in the economic well-being of a population.

Economic Growth and Economic Development

Economic growth is a recent phenomenon in human history. It began with the industrial revolution in Britain at the end of the 18th century. This progress spread to Europe and North America in the 19th century, accelerating as it travelled. In the 20th century, particularly in the second half, it spread and accelerated again.

Till the 1960s, the term 'economic development' was often used as a synonym of economic growth, the measure for the latter being the rise in per capita GNP in real terms. According to C.P. Kindleberger,[4] "Whereas economic growth merely refers to a rise in output, economic development implies changes in technological and institutional organisation of production as well as distributive pattern of income." *Thus, economic development is a broader concept than economic growth.* Compared to the objective of development, economic growth may be easy to realise. By larger mobilisation of resources and raising their productivity, output levels can be raised. The process of development is far more extensive. Apart from the rise in output, it involves changes in the composition of output as well as a shift in the allocation of productive resources to ensure social justice.

In some of the underdeveloped countries, the process of economic growth has been accompanied by economic development. But this may

3. Todaro, Michael (2004). *Economic Development in the Third World* (8th edition), ch.1. Delhi: Pearson Education (Singapore) Pvt. Ltd.
4. Kindleberger, C.P. (1965). *Economic Development* (2nd edition), ch. 1.

not be the case always. *While there can be growth without development, development without growth is unconceivable*.

The *Growth Report* (2008) emphasises that growth is not an end in itself. It is, instead, a means to several ends that matter profoundly to individuals and societies. Growth is, above all, the surest way to free a society from poverty. Without it, a lack of material resources will tend to dominate everything else, narrowing people's horizons depriving them of the chance to fulfil their potential. Prosperity on the other hand, frees people to make choices, and allows a more equal distribution of opportunities.

Development as a Multi-dimensional Process

According to Todaro, "Development must, therefore, be conceived of as a multi-dimensional process involving major changes in social structures, popular attitudes and national institutions, as well as the acceleration of economic growth, the reduction of inequality and the eradication of absolute poverty. Development, in its essence, must represent the whole gamut of change by which an entire social system, tuned to the diverse basic needs and desires of individuals and social groups within that system, moves away from a condition of life widely perceived as unsatisfactory, towards a situation or condition of life as materially and spiritually better."

According to Goulet[5], at least three basic components as core values should serve as a conceptual basis and practical guidelines for understanding the "inner" meaning of development. These core values—sustenance, self-esteem and freedom—represent common goals sought by all individuals and societies. They relate to fundamental human needs that find their expression in almost all societies and cultures at all times.

Three Core Values of Development

Sustenance: The life-sustaining basic human needs include food, shelter, health and protection. When any one of these is absent or in critically short supply, a condition of absolute "underdevelopment" exists.

Self-esteem: A second universal component of good life is self esteem—a sense of worth and self-respect—of not being used as a tool by others for their own ends. Due to the significance attached to material values in developed nations, worthiness and esteem are now-a-days

5. Goulet, Denis (1971). *The Cruel Choice: A New Concept in the Theory of Development*. New York: Atheneum. pp. 87-94.

increasingly conferred only on countries that possess economic wealth and technological power—those that have developed.

Now-a-days, the Third World seeks development in order to gain the esteem which is denied to societies living in a state of disgraceful 'underdevelopment'. Development is legitimised as a goal because it is an important, perhaps even an indispensable, way of gaining esteem.[6]

Freedom from Servitude—To be Able to Choose: Arthur Lewis[7] stressed the relationship between economic growth and freedom from servitude when he concluded that "the advantage of economic growth is not that wealth increases happiness, but that it increases the range of human choice". Wealth can enable a person to gain greater control over nature and his physical environment than they would have if they remained poor. It also gives them the freedom to choose greater leisure. The concept of human freedom should encompass various components of political freedom, freedom of expression, political participation and equality of opportunity.

Development, Freedom and Opportunities

According to Drèze and Sen, "One way of seeing development is in terms of the expansion of the real freedoms that the citizens enjoy to pursue the objectives they have reason to value, and in this sense the expansion of human capability can be, broadly, seen as the central feature of the process of development."[8]

'Capability' refers to the alternative combinations of functionings from which a person can choose. Thus, the notion of capability is essentially one of freedom—the range of options a person has in deciding what kind of life to lead.

The expansion of human capabilities can clearly be enhanced by economic growth (even in the limited sense of growth of real income per head), but: (1) there are many influences other than economic growth that work in that direction, and (2) the impact of economic growth on human capabilities can be extremely variable, depending on the nature of that growth (for example, how equitable and employment-intensive it is, and whether the economic gains from growth are used to address the deprivations of the most needy).

---

6. Goulet *op.cit.*
7. Lewis, W. Arthur (1963). "Is Economic Growth Desirable?" in Allen and Unwin (eds.), *Theory of Economic Growth*. London. p. 420.
8. Drèze, Jean and Amartya Sen (2005). *India Development and Participation*, ch. 2. Delhi: Oxford University Press.

Human Development

The first *Human Development Report* (HDR) published by the United Nations Development Programme (UNDP) focused on the new paradigm of development that puts people at the centre of development. The concept, developed by Mahbub ul Haq and Amartya Sen, is defined as 'the process of enlarging people's choices'. Economic growth is considered only a means of capability expansion and not as an end in itself.

Such a paradigm of development enables all individuals to enlarge their human capabilities to the full and to put these capabilities to their best use in all fields—economic, social, cultural and political. It also protects the options of the unborn generations. It does not run-down the natural resource base needed for sustaining development in the future.

Human Development Index

The Human Development Index (HDI), used in the HDRs to compare countries in the world, has been designed as an alternative to per capita income, the single most commonly used measure to evaluate development outcomes thus far. The index includes three important choices:

(i) Longevity measured by life expectancy at birth.

(ii) Educational attainment as measured by adult literacy rate and gross enrolment ratio GER (primary, secondary and tertiary level combined).

(iii) Adjusted real GDP per capita—PPP stands for purchasing power parity. PPP GDP is calculated after eliminating price differences among countries.

Several crucial decisions were taken with respect to the HDI by Mahbub ul Haq and Amartya Sen, its principal architects. The first was that it should reflect human capabilities. Second, it should include only a limited number of variables to keep it 'simple and manageable'. Third, a composite index would be prepared rather than several separate indices. Fourth, the HDI would cover both social and economic aspects and finally, the coverage and methodology of the HDI would be kept flexible (Haq, 1995).

Three features of the HDI—its simplicity, universality and plurality—have contributed to the emergence of the HDI as a strong alternative evaluative measure of development outcomes.[9]

---

9. Prabhu, K. Seeta (2007). "Human Development Index", in Kaushik Basu (ed.) *Oxford Companion to Economics in India.*

The HDI value indicates how far a country has gone to attain certain defined goals: an average life span of 85 years, access to education for all and a decent standard of living. The maximum and minimum values for each variable, which are fixed, are reduced to scale between 0 and 1.

Countries are classified into three groups:

(1) High human development countries—Countries with HDI values of 0.800 and above.

(2) Medium human development countries—Countries with HDI values of 0.500 to 0.799.

(3) Low human development countries—Countries with HDI values below 0.500.

Sustainable Human Development

Sustainable human development addresses both inter-generational and intra-generational equity—enabling all generations, present and future to make the best use of their potential capabilities. In the final analysis, sustainable human development is *pro-people, pro-jobs and pro-nature*. It gives the highest priority to poverty reduction, productive employment, social integration and environmental regeneration. It accelerates economic growth and translates it into improvements in human lives, without destroying the natural capital needed to protect the opportunities of future generations.

The strongest argument for protecting the environment is the ethical need to guarantee the future generations opportunities similar to the ones previous generations have enjoyed. This guarantee is the foundation of 'Sustainable Development'.

The principal goal of development policy is to create sustainable improvements in the quality of life for all people. Sustainable development has many objectives. Insofar as raising per capita income improves people's living standards, it is one among many development objectives. The aim of lifting living standards encompasses a number of more specific goals, bettering people's health and educational opportunities, giving every one the chance to participate in public life, helping to ensure a clean environment, promoting inter-generational equity and much more.[10]

10. The World Bank (2000). *World Development Report 1999-2000*. p.13.

What Makes Development Unsustainable?

When increase in GNP is brought about through depletion of resources under unhealthy environmental conditions by the present generation, the future generations will be left with much depleted resource to produce output under polluted environmental conditions adversely affecting their health and efficiency. Under such circumstances, the rate of economic development in future is bound to fall. Thus, when we are producing more at the cost of future generations the present level of development is not sustainable i.e., we will not be able to maintain it in future.

Sustainable Development and Environmental Accounting

Environmentalists have used the term 'sustainability' in an attempt to clarify the desired balance between economic growth on the one hand and environmental preservation on the other. Although there are many definitions, basically sustainability refers to "meeting the needs of the present generation without compromising the needs of future generations." For economists, a development path is sustainable if the stock of overall capital assets remains constant or rises over time. Implicit in these statements is the fact that future growth and overall quality of life are critically dependent on the quality of the environment. The natural resource base of a country and the quality of its air, water and land represents a common heritage for all generations. To destroy that endowment indiscriminately in the pursuit of short-term economic goals penalises both present and especially, future generations. It is therefore important that development policy makers incorporate some form of environmental accounting into their decisions.

In light of rising consumption levels worldwide combined with high rates of population growth, the realisation of sustainable development will be a major challenge. From present information concerning rapid destruction of many of the world's resources, it is clear that meeting the needs of a world population that is projected to grow by an additional 3 billion in the next 50 years will require radical and early changes in consumption and production patterns (Todaro, 2004).

Population, Resources and the Environment

Rapidly growing populations have led to land, water and fuelwood shortages in rural areas and to urban health crises resulting from lack of sanitation and clean water. In many of the poorest regions of the globe, it is clear that increasing population density has contributed to severe and accelerating degradation of the very resources that these growing populations depend on for survival.

To meet expanding LDC needs, environmental devastation must be halted and the productivity of existing resources stretched further so as to benefit more people.

Poverty and the Environment

It is true that environmental destruction and high fertility go hand in hand, they are both the direct outcome of a third factor i.e., absolute poverty. For environmental policies to succeed in developing countries, they must first address the issues of landlessness, poverty and lack of access to institutional resources. Insecure land tenure rights, lack of credit and inputs, and absence of information often prevent the poor from making resource-augmenting investments that would help preserve the environmental assets from which they derive their livelihood. Hence, preventing environmental degradation is more often a matter of providing institutional support to the poor than fighting an inevitable process of decay.

Growth *versus* the Environment

Evidence indicates that the worst perpetrators of environmental destruction are the billion richest and billion poorest people on earth. It has even been suggested that the bottom billion are more destructive than all four billion people in between. It follows that increasing the economic status of the poorest group would provide an environmental windfall.

Rural Development and the Environment

To meet the expanded food needs of rapidly growing LDC populations, it is estimated that food production in developing countries will have to double by 2010. Because land in many areas of the developing world is being unsustainably over-exploited by existing populations, meeting these output targets will require radical changes in the distribution, use and quantity of resources available to the agricultural sector. And because women are frequently the caretakers of rural resources such as forests and water supplies and provide much of the agricultural supply of labour, it is of primary importance that they be integrated into environmental programmes. In addition, poverty alleviation efforts must target women's economic status in particular in order to reduce their dependence on unsustainable methods of production.

Urban Development and the Environment

Congestion, vehicular and industrial emissions, and poorly ventilated household stoves also inflate the tremendously high environmental costs of urban crowding. Research reveals that the urban environment appears to worsen at a faster rate than urban population size increases, so that the marginal environmental cost of additional residents rises over time.[11]

Global Warming and Climate Changing

As total world population grows and incomes rise, net global environmental degradation is likely to worsen. We know that the world is warming and that the average global temperature has increased by around 0.7°C (1.3°F) since the advent of the industrial era. We know also that the trend is accelerating: average global mean temperature is rising at 0.2°C every decade. With the global rise in temperature, local rainfall patterns are changing, ecological zones are shifting, the seas are warming and ice caps are melting. Small-scale farmers have to cope with losses caused by more intense storms, floods and sea surges.

Climate change will be one of the defining forces shaping prospects for human development during the 21st century. Through its impact on ecology, rainfall, temperature and weather systems, global warming will directly affect all countries. Nobody will be immune to its consequences. However, some countries and people are more vulnerable than others. In the long term, the whole of humanity faces risks but more immediately, the risks and vulnerabilities are skewed towards the world's poorest people.[12]

Rich nations must show leadership and acknowledge their historic responsibility. Their citizens leave the biggest carbon footprint in the earth's atmosphere. Moreover, they have the financial and technological capabilities needed to make deep and early cuts in carbon emissions. None of this means that mitigation has to be left to the rich world. Indeed, one of the most urgent priorities is international cooperation on technology transfer to enable developing countries to make the transition to low-carbon energy systems.

There are even fears that what can be prevented now may become close to irreversible if no preventive action is taken without delay, no matter how much the future generations might be ready to spend to

11. See World Resources Institute (1996). *World Resources, 1996-97: The Urban Environment.* New York: Oxford University Press.
12. UNDP (2008). *Human Development Report 2007-08* (ch. 1).

reverse the catastrophe. Some of these predicaments may be particularly damaging for the developing world (for example, the submerging of parts of Bangladesh or the whole of the Maldives due to rising sea levels).

The Indian Case

The record of economic and social development in India since Independence, though highly uneven and far from exemplary, includes substantial overall progress in many fields. The same period, however, has also been one of formidable environmental plunder—deforestation, falling groundwater tables, polluted rivers and ponds as well as polluted air that we breathe.

In view of these contrary trends, there has been a temptation in public discussions to think of 'development' and 'environment' in antagonistic terms. Many of these deteriorating environmental trends are clearly linked with heightened economic activity, e.g., industrial growth, increased energy consumption, more intensive irrigation, commercial felling of trees and other such activities that tend to be linked with economic expansion. 'Development' is, thus, held responsible, for the damage. On the other side, environmental activists are often accused of being 'anti-development', since the advocates of accelerated growth often see environmentalists as being unwelcoming (if not obstructive) of economic progress for fear of its adverse environmental impact. Drèze and Sen do not agree with the confrontational view, which places development and environment on a collisional path. According to them, many human freedoms and components of the quality of life are dependent on the integrity of the environment (involving the air we breathe, the water we drink, the epidemiological surroundings in which we live and so on), development cannot but be sensitive to the quality of the environment. The opportunity to live the kind of lives that people value—and have reason to value—depends *inter alia* on the nature and robustness of the environment. In this sense, development has to be environment-inclusive.

How to Protect Environment

While human activities that accompany the process of development may have destructive consequences, it is also within human power to enhance and improve the environment in which we live. For example, greater female education and women's employment can help to reduce population growth and the pressure on environmental resources. Similarly, the spread of school education and improvements in its quality can make us more environment-conscious. Better communication and a richer media can also make us more aware of the need for environment-oriented thinking. It is easy to find many other examples of such interconnections. In general, seeing development in terms of increasing the effective freedom of human beings brings the constructive agency of people in environment-friendly activities directly within the domain of developmental achievements. Development is empowering and that power can be used to preserve and enrich the environment.

The assessment of development should be inclusive of environmental concerns. We must also take note of the various ways in which the process of development may influence the nature of the environment and the values that are invoked in assessing it. This recognition does not, in any way, change the basic fact that the process of economic development can also have very destructive environmental consequences, sometimes even swamping the constructive perspective. But it is important to see the relationship between development and the environment in an adequately broad way, taking note of the constructive prospects as well as destructive possibilities.

Consequences of Environmental Plunder

What, then, are the main reasons for being concerned about environmental degradation in India and its relation with current patterns of development? Are there real reasons for disquiet? There, certainly, are overwhelming reasons for this concern.

First, environmental degradation has compromised or 'undone' many of the improvements that were otherwise made possible by greater economic prosperity. For instance, it is arguable that, due to rising congestion and pollution, the quality of life in some of India's larger cities is lower today than it was 20 years ago, in spite of a large increase in per capita incomes. In rural areas, too, environmental degradation had often considerably diluted if not defeated the gains of economic development. In districts such as Kalahandi in Orissa, for instance, the collapse of the environmental base—especially forests—has undermined people's traditional livelihoods and forced a large proportion of the workforce into seasonal or permanent migration (Drèze, 2001). While Kalahandi occasionally makes headlines for extreme cases of starvation (if not 'famine'), there is a much larger story behind the headlines, in which environmental degradation plays a major role as a causal antecedent of chronic hunger and deprivation (Drèze and Sen, 2005).

Second, the present trends of environmental decline are not only intolerable already, they are also incompatible with the basic requirements of sustainable development. To illustrate, air pollution levels in Delhi are already much above WHO standards, yet the number of motorised vehicles—which account for the bulk of the problem—continues to grow at more than 10 per cent per year. Clearly, something needs to be done, and has to be done soon, given the cumulative effects of this growth. Similarly, present trends of rapid decline of groundwater tables in large parts of the country are utterly unsustainable and call for urgent attention.

Third, in many cases environmental plunder is an infringement of distributive justice and the basic rights of the underprivileged. In urban areas, for instance, a minority of car owners cause massive pollution, congestion, noise, tension and accidents—all at the expense of the public at large. The people whose lives are impoverished and shattered in this way are often among the poorest in the society, from street vendors to pavement dwellers.

The distributive aspects of environmental plunder have a gender dimension, too. The well-being and freedom of many rural Indian women depend vitally on environmental resources, including convenient access to water, fodder and fuel, and this connection is often far closer than those that link men to these environmental resources. As a result, women frequently suffer disproportionately from environmental degradation.

Public Policy

Protection of the environment has to be a central part of any sustainable inclusive growth strategy. This aspect of development is especially important in the Eleventh Plan when consciousness of the dangers of environmental degradation has increased greatly. Population growth, urbanisation and energy-intensive technologies have resulted in injecting a heavy load of pollutants into the environment. More recently, the issue assumed special importance because of the accumulation of evidence of global warming and the associated climate change that it is likely to bring (Eleventh Plan).[13]

State intervention to halt environmental degradation in India has been so far rather weak in comparison with the magnitude of the problem. In fact, not only has public policy tolerated environmental plunder for a long time, it has even, in many cases, actively encouraged it. Government projects (from dams and mines to firing ranges and nuclear tests) are themselves a major cause of environmental damage. Public policy has often subsidised or otherwise encouraged the

13. Planning Commission (2008). *Eleventh Five Year Plan 2007-2012*, ch. 9, Government of India, Vol. 1.

destruction of the environment by private parties. For instance, the depletion of groundwater resources (especially by large farmers) has been accelerated by electricity subsidies, sugarcane subsidies and plentiful credit for energised water extraction devices.

Environmental irresponsibility in public policy has both political and ideological roots. To start with, environmental irresponsibility frequently draws on the often-repeated prejudice that a little bit of environmental vandalism is the price one has to pay for economic development, at least in its early stages. Some have even argued that environmental protection is a 'bourgeois' or 'western' concern, best addressed after economic prosperity has been achieved. This carries with it the suggestion that meanwhile, environmental degradation should be tolerated.

Public policy in India has tended to be heavily influenced by powerful lobbies that thrive on the private appropriation of environmental resources: mining companies, timber contractors, sugarcane mills, car manufacturers, the plastic industry, to name a few. Sugarcane subsidies, for instance, have far more to do with the political influence of large farmers and mill owners than with the merits of the case. Similarly, public regulation of the 'polybag' has been fiercely opposed by the plastic industry.

Against this background of irresponsibility and apathy, environmental activists have tended to seek help from the judiciary. The nineties have seen an unprecedented wave of 'public interest litigations' on environmental matters. In some cases (e.g., relating to pollution in Delhi), judgements favourable to the environmental cause have been obtained. 'Judicial activism', however, has important limitations as a means of environmental protection.

Judicial activism has played a fruitful role in generating public awareness of, and media interest in, environmental problems, and in giving some strength (indeed a much needed strength) to environmental pressure groups. However, judicial activism on its own is not an adequate and sustainable basis for environmental protection. A more comprehensive approach is needed, which must also incorporate other ways of giving environmental problems the attention they deserve.

We still have a long way to go, but environmental activism has gained some considerable ground in India today, and shows promise of advancing more.

An important feature of any environmental strategy is that environmental objectives require action in several areas, which typically lie in the purview of different ministries. The Ministry of Environment and Forests (MoEF) has the important role of monitoring the development process and its environmental impact in a perspective of sustainable development and to devise suitable regulatory structures to achieve the desired results. While this role is crucial, environmental objectives can only be achieved if environmental concerns are internalised in policymaking in a large number of sectors. This would require sharing of responsibility at all levels of government and across sectors with respect to monitoring of pollution, enforcement of regulations, and development of programmes for mitigation and abatement. Regulatory enforcement must also be combined with incentives, including market and fiscal mechanisms to encourage both industry and people in their day-to-day working lives to act in a manner responsive to environmental concerns. Sustainable use of natural resources also requires community participation with a responsible role assigned to the communities for conservation. (Eleventh Plan)

India is a party to the United Nations Framework Convention on Climate Change (UNFCCC) and its Kyoto Protocol. The Protocol provides for three mechanisms that enable the developed countries with quantified emission limitation and reduction commitments to acquire greenhouse gas reduction credits from activities outside their own boundaries at relatively lesser costs. These are Joint Implementation, Clean Development Mechanism (CDM) and Emission Trading. Only CDM is applicable to developing countries like India. Under the Clean Development Mechanism, a developed country would take up greenhouse gas reduction project activities in a developing country where the costs of greenhouse gas reduction project activities are usually much lower.

Underdevelopment: Meaning and Characteristics

The term *underdevelopment* is relative. UN experts have defined an underdeveloped country as one having real per capita income lower than per capita real income of the USA, Canada, Australia and Western Europe.[14] The World Bank in its *World Development Report*[15] (2009) classified the various countries on the basis of per capita gross national income (GNI).

14. United Nations (1951). *Measures of Economic Development of Underdeveloped Countries*. p. 3.
15. *World Development Report*, 2009.

(i) Low income countries with GNI per capita $ 578 or less (PPP GNI per capita $ 1,494 or less).

(ii) Middle income with per capita GNI $ 2872 (PPP GNI per capita $ 5952). Within middle income, there are lower middle income and upper middle income countries.

Lower-middle income countries with per capita GNI $ 1,887 (PPP per capita $ 4,543).

Upper middle income countries with GNI per capita $ 6,987 (PPP per capita $ 11,868).

(iii) High income countries with per capita GNI of $ 37,566 or more (PPP per capita $ 36,100 or more).

According to data given in the *World Development Report 2009*, in 2007, low income countries accounted for about 19.6 per cent of the world population but contribtued only 2.9 per cent to total world PPP GNI. The middle income countries constituted 64.4 per cent of world population but accounted for about 39 per cent of world PPP GNI. These two groups, popularly described as developing economies or underdeveloped econmies, comprise 84 per cent of the world population but account for about 42 per cent of world PPP GNI. Most countries of Asia, Africa, Latin America and some countries of Europe are included in them.

The high income economies, comprising 15.9 per cent of world population, contribute 58 per cent to world PPP GNI.

TABLE – 1.1

DISTRIBUTION OF WORLD POPULATION AND WORLD GNI AMONG VARIOUS GROUPS OF COUNTRIES (2007)

	Population 2007	*GNI 2007 (Billion $) PPP*	*GNI 2007 (per capita) $ PPP*	*Average Annual Growth of Population (2000-2007)*
World	6612	65144	9852	1.2
Low Income Countries	1296	1935	1494	2.2
Middle Income Countries	4260	25354	5952	1.0
Low and Middle Income Combined	5556	27284	4911	1.3
High Income Countries	1056	38134	36100	0.7
India	**1123**	**3078**	**2740**	**1.4**

Source: World Development Report, 2009.

One may make the following observation with regard to this UN classifications of developed and underdeveloped/developing countries on the basis of per capita income. There is gross inequality of income between the rich and the poor countries and this gap is widening over the years. All high income countries are not necessarily developed countries as Joan Robinson remarked, "For several of the Arab States, GNP per capita suddenly jumped to levels which exceeded that of the richest western states yet in these countries are found some of the poorest and least developed communities in the world."

As modern development economics defined development as a process involving elimination of poverty, income enequality and unemployment, underdevelopment in this framework would be a situation characterised by the worst kind of depreivation. Michael Todaro while defining underdevelopment in terms of poverty, states that, "Underdeveloment is a real fact of life for over two billion people of the world."[16]

A different approach to underdevelopment is provided by Jacob Viner. Accoding to Viner, development potential of a country is a much better criterion to judge the extent of its underdevelopment. He defined an underdeveloped country as the one "which has good ptoential for using more capital or more labour or more available natural resources or all of these, to support its population on a higher level of living." The definition of an underdeveloped country given by the Indian Planning Commission in its Five Year Plan is similar to the one given by Jacob Viner. "An underdeveloped country's economy is characterised by the existence, in greater or lesser degree, of unutilised or underutilised manpower on the one hand and of unexploited natural resources on the other. This state of affairs may be due to stagnancy of techniques or to certain inhibiting socio-economic factors which prevent the more dynamic forces in an economy from asserting themselves."[17]

Common Characteristics of Underdeveloped Countries

The underdeveloped or the developing countries, as these are popularly known, inspite of their diverse structure, have some common characteristics. Todaro classifies these common characteristics into six broad categories:[18]

16. Todaro, P. Michael (1983). *Economic Development of the Third World*, Second edition. New York: Longman.
17. Government of India, Planning Commission (1952). The First Five Year Plan, Ch. 1, p. 7, New Delhi.
18. Todaro, P. Michael (2004), *op cit*.

1. Low levels of living.
2. Low levels of productivity.
3. High rates of population growth and dependency burden.
4. High and rising level of unemployment and underemployment.
5. Significant dependence on agricultural production and primary products exports.
6. Dominance, dependence and vulnerability in international relations.

1. Low Levels of Living

In developing nations, general levels of living tend to be low for the vast majority of people. These low levels of living are manifested in the form of low incomes (poverty), inadequate housing, poor health, limited or low education, high infant mortality and low life expectancy.

The GNP per capita is often used as a summary index of the relative economic well-being of people in different nations. On account of low per capita income, population suffers from poor health, low education, high infant mortality and low life expectancy.

TABLE – 1.2

INDIA'S GLOBAL POSITION ON HUMAN DEVELOPMENT 2006

Country	*HDI Index*	*GDP Per Capita (US $PPP)*	*Life Expectancy at Birth (yrs.)*	*Adult Literacy Rate (% aged 15 yrs. & above)*	*Combined Gross Enrol. Ratio in Education (%)*
China	0.762(94)	4,682(104)	72.7(71)	93.0(81)	68.7(113)
India	0.609(132)	2,489(126)	64.1(127)	65.2(148)	61.0(134)

Source: Government of India, *Economic Survey 2008-09.*

In India, at the time of Independence, the life expectancy at birth was 32 and literacy was only 17 per cent. Poverty ratio i.e., percentage of population below poverty line was above 50 per cent. As a result of planned economic development during the last six decades, expectation of life has improved to 63 years in 2006 while the average for middle income countries is 67. Literacy rate has improved to 61 per cent against the average of 90 in middle income countries and 61 in low income countries. Poverty ratio has also declined considerably from more than 50 per cent to under 20 per cent but the total number of poor is still very high—220 million (10th Plan). Inspite of significant improvement in various human development indicators, India's rank is still low in several of these indicators.

2. Low Levels of Productivity

Throughout the developing world, levels of labour productivity are extremely low compared with those in developed countries. Low level of living and low productivity are self-reinforcing social and economic phenomenon in Third World countries and as such, are the principal manifestation of, and contributors to, their development. Myrdal's well known theory of "circular and cumulative causation" in underdeveloped countries is based on the interaction between low living levels and low productivity.

Low productivity is due to low level of technology. The sharp differences in productivity between developed and underdeveloped nations can be traced to the level of technology in these countries. Productivity level in Indian economy has been low on account of backward or poor technology and this applies to all sectors of the economy—whether it is agriculture, industry or the tertiary sector.

A comparison of productivity levels in Indian agriculture with the levels in other countries shows how low the productivity in Indian agriculture is. Productivity of wheat in India is about 35 per cent of the productivity in France. It is 66 per cent (i.e., less than two-thirds) of the productivity in comparison to another developing country, China. As far as rice is concerned, productivity in India is 46 per cent of the productivity in China and Japan (i.e., less than half). The productivity of cotton in India is one-third of the productivity in China. Even in comparison to Pakistan, productivity of cotton in India is just 61 per cent. As far as groundnut is concerned, productivity in India is 34 per cent of the productivity in USA, 40 per cent of the productivity in China and 51 per cent of the productivity in Argentina. Similar conclusions hold for most of the other crops.[19] The low levels of productivity in Indian agriculture point to the possibilities of increasing productivity by adopting appropriate strategies and policies.

International comparisons reveal a wide gulf in India's performance between achievements in output and productivity. While India compares favourably in terms of total output, it compares poorly in terms of yield per hectare (See Ch. 10).

19. Tata Services Ltd., *Statistical Outline of India*, 1998-99 .

3. High Rate of Population Growth and Dependency Burden

Fast growing population in the Third World is both a cause and effect of underdevelopment. These countries have effectively brought down the mortality rates but birth rates continue to be high due to wide spread poverty, ignorance and social and religious factors. Due to high birth rate, the dependency burden is about half of the population as against one-fourth in developed countries. The active labour force has to support almost twice as many children as it does in richer countries. Population has been growing in Third World countries in the range of 2 to 3.5 per cent per annum as compared to less than 1 per cent in developed countries. In India, for instance, the rate of growth of population increased from 1.25 per cent per annum in 1951 to 2.5 per cent in 1981. It started declining only thereafter and 1991 census recorded a growth rate of 2 per cent with children under the age 15 forming 38 per cent of the total population. Average annual growth rate during 2000-2007 has been estimated at 1.4 per cent as compared to 0.7 per cent for high income countries, 1.0 per cent for middle income and 2.2 per cent for low income countries (WDR, 2009).

4. High and Rising Levels of Unemployment and Underemployment

One of the principal manifestations of and factors contributing to the low level of living in developing nations is their relatively inadequate and inefficient utilisation of labour in comparison with the developed nations. Current rates of open unemployment in Third World average from 10 to 15 per cent and when the underemployed are added to the openly unemployed, almost 30 per cent of the combined urban and rural labour force in Third World nations is under-utilised.[20]

With *low developed countries'* population growing rapidly, their labour force will also be accelerating for some time to come. This means that jobs will have to be created at equivalent rates simply to keep pace with the growth of labour supply.

Thus, the need for providing work opportunities for the growing labour force and also to reduce the base level of unemployment significantly, assumes great importance so as to avoid the social tensions that arise from growing unemployment and underemployment.

---

20 Todaro, P. Michael (2004). *op cit.*

5. Substantial Dependence on Agricultural Production and Primary Product Exports

The vast majority of people in Third World nations live and work in rural area. Almost 80 per cent are rurally based compared with less than 35 per cent in economically developed countries. The proportion of labour force engaged in agriculture in less developed countries is 66 per cent compared with 21 per cent for developed nations. Moreover, agriculture contributes about 32 per cent to the GNP of the former while it accounts for only 8 per cent of GNP of the latter.

The basic reason for the concentration of people and production in agricultural and other primary production activities in developing countries is the simple fact that for the low income levels, the first priority is for food, clothing and shelter. Agricultural productivity is low not only because of the large number of people in relation to available land but also because in *lower development countries* agriculture is often characterised by primitive technologies, poor organisation and limited physical and human capital inputs.

In India, the predominance of the primary sector is reflected in the contribution of this sector to GDP and employment in the economy. In 1951, the contribution of primary sector to India's GDP was 57 per cent and to employment 73 per cent. Even today, primary sector provides employment to about 60 per cent of the workforce and its contribution to GDP is less than 20 per cent as compared with 3 per cent of workforce engaged in primary sector in the UK and 4 per cent in USA contributing about 2 per cent to their GDP. Indian economy is in transition from underdevelopment to a developing economy.

6. Dominance, Dependence and Vulnerability in International Relations

For many less developed countries, a significant factor contributing to the persistence of low levels of living, rising unemployment and growing income inequality is the highly unequal distribution of economic and political power between poor and rich nations. These unequal strengths are manifested not only in the dominant power of rich nations to control the pattern of international trade but also in their ability often to dictate the terms in which technology, foreign aid and private capital are transferred to developing countries.

Examples include the transfer of often inappropriate educational structures, curricular and school systems; the formation of Western-style trade unions; the organisation and orientation of health services also following the Western model; and finally, the structure and operation of public, bureaucratic and administrative system that also may be inconsistent with the priority needs and the available manpower supplies in developing nations. Of even greater potential significance may be the influence of rich-country's social and economic standards on developing-country salary scales, elite lifestyles and general attitudes towards the private accumulation of wealth. Such attitudes can often breed corruption and economic plunder by a privileged minority.

The net effect of all these factors is to create a situation of 'vulnerability' among Third World nations in which forces largely outside their control can have decisive and dominating influences on their overall economic and social well-being.

According to Michael Todaro, the phenomenon of underdevelopment needs to be viewed in a national and an international context. Economic and social forces, both internal and external, are responsible for the poverty, inequality and low productivity that commonly characterise most Third World nations. The successful pursuit of economic and social development will require not only the formulation of appropriate strategies within the Third World but also a modification of the present international economic order to make it more responsive to the development needs of poor nations.

Nature of Indian Economy

Indian economy is in transition from underdeveloped to a developing economy since 1951 when India embarked on a programme of planned economic development of the country.

Indian economy certainly had all the characteristics of an underdeveloped economy at the time of Independence but the planned economic development during the last six decades has definitely brought Indian economy in the category of developing economies, coming closer to middle income category countries. Indeed, in terms of growth, India performed much better than the industrialised countries which experienced a slowdown in growth, the transition economies which did badly, and much of the developing world. And it was only east Asia, particulary China, which performed better (See Appendix A1.1).

India has been widely heralded as a success story for globalisation. Over the past two decades, the country has moved into the premier league of world economic growth; high-technology exports are booming and India's emerging middle-class consumers have become a magnet for foreign investors.

Why has accelerated income growth not moved India onto a faster poverty reduction path? Extreme poverty is concentrated in rural areas of the northern poverty-belt states, including Bihar, Madhya Pradesh, Uttar Pradesh and West Bengal, while income growth has been most dynamic in other states, urban areas and the service sectors. While rural poverty has fallen rapidly in some states, such as Gujarat and Tamil Nadu, less progress has been achieved in the northern states. At the national level, rural unemployment is rising, agricultural output is increasing at less than 2 per cent a year, agricultural wages are stagnating and growth is virtually 'jobless'.

The deeper problem facing India is its human development legacy. In particular, pervasive gender inequalities, rural poverty and inequalities between states, is undermining the potential for converting growth into human development.

Perhaps the starkest gender inequality is revealed by this simple fact: girls aged 1-5 are 50 per cent more likely to die than boys. This fact translates into 130,000 'missing' girls. Female mortality rates remain higher than male mortality rates through age 30, reversing the typical demographic pattern. These gender differences reflect a widespread preference for sons, particularly in northern states. Girls, less valued than their brothers, are often brought to health facilities in more advanced stages of illness, taken to less qualified doctors and have less money spent on their health care. The low status and educational disadvantage suffered by women have a direct bearing on their health and their children's. About one-third of India's children are underweight at birth, reflecting poor maternal health.

Translating economic success into human development advances will require public policies aimed explicitly at broadening the distribution of benefits from growth and global integration, increased public investment in rural areas and services and—above all—political leadership to end poor governance and address the underlying causes of gender inequality.

With the objective of inclusive growth taking centre stage, the Government has strengthened its efforts for social sector development in recent years. Expenditures of the Government of India on social services and rural development have more than doubled over the last four years. Impressive outlays on education, health, water supply and housing indicate the emphasis which Government places on these sectors. These expenditures have supplemented sustained high level of economic growth in achieving better social sector performance and improvement in the quality of life. Several initiatives have been launched, especially for the poor. Programmes like the National Rural Employment Guarantee Scheme, Pradhan Mantri Gram Sadak Yojana, Aam Aadmi Bima Yojana and Rashtriya Swasthya Bima Yojana, can go a long way in improving the living conditions of the common man in the remotest part of the country. Proper implementation of these programmes is essential. Consequently, the role of states and district administrations responsible for the implementation of the welfare schemes is vital.

Along with higher economic growth and poverty reduction, there has been an improvement in many important social indicators like life expectancy, infant mortality rate and gross enrolment ratios at primary level of education. However, disparities continue at the state and regional level. The Eleventh Five Year Plan also aims at reducing poverty and the disparities across regions and communities.

Questions

1. (a) What is sustainable development?

   (b) What are the causes of environmental problem?

   (c) Discuss the role of environmental protection in sustainable development. *[B.A. (P) 2009]*

2. Distinguish between a 'developing' and a 'developed' economy. Is India a developing economy? *[B.A. (P) 2003, 2004, 2008]*

3. Examine the salient features of the Indian economy in the post 2000 period. Compare it with the Indian economy on the eve of Independence. *[B.Com. (P) 2006]*

4. Distinguish between a 'developing' and a 'developed' economy. Examine the salient features of India as a developing economy. *[B.Com. (P), 2001: B.A. (P) 2006]*

5. What are the salient features of an underdeveloped economy? How far are these features present in the Indian economy? *[B.A. (P) 2004; B.Com. (P) 2004]*

6. Distinguish between developed and underdeveloped economies. Why do some economies grow faster than others? *[B.A. (P) 2004]*

7. Examine the salient characteristics of a 'Developing Economy'. Would you consider India as a developing economy? *[B.A. (P) 2003]*

APPENDIX – A1.1

INDIAN ECONOMY: SOME COMPARATIVE BASIC FACTS

HDI Index *Rank*		*Population Million 2007*	*Average Annual % Growth 2000-2007*	*PPP GNI $ Per Capita 2007*	*GDP Per Capita % Growth 2006-07*	*Life Expectancy at Birth (yrs.)* *Male 2006*	*Female 2006*	*Adult Literacy Rate % Ages 15 and Above 2005*
609 (132)	**India**	**1123**	**1.4**	**2740**	**7.7**	**63**	**66**	**61**
762 (94)	China	1320	0.6	5370	11.2	70	74	91
Low HDI (Below 0.500)	Low Income Countries	1296	2.2	1494	4.3	56	58	61
Middle HDI (0.500-0.799)	Middle Income Countries	4260	1.0	5952	6.9	67	71	90
High HDI (0.800 and above)	High Income Countries	1056	0.7	36100	2.0	76	82	99
	World	6612	1.2	9852	2.6	66	70	82

Source: World Development Report, 2009.

2

Factors in Development

Introduction

ECONOMIC development implies a process of securing higher levels of productivity in all the sectors of the economy which in turn is a function of the level of investment and the level of technology. For raising the level of technology, the economy has to have more and more of capital formation. But it must be emphasised that capital though necessary, is not a sufficient condition for economic development which depends on such non-economic factors as social attitudes, political conditions and natural endowments.

Economic Factors

Among economic factors, the major factors which determine the levels and tempo of development in an economy are natural resources, capital formation, technical progress, entrepreneurship and population growth.

(1) Natural Resources: Abundance of natural resources provide a base for rapid economic development. However, it does not mean that countries having natural resources in abundance are among the developed nations. While on the one hand we have examples of developed countries like USA, Canada, Australia, New Zealand having abundance of natural resources, on the other hand, we also have examples of many countries in South America and Africa having abundant natural resources and yet remaining underdeveloped countries. In these countries, rich natural resources have not been fully exploited due to absence of other necessary factors such as adequate supply of capital and technology.

It may also be pointed out that inadequate domestic availability of natural resources does not necessarily mean that a country would remain underdeveloped. Japan has made rapid progress by overcoming the lower availability of natural products by synthetic substitutes. While synthetic substitutes help in overcoming to some extent the shortage of natural resources, they cannot facilitate the development to the same extent as the abundant availability of natural resources. In India, the efforts towards expanding irrigation and power generation through multipurpose projects and dams is a good example of proper utilisation of existing resources while exploration for oil under land and under sea is an effort to discover new resources.

(2) Capital Formation: Economic development consists of the introduction of new combinations of factors of production which tend to increase the productivity of labour. Improvement in productivity in turn requires development and application of new techniques of production and better utilisation of human resources. To develop new techniques and human resources, the rate of capital formation has to be raised. Without adequate availability of capital, neither technical progress nor the development of human resources can possibly be achieved. Capital formation is possible when the society is channelising a part of its resources to the production of capital goods, *viz.*, tools, implements, machines, transport equipment and such other items as would enlarge the productive potential of a country. The size of a country's capital stock also governs the level of technology. Latest technology and automatic devices of production require huge capital investment. A capital-poor country cannot afford such technology and therefore, techniques of production in such an economy are going to remain primitive.

In view of the fast growing population—a feature that characterises all the underdeveloped countries—the rate of capital accumulation must also be correspondingly higher so that a country can provide maintenance and equipment to the additional people and thus maintain the per capita income at least at the previous level. In a country aspiring to raise the level of per capita income, the rate of capital accumulation must be kept higher than the rate of population growth. Thus, in view of the rapidly increasing population and the necessity of improving technology in the backward countries, a large increase in capital formation is most urgently required.

However, underdeveloped countries find it extremely difficult to step up the rate of capital formation. Their savings are very low—practically non-existent and the capital market is hardly developed. The consequent lower supply of capital results in low productivity which further reduces income and thereby impairs the capacity to save. Further, with low income and lower purchasing power in the hands of the people, the size of the market shrinks which reduces the inducement to invest. Thus, lower savings combined with smaller investment results in perpetual backwardness of the underdeveloped economies.

(3) Technological Progress: Technological changes are the most important factors in the process of economic growth. Technological changes are related to production, processing, marketing and distribution. Changes in technology lead to increase in productivity of labour, capital and other factors of production. The technological changes not only reduce the cost of production, but also increase the quality of the product; besides, new products are produced creating a demand for them. The basis for technological change is the scientific discovery and invention. When an invention is applied in production, it is called innovation leading to improvement. Japan stands a typical example to prove that vast economic development could be achieved through improved technology. The developing countries are benefiting from the vast knowledge acquired by advanced countries in the field of science and technology. Technological change would enable the productive units to go in for specialisation and division of labour which would in turn increase the productivity. Underdeveloped countries have lagged behind in the use of modern technology. But the adoption of new technology again requires huge amounts of investment to buy new equipment. Capital is, thus, an important factor that inhibits or promotes growth.

Technology Transfer: The *Growth Report* (2008) points out that in all the cases of sustained high growth, the economies have rapidly absorbed know-how, technology and more generally, knowledge from the rest of the world. These economies did not have to originate much of this knowledge, but they did have to assimilate it at a tremendous pace. Economies can learn faster than they can invent. Knowledge acquired from the global economy is thus the fundamental basis of economic catch up and sustained growth.

Knowledge does not only consist of ideas for making more things, cheaper things or new things. It includes the accumulated wisdom of human and social experience—as historians and social scientists interpret and reinterpret it. For example, the "invention" of the separation of powers between three branches of government, and the checks and balances it ensures, is possibly one of the most creative and influential innovations of the last few centuries. Many other institutional innovations have been tried and refined through trial and error, and have helped achieve economic and social goals more efficiently and fairly.

To economists, these ideas all share one characteristic: they are "nonrival." If you use or "consume" an idea, it does not stop me from also using it. Thomas Jefferson made a famous analogy with the light of a candle: If you light your candle with mine, it does not darken my flame.[1]

The value of knowledge in the global economy is high and rising. Indeed, the progress of the advanced economies depends mainly on innovation and new ideas. Technology also spreads more quickly now from the countries where it is invented to other parts of the world. For example, it took over 90 years after its invention for the telegram to spread to 80 per cent of developing countries. It took only 16 years for the mobile phone to do so.

What can developing economies do to ensure that they learn—to ensure that productive and institutional knowledge is transferred to them?

One known channel is foreign direct investment (FDI). FDI can bring a familiarity with foreign production techniques, overseas markets and international supply chains. This expertise may be worth more than the capital itself. In developing countries, FDI is a small fraction of total investment. But because of the knowledge transfer it normally carries with it, its importance is much larger than its fractional contribution to total investment.

Foreign education, particularly higher education, has proved to be an important channel of knowledge transfer. One of the first actions Japan took during the Meiji Restoration was to bring experts from the United States and Europe, and to send Japanese students to Western universities. A more recent and well-known example is China when it started reforms. At the invitation of leaders and officials from the Chinese government, a stream of foreign experts visited the country to help them learn about the workings of a market economy, the institutions underpinning it and its responses to change. At the same time, a stream of Chinese students left to be trained in the US and European universities. By studying abroad, students acquire international contacts, which will help them remain abreast of new thinking long after they have left the classroom.[2]

1. *The Growth Report: Strategies for Sustained Growth and Inclusive Development*, Commission on Growth and Development.
2. ibid.

(4) Human Factors: Rate of growth of population has been an important factor in modern economic growth. Mere growth in the size of the population would not lead to economic development. It depends on the efficiency of the people. According to Kuznets, the population of Europe increased more than four-fold within a period of two centuries (1750-1950), while the population of the remaining world increased just by 200 per cent. This phenomenal increase of population in European countries was not detrimental to economic progress; on the other hand it was helpful for them to increase their per capita GNP. During this period, a four-fold increase in population had resulted in ten-fold increase in GNP per capita of European countries. This is attributed to the human factor. This is also due to increased efficiency of labour force what we call human capital formation. This could be achieved by good expenditure on health, education, sanitation and on social services and security measures. But in backward economies, increase in population is a great hindrance to the economic development. Hence, family planning and control of population should form part and parcel of economic development and planning in developing countries.

Human Capital: Investments in the health, knowledge and skills of the people—human capital—are as important as investments in the more visible, physical capital of the country.

Education may influence the economy in subtle ways, interacting with other factors. For example, India turned out world-class engineers and scientists for decades before its economy took off. This investment in skills yielded limited economic results until India discovered a global demand for software services (a demand which has since broadened to include outsourced research-and-development and a wide array of services delivered over the Internet).

Investments in human capital will generate opportunities for growth including opportunities unforeseen at the time of the investment. But as India's experience demonstrates, those investments do not translate mechanically into growth. Other factors can intervene.

Education: Every country that sustained high growth for long periods put substantial effort into schooling its citizens and deepening its human capital.

Non-Economic Factors

Non-economic factors are as powerful if not more powerful than economic factors in influencing the extent of economic development and growth. According to Nurkse, "Economic development has much to do with human endowments, social attitude, political conditions and historical accidents."

1. Social Factors: Social and cultural factors have influenced economic growth all over the world. In the western countries, education and their culture led to the spirit of physical adventure and discoveries leading to the rise of new mercantile classes who were interested in savings and investments and in undertaking risks in order to earn lot of profits. This spirit was responsible for Industrial Revolution in European countries in 18th and 19th centuries. In underdeveloped countries, the activities of the people would be based on tradition religion and customs. In such countries, the family would be the primary economic and social unit, and relationships would be personal and patriarchal; and decisions would be influenced by caste, clan, creed and religion at the social level. If economic development is to take place, social attitudes, values and institutions will have to be changed.

Mass participation in development programmes is a pre-condition for accelerating the growth process. However, people show interest in the development activity only when they feel that the fruits of growth will be fairly distributed. Experiences from a number of countries suggest that whenever the defective social organisation allows some elite groups to appropriate the benefits of growth, the general mass of people develop apathy towards states's development programmes. Under the circumstances, it is futile to hope that masses will participate in the development projects undertaken by the state.

Taking the case of India, the wide-ranging nature of the reforms that are required in India, are not only in economic matters but also in the social and political domains. There is urgent need not only for more efficient and equitable economic institutions, but also for uprooting corruption, protecting the environment, eradicating caste inequalities, preventing human rights violations, restoring the credibility of the legal system, halting the criminalisation of politics (to cite a few major concerns).

(2) Political Factors/Political Freedom: Political and administrative factors also help in modern economic growth. Enlightened electorates, educated politicians and morally straight administrators would ensure greater economic development and growth. Weak political structure, instability, corrupt politicians, officials and inefficient administration would be a hindrance to economic development. Lewis points out, "No country has made progress without positive stimulus from intelligent Governments."

Political freedom is an essential condition for the economic development of a country.

Looking to the world history of modern times, one learns that the process of development and underdevelopment are interlinked and it is wrong to view them in isolation. We all know that the underdevelopment of India, Pakistan, Bangladesh, Sri Lanka, Malaysia, Kenya and a few other countries, which were in the past British colonies, was linked with the development of England. England recklessly exploited them and appropriated a large portion of their economic surplus. This made a significant contribution to Britain's economic development. The colonies, however, were forced to remain backward in the process.

Dadabhai Naoroji has also explained in his classic work *Poverty and Un-British Rule in India* that the drain of wealth from India under the British was the major cause of the increase in poverty in India during that period, which in turn arrested the economic development of the country. Bipan Chandra's work lends powerful support to Naoroji's views on the country's underdevelopment during the British period.

(3) Leadership and Governance: The *Growth Report* (2008) states, "Growth is about more than economics. It also requires committed, credible, and capable governments... The high-growth economies typically built their prosperity on sturdy political foundations".

In the fast-growing economies, policy makers understood that successful development entails a decades-long commitment, and a fundamental bargain between the present and the future. Even at very high growth rates of 7-10 per cent, it takes decades for a country to make the leap from low to relatively high incomes.

During this long period of transition, citizens must forgo consumption today in return for higher standards of living tomorrow. This bargain will be accepted only if the country's policy makers communicate a credible vision of the future and a strategy for getting there. They must be trusted as stewards of the economy and their promises of future rewards must be believed. Their promise must also be inclusive, leaving citizens confident that they and their children will share in the benefits.

Such leadership requires patience and a long planning horizon. In several cases, fast-growing economies were overseen by a single-party government that could expect to remain in power for decades to come. In a multiparty democracy, on the other hand, governments typically look no further than the next election. But democracies can nonetheless preside over remarkable passages of growth. Today's India is the most prominent example.

Committed to the goal of high growth, governments should be pragmatic in their pursuit of it. The policy makers who succeeded in sustaining high growth were prepared to try, fail and learn. Singapore, for example, did not turn outward until it had first tried turning inward, encouraging domestic firms to compete with industrial imports. Same has been the case with India.

(4) The Role of Government: The Commission on Growth and Development in its Report (2008) reviewing the cases of high, sustained growth in the post-war period have emphasised the role of committed, credible and reliable governments in these countries.

What should governments do? What is the optimal size of the state and what are its proper responsibilities? More ink has been spilled on this question than any other in development.

One view is that governments should do as little as possible. "That government is best which governs least". Arthur Lewis observed that, "Governments may fail either because they do too little, or because they do too much". Some countries, for example, suffer from too little public investment; others, from too much government regulation. Some suffer from both problems simultaneously. In India, for example, the first priority in the 1990s was for the government to do less, dismantling the excesses of the licence-and-permit Raj. Now the government is trying to do more, making up for years of underinvestment in public infrastructure.

The *Growth Report* remarks, "A preoccupation with the size of government can also distract attention from its effectiveness. The task is to improve the effectiveness of government institutions rather than stripping them of their tasks." Governments should not do nothing, out of a fear of failure. They should test policies, and be quick to learn from failure.

Effective Government: It may be emphasised that government is not only a policy maker, it is also a service provider, an investor, an arbitrator and an employer, often a big one. And while a government's choice of policies matters a great deal, it is also important that it implements those policies well.

Where the government provides a service, it should be forced to compete with alternative providers from the private or non-profit sectors. In addition, it should collect feedback from the citizens it serves. Where this is not possible or not sufficient, bureaucracies should also be subject to periodic scrutiny by an independent evaluator. These evaluators should aim to identify and remove some of the redundant layers that bureaucracies collect over the years.

(5) Institutions: Institutions have been defined as the rules of the game of a society or more formally are the humanly devised constraints that structure human interaction. They include both formal rules (statute law, common law, regulations) and informal constraints (conventions, norms of behaviour and self-imposed codes of conduct), and the enforcement characteristics of both. While the formal rules can be changed overnight, the informal norms change only gradually. Changes in formal laws and rules are in the direct control of public policy. There is however a much larger agenda of change required, which involves education, social action and the development of civil society. Because formal rules will work only if they are accompanied by matching developments in the informal structures of interaction.[3]

The Government, The State and The Market: Although the competing virtues of the market mechanism and governmental action have been much discussed in the literature, the comparative merits of the two forms of economic decision are so thoroughly context-dependent that it makes little sense to espouse a *general* 'pro state' or 'pro market' view. For proper understanding, the distinction between the state and the government may be of some significance. The state is, in many ways, a broader concept, which includes the government, the legislature that votes on public rules, the political system that regulates elections, the role that is given to opposition parties, and the basic political rights that are upheld by the judiciary. A democratic state makes it exceedingly difficult for the ruling government to be unresponsive to the needs and values of the population at large.[4]

There is a similar question about the context-dependence of the role of the market mechanism.

There is a close interdependence between markets and governance. In particular, the operation and successes of the market mechanism can be deeply influenced by the nature of governmental arrangements and actions that go with it. As Basu puts it, "There is no escape from the need for purposive, intelligent action from government. Government or

---

3. *The Growth Report, op cit.*
4. Drèze, J. and A. Sen (2002). *India: Development and Participation*, Ch.2. Oxford University Press.

good governance, is a concommitant of efficient markets, not a substitute."[5]

Markets can hardly function in the absence of legal provisions and justifiable rights to property and contractual entitlements. The disastrous results of indiscriminate liberalisation and wholesale privatisation in Russia in the 1990s illustrate the penalties of ignoring the basic recognition that the effective functioning of the market mechanism is highly contingent on adequate institutional foundations.

Also, the government may have a major role in initiating and facilitating market-reliant economic growth. We have examples of such successful capitalist countries as Germany and Japan. More recently, the role of the government has received much attention in interpreting the so-called 'East Asian miracle'—the remarkable economic success of the newly industrialising countries in East Asia (in particular South Korea, Taiwan, Hong Kong, Singapore and more recently, China and Thailand).

In fact, there is a deep complementarity between market efficiency and state action. The performance of the market is highly contingent on various forms of state action, from the provision of an adequate legal framework to redistributive policies. One implication of these complementarities is that liberalisation does not necessarily diminish the importance of state action. This applies even to regulation itself, insofar as a relaxation of one type of rules often calls for developing new rules of a different type. For instance, allowing private entry into new sectors (such as medical insurance or electricity distribution), which may be considered as a form of deregulation, calls for an adequate overseeing framework, especially if these sectors have features (e.g. economies of scale, information asymmetries, pervasive externalities) that interfere with the efficiency of the market mechanism. Even in western 'market economies', including the United States, this necessity is well recognised.

Cooperative Action: Besides state intervention and the market mechanism, there is the third alternative way of coordinating economic activity i.e., cooperative action.

Development itself opens up new opportunities for social cooperation. The recent expansion of cooperative action on a global scale (involving concerns such as environmental protection, the debt crisis and world peace) is one example of this process.

---

5. Basu, Kaushik (ed.) (2004). *India's Emerging Economy: Performance and Prospects in the 1990s and Beyond*, Ch 1. Oxford University Press.

Just as the state and the market are highly complementary institutions (even though they are often seen in antagonistic terms), a similar relation holds between cooperative action on the one hand and the state or the market on the other. In a democratic society, the priorities and actions of the state depend on organised public demands, and other aspects of a broad political process in which cooperative action plays a crucial part. Conversely, what cooperative action can achieve depends to a considerable extent on the opportunities created through state action, e.g., the level of education in the community, the accountability of government institutions and the legal framework of civic associations.

Thus, cooperative action and market institutions are often compatible or even complementary. For instance, the efficiency of the market mechanism can be greatly enhanced by cooperative social norms that reduce so-called 'transaction costs'. Indeed, markets can flourish more easily when contracts are not typically broken and do not have to be rescued by litigation.

Conclusion

Economic development is not a purely economic phenomenon but interacts with social, political and cultural development at all stages. The key to development, according to Cairncross, lies in men's minds, in the institutions in which their thinking finds expression and in the play of opportunity on ideas and institutions. The values, attitudes, motivation and institution of any society, the level of education, prevailing religious beliefs, standard of conduct in business and government, freedom from civil commotion and strife, competence and dedication of those in authority and so on, are bound to exercise a major influence on growth. All these constitute non-economic factors of development.

Questions

1. Distinguish between 'economic development' and 'economic growth'. What are the main factors which determine economic development? *[B.A. (P) 2006, 2007]*
2. Write a short note on Factors in Economic Development. *[B.A. (P) 2003; B.Com 2007]*
3. India's economic development has been "hindered by social, political and religious factors." Discuss. *[B.Com (P) 2006]*
4. "Growth is necessary but not sufficient condition for development." Explain. What are the factors affecting economic development of a country? *[B.Com. (P) 2003]*

3

Capital Formation

What is Capital Formation?

ACCORDING to Nurkse, "The meaning of capital formation is that a society does not apply the whole of the current productive activity to the needs and desires of immediate consumption, but directs a part of it to the making of capital goods, tools and equipment, machines and transport facilities, plants and all the various forms of real capital that can so greatly increase the efficiency of productive efforts."

Process of Capital Formation

The process of capital formation involves three distinct though interdependent activities. The first thing that is required for capital formation is saving. It is through this activity that a part of the resources is withdrawn from current composition so as to increase the volume of real saving in the economies. But most people who have savings in any society are not the ones who make investments. Their savings are to be mobilised, if they are to be used for productive purposes. Thus requires a widespread networking of the banking, insurance and other financial institutions which will mobilise public savings. Thus, in the process of capital formation, the second activity is finance. The third is investment itself, the activity that raises the productive capacity of any country.

Role of Capital Formation

(i) Capital Formation and Technical Progress

Economic development consists of the introduction of new combinations of factors of production which tend to increase the productivity of labour. Improvement in productivity in turn requires development and application of new techniques of production and better utilisation of human resources. To develop new techniques and human resources, the rate of capital formation has to be raised. Without adequate availability of capital, neither technical progress nor the development of human resources can possibly be achieved.

Capital formation is possible when the society is channelising a part of its resources to the production of capital goods, *viz.*, tools, implements, machines, transport equipment and such other items as would enlarge the productive potential of a country. The size of a country's capital stock also governs the level of technology. Latest technology and automatic devices of production require huge capital investment. A capital-poor country cannot afford such technology and therefore, techniques of production in such an economy are going to remain primitive.

(ii) Capital Formation for Raising GNP and Per Capita Income

In view of the fast growing population—a feature that characterises all the underdeveloped countries—the rate of capital accumulation must also be correspondingly higher so that a country can provide maintenance and equipment to the additional people and thus maintain the per capita income at least at the previous level. In a country aspiring to raise the level of per capita income, the rate of capital accumulation must be kept higher than the rate of population growth. Thus, in view of the rapidly increasing population and the necessity of improving technology in the backward countries, a large increase in capital formation is most urgently required.

(iii) Capital Formation for Fuller Utilisation of Natural Resources

High rate of capital formation is necessary to make the full use of natural resources available in a country. For example, India has vast mineral wealth, huge water resources in the form of a large number of rivers, fertile land, forest wealth etc. Under planned economic development of the country, rate of capital formation has been stepped up and more capital is devoted to the use of natural resources. India's success in exploration and production of substantial quantity of petroleum, coal, iron ore, etc., is due to use of more capital, equipment, machinery and other resources on mining and minerals. Consruction of multipurpose river valley projects is an example of capital employed for making better use of water resources.

(iv) Capital Formation for Improvement in Labour Efficiency

Increase in stock of capital enable labour to work with greater efficiency. Efficiency of labour depends to a large extent on the nature and type of equipment with which it works. Capital formation, by improving the quantity and quality of equipment available for labour to work with, contributes a lot to increasing efficiency and productivity.

(v) Capital Formation will Increase Supply as well as Demand for Goods and Services

Capital formation helps to increase production and its demand. Increased rate of capital formation has a dual role in increasing the tempo of economic development. On one side, capital increases productive capacity and expands volume of goods and services produced. On the other side capital formation means increased rate of investment. Investment, in turn, creates income for those who work on capital projects—on dams, roads or building of plants and factories. This increased income creates additional demand for goods and services. Thus, capital results in additions to production as well as addition to demand for the goods produced. In this way, the process of production continues to expand as market demand continues to increase. Higher production and greater sales keep the economy moving on the path of rapid economic development.

Problem of Capital Formation

However, underdeveloped countries find it extremely difficult to step up the rate of capital formation. Their savings are very low—practically non-existent and the capital market is hardly developed. The consequent lower supply of capital results in low productivity which further reduces income and thereby impairs the capacity to save. Further, with low income and lower purchasing power in the hands of the people, the size of the market shrinks which reduces the inducement to invest. Thus, lower savings combined with smaller investment results in perpetual backwardness of the underdeveloped economies.

The Vicious Circle of Poverty

Ragner Nurkse explains the problem of capital formation in underdeveloped countries through the vicious circle of poverty. To quote Nurkse: "Vicious circle of poverty implies a circular constellation of forces tending to act and react upon each other in such a way as to keep a poor country in a state of poverty."[1] To clarify this, Nurkse takes a poor man as his example. Owing to inadequate diet, a poor man remains weak which reduces his efficiency or capacity to work and thus lowers his earnings. As a consequence of lower income, the poor man continues to grow weaker and inefficient thereby perpetuating his

1. Nurkse, Ragnar. *Problems of Capital Formation in the Underdeveloped Countries*, p. 2.

poverty. This example of a poor individual can be generalised to enfold a country as a whole because a country's income depends on the efficiency of the individuals in the country. Therefore, Nurkse concludes that "a country is poor because it is poor".

The vicious circle of poverty constantly holds the capital formation at lower levels. Thus, the vicious circle of poverty operates both on the supply as well as demand side of capital formation in the underdeveloped countries.

Supply of Capital

Underdeveloped countries are characterised as low income countries. Low incomes reduce people's capacity to save. When the volume of saving is low, investment also remains low. Further inadequate availability of investment funds prevents the introduction and use of modern technology thereby keeping the country technologically backward. Primitive techniques of production further reduces the level of productivity and hence keeps the level of income permanently low. Thus, low income is the result of low productivity and low productivity is a consequence of shortage of capital which in turn is the result of low saving capacity and low saving capacity in turn is a consequence of low real income.

VICIOUS CIRCLE OF POVERTY : *Supply Side*

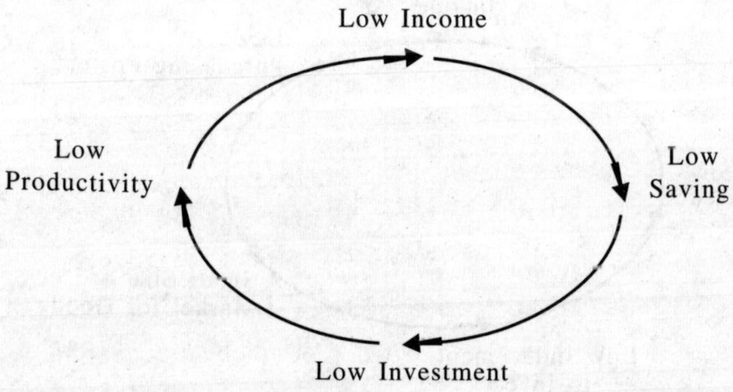

To quote Nurkse, "On the supply side, there is a small capacity to save resulting from the low level of real income. The low real income is a reflection of low productivity which, in turn, is largely due to the lack of capital. The lack of capital is the result of small capacity to save and so the circle is complete."[2]

2. Nurkse *op cit.* p. 5.

Demand for Capital

It is not merely the supply of capital that is scarce in the underdeveloped countries but the demand for capital also is not much. Demand for capital is a measure of people's desire to introduce and utilise new techniques, modern equipment and machinery in the productive process. The degree of demand for capital goods obviously depends on the extent of consumers demand for the goods produced with the help of capital goods.

Due to low level of productivity and therefore low per capita real income, people have low purchasing power i.e., they lack capacity to buy these goods from the market. The low demand for consumer goods hardly offers any inducement to the producer to invest in capital goods. Thus, in the absence of sufficient inducement to invest, the rate of investment stagnates keeping the productivity levels low and thereby perpetuating low real income. In the words of Nurkse, "On the demand side, the inducement to invest may be low because of the small buying power of the people which is due to their low real income, which again is due to low productivity. The low productivity, however, is a result of the small amount of capital used in production, which in turn may be caused at least partially by the small inducement to invest."[3]

VICIOUS CIRCLE OF POVERTY : *Demand Side*

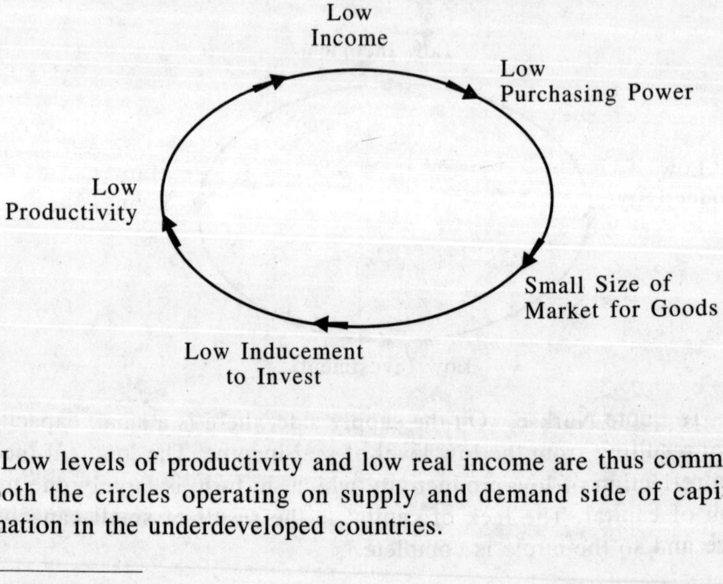

Low levels of productivity and low real income are thus common to both the circles operating on supply and demand side of capital formation in the underdeveloped countries.

3. Nurkse *op cit.* p. 5.

Size of Market and Inducement to Invest

As already pointed out, in underdeveloped countries, not only supply of capital is scarce but demand for capital too is very small. It sounds paradoxical that in underdeveloped countries there should be paucity of demand for capital. Now, the problem is, how the size of the market can be expanded or enlarged. In this regard, we have to examine the factors determining the size of the market. Nurkse enumerates a number of important factors such as, monetary expansion, salesmanship and advertisement, size of the country and its population, trade barriers and the level of productivity. After examining all the factors, he singles out the level of productivity as the most significant determinent of the size of the market. Let us briefly examine these factors:

Monetary Expansion – It is generally believed that the market can expand if the quantity of money in the market is increased. The increased monetary circulation will raise the volume of purchases and sales. But in underdeveloped countries, it is not possible to secure an expansion in the size of the market merely by increasing the supply of money. In underdeveloped countries, because of the inelastic nature of supply position in agriculture and rigidities in the economic system, it is not possible to increase production within a short period of time. Expansion of money supply under such conditions will only result in the rising prices.

Salesmanship and Advertisement – Efficient salesmanship and effective advertisement do contribute to the expansion of the market but these devices have their own limitations. The individual firms, no doubt, can boost up their sales through publicity and advertisement but ultimately, it is the total purchasing power of the people that determines the overall sales. Because of low income and low purchasing power, the ultimate demand for goods in the market is bound to remain low. What happens in such a situation is that some firms are able to increase their sales at the expense of others leaving the overall level of sales remaining the same.

Population – It is commonly believed that larger the number of people in a country, the higher shall be the extent of demand enlarging the size of the market. But, according to Nurkse, population plays only a limited role in determining the size of the market. A country with large population but low national income and consequently low per capita income and low purchasing power will have a low level of demand. The extent of demand depends upon real purchasing power of the people and not on the size of population. The basic reason is that the poverty ridden people in the underdeveloped countries cannot even think of buying those goods in the market which are regarded as essential part of life in advanced countries.

Geographical Area – Similarly, the geographical area of the country hardly has any bearing on the size of the market. A country with large geographical area inhabited by poor people will not have a large market.

Cost of Transport and Tariff Barriers – The abolition of trade barriers and efficient transport system is likely to reduce cost of goods and create more demand for them. But these measures alone cannot bring about a significant expansion in the existing market. Ultimately, the size of the market or the level of demand depends on real income and the purchasing power of the people. In the poor countries, it is the low real income and low purchasing power that are the real impediments to the expansion of market. The reduced cost of transport and the removal of tariff barriers can only be of a limited help.

To sum up, it can be said that monetary expansion, size of population, geographical area of a country, effective advertisement and salesmanship, reduction in cost of transport, removal of tariff barriers etc., are not very effective means in securing the expansion of the size of the market, though their importance cannot be ignored.

Level of Productivity—A Crucial Determinant of Size of the Market

According to Nurkse, "The crucial determinant of the size of market is productivity". In his view, a significant expansion in the size of the market can only be brought about with improvement in productivity of the people. While discussing the vicious circle of poverty on the demand side, it was observed that it is the low level of productivity that keeps down the level of real income and purchasing power of the people and this limits the demand for goods and restricts the growth of the market. But if productivity is increased, the level of real income and purchasing power will also rise which will generate more demand for goods and thus, lead to an expansion in the size of the market.

The level of productivity depends on the level of technology. The larger the use of machinery and capital-intensive techniques in the process of production, the higher shall be the level of productivity which shall yield higher incomes to the people as well as large quantities of goods, thereby keeping both the demand and supply at a high level in the market. On the other hand, in underdeveloped countries because of low level of productivity, the supply and demand both remain low, resulting in the small size of the market. The size of the market can be expanded only by an increase in productivity as Nurkse observes "Capacity to buy means capacity to produce". In a country where people cannot produce much because of low productivity, they will surely be not in a position to buy more because of low incomes resulting from low productivity. Hence, low productivity works both on demand and supply sides in keeping the size of the market perpetually small.

It is clear from the above that the size of the market can be expanded by raising the level of productivity. Productivity in turn depends on the use of capital which is inhibited in underdeveloped economies by the low inducement to invest. Therefore, the basic question now is, how to increase the inducement to invest so that people use more capital in production so as to bring about improvement in their productivity. According to Nurkse, if in the underdeveloped countries a large number of industries are set up simultaneously, this is likely to expand the size of the market. This proposition of Nurkse is known as the theory of Balanced Growth.

Theory of Balanced Growth

The theory of 'Balanced Growth' has been put forward as a solution to the problem of vicious circle of poverty on the demand side of capital formation. To break this vicious circle, the theory of balanced growth advocates a simultaneous setting up of a large number of mutually complementary industries that would generate demand for each other's products and thus expand the size of the market and increase inducement to invest.

Rosenstein Rodan gave the earliest version of the balanced growth theory. He observed that in underdeveloped countries, no new industry has a chance to survive due to limited size of market demand. Thus, if for example, a shoe factory is set up employing a hundred workers, the chances are that it would soon close down due to lack of demand for shoes. But if in place of one factory, we simultaneously set up, say, one hundred factories employing thousands of workers, the chances are that all these factories would survive. This is because the additional income in the hands of these workers arising from their employment, will create additional demand in the market as they spend money on various products produced by these industries. Thus, demand for shoes as well as for goods produced by other industries increases that enables all of them to survive and grow. Nurkse agreed with Rosenstein Rodan and put forward the balanced growth theory on similar lines but enlarged the scope of the balanced growth programme to include many more industrial sectors.

According to Nurkse, the only way to remove the obstacles arising out of the small size of the market is "more or less synchronised application of capital to a wide range of different industries".[4] The people working in these industries will be buyers of each others' produce. Accordingly, each individual industry shall create a demand for the goods of the others. The essence of Nurkse's theory is that if large investment is undertaken in the mutually dependent industries, the vicious circle of poverty can be broken and the country can look forward to the economic advancement.

The Big Push Theory

The balanced growth theory has another version called the Big Push Theory. This theory, apart from suggesting the balanced development of the consumer goods industries and the social overhead capital, underlines the importance of simultaneously undertaking investment in the capital goods industries as well. The necessity for maintaining a balance between consumer goods industries and capital goods industries arises because of their technical complementarity. Generally, this complementarity is more pronounced in the capital goods industries which are dependent on consumer goods industries for the supply of their finished and semi-finished products, machinery and other types of capital equipment.

The "Big Push Theory" presents a comprehensive programme of economic development in which the following balances have to be maintained:

(i) A horizontal balance among the consumer goods industries according to expected emerging patterns of demand so that with the expansion in demand, the supply is increased accordingly.

(ii) A balance between the social overhead capital and productive activities so that one may not suffer in the absence of the others.

(iii) A vertical balance between the consumer goods industries and the capital goods industries according to their degree of technical complementarity so that external economies can be fully reaped.

According to this theory, to take full advantage of external economies, all investments in all the interdependent industries should

4. Nurkse *op. cit.* p. 11.

be made in accordance with a well chalked out plan of economic development.

This 'balanced growth' or simultaneous development of many industries would require mobilisation of large amounts of resources at one time. According to Rosenstein Rodan and Nurkse, poor developing economies were characterised by a large surplus of labour employed at zero marginal cost in the traditional sector. Under this assumption of disguised unemployment, the labour supply would create no major bottleneck to a 'great leap forward' in industrialisation.

The key to the success of the balanced growth strategy would, of course, be to mobilise sufficient funds for simultaneous development of many industries.

Weaknesses of the Theory of Balanced Growth

The theory of balanced growth suffers from inherent weaknesses. Singer[5] has expressed his doubts about the practicability of balanced growth doctrine. According to him, if underdeveloped countries are to launch a large investment package in industries without paying much attention to agriculture, they are bound to run into difficulties. To avoid food and raw material shortage, the big push in industry will have to be accompanied by a big push in agriculture as well. But when we think of such a large and varied package of industrial investment and investment in agriculture at the same time, it creates serious doubts about the capacity of the underdeveloped countries to follow the path of balanced growth. As he says, "The resources required for carrying out the policy of balanced growth are of such order of magnitude that a country disposing of such resources would infact not be underdeveloped."

In underdeveloped countries, there is an acute shortage of capital and other resources. To suggest that they can move on the path of economic progress by massive investment simultaneously in all sectors appears totally impractical. In fact, the balanced growth doctrine requires huge amounts of precisely these resources whose limited availability is the basic characteristic of the underdeveloped economies.

A major weakness of the balanced growth theory is that it completely ignores the fundamental problems of scarcity of capital resources facing the underdeveloped countries. The theory seems to believe that all the required resources are available in sufficient quantities and the only problem before the backward countries is how

5. Singer, *Concept of Balanced Growth and Economic Development.*

to use them in accordance with a calculated programme of economic development. In fact, scarcity of resources is the basic problem of underdeveloped countries. Thus, underdeveloped countries cannot afford balanced growth programmes. They will have to fall back upon a strategy involving unbalanced growth.

Theory of Unbalanced Growth

Prof. Hirschman, the leading exponent of the theory of unbalanced growth argues that a deliberate unbalancing of the economy in accordance with predesigned strategy is the best way to achieve economic growth. "An ideal situation obtains when one disequilibrium calls forth a development move which in turn leads to a similar disequilibrium and soon ad-infinitum." He observes that development has proceeded in this way with "growth being communicated from the leading sectors of the economy to the followers, from one industry to another, from one firm to another". Development process is a chain of disequilibrium that must be kept alive and the task of development policy is to maintain tension, disproportions and disequilibria.

Hirschman's theory of unbalanced growth is based on the following propositions:

(a) That technical complementarity is found among the various industries but in the case of some of them, the degree of complementarity is more than the other. Therefore, the programme for economic development should aim at the establishment of those industries where these complementarities happen to be the greatest.

(b) That a simultaneous investment in a number of complementary industries according to the programme of balanced growth may achieve a once for all increase in national income. But after this, the economy will become stabilised at a higher level without any movement forward. The objective of development is not only to achieve a once for all increase in national income, rather this process of income propogation must continue year after year. In order to see that the development process moves on continuously, it is necessary to create and maintain deliberate imbalances in the economy. To create these imbalances, Hirschman suggests investment either in Social Overhead Capital (SOC) or in Directly Productive Activities (DPA).

Social overhead capital is defined as "comprising all those basic services without which primary, secondary and tertiary productive activities can not function". This includes investment in education, public health, transport and communications, irrigation, drainage etc. Large investment in SOC will encourage investment in DPA by providing cheap inputs to agriculture and industry e.g., cheap electricity and power supply may encourage the development of industries both large and small and may stimulate activity in other sectors as well. To quote Hirschman, "Investment in SOC is advocated not because of its direct effect on final output, but because it permits and infact invites DPA to come in some SOC investment as a prerequisite of DPA investment."

Imbalances in the economy can also be created by investment in directly productive activities such as investment in manufacturing industries and constructional activities. Expansion in investment in DPA without the corresponding expansion in SOC will lead to increase in cost of production in view of inadequate availability of overhead facilities. In such a situation, pressures are likely to be exerted and the government may step in and undertake investment in SOC for creating the necessary infrastructure which would lead to an all-round development of the economy.

The sequence of development from SOC to DPA is known as development via excess capacity. The second sequence *viz.*, from DPA to SOC is called development via shortages. Development via excess capacity of SOC is more continuous and smooth than development via shortages of SOC. According to Hirschman, "Development *via* shortages is an instance of disorderly compulsive sequence while that with excess SOC capacity is essentially permissive."

Every investment project has both forward linkages (it may encourage investment in subsequent stage of production) and backward linkages (it may encourage investment in earlier stages of production) and the task of development policy is to find out projects with the maximum total linkage. Hirschman has worked out the forward and the backward linkage in case of number of industries and on the basis of that, the maximum linkage exists in the case of intermediate manufacturing industries. Therefore, if investment is made in such industries, it is bound to affect the demand and supply positions in other sectors of the economy and thus leading to their expansion as well.

Balanced Growth or Unbalanced Growth?

After having discussed both the theories of balanced growth and unbalanced growth, the natural question to ask is which of these is more appropriate or largely feasible for bringing about a rapid development in the underdeveloped countries. Prof. Hirschman observes the balanced growth theory makes an impossible demand on the limited resources of the underdeveloped countries by asking them to simultaneously start investing in a number of complimentary industries which require a huge amount of capital, technical know-how and efficient organisational ability. If these countries were in a position to do so, they would surely not have remained underdeveloped till now. He feels that supply of these factors can be increased only over a long period of time and hence, the minimum objectives of development policy should be to create the right type of imbalances which exert pressure on the different sectors of the economy, thus, automatically moving the country on the path of development. The case of unbalanced growth is based primarily on the impracticability of the balanced growth because of the non-availability of adequate resources, particularly of capital, in these countries.

The case for balanced growth on the other hand gets strengthened when one realises that stagnation in underdeveloped economies is deep rooted due to structural disequilibrium in its economy. Sustained growth requires a harmonious development of various complementary sectors but again the question arises—Do these economies have enough of resources to invest simultaneously in all the sectors? Thus, the case of unbalanced growth is based primarily on the impracticability of the balanced growth because of the non-availability of adequate resources of capital in these countries.

Supply-Side of Capital Formation

On the supply side there is need to raise the ability and willingness to save. Ability to save can be increased only through increase in real per capita income but willingness to save can be raised through various incentives like offering higher rates of interest, promoting various schemes of savings.

Promoting Voluntary Savings

Arthur Lewis regards increasing the rate of saving from 5 per cent per annum (as generally found in many developing countries) to 12 per cent per annum as the central problem of economic growth. This will require a substantial expansion of commercial banks, cooperative institutions and savings banks to tap resources for development.

Disguised Unemployment and Capital Formation

In underdeveloped countries, there is an excessive number of people working in agriculture and if some of them are taken away from this sector, it would not adversely affect agricultural production. Since these surplus workers by implication do not contribute anything to the agricultural production, technically speaking, they are unemployed. This type of unemployment is known as disguised unemployment. According to Nurkse, disguised unemployment exists when "even with unchanged techniques of agriculture, a large part of population engaged in agriculture could be removed without reducing agricultural output". Hence, all those people who are working but whose marginal productivity is zero are regarded as disguisedly unemployed.

Disguised unemployment is commonly found in the case of family employment, this concept is generally not applicable in the context of wage labour because in the case of wage labourer, wage rate cannot be more than the marginal productivity of the workers.

In the underdeveloped countries, quite a large portion of the working force remain idle because of disguised unemployment. According to Nurkse if this surplus labour is taken away from agriculture and used in building irrigation projects, roads, railways, canals, factories, etc., this labour becomes productive and helps in the capital formation of the country. But the question arises, from where are we going to get the resources and means of subsistence for the people who will now be working on these capital projects. According to Nurkse, the use of disguised unemployment for capital formation could be financed from within the system itself. He explains this with an example: supposing that six number of a family are working on a field and that if two of them are taken away from there and the total output remains the same, then these two are in the state of disguised unemployment. These two unproductive workers were being fed on the family farm. When they start working on capital formation projects, if their share could be taken away to feed them at the site of their work, the concealed saving will become effective saving because without any extra expenditure these people would add to the capital of the nation. The unproductive workers in agriculture will become productive workers on the capital projects whereas the expenditure on their consumption would remain the same.

However, in the process of transfer of people from the village to the site of work, some leakages emerge in the potential savings as a result of which total amount of saving that is available for capital formation becomes smaller. These leakages are:

(i) Consumption of people who stay back in farm may increase. Thus, this food surplus which has been designed as (concealed savings) will not be as much as it was supposed to be. According to Nurkse, "Everything depends on the mobilisation of the concealed saving potential in the shape of food surplus that becomes available to the productive peasants when their unproductive dependents go away. This mobilisation will be incomplete if the remaining peasants cannot be stopped from eating more than before."

(ii) Consumption by the transferred labour may increase. It is also possible that the people who are taken to the capital project may also increase their consumption as now they are subject to hard work while earlier on farm they may not be doing much work. Hence, a part of the existing food surplus (or the concealed saving potential) shall be utilised for meeting the extra consumption requirements.

(iii) *Cost of transport*: The food surpluses have to be collected from the village and taken to the site of capital formation which will involve transportation cost. This expenditure on transport is again a leakage from the saving which would reduce the amount available for capital formation. Although, this leakage can be stopped or minimised if the capital projects are started somewhere near the village themselves. However, it is not possible to entirely plug these leakages.

Role of Complementary Savings in Capital Formation

However, if this decrease in potential savings resulting from these leakages can be compensated by mobilisation of additional savings from outside, the people can be fruitfully engaged on the capital projects. These savings can be obtained either from the people living in urban areas within the country or in the form of foreign aid. As Nurkse points out, "Even if there is a leakage in the subsistence fund, provided that it can be covered by means of resources obtained from outside system, it will be possible to mobilise the whole or part of disguised unemployed for the purpose of capital formation."[6]

Financing Capital Formation

Financing of capital projects has two aspects: (a) making available to the workers food and other necessary items of consumption and

6. Nurkse *op. cit* p. 32.

(b) providing them the necessary capital goods, tools and implements. As far as (a) is concerned, it is necessary that the surplus available on the farms after these unproductive workers have left, should be mobilised either in the form of compulsory taxation of agricultural produce or through an increase in land revenue. For example, in Japan, in the early stages of their development, farmers were subjected to a very heavy land revenue. On the other hand in Soviet Russia, agricultural surplus was collected through compulsory taxation. Whatever methods of mopping up the agricultural surplus is applied, the fact remains that for the utilisation of disguised unemployment and digging out the concealed saving therein, the government will have to adopt some strong measures for procuring such a large surplus of agricultural produce.

The other aspect of capital formation is to make available to workers tools, implements and other necessary capital equipment. One way out is that these workers, before they are actually engaged in capital projects, may sit down and make the necessary equipment which is to be used on the capital project or that such implements are imported from other countries. In this context, Nurkse pointed out: "In over populated countries, in building a road, for instance, it would be fantastically uneconomic to equip each worker with a bulldozer. In such countries, one can see river dams being built by men and women carrying earth on their head-baskets. The same degree of capital intensity as in economically advanced countries should be neither desirable nor permitted."

Another source of obtaining capital equipment has also been suggested by Nurkse. He believes that in underdeveloped economies, not only labour is suffering from disguised unemployment, but the same is true for capital equipment in agriculture. Because of small size of fields and their fragmentation, each farmer is obliged to keep a minimum quantity of capital equipment in the form of spades, cattle, carts, etc. Through proper organisation of agriculture, this equipment can be made available for being used on capital projects.

From the above analysis, one can conclude that through certain organisational reforms, disguisedly unemployed labour can be fruitfully used on the capital projects, thereby substantially contributing to the productive efficiency of the economy.

The Demonstration Effect

Shortage of capital in the underdeveloped countries is the most serious obstacle in the way of their economic development. We have seen that in such countries the level of real income is low which results in low capacity to save and therefore, low capital formation, low productivity and low real income.

In their effort to raise the rate of saving from the prevalent low levels, underdeveloped countries are faced with the problem of demonstration effect. Nurkse points out that with increase in the level of productivity and real income, the consumption pattern of the people may undergo such changes that savings instead of becoming easier may infact become far more difficult. Here in lies the new theory of consumption according to which the capacity of the people to save does not depend only on the level of their own income but also on the income levels of other people with whom they come into contact. When an individual observes that the people around him are enjoying more of comforts and luxuries, he naturally feels that he too would like to live in the same manner as and when he can afford to do so. Consequently, when his income increases, his consumption expenditure also increases. This tendency of an individual's or a nations consumption to increase under the impact of the superior consumption levels of the others as named is Duesenbery or 'Demonstration Effect'. As Nurkse puts it, "When people come into natural contact with superior goods or superior patterns of consumption, with new articles or new ways of mceting old wants, they are apt to feel, after a while, certain restlessness and dissatisfaction. Their knowledge is extended, their imagination stimulated; new desires are aroused, the propensity to consume is shifted upwards". The operation of demonstration effect on consumption is confirmed by the statistical evidence put forward by Simon Kuznets. According to him, the real income of USA increased three times between 1890 and 1920 but the ratio of national saving during this period has become even lower than before. The reason for this decline in saving ratio is that by coming into contact with higher consumption levels and better ways of living, their consumption expenditure increased faster than the rate at which their incomes increased.

Nurkse says, "The amount of saving by an individual depends not only and perhaps not even mainly on the absolute level of real income, but also on the ratio of his incomc to the superior income level of other people with whom he may come into contact."

According to Nurkse, the demonstration effect which influences the consumption and living levels of the individuals belonging to various income groups within the same country also operates between the countries which are at different levels of economic prosperity. In an open economy, people in the poor countries invariably try to copy the levels of living prevailing in the prosperous countries.

The demonstration effect operates at the international level because of two major reasons namely: (i) existence of inequalities in the level of consumption and living between the advanced and backward countries and (ii) the increasing consciousness among the people about the superior levels of living in advanced countries.

Inequalities in the real income and consumption have increased considerably during the past few decades. There has been no doubt an improvement in the level of living of the poor countries but the standard of living in advanced countries have progressed at a much rapid rate and so have inequalities.

Demonstration Effect and Propensity to Save

It has been brought out in the above analysis that demonstration effect adversely affects the savings of the people in the underdeveloped countries. Any increase in their income certainly increases their ability to save but it does not necessarily increase their willingness to save. Demonstration effect not only reduces the flow of voluntary savings, it also makes it difficult for the government to mobilise compulsory savings in the form of taxes.

TABLE – 3.1

DISTRIBUTION OF WORLD INCOME

	GNI (Billion US $) 2007		*Total Population (million) 2007*		*GNI Per Capita (US $) 2007*
1. Low Income Economies	748.8	(6.39)	1296	(19.6)	578
2. Middle Income Economies	12234.7	(15.31)	4260	(64.4)	2872
3. High Income Economies	39682.1	(78.3)	1056	(16.0)	37566
World	52621.4	(100.0)	6612	(100.0)	7958
India	**1069.4**	**(1.46)**	**1123**	**(16.9)**	**950**

Source: Compiled from *World Development Report*, 2009.

Demonstration effect also has its adverse effects on balance of payments as Nurkse puts it: "The poor nations, in contact with the rich, feel constantly impelled to keep their money incomes and outlays above what is warranted by their own capacity to produce. This results in inflationary pressures at home and a persistent tendency towards disequilibrium in the balance of payments."[7]

Positive Aspect

Demonstration effect has a positive aspect also. Higher demand for consumption goods may create incentives for more investment both in consumer goods and capital goods industries. Also, it may increase people's incentive to work. When people try to emulate higher living standards, they need to work hard and earn more to pay for such consumption. Further, along with superior consumption, knowledge about superior techniques of production is also transmitted from advanced countries to the underdeveloped countries which may help them in raising their levels of productivity.

Measures to Restrict the Adverse Effects

1. *Economic Isolation* – It is an extreme measure and Nurkse terms economic isolation as defeatist solution. According to him, economic isolation promotes stagnation. Contact with the outside world and higher living standards will help the economy. The adverse impact of demonstration effect can be reduced or weakened through appropriate policies directed towards controlling and discouraging domestic production and consumption of luxury goods, restricting the import of luxury goods.

2. *Foreign Aid* – Another method of checking the adverse influence of demonstration effect is making available to the poor countries sufficient quantities of foreign aid for meeting their requirements. With foreign aid, the work of capital formation becomes easier and balance of payment difficulties minimised. But the magnitude of foreign aid received by the poor countries does not infact depend on the extent of their poverty or the magnitude of their requirements, it is generally determined by political consideration. As Nurkse has pointed out, "Inter-governmental grants are inevitably matters of international political economy: if not deliberate instruments of foreign policy, they are at any rate shaped by the tactility of a country's relation with other nations. Such transfers as

7. Nurkse *op. cit.* p. 38.

may occur will inevitably be based in part on the shifting ground of political expediency."[8]

Foreign Capital and Economic Development

A country can obtain capital from two sources: (a) internal or domestic sources and (b) international transfers of capital. In the underdeveloped countries, the per capita real income being very low, not much of saving for capital formation can be obtained from the internal sources. Even those people who have the capacity to save do not save much because of the operation of the demonstration effect which enhances their consumption level and weakens their propensity to save. Also, the underdeveloped countries may not have the know-how to produce the capital goods. These goods may, therefore, have to be imported from the advanced industrial nations. But in view of the persistent balance of payment difficulties faced by these countries, large scale import of capital goods may be very difficult. Therefore, for initiating the process of economic development, the underdeveloped countries are obliged to depend on external sources of capital. Foreign capital, by complimenting the domestic capital availability, will make the process of economic development easier and quicker.

International transfer of capital takes place broadly through: (a) foreign direct investment and (b) international loans and grants.

Foreign direct investments have been the largest source of finance for developing countries and, according to World Bank Report on Global Development Finance, 1999, is likely to remain the largest source in foreseeable future.

The inflows of FDI to developing countries are highly concentrated, with Latin America and China being the major recipients in the lst 10 years. In aggregate terms, FDI to developing countries has been volatile. Between the mid-1990s and the early 2000s, inflows declined from 35 per cent of total world FDI to 10 per cent. FDI inflows have now recovered and are hovering around 30 per cent of the world total.

Since the mid-1990s, private capital flows to developing countries have declined and developing countries now are net savers. The exception is FDI, whose role in recent years has increased, in both absolute and relative terms.

---

8. Nurkse *op. cit.* p. 40.

After reaching over 25 per cent of the world total in the early 1990s, private capital flows into developing countries are a small and declining portion of all private capital flows.[9]

Private Foreign Investment: Some Pros and Cons for Development

According to Michael Todaro, few areas in the economics of development arouse so much controversy and are subject to such varying degrees of interpretation as the question of the benefits and costs of private foreign investment. The basic arguments for and against the development impact of private foreign investment can be summarised as follows:

Foreign private investment is typically seen as a way of filling in gaps between the domestically available supplies of savings, foreign exchange, government revenue and skills, and the planned level of these resources necessary to achieve development targets. To give a simple example of the "savings-investment gap" analysis : supposing the planned rate of growth of output is 7 per cent annually and the capital output rate is three, then the needed rate of saving is 21 per cent. If the saving that can be domestically mobilised is 16 per cent, then a saving gap equal to 5 per cent can be said to exist. If the nation can fill this gap with foreign financial resources, it will better be able to achieve its targeted rate of growth. Thus, the first and foremost contribution of private foreign investment to national development is its role in filling the resource gap between targeted investment and locally mobilised savings.

A second contribution, similar to the first, is its contribution to filling the gap between targeted foreign exchange requirements and those derived from net export earnings plus net public foreign aid. This is the so-called forcign exchange or trade gap.

An inflow of private foreign capital can also help to remove the deficit in the balance of payments over time if the foreign owned enterprise can generate a net positive flow of export earnings.

The third gap supposed to be filled by foreign investment is the gap between targeted governmental tax revenues and locally raised taxes. By taxing the profits of these enterprises, LDC governments are able to mobilise public financial resources for development projects.

---

9. *The Growth Report: Strategies for Sustained Growth and Inclusive Development*, Commission on Growth and Development.

Fourth and final, there is the gap in management, entrepreneurship, technology and skill. Foreign enterprises are believed to supply a package of needed resources including management experience, entrepreneurial abilities and technological skills which can then be transferred to their local counterparts by means of training programmes or the process of learning by doing. Further, these enterprises bring with them the most sophisticated technological knowledge about production processes while transferring modern machinery and equipment to capital-poor Third World countries. Such transfers of knowledge, skills and technology are assumed to be both desirable and productive to the recipient nations.

Arguments Against Private Foreign Investment

The Third World countries have commonly raised the following objections against private foreign investment :

1. Their impact on development is very uneven, and in many situations MNC activities reinforce dualistic economic structures and accentuate income inequalities. They tend to promote the interests of the small number of well-paid modern-sector workers against the interests of the rest by widening wage differentials. They divert resources away from needed food production to the manufacture of sophisticated products catering primarily for the demands of local elites. And they tend to worsen the imbalance between rural and urban economic opportunities by locating primarily in urban areas and contributing to the accelerated flow of rural-urban migration.
2. They typically produce inappropriate products (meant for small rich minority of the local population), stimulate inappropriate consumption patterns through advertising and their monopolistic market power, and do this all with inappropriate (capital intensive) technologies of production. This is perhaps the major area of criticism of private direct investment particularly of multinationals.
3. As a result of 1 and 2, local resources tend to be allocated towards socially undesirable projects. This in turn aggravates the already sizeable inequality between rich and poor and the serious imbalance between urban and rural economic opportunities.
4. MNCs use their economic power to influence government policies in directions unfavourable to development. They are able to extract sizeable economic and political concessions from

competing LDC governments in the form of excessive protection, tax rebates, investment allowances, and the cheap provision of factory sites and essential social services. Also, these MNCs can avoid much local taxation by artificially inflating the price it pays for intermediate products purchased from overseas affiliates so as to lower its stated local profits.

5. MNCs may damage host economies by suppressing domestic entrepreneurship and using their superior knowledge, worldwide contacts, advertising skills to drive out local competitors and inhibit the emergence of small scale local enterprises.

Summing up the pros and cons of foreign private investment, Todaro observes that, "the real debate ultimately centres on different ideological and value judgements about the nature and meaning of development and the principal sources from which it springs." The advocates of private foreign investment tend to be "free-market, private enterprise, *laissez-faire*" proponents. Those who argue against foreign capital particularly, the activities of MNCs are often motivated by a sense of the importance of national control over domestic economic activities. According to Todaro, the only really valid conclusion is that private foreign investment can be an important stimulus to economic and social development so long as the interests of both MNCs and host country governments coincide. By the strengthening of the relative bargaining powers of host-country governments through their coordinated activities, the private foreign investment can better fit the long-term development needs and priorities of poor nations.

Foreign Aid

In addition to export earnings and private foreign investment, another major source of Third World foreign exchange is bilateral and multilateral development assistance, known also as foreign aid.

Economists have defined foreign aid, therefore, as any flow of capital to LDCs which meets two criteria: (1) its objective should be non-commercial from the point of view of the donor; and (2) it should be characterised by "concessional" terms, that is, the interest rate and repayment period for borrowed capital should be "softer" (less stringent) than commercial terms. Even this definition can sometimes be inappropriate since it could include military aid, which is both non commercial and concessional. Normally, however, military aid is excluded from international measurements of foreign aid flows. The concept of foreign aid that is now widely used and accepted is one which encompasses all official grants and concessional loans, in currency or in kind, which are broadly aimed at transferring resources from developed to less developed nations (and more recently, from OPEC to other Third World countries) on developmental and/or income distributional grounds. Unfortunately, there often is a thin line separating purely "developmental" grants and loans from those ultimately motivated by security and/or commercial interests.

Aid can be "tied" either by source (i.e., loans and/or grants have to be spent on the purchase of donor country goods or services) or by project (funds cannot be spent on raw materials and intermediate products). In either case the 'real value' of the aid is reduced because the specified source is likely to be an expensive supplier. Otherwise there would be no need to 'tie' the aid. Additionally, aid may be tied to the import of capital-intensive equipment, which may impose an additional real resource cost—in the form of higher unemployment—to the recipient nation. Or the project itself may require purchase of new machinery and equipment from monopolistic suppliers while existing productive equipment in the same industry is being operated at very low levels of capacity.

Because foreign aid is seen differently by donor and recipient countries, we must first analyse the giving and receiving process from these two often contradictory viewpoints.

Why Donors Give Aid

Donor countries give aid primarily because it is in their political, strategic and/or economic self-interest to do so. While some development assistance may be motivated by moral and humanitarian reasons to assist the less fortunate (e.g. emergency relief programmes), there is no historical evidence to suggest that over longer periods of time donor nations assist others without expecting in return some corresponding benefits (political, economic, military, etc.). We can therefore characterise the foreign aid motivations of donor nations into two broad, but often interrelated, categories: political and economic.

Economic Motivations :
Two-Gap Models and Other Criteria

Within the broad context of political and strategic priorities, foreign aid programmes of the developed nations have had a strong economic rationale. In fact, while the political motivation may have been of paramount importance, the economic rationale was at least given greater lip-service as the overriding motivation for assistance.

The principal economic arguments advanced in support of foreign aid are as follows:

Foreign Exchange Constraints. External finance (both loans and grants) can play a critical role in supplementing domestic resources in order to relieve savings or foreign exchange bottlenecks.

The basic argument of the two-gap model is that most developing countries are faced either with a shortage of domestic savings to match investment opportunities or a shortage of foreign exchange to finance needed imports of capital and intermediate goods.

Growth and Savings. External assistance also is assumed to facilitate and accelerate the process of development by generating *additional* domestic savings as a result of the higher growth rates which it is presumed to induce. Eventually it is hoped that the need for concessional aid will disappear as local resources become sufficient to give the development process a self-sustaining character.

Why LDC Recipients Accept Aid

The major reason is clearly economic in concept and practice. Third World countries have often tended to accept uncritically the proposition, typically advanced by developed-country economists, taught in all universities development courses, and supported by reference to 'success' cases like Taiwan, Israel and South Korea to the exclusion of many more 'failures', that aid is a crucial and essential ingredient in the development process. It supplements scarce domestic resources; it helps to transform the economy structurally; and it contributes to the achievement of LDC takeoffs into self-sustaining economic growth. Thus, the economic rationale for aid in LDCs is based largely on their acceptance of the donor's perceptions of what they, the poor countries, require to promote their economic development.

The basic area of conflict arises, therefore, not out of any disagreement about the role of aid but about its amount and conditions. LDCs, naturally, would like to have more aid in the form of outright grants or long-term low-cost loans with a minimum of strings attached. This means the abolition of tying aid to donor exports and the granting of greater latitude to recipient countries to decide for themselves what is in their best long-run development interests.

The two minor, though still important, motivations for LDCs to seek aid are political and moral. In some countries, aid is seen by both donor and recipient as providing greater political leverage to the existing leadership to suppress opposition and maintain itself in power.

Once aid is accepted, the ability of recipient governments to extricate themselves from implied political and/or economic obligations to donors and prevent donor governments from interfering in their internal affairs can be greatly diminished.

Finally, we come to the moral motivation. Many proponents of foreign aid in both developed and developing countries believe that rich nations have an obligation to support the economic and social development of the Third World. They then go on to link this moral obligation with the need for greater LDC autonomy with respect to the allocation and use of aid funds.

The Effects of Aid

The controversy over the economic effects of aid like that related to private foreign investment is fraught with disagreements. On one side are the "economic traditionalists" who argue that aid has indeed helped to promote growth and structural transformation in many LDCs.[10] Others have argued that aid does not promote faster growth but may in fact retard it by substituting for, rather than, supplementing domestic savings and investment and by excerbating LDC balance of payments deficits as a result of rising debt repayment obligations,[11] and tying aid to donor-country exports.

Aid is further criticised for focusing on and stimulating the growth of the modern sector, thereby increasing the gap in living standards between the rich and the poor in Third World countries. Some would even assert that foreign aid has been a positive force for anti-development in the sense that it both retards growth through reduced savings and worsens income inequalities.[12] Rather than relieving economic bottlenecks and filling gaps, aid (and for that matter, private foreign assistance) not only widens existing savings and foreign exchange resource gaps but may even create new ones (e.g., urban-rural or modern sector-traditional sector gaps).

Recent Trends in Aid :
The Decline in Concessional Finance

On the donor side, there has been growing disenchantment in recent years with foreign aid as domestic issues like inflation, unemployment and balance of payments problems gain increasing priority over international cold war politics. One often hears the expression "aid

10. Nurkse *op. cit.* p 45.
11. Nurkse *op. cit.* p. 70.
12. Nurkse *op. cit.* p. 80-81.

weariness" used to describe the attitudes of developed countries toward foreign assistance.

Net concessional assistance to developing countries totalled $ 32.7 billion in 1998, i.e., $ 12 billion below the 1990 level.

Aid Effectiveness :
The Relationship between Aid and Growth

The decline in aid over the 1990s has been driven, in part, by growing skepticism in donor countries over the contribution of aid to growth. Many developing countries have become more aid-dependent since the 1970s. While official assistance has fallen steadily in the 1990s, assistance actually rose strongly during the 1980s; net concessional flows to all developing countries increased from $ 25 billion in 1980 to $ 45 billion in 1990.

The 1990s have also witnessed a reconsideration of the contribution of aid to economic growth. Past theories emphasised the role of foreign aid in financing the gap between domestic savings and investment needed to attain a certain growth target. However, empirical studies consistently found a weak relationship between aid and investment and little impact of aid on growth.

A study of 56 developing countries found little connection between aid and per capita growth (Burnside and Dollar, 1997). However, among countries in this sample that had good economic management (as measured by inflation, the budget deficit, trade regime, effectiveness of the legal system, competence of the bureaucracy and extent of corruption), the connection was much stronger: those receiving substantial amounts of aid achieved per capita growth rates of 3.7 per cent, while countries that received little aid grew at only 2.2 per cent. By contrast, the impact of aid was insignificant for countries with bad economic management. These results support the view that aid does matter, but only in countries that have a good policy and institutional environment.

Does aid help promote good policies? Much development aid, including the World Bank's assistance, has been devoted to encouraging policy reforms and strengthening institutions—but the record of success is mixed.

The experience of Zambia illustrates the failure of aid to promote good policies and its ineffectiveness in a bad policy environment. The amount of aid received by Zambia increased from 0.2 per cent of GDP in the early 1970s to 8 per cent in the early 1990s, while policies deteriorated. Real GDP per capita was 8.5 per cent of U.S. income in 1966, but only 3.8 per cent in 1990.

Aid and Poverty

But how effective is aid in reducing poverty? Collier and Dollar (1998) estimate that without aid there would be an additional 30 million poor people in developing countries each year (based on a poverty line of $ 2 a day). However, they further estimate that increasing the allocation of aid to countries in which the policy environment is strong and the income elasticity of poverty is high could substantially increase the number of people who escape poverty, perhaps by an additional 50 million people per year. This calculation equalises the marginal cost (in terms of aid) of lifting someone above the poverty line in each country. To achieve such a large poverty reduction with the current allocation of aid, they estimate that the total volume of aid would need to increase by fourfold.

One reason why the optimal allocation of aid is not achieved is that donors tend to phase out aid from reforming countries as the growth rate takes off. Also, they tend to divert aid to where the poverty problem is acute, but possibly insoluble because of the weak policy environment.

Many developing countries have indeed improved their policy environment during the 1990s. According to the World Banks' ratings, average policy performance has improved significantly in both Sub Saharan Africa and South Asia, and is now better than at any time in the previous quarter century. Some 2 billion out of a total of 2.7 billion poor live in 32 countries and that in the 1990s they have adopted a good policy environment (for example, Ethiopia, India, Mali and Uganda).

Questions

1. Distinguish between balanced growth and unbalanced growth Which strategy would you recommend for a developing country like India? Give reasons. *[B.Com. (P) 1999: B.A. (P) 2000, 2006]*
2. Write short note on capital formation in India. *[B.A. (P) 2005]*
3. Analyse the problem of disguised unemployment. In this context, examine the problems involved in using disguised unemployment as a source of cost-free capital formation. *[B.Com. (P) 2005]*
4. Write short note on Demonstration effects. *[B.Com. (P) 2005]*
5. Write a short note on merits and demerits of unbalanced growth strategy. *[B.Com. (P) 2003, 2005]*

6. Write short note on 'Disguised unemployment as a source of capital formation. *[B.A. (P) 2003; B.Com. (P) 2005]*
7. Explain 'vicious circle of poverty'. Show how it can be broken from the demand and supply side. *[B.Com. (P) 2005]*
8. Write a short note on Balanced vs. Unbalanced Growth. *[B.Com. (P) 1999, 2001, 2005]*
9. Examine the strategy of unbalanced growth. Discuss its merits and Demerits. *[B.Com. (P) 2001; B.A. (P) 2004]*
10. Differentiate between the concepts of Balanced and Unbalanced growth. Which of the two would you advocate in solving the problems of capital formation in India? *[B.A. (P) 2003]*
11. Write a short note on disguised unemployment as saving potential. *[B.Com. (P) 2000, 2003]*
12. Explain the Nurkesean strategy of using disguised unemployment as a source of capital formation. How far is this strategy feasible in India? *[B.A. (P) 2001]*
13. Discuss balanced growth as a strategy to break vicious circle of poverty. How suitable is this strategy for India? *[B.Com. (P) 2000]*

4

Population and Economic Development

IN recent years, there has been an increasing focus on the relationship between population growth and economic development. The most difficult problem for such an analysis is to be able to separate cause from effect. Does economic development accelerate or retard population growth or does population growth contribute to or retard economic development? What are the linkages and how strong they are and in what direction do they operate?

Economic Development and Population Growth

The Theory of Demographic Transition

The theory of demographic transition attempts to explain why all contemporary developed nations have more or less passed through the same three stages of population growth. Before their economic modernisation, these countries, for centuries, had stable or very slow growing population as a result of a combination of high birth rate and almost equally high death rate. With economic development resulting in higher incomes, improved public health facilities, there was a marked decline in mortality that gradually raised life expectancy from under 40 years to over 60 years. However, the decline in death rate was not immediately accompanied by a decline in fertility. With declining death rate but birth rate not falling correspondingly, these countries passed through stage two, marking the beginning of demographic transition i.e., transition from stable or slow growing population to rapidly increasing number. Finally, stage three is reached when the forces and influences of modernisation and economic development cause fertility to decline so that eventually, falling birth rate converge with lower death rate leaving little or no population growth.[1] Thus, how does economic development affect population growth can be explained through the theory of demographic transition.

The Microeconomic Theory of Fertility

In recent years, economists have begun to look more closely at the micro economic determinants of family fertility. They have utilised the principles of economy and optimisation to explain family size decisions. In deciding whether or not to have additional children, parents are assumed to weigh economic benefits against costs. The principle of benefits are the expected income from child labour usually on the farm and their family support for elderly parents. Balance against these benefits are the two principle elements of costs: (1) The opportunity cost of mother's time, the income she could earn if she were not at home caring for her children. (2) The cost of educating children that is the trade off between having fewer 'high quality' high cost, educated children with high income earning potentials *versus* more 'low quality', low cost, uneducated children with much lower earning prospects.

Statistical studies have shown that birth rates among the poor are likely to fall where there is—

(i) An increase in the education of women and consequent change in their role and status.

(ii) An increase in female non-agricultural wage employment opportunities which raises the price or cost of their traditional child bearing activities.

(iii) A rise in family income through increase in direct employment and earning of husband and wife and or redistribution of income and assets from rich to poor.

(iv) A reduction in infant mortality through expanded public health programme and better nutritional status for both parent and child.

(v) The development of old age and social security systems to bridge the economic dependence of parents on their offsprings.

Thus, efforts to make jobs, education and health more broadly available to poverty groups in Third World countries will not only

1. Todaro, Michael (2004). *Economic Development in the Third World* (8th edition). Delhi: Pearson Education (Singapore) Pte. Ltd.

contribute to their income and physical well-being but it can also contribute substantially to their motivation for smaller families which is vital to reducing growth rates.

How Does Population Growth Affect Economic Development?

So far we have tried to analyse the effect of economic development on population growth, now let us examine how does population growth affect economic development? We may begin by asking the question how does population growth affect the net national product?

Until recently, the literature of economic demography drew attention to two main relationships through which population growth affect the economy, what we may call : (i) the 'saving effect' and (ii) 'composition of investment effect'.[2] The former of these argues that savings are reduced by population growth because of the so-called burden of dependency. With high fertility and declining mortality in younger and older age groups, the population acquires an increasing proportion of people in the non-working age groups relative to those of working age. Since all must consume, in the absence of increasing output per worker, saving per head must fall. Even if productivity is increasing, savings are less than they would be with a smaller number of dependents per worker.

The investment argument is like this: with increasing population, a share of investible resources has to be devoted to reproducing for additional people unproductive facilities, duplication of social services which would be unnecessary if population were not growing. A number of studies starting with Coale and Hoover have shown through comparison of high and low fertility paths that there have been greater growth of GNP with the lesser rate of population growth. Robert Cassen has raised doubts on the validity of the above saving and investments effect. He argues, if bulk of savings in poor countries come from small wealthy class whose fertility is low and if cost of additional children are met out of consumption rather than saving, the saving cost of additional children would be quite inconsiderable.

In the macroeconomic picture, if population growth leads to slower growth of output, then one would expect slower growth of saving but to avoid circularity, the negative effect of population on GNP growth must be established independently of the saving effect. Similarly, regarding the composition of investment effect, Cassen observes that one important area which has not been incorporated in the existing

2. Cassen, R.H. *India, Population, Economy and Society*, ch.4, p. 221.

demographic models is the question of changing composition of the resource costs of producing basic consumption goods, that is food. As long as a society can increase agricultural output by mainly labour using means, the chief resource to feed growing population is provided by the population itself, the capital required is circulating capital, wage good to support the labour force. But a point is reached where required increases in agricultural output necessitated yield improving inputs which are expensive in both capital and foreign exchange. Just as Coale and Hoover model argued that with slower population growth more capital would have been available for raising per worker productivity because of reduced welfare expenditure, similarly Cassen argues that more capital and foreign exchange would have been available from reduction in expenditure devoted to raising agricultural output.

The composition of investment argument according to Cassen is really quite general. Wherever population growth requires increase in production, which in turn require investment, a lesser rate of population growth would release investible funds for use elsewhere. One fails to understand why past models have concentrated on welfare investment. Food production is in fact the least postponable of all forms of population-related output needs and if agriculture enters a phase of fundamental alteration in production function or in other words changing resource requirements for additional output, this can be a major burden of population growth. India reached this stage since mid-1960s when increases in agricultural output had to be brought out by yield improving technology which is capital-intensive instead of increasing acreage. The biggest problem for India if current trend continues is the increasing share of investible surplus that will be taken up by food needs of the growing population.

According to K. Sundaram, the implications of growing demographic pressures in India for the process of development in general and the progress towards poverty eradication become clearer once we focus on the labour force consequences of population growth. The sheer magnitude of the addition to workforce brings to the fore the capital constraints in raising the productivity of the labour force. The capital requirement of equipping the labour force would be astronomically large.[3]

The labour force expansion also puts direct pressure on the single most important natural resource in a predominantly agrarian economy, namely, land. Admittedly, the effective supply of land can be augmented

3. Sundaram, K. (1999-2000). "Demography and Development", in Uma Kapila (ed.), *Indian Economy Since Independence*. New Delhi: Academic Foundation.

by the use of reproducible capital. Irrigation is the most obvious example making it possible to increase the gross cropped area. The inadequate expansion of gross cropped area and of the irrigated area reflects the fact that the irrigation system has not expanded even up to the limits of currently known irrigation potential. This again is a manifestation of the inadequacy of capital resources. Further, it may be emphasised that even if currently known irrigation potential is fully utilised, it will leave a good chunk of the net sown area dependent on rain which may or may not be adequate. Thus, the moisture availability may act as an independent constraint on raising agricultural productivity and hence on overall economic development.

While Sundaram has analysed the implications for growing demographic pressures in India for the process of development in general, Pravin Visaria has focused on the demographic aspects of development. The process of development has brought about a remarkable decline in mortality level. Of course, the decline in the level of fertility has not been large enough to lower the rate of natural increase of the population. According to Pravin Visaria, despite several limitations, the family planning programme has undoubtedly contributed to the observed decline in the total fertility rates and the birth rate. It has also helped to offset the possible increase in marital fertility rates that could have resulted from the decline in mortality and the incidence of widowhood. But for the family planning programme, the rate of growth of India's population could have risen sharply as has happened in several African countries where the growth of population has been 3.6 and 3.8 per cent during 1985-1990. The population of India's neighbours, Bangladesh and Pakistan, has too been growing at an annual rate of 2.7 to 3.4 per cent. By comparison, India seems to have done better and the rate of growth of population has remained stable at a moderate level.

The level of fertility is an integral aspect of development, universely related to the latter. The classical model of demographic transition postulates a link between a desire for fewer children and change in macro developmental variables such as urbanisation, industrialisation, literacy and education, and the status and role of women (Coale, 1973; Friedman, 1982). A United Nation's study (1963) has added means of communication to the list. Significant changes in these variables subsumed under 'modernisation' do constitute sufficient conditions but there are multiple pathways to the eventual similiarity of the levels of fertility and mortality. There are lessons to be learnt from the experience of Kerala and Tamil Nadu which have already attained the replacement level of fertility (or a net reproduction rate of one) by 1988. An almost universal female literacy and a low level of infant and child mortality and the high status of women are considered crucial in the decline in fertility in Kerala. The decline in fertility in Tamil Nadu has been attributed to support for both increase in the age at marriage and an imaginative programme of information, education and communication (IEC).

Quite apart from the two southern states that have already lowered their fertility below the replacement level, the diversity of situation in India's heterogenous society needs to be taken into account. In a country with over 575,000 villages and 4700 urban centres, the means of modifying traditional behaviour have to be adapted to the local conditions.

India's Demographic Transition

Table 4.1 suggest that the country's demographic transition really began, rather hesitatingly, with a reduction in the average death rate during the 1920s and 1930s. These decades saw a decline in the frequency and scale of major famines and epidemics, which previously had made people's lives so incredibly precarious. As a result, there was a modest increase in life expectancy. And, with a prevailing crude birth rate of about 45 per thousand, these small gains in mortality were sufficient to raise the average annual rate of population growth to over one per cent per year during the 1920s, the 1930s and the 1940s.

At the time of its Independence in 1947, India's population was about 345 million. Life expectancy was around 33 years and the TFR was close to six births. The decades following the 1940s have seen great changes.

The most important change relates to mortality. Immediately after Independence, the Government of India placed great stress upon improving the health of its people. As a result, death rates have fallen almost everywhere, more or less continuously. At the start of the twenty first century, life expectancy is almost double that of 1947 (about 67 years for females and 64 years for males 2001-2006).

The reduction in the death rate after 1947 resulted in a significant rise in the rate of population growth, which reached almost 2 per cent during 1951-1961. In the following three decades, it remained fairly constant at around 2.2 per cent. The birth rate was more resistant to change than the death rate. It was only during the 1991-2001 intercensal decade that the birth rate fell faster than the death rate—so bringing about a significant decline in the rate of population growth.

TABLE – 4.1

KEY POPULATION STATISTICS OF INDIA, 1901-2001[4]

Census Year	*Total Population (million)*	*Average Annual Growth Rate (per cent)*	*Birth Rate*	*Death Rate*	*Rate of Natural Increase*	*Sex Ratio (males per 1000 females)*	*Per Cent of Urban Population*
1901	238.3	0.3	49.2	42.6	6.6	1029	10.8
1911	252.0	0.6	48.1	47.2	0.9	1038	10.3
1921	251.2	N	46.2	36.3	9.9	1047	11.2
1931	278.9	1.1	45.2	31.2	14.0	1053	12.0
1941	318.5	1.3	39.9	27.4	12.5	1058	13.9
1951	361.0	1.3	40.9	22.8	18.1	1057	17.3
1961	439.1	2.0	40.0	17.8	22.2	1063	18.0
1971	548.2	2.2[b]	37.8	15.4	22.4	1075	19.9
1981	683.3	2.2[b]	33.8	12.3	21.5	1071	23.3[a]
1991	846.3	2.1	30.6	10.3	20.3	1067	25.7
2001	1027	1.9	25.8	8.5	13.3	1072	27.8

Note: a Includes only an estimate for Assam.
b Growth rate for 1961-1971 and 1971-1981 take account of the fact that the reference data of the 1971 Census was 1 April, whereas that of the 1981 Census (like the 1951 and 1961 Census) was 1 March.
N: Negligible.

4. Visaria, Pravin (2008-09). "Demographic Aspects of Development: The Indian Experience", in Uma Kapila (ed.), *Indian Economy Since Independence*. New Delhi: Academic Foundation.

Although the 'total fertility rate' (the average number of births per couple) for India as a whole is still well above the 'replacement level' (around 2.1), fertility in India has fallen quite sharply in recent decades, from around 6 in 1961 to 3 in 2001 and 2.8 in 2006.

According to Drèze and Sen (2002), in order to interpret these contrasting trends (continuing rapid population growth on the one hand, and declining fertility rates on the other), population growth has to be placed in the context of the 'demographic transition' from high to low fertility and mortality rates. In the initial phases of this transition, death rates typically fall faster than birth rates so that the rate of population growth increases: in India, for instance, it increased from virtually zero at the beginning of the twentieth century to 2.2 per cent per year in the 1960s and 1970s. As the transition progresses, the rate of decline of birth rates gradually overtakes that of death rates, leading to a decline in the growth rate of population, as began to happen in India about 20 years ago. In some individual states, it happened much earlier.

The decline of population growth, though relatively recent, can be expected to accelerate in the relatively near future, not only due to steadily falling fertility rates but also because of ongoing changes in the age structure of the population. Viewed in the context of this demographic transition, current patterns of population growth appears, less alarming. Indeed, India is now well into the last phase of its demographic transition, involving falling populaton growth and sustained progresss towards 'population stabilisation' (which is expected to occur around the middle of this century), and there is certainly no evidence that a 'population bomb' is ticking away. This does not, of course, detract from the need for concern about rapid population growth at this time, or from the possibility of accelerating the demographic transition through supportive public policy (Drèze and Sen, 2002).

Growth of Population

The major causes responsible for the high growth of population in India fall into two groups: (i) those responsible for persistence of high fertility indirected by high birth rate and (ii) those responsible for decling mortality as indicated by falling death rate.

Causes of High Birth Rate

Social Factors

Social factors like universality of marriage and marriage at young age, joint family system, preference for a son result in high birth rate.

Economic Factors

Economic factors such as widespread poverty, high infant mortality and children as an insurance have also contributed to high birth rate.

Poverty

Among poverty groups not much money is spent on the upbringing of the children and hence, they are not much of a liability. Rather they start earning at an early age by doing some work on farms or take up some odd jobs in urban industrial areas. Hence, they add to family income and prove an asset to the family. Among poor families, additional children do not add to any burden, rather they provide helping hands for the family.

Lack of Social Security

Further, low survival rate among infants also encourages high birth rate. As social security like old age pension is not available to the poor masses in India, they expect their children to look after them in their old age. But since infant mortality rate (death rate among infants or very small children) is very high, people like to raise larger families so that some of them survive to look after parents in the old age. Thus, absence of social security combined with high infant mortality contribute to high birth rate. Because of lack of savings due to poverty, a large number of children act like insurance for their parents.

Illiteracy, Ignorance and Belief in Fate

Illiteracy is widespread in India. Illiterate and ignorant people thus accept every child as a will of God and would never think of interfering with His will. This increases the birth rate in India. Moreover, illiterate population does not realise the problems caused by increasing population or the means to keep family size in reasonable limits.

Ineffective Family Planning

Thus, high birth rate in India is the result of a whole lot of social, economic, religious and cultural factors. Unless a change is brought about in our attitude through social and cultural changes by spread of education and enlightenment or through economic and political pressure, not much decline can be expected in the prevailing high birth rate.

Fertility Rate

Fertility rate is a more scientific explanation of population growth rate than the birth rate. The birth rate, which measures the number of live births per thousand of population, is only a crude measure and thus called crude birth rate. It is crude because it associates the total number of live births with total population, whether young or old, male or female or whether they belong to reproductive age group or not.

Total fertility rate (TFR) on the other hand, measures the average number of children born to a woman up to the end of reproductive period. TFR, which was around 6 during 1951-52 declined to 5.3 during 1970-1972, 4.5 during 1980-1982, and 3.6 in 1990-1992 and 2.8 in 2006. Thus, though there has been some decline in TFR, it has not been large enough to much reduce natural growth rate of population in the face of continued decline in mortality rate. TFR in turn depends upon proportion of the married population, age at marriage and the number of children born per married women in course of her reproductive period.

Fertility rates vary radically across the country—between regions, between states and between districts. For example, for the state of Kerala as a whole—consisting of 14 districts—the average fertility rate is now around 1.8, which is lower than the rates for China and USA, and comparable with those of some West European countries such as Britain and France. In fact, the fertility rate is also below the replacement level already for Tamil Nadu, and demographic calculations suggest that several other states (including Andhra Pradesh, Himachal Pradesh, Gujarat, Punjab and West Bengal) will have below-replacement fertility rates within the next five years or so.

In general, however, the seriousness of the population issue must not be dismissed. Given the density of pupulation that India already has, the environmental and social implications of further significant expansion can indeed be potentially grave.

Causes of Decline in Death Rate

In the early years of 20th century, death rate was very high. It was 42.6 per thousand during 1901-1910 and further increased to 47.2 per thousand during 1911-1920, but came down slowly to 36.3 per thousand in 1921-1930 and remained above 31 per thousand during 1931-1940. However, since the planned economic development of the country, there is a sharp decline in death rate from about 27 per thousand in 1941-1950 to 8.5 per thousand during 1991-2000. The current level is 7.4 (2007).[5] This decline in death rate was slow and gradual in the earlier decades but became progressively sharper after 1951.

5. Government of India, *Economic Survey* 2008-09.

Control of Epidemics

In the earlier years of the 20th century, epidemics like plague, smallpox, malaria, etc., took a heavy toll of life. But with increasing availability of effective medicines and improvement in health care facilities, these epidemics have been controlled. This has contributed to a substantial reduction in the death rate.

Control of Famines

Famines which occured in India frequently and with marked regularity, took a heavy toll of life. The Bengal famine of 1943 for example caused thousands of starvation deaths while millions of people fled to other parts of the country in search of food. With the improvement in the means of transport and communications, spread of famines has been effectively checked. Of course, sometimes famine like conditions do occur in some parts of the country, as had happened during the year 2000 AD in parts of Gujarat and Rajasthan, yet effective measures to make supply of food available in these areas prevented any starvation deaths. Control of famines has been an important factor in the decline of death rate.

Improved Medical Facilities

With the increased investment in health and medical care facilities, many new hospitals have come up and a large number of dispensaries have been opened even in far-flung rural areas. Thus, an increasingly greater proportion of population is now being provided medical facilities. This has improved health and prevented deaths due to timely availability of medical aid.

Spread of Maternity Homes

With spread of maternity homes where trained staff looks after child birth, deaths at the time of delivery have been largely prevented.

Impact of Economic Development

Under the impact of development, incomes and living standards of people have improved. This has improved their health and nutritional levels and made them less prone to disease and early death. Improvement in personal hygiene and sanitary conditions which go with better living standard have prevented the spread of communicable diseases. Education has made them aware of preventive measures that ensure disease-free life. Thus, the impact of overall development has been to promote better health and longer life. The life expentancy at birth (number of years a new born child is expected to live) has gone up from 32 years in 1950-51 to nearly 62.6 years for males and 64.2 years for females in 2006-07. This shows that now on, an average people live longer. Special programmes aimed at improving income and living standards of the poorer sections of society, provision of basic needs such as pure drinking water, health care facilities, houses for the homeless, etc., have all contributed to better life and lower death rate.

Thus, the social, economic, political, epidemiological and other developments that have underpinned the sustained mortality improvement of recent decades are many and complex. However, the increased control of many infectious and parasitic diseases (e.g. smallpox, malaria, cholera), the spread of immunisation coverage (especially with the Expanded Programme of Immunisation introduced around 1978), general progress in improving sanitation and water supplies, increased levels of education in the population, and a very considerable expansion of health facilities, have all been significant parts of the explanation for the sustained improvement in mortality.

India Vision 2020, Report of the Planning Commission[6] states that India's population would be 1331 million (133 crore) by the year 2020. The current and the projected increase in population growth rate is due to large size of population in the reproductive age group, high fertility rate due to unmet needs of contraception and also high wanted fertility due to high infant mortality rates. Effective steps and appropriate policies with regard to these issues thus, need to be devised and implemented to meet the growing population challenge.

Efforts must therefore, be made to reduce the growth rate of population. As there is still some scope for further reduction in death rate in India, therefore, all our efforts are needed to effectively reduce birth rate to stem the tide of rapidly increasing population.

Measures to Reduce Birth Rate

Here, we may just list some of the measures which can help to reduce birth rate and thereby check the growth rate of population.

1. **Spread of education** particularly female education as we have before us the experience of Kerala and Tamil Nadu.
2. **Increase in female wage employment:** Female education and their gainful employment will raise the status of women which will have positive effect on achiveing small family norm.

6. Planning Commission (2003). *India Vision 2020*. New Delhi: Academic Foundation.

3. **Provision of old age pension and social security** which will reduce the dependence of parents on their children.

4. **Reduction in infant mortality** i.e., death rate of infants and small children through expanded public health programmes and better nutritional standards by ensuring longevity of life for new born children will help in reducing birth rate.

5. **Family planning:** Family planning means planned parenthood where the parents decide to keep their family small by giving birth to one or two children at proper intervals. The idea is to have a baby by choice and not by chance. Young married couples make use of various birth control devices to limit size of their families. Acceptance of family planning and one or two child norm by a large section of our population in the reproductive age group can help reduce birth rate substantially.

6. **Incentives for small families:** Such incentives as preference in government jobs, housing and other loans at low interest rates, preference in allotment of accommodation to people with small families can have a great impact on cutting down the birth rate. A scheme of disincentive to people with large families can also be devised so that the policy of carrot and stick can yield the desired fall in population growth rate.

Concerns about Population Growth

Although we need not worry about Malthusian fears that population growth in India is outstripping—or will soon outstrip—the growth of food supply but one cannot deny the fact of the widespread prevalence of hunger in India.

There is little evidence that the problem of producing enough food to keep up with population growth is a real problem now—or in the foreseeable future. That does not, however, obviate the need for concern about rapid population growth. First, as far as food is concerned, the extra demand for food in India will come not only from population growth, but also from the enhancement of the quantity and quality of food consumed per unit of population. It is the cumulative effects that we have to look at. The incidence of nutritional deprivation in India is among the highest in the world. General undernourishment—what is sometimes called 'protein-energy malnutrition'—is nearly twice as high in India as in Sub-Saharan Africa on the average. Judged in terms of the usual standards of retardation in weight for age, the proportion of undernourished children in Africa is 20 to 40 per cent, whereas the percentage of undernourished Indian children is very high 40 to 60 per cent. The proportion of 'severely undernourished' children in India is above 20 per cent in the larger north Indian states (based on the weight-for-age criterion).

As Indians acquire greater purchasing power, and as the biases against particular groups (such as young girls) diminish, the size and composition of food consumption per head will have to change. The challenges of food production and food availability in India have to be seen in that light, rather than in terms of the old Malthusian comparison between the growth of total population and that of aggregate food production (Drèze and Sen, 2002).

Second, the pressure on environmental resources is no less serious than perspective of food production and consumption. We have sufficient evidence of rapid deterioration of the local environment across the country (in addition to India's contribution to global environmental degradation), with a wide range of adversities, varying from overcrowding of habitat and increases in manmade pollution to the denuding of forests and vegetation.

Third, rapid population growth leads to excessive pressure not only on the environment but also on the social infrastructure, including sewage systems, hospital facilities, railway networks, power grids, garbage processing plants, and many other components of the 'stock' of public amenities. When public authorities are constantly racing to bring this stock in line with a larger population, there is much less room for qualitative improvements in public facilities. This phenomenon is clearly visible in some urban agglomerations, the rapid growth of which has gone hand in hand with a qualitative deterioration of the social infrastructure.

Fourth, there is a compounding of the impact of population growth and economic growth. In all the spheres of concern to which we have already referred (food and nutritional adequacy, environmental degradation, infrastructural pressure, etc.), we have to look at the cumulative effects of growth in population size and increase in economic activity.

"To summarise, concern about population growth must not be simply dismissed as groundless. The size of the Indian population is already large, and its continued rapid expansion can certainly be a source of anxiety for the environment, in addition to the problems it raises for improving the living standard and economic and social well-being of the people. And yet the population situation is not as terrifying as it is sometimes made to look, based on the citation of selectively chosen statistics (or non-statistics). First, food supply has not been falling behind population—quite firmly to the contrary. The possibility of accommodating considerable increases in food consumption per head—both quantitative and qualitative—is still quite favourable. Second, the fertility rate is falling quite rapidly, and may decline faster still with sensible policies, especially related to child health and women's empowerment. Third, the fertility rate varies widely between different regions in India, and there is much to learn from those that have already achieved low fertility rates, and also much evidence that these achievements are indeed spreading to other regions as well" (Drèze and Sen, 2002).

Gender Equity and the Demographic Transition

There is much evidence now, based on inter-country comparisons as well as inter-regional contrasts within India, that women's empowerment (through employment, education, property rights, etc.) can have a very strong effect in reducing fertility rates. Speedy fertility declines in the states of Kerala, Tamil Nadu or Himachal Pradesh in India can be firmly linked to the rapid enhancement of female education and other sources of empowerment of young women. In fact, the principal variables that seem to account for inter-district variations in fertility rates in India are directly linked to women's empowerment, in particular female literacy and women's participation in gainful employment.

Female literacy not only has a strong impact in reducing child mortality rates, which in itself is a great result, it additionally also contributes to reducing fertility. Similarly, the promotion of women's employment opportunities and related sources of empowerment contribute to their security in old age, and offer some protection from the adversities of widowhood. These, again, are important achievements in themselves, and also make a further contribution to fertility decline, insofar as the fear of old-age insecurity often slows down the adoption of small family norms.

Population Policy since 1947

The debate about population growth and family planning received impetus in the late 1940s not only due to the publication of the Bhore Committee Report, but also because of the occurrence of several poor harvests which necessitated the importation of food. Moreover, the 1951 Census revealed significant demographic growth. It was against this background that Nehru announced that India would initiate a national family planning programme. The final document of the First Five Year Plan, presented to Parliament in 1952, referred specifically to a programme for 'family limitation and population control'. Thus, India became the first country in the world to adopt an official national population policy in support of family planning (Caldwell, 1998; Visaria and Jain, 1976).

During the 1950s, the government allocated modest sums of money to the population programme. At that time, many people had reservations about the promotion of modern contraception. Also as India was a *pioneer*, there was little previous experience on which to draw. However, there were other significant developments in the 1950s. There was increasing achievement in promoting contraception in the larger towns. The government of Madras state began endorsing vasectomy with success, and it was soon followed by Kerala, Mysore and Maharashtra. Madras also began making compensation payments to poor people who were sterilised. By the time of the Third Five Year Plan (1961-1966) the 'objective of stabilising the growth of population (within) a reasonable period' was put 'at the very centre of India's planned development'. The Third Plan document also noted the important role that voluntary sterilisation might make towards achieving this. The budgetary outlay was significantly increased. Sterilisation camps began to be used to promote vasectomy. There was also a shift in the emphasis of family planning delivery, from a clinic-based approach to a wider community extension strategy.

The period of the Fourth Five Year Plan (1969-1974) saw increased concern over the rate of demographic growth. The 1971 Census showed a decadal increment of 109 million. Consequently, there was an increased emphasis upon targets, compensation payments and male sterilisation. This continued into the Fifth Plan, and culminated in the atmosphere of urgency which characterised Indira Gandhi's declaration of Emergency in 1975-1977. The language of the 1976 National Population Policy as quoted in Cassen (1978: 182) is revealing of the time:

"The wait for education and economic development to bring about a drop in fertility is not a practical solution. The very increase in population makes economic development slow and more difficult of achievement. The time factor is so pressing, and the population growth so formidable, that we have to get out of this vicious circle through a direct assault upon this problem as a national commitment."

The Emergency saw a massive increase in vasectomies. But there was later a backlash against the programme, particularly in the northern states, which lasted into the 1980s. Subsequently, although the government family welfare programme has continued to emphasise sterilisation, it has been mainly tubectomy which has been provided.

The rhetoric of population control largely disappeared with the Sixth Plan (1980-1985). Since the Seventh Plan in particular (1986-1990), there has been increasing recognition of the requirements: to tailor the family welfare programme to the conditions prevailing in individual states; to adopt a multi-sectoral approach which recognises the linkages between birth control and programmes in other areas (such as education); and to involve the private sector more in contraceptive delivery. Incentive payments and targets have largely been eliminated. Furthermore, following the 1994 Cairo Population Conference, emphasis has now greater shifted to the reproductive health needs of women.

National Population Policy, 2000

The National Population Policy, 2000 aims at achieving net replacement levels of total fertility rate by 2010 through vigorous implementation of inter-sectoral operational strategies. The long-term objective is to achieve population stabilisation by 2045, at a level consistent with the requirements of sustainable economic growth, social development and environment protection. Crude birth rate has come down, but needs to come down faster in view of the declining crude death rate (Table 4.2).

Objectives of National Population Policy

The immediate objective of the NPP 2000 is to address the unmet needs for contraception, health care infrastructure and health personnel, and to provide integrated service delivery for basic reproductive and child health care. The medium-term objective is to bring the TFR to replacement levels by 2010, through vigorous implementation of inter sectoral operational strategies. The long-term objective is to achieve a stable population by 2045, at a level consistent with the requirements of sustainable economic growth, social development and environmental protection.

TABLE – 4.2

INDIA — SELECTED HEALTH INDICATORS

Sl. No.	*Parameter*	*1951*	*1981*	*1991*	*Current Level*
1.	Crude Birth Rate (Per 1000 population)	40.8	33.9	29.5	23.1 (2007)
2.	Crude Death Rate (Per 1000 population)	25.1	12.5	9.8	7.4 (2007)
3.	Total Fertility Rate (TFR) (Per woman)	6.0	4.5	3.6	2.8 (2006)
4.	Maternal Mortality Ratio (MMR) (Per 100,000 live births)	NA	NA	437 (1992-93)	254 (2001-2004)
5.	Infant Mortality Rate (IMR) (Per 1000 live births)	146 (1951-1961)	110	80	53 (2007)
6.	Child (0-4) Mortality Rate (Per 1000 children)	57.3 (1972)	41.2	26.5	17.0 (2006)
7.	Couple Protection Rate (per cent)*	10.4 (1971)	22.8	44.1	48.2 (1998-99)
8.	Life Expectancy at Birth				
	8.1 Male	37.2	55.4 (1981-1985)	59 (1989-1993)	62.6 (2002-2006)
	8.2 Female	36.2	55.7	59.7 (1991-1995)	64.2 (2002-2006)

Note: The dates in the brackets indicate years for which latest information is available.
* National Family Health Survey NA: Not Available.

Source: Ministry of Health & Family Welfare and Office of the Registrar General, India. *Economic Survey* 2008-09.

TABLE – 4.3

INDIA: POPULATION PROJECTIONS

(In Millions)

Year	*2001*	*2006*	*2011*	*2016*	*2021*	*2026*
Total	1,029	1,112	1,193	1,269	1,340	1,400
Below 15 Years	365*(364)	357	347	340	337	327
15-64 Years	619*(613)	699	780	851	908	957
Above 65 Years	45*(49)	56	66	78	95	116

Notes: * Figures are as per smoothing of age-groups for working out population projections. Figures in parenthesis are as per Census of India 2001. These figures will not tally with the total since 'age not stated' is excluded.
2001 figures exclude the population of Paomata, Mao-Maram and Purul sub-divisions of Senapati district of Manipur.

Source : Population Projections for India and States 2001-2026 – Census of India 2001: Report of the Technical Group on Population Projections constituted by the National Commission on Population, May 2006.

In pursuance of these objectives, the following National Socio Demographic Goals to be achieved in each case by 2010 are formulated:

BOX – 4.1

NATIONAL SOCIO-DEMOGRAPHIC GOALS FOR 2010

(1) Address the unmet needs for basic reproductive and child health services, supplies and infrastructure.

(2) Make school education up to age 14 free and compulsory, and reduce drop-outs at primary and secondary school levels to below 20 per cent for both boys and girls.

(3) Reduce infant mortality rate to below 30 per 1000 live births.

(4) Reduce maternal mortality ratio to below 100 per 100,000 live births.

(5) Achieve universal immunisation of children against all vaccine preventable diseases.

(6) Promote delayed marriage for girls, not earlier than age 18 and preferably after 20 years of age.

(7) Achieve 80 per cent institutional deliveries and 100 per cent deliveries by trained persons.

(8) Achieve universal access to information/counseling, and services for fertility regulation and contraception with a wide basket of choices.

(9) Achieve 100 per cent registration of births, deaths, marriage and pregnancy.

(10) Contain the spread of Acquired Immune Deficiency Syndrome (AIDS), and promote greater integration between the management of reproductive tract infections (RTI) and sexually transmitted infections (STI) and the National AIDS Control Organisation.

(11) Prevent and control communicable diseases.

(12) Integrate Indian Systems of Medicine (ISM) in the provision of reproductive and child health services, and in reaching out to households.

(13) Promote vigorously the small family norm to achieve replacement levels of TFR.

(14) Bring about convergence in implementation of related social sector programmes so that family welfare becomes a people centred programme.

If the NPP 2000 is fully implemented, we anticipate a population of 1107 million (110 crore) in 2010, instead of 1162 million (116 crore) projected by the Technical Group on Population Projections.

The well-known 'demographic dividend' will manifest in the proportion of population in the working age group of 15-64 years increasing steadily from 62.9 per cent in 2006 to 68.4 per cent in 2026. The actual tapping of this demographic dividend will, however, depend a lot on ensuring proper health care and other human resource development such as education.

TABLE – 4.4

INDIA'S GLOBAL POSITION IN TERMS OF SOCIO-DEMOGRAPHIC PARAMETERS

Country	*Life Expectancy at Birth (years)*	*Under-five Mortality Rate (per 1,000 live births)*		*Infant Mortality Rate (per 1,000 live births)*		*Maternal Mortality Ratio (per 100,000 live births)*
	2000-2005	*1990*	*2005*	*1990*	*2005*	*2005*
China	72	49	27	38	23	45
India	63	123	74	80	56	450
Nepal	61	145	74	100	56	830
Pakistan	63	128	99	96	79	320
Sri Lanka	71	23	14	19	12	58
Bangladesh	62	144	73	96	54	570
South Asia	63	126	80	84	60	NA

Note : NA : Not available.

Source : UNDP, *Human Development Report* 2007-08.

In spite of the progress achieved in these parameters of health, family welfare and population growth, we still lag behind some developing countries like China, Sri Lanka and many South Asian countries with regard to social indicators of progress. Thus, for example, life expectancy at birth in the year 2005 was 72 years in China, 71.1 years in Sri Lanka as against 63 years in India. Infant mortality rate in 2005 was only 23 per thousand in China and just 12 per thousand in Sri Lanka as against 56 per thousand live birth in India. Other parameters of socio demographic progress show a similar picture.

Among the major states, the states of Kerala and Tamil Nadu have already achieved the replacement level of fertility *viz.*, TFR of 2.1, while the states of Andhra Pradesh, Gujarat, Karnataka, Maharashtra, Orissa, Punjab and West Bengal, having a TFR in the rang of 2.2 to 3.0 are in the direction of achieving the replacement level of fertility. There are a few states, namely, Assam, Haryana and Madhya Pradesh, which are having a TFR in the range of 3.1 to 4.0 while the states of Bihar, Rajasthan and Uttar Pradesh have recorded TFRs in the range of 4.1 to 4.7 as per the Sample Registration System, 1999.

The National Population Stabilisation Fund (NPSF) was renamed and registered as Janasankhya Sthirata Kosh (JSK) in June 2003. The objective of JSK is to facilitate the attainment of the goals of National Population Policy (NPP), 2000. The Fund will support projects, schemes, initiatives and innovative ideas, designed to help population stabilisation both in the government and voluntary sectors, and provide a window for canalising monies through voluntary contributions from individuals, industry, trade organisations and other legal entities in furtherance of this national cause. A contribution of Rs. 100 crore has been made out of plan budget.

Striving towards population stabilisation is not the sole responsibility of any one agency or the government. The private sector, the non government organisations (NGOs), the Panchayati Raj Institutions, the municipal bodies, etc., should all actively work to achieve this objective. The private sector contains a huge untapped potential for increasing coverage of population control and family welfare services. "The industry can, and should play a major role in hastening our progress towards population stabilisation. In addition to providing Family Welfare Services to their employees they should reach out to the needy in the locality."

Implications of Mortality Decline for the Future

India will face many health challenges in the first quarter of the twenty-first century. The control of major communicable diseases like malaria and TB will require considerable financial and administrative resources, concerted efforts and political will. The country must also increase rapidly its levels of basic immunisation coverage for the major preventable diseases of childhood. Health sector reforms will need to address the significant disparities which exist in relation to the availability of basic health care facilities; this must involve increased investment in rural areas and in those states which are presently under-served.

Levels of mortality in India will probably continue to improve in the period 2001-2026. However, the objectives specified in the National Population Policy of 2000—such as reducing the IMR to 30 and the MMR to 100 by the year 2010 (Ministry of Health and Family Welfare 2000b: 2)—seem rather unrealistic (Dyson *et al.*, 2004).

Socio-economic progress—in particular, rises in levels of education and average incomes and improvements in infrastructure—should also contribute to a continuing reduction in mortality from certain types of infectious disease, such as some forms of diarrhoea and respiratory infection. Fertility decline too should bring benefits to the conditions influencing maternal and child death rates.

However, there will be health problems related to urbanisation, changes in lifestyles and, especially over the longer run, population ageing.

Urbanisation and Economic Development

Economic development is generally associated with the growth of urbanisation. Urbanisation refers to the movement of population from villages to towns and cities that offer more productive avenues of employment than the traditional primitive agricultural sector of the economy. The urban areas *viz.*, towns and cities are the major centres of industrial and commercial activity. With economic development there is a rapid expansion in industry trade and commerce in urban areas. Consequently, more avenues of earning and better opportunities of employment are created which attract people from rural areas. The process of urbanisation is thus intimately linked up with the process of economic development. Economic growth speeds up the process of urbanisation and therefore, extent of urbanisation in a country is sometimes taken as an index of its economic development.

During the first half of the 20th century, India passed through a period of economic stagnation. Consequently, the extent of urbanisation was very limited. Urban population which accounted for 11 per cent of total population in 1901 reached the figure of 14 per cent in 1941. With a very liberal definition of the urban area adopted in 1951, urban population became 17.6 per cent of total population. Much of the increase, therefore, was statistical. This explains why the adoption of a little more strict definition of the urban area in 1961 census resulted in recording a very small increase in the urban population and it was estimated at 18.3 per cent of total population. The 1981 census has also continued with the definition adopted in 1971, both from the point of view of administrative convenience and maintenance of comparability.

In the 1971, 1981, 1991 and 2001 censuses, an urban area has thus been defined as follows:

(a) all places with a municipality, corporation, cantonment board or notified town area committee,

(b) all other places which satisfy the following criteria:

i) a minimum population of 5,000;

ii) at least 75 per cent of male working population engaged in non-agricultural pursuits; and

iii) a density of population of at least 400 persons per sq. km.

The definition of the 'urban area' though very strict as compared to definitions adopted in earlier censuses is still not comparable with the definition of urban area provided in other countries. For instance, in Japan, a place having 30,000 or more inhabitants is classified as urban area.

Urbanisation Trends in India

The population data on rural and urban distribution provided by the 2001 Census reveal a distinct increase in the proportion of urban in India. In 2001 urban population of India was 27.78 per cent as against 23.34 per cent in 1981. Since 1951, urban population in India has steadily increased and as a consequence the proportion of urban population to total population has risen from 17.3 per cent in 1951 to 27.78 per cent of the total population in 2001. During the 1951-2001 period annual growth rate of urban population has shown no clear trend. Between 1921 and 1951 the rate of growth of urban population steadily increased. The process of urbanisation, however, slowed down between 1951 and 1961. This trend was reversed after 1961 and for two decades the rate of growth of urban population once again showed a tendency to rise. The annual rate of growth of urban population declined during 1991-2001 and was 2.71 per cent as against 3.70 per cent during 1971-1981 and 3.11 per cent during 1981-1991.

In interpreting the data on rural-urban distribution of population, great care is required as the concept of urban area is not the same under various censuses. The number of towns has fluctuated from decade to decade on account of changes in the definitions and concepts. In the 1961 Census certain towns were declassified, as a result of which the number of towns had declined from 3,060 in 1951 to 2,700 in 1961. However, the data for 1971, 1981, 1991 and 2001 are comparable, as the definition of an urban unit adopted in the 1971 Census was also followed in the 1981, 1991 and 2001 Censuses. Hence, it is not difficult to see that 1961 onwards the number of towns has steadily increased. From 2,700 in 1961 the number of towns increased to 3,126 in 1971, to 3,378 in 1981, to 3,768 in 1991 and to 5,545 in 2001.

TABLE – 4.5

SUMMARY MEASURES OF INDIA'S URBANISATION

Census	*Population (Millions)*	*Urban Population (Millions)*	*Annual Population Growth Rate (%)*		
			Total	*Urban*	*Rural*
1951	361.0	62.4	-	-	-
1961	439.1	78.9	1.96	2.34	1.88
1971	548.2	109.1	2.22	3.24	1.98
1981	683.3	159.5	2.70	3.79	1.77
1991	846.3	217.6	2.14	3.11	1.83
2001	1,023.0	285.3	1.94	2.71	1.65

Source: Tim Dyson and Pravin Visaria (2004). "Migration and Urbanisation: Retrospect and Prospects" in Tim Dyson, Robert Cassen and Leela Visaria (eds.) *Twenty First Century India*. Table 6.4, p. 116, New Delhi.

Stable Structure of Urban Settlements: A notable feature of the urbanisation process witnessed in the twentieth century is the very stable structure of urban settlements. Since 1951 the urban population of the country has grown 4.58 times and yet the number of towns has increased by only 150 per cent. In other words, the population of existing towns has increased significantly and thus they have grown in size. The number of villages graduating into town status over the period is not very large.

The stability in the structure of urban settlements reflects built-in resistance to change in socio-economic structure of the country. For centuries, most of the regions had settled cultivation as a consequence of which a very stable structure of rural settlements emerged in this country. In fact, majority of villages had existed for a long period with more or less stable population. The small towns (again stable in size) served villages as market and service centres. Apart from small towns there is "a hierarchy of settlements in each region and sub-region, and it appears that this hierarchy has remained stable for a long time". Urban growth that then takes place is largely by accretion to existing towns rather than by emerging of new towns. In future, whether this stable structure of urban settlements will survive is difficult to say. Some experts believe that in areas where towns are at present sparsely distributed a large number of new urban settlements may appear in future as a result of population growth. In other areas, the possibility of a large number of villages graduating into towns cannot be ruled out. This transformation would take place particularly in those villages where small scale industries are being set up.

Pattern of Growth of Towns by Size-Classes

It is customary in Indian censuses to classify towns into the following six classes according to population size. Table 4.6 shows population by class of town in 2001.

TABLE – 4.6

INDIA'S URBAN POPULATION BY CLASS OF TOWN—2001 CENSUS

Class of Town		*Population in (Million) 2001*
Class I	Population of 100,000 and Above	1,78,224
Class II	Population of 50,000 to 99,999	34,452
Class III	Population of 20,000 to 49,999	42,119
Class IV	Population of 10,000 to 19,999	22,593
Class V	Population of 5,000 to 9,999	7,890
Class VI	Population of less than 5,000	842
All Classes	2,86,120	
Urban Population as Percentage to Total Population		27.82

Source: Registrar General & Census Commissioner of India, *Census of India*, 2001.

In accordance with the experience of developed countries, population in India has tended to concentrate in Class I towns (according to Indian census convention, all such towns are known as cities). Again, like in developed countries, in India, the maximum concentration of urban population is found in the largest urban centres within cities, especially in cities with population more than ten lakhs each (also known as million plus cities).

Migration of Rural Population to Urban Areas in India

During the 1951-2001 period, India's population had increased at the rate of 2.12 per cent per annum while in the same period urban population increased at the rate of 3.1 per cent per annum as against 1.8 per cent per annum increase in the rural population. The birth rate in India in the urban areas has always been lower as compared to the birth rate in the rural areas. In 2000, urban birth rate was 20.7 per 1,000 population as against 27.6 in the rural areas. Hence, the higher rate of population growth in the urban areas is due to migration of rural population to cities. It has been estimated that around 45 per cent of the annual increase in urban population is due to migration.

Since Independence, there has been explosive growth of big cities due to migration. For example, population of Bangalore increased by 75.6 per cent during 1971-1981. Population of Asansol in West Bengal increased by 108.7 per cent, of Faridabad in Haryana by 85.5 per cent, of Guwahati in Assam by 188.3 per cent, of Thane in Maharashtra by 105.9 per cent, of Visakhapatnam in Andhra Pradesh by 75.0 per cent and of Bhubaneswar in Orissa by 87.7 per cent during 1981-1991. Similarly, population of Surat in Gujarat increased by 85.1 per cent and of Nasik in Maharashtra by 58.9 per cent during 1991-2001. Many other big cities have also recorded very high rates of population growth in different decades. As a result, class I cities with a population of 1,00,000 and above accounted for 73.7 per cent of the total urban population in 2001 as against 44.6 per cent in 1951.

Causes of Migration

The factors influencing rural-urban migration are varied and complex. In earlier times, migration from rural to urban areas was largely on account of non-economic factors, such as social, physical, demographic, cultural and communication factors. In villages, social organisations are rigid and in the past people who wanted to break away from these organisations used to migrate to cities. Climatic and meteorological disasters like floods and droughts often compelled the people to leave villages. In recent times, with the decline in mortality rates which resulted in rapid population growth in rural areas, young people have shown a tendency to look for jobs in the cities. Improved transportation, urban oriented education and modernising impact of cinema, radio and television have also induced migration of people from rural to urban areas.

All these non-economic factors are even now relevant. However, now there is widespread agreement among economists and sociologists that migration is caused mainly by economic factors. These include "push" from subsistence agriculture and "pull" of relatively high urban wages and "push back" toward rural areas as a result of high urban unemployment.

1. Push from subsistence agriculture: In India, for agricultural workers and small and marginal farmers, agriculture is a subsistence activity. Small and marginal farmers possess small holdings which often do not ensure productive employment to all the adult male members of the household. On small holdings there is considerable amount of disguised unemployment which implies that productivity of many persons working on these farms is almost nil. These persons all the time feel pressure to migrate to cities. Even activities allied to agriculture have not received the required attention. Dairying and poultry farming are now being encouraged. Some attention is being given to the development of rural infrastructure. The fact, nevertheless, remains that the growth of new jobs in the countryside is slower than the rate of workforce growth. Therefore, a large migration of rural population to cities is due to the 'push' factor.

2. Pull of relatively high urban wages: Urban wages are generally higher as compared to rural wages. In the countryside wages are traditionally determined and are low. Since it is not easy to organise agricultural workers, they rarely get wages which could be considered as just and fair. There is no administrative system whereby the government can assure that agricultural workers are paid the minimum wages. In contrast, industrial workers in the cities get fair wages. The interest of the workers employed in the organised sectors is also protected by the trade unions. Even in the unorganised and informal sectors the exploitation of workers is far less than in agriculture. Therefore, 'pull' of relatively high urban wages is quite strong and a large number of people , particularly the young men and women, keep on migrating to the cities.

3. Push back toward rural areas: Though cities provide jobs in both organised and unorganised sectors at relatively high wages, they cannot absorb all the people seeking jobs in productive activities. In India, it has been observed that the rate of urban unemployment is generally higher than the rate of rural unemployment. The main reason for the higher rate of unemployment in the urban areas is rural-urban migration. It is true that during the planning period, new industries have been set up in cities and fresh job opportunities have been created. Development of infrastructure, expansion of the financial sector and administration have also allowed absorption of a large number of workers. But India's experience in recent years has been that rates of rural-urban migration have exceeded rates of urban job creation and surpassed greatly the absorption capacity of both industry and urban social services. As a result, sometimes there is some 'push back' toward rural areas. This implies that out of a large number of migrants from rural to urban areas, some of those who are unable to find work in cities go back to villages.

Problems due to Urbanisation

The fact that urbanisation has been caused by 'push' factors have given rise to a number of problems like overcrowding in urban areas and sheer inadequancy of infrastructure and various civil services. The level of economic development in urban areas has been inadequate in relation to the scale and pace of demographic growth.

While it is admitted that the proportion of urbanisation is very low in India as compared to other developed countries and further that the future projections see a sizeable increase in urban population, there is a need to adopt a cautious approach in this direction. Two lines of action need attention.

One, if the existing spatial pattern of urbanisation is allowed to continue, urban growth would further get concentrated in bigh cities, which are already bursting at the seams. There is an urgent need to reverse this process and devise alternative development strategies to save the country from the bane of lopsided urbanisation.

Two, it is necessary to provide infrastructure and basic amenities in rural areas. Kerala experience can be a good guide for future planning. Infrastructural amenities like transportation, communications, electric power supply, drinking water facilities, etc., are well-developed in rural Kerala. Advancement in social overheads such as education, health and other welfare activities in rural Kerala, stands out conspiciously when compared to the similar situation in other states. As a result, mass migration from villages to towns in search of employment opportunities and civic amenities seen in all other parts of the country particularly in the big metropolitan cities is almost absent in Kerala. This holds both a promise and challenge for the rest of India.

Urbanisation: Not an Unmixed Blessing

Urbanisation makes a positive contribution to country's economy. Apart from being major industrial and commercial centres that offer more of income and employment, the urban centres offer more and better education and health facilities and in general provide a better quality of life.

But in India, rapid urbanisation has created a number of problems. Excessive concentration of population in cities has created unbearable pressure on housing and civic facilities. Thus, urban slums have grown and environment has got polluted posing danger to life and health of city dwellers.

Thus, urbanisation is not an unmixed blessing as uncontrolled urbanisation gives rise to innumerable problems. For this, industry and trade should be dispersed and employment facilities provided in rural areas so that the process of rural-urban migration gets reversed.

Economic Development and Occupational Structure

Occupational structure means the distribution of workforce in different occupations. Economic development brings out changes in the distribution of workforce. In an underdeveloped country, large proportion of workforce is engaged in the primary sector—any where between 60 to 70 per cent. With economic development, workforce shifts from primary to secondary and tertiary sectors. The reasons for such a change are:

(1) With rise in income, demand for agricultural goods does not rise proportionately because of low income elasticity of demand for food and other basic goods coming from agriculture. On the other hand, rise in income brings about large increase in demand for industrial goods and services creating demand for labour in manufacturing and services sectors.

(ii) Economic development makes available more capital and better techniques in agriculture so that productivity of land and labour increases in agriculture, thus releasing the labourforce from agriculture. On the other hand, with increased demand for industrial products, demand for labour in industrial and services sector will increase.

Table 4.7 below presents changes in India's occupational structure since 1951.

TABLE – 4.7

OCCUPATIONAL DISTRIBUTION OF WORKING POPULATION IN INDIA

Sector	*1951*	*1971*	*1981*	*1991*	*2001*	*2004-05*
Primary Sector	72.1	72.1	68.7	65.0	60.4	58.4
Secondary Sector	10.7	11.2	13.5	15.0	15.8	18.2
Tertiary Sector	17.2	16.7	17.8	20.0	23.8	24.8

Till 1971, there was hardly any change in the occupational structure. However, during the last three decades, there have been definite changes in occupational structure in line with changes witnessed in other developed countries although the changes is not in so pronounced. There has been some shift in working population from primary sector to secondary sector and to tertiary sector.

As one would expect, we have a continuation of the long term trend of a decline in the share of agriculture and allied activities and at the present pace of decline, another decade may see the share of agriculture in employment going below the 50 per cent mark. Despite this sizeable decline in its share, the absolute number of workers in this sector has increased by nearly 18 million i.e., over 30 per cent of the incremental workforce. The secondary sector has increased its share from 15.8 per cent in 2001 to 18.2 per cent 2004-05. This sector added over 20 million to its workforce and accounted for 35 per cent of incremental workforce.

Overall, the share of services sector went up only slightly from 23.7 per cent to 24.8 per cent.

From a careful study of the economic history of the various countries where occupational structure has undergone a significant change in a relatively short period, one would realise that the contribution of three factors, *viz.*, a rapid decline in the rate of population growth, considerable increase in labour productivity in agriculture and a spurt in growth of industries were the foremost. In India, none of the three factors existed during the period beginning from 1951. In the first place, rate of population growth instead of declining rose so much that the decision makers in the government and also the Planning Commission were taken by surprise. On the assumption that the rate of population growth would remain below 2.0 per cent per annum, the Planning Commission in the mid-1950s had hoped that by 1975-76, the proportion of agricultural labour force to the total labour force would come down to 60 per cent or so.[7] This could happen only in 2001. It took us 25 years more to reach the level which was to be achieved by 1975-76. These calculations were, however, upset as a result of population explosion.

Secondly, even now Indian agriculture is very much traditional and the productivity of labour in it is low. During the past four decades, increase in productivity has bet been enough to release large manpower that should seek employment outside the agricultural sector.

Apart from releasing manpower, a rise in labour productivity in agriculture widens the market for manufactures in the rural sector, which in turn provides inducement to industrialisation.

Finally, since the beginning of planning the pace of industrialisation has been slow, and for nearly one and a half decades beginning from the mid-1960s this sector suffered from near stagnation.

---

7. Krishnamurty, J. (1984). "Changes in the Indian Work Force", *Economic and Political Weekly*, p. 2128, December 15.

A shift away from agriculture since the 1970s is certainly an encouraging development. If this process continues in the future, the occupational structure might undergo a significant change in the coming years. On the basis of existing evidence Krishnamurty, however, feels that the extent to which this process of change is related to rising share of manufacturing reflecting positive growth forces in the economy cannot be determined. Further, "if the Indian rural labour force is becoming progressively casualised (and the NSS results suggest a similar process is on in urban India), the declining share of agriculture could reflect at least in part, the growing inability of agriculture to take on the increased numbers added to the labour force. This in turn could be due to not only demographic pressures but adverse trends in the agrarian sector". Krishnamurty admits that if more and more small and marginal farmers are being pushed out of agriculture because their land base is becoming smaller, then this cannot be looked upon as a happy situation.

The Future

According to Dyson[8], during the next few decades India's population will continue to grow, although at a slowing rate; it will continue to urbanise; and it will start to age (though gradually at first).

The near-term future is largely determined. Demography allows us to forecast, for example, that the results of the 2011 Census will reveal a population that is close to 1.2 billion, and that the associated population growth rate during the 2001-2011 intercensal decade will be around 1.6 per cent per year. Also, the country's level of urbanisation in 2011 will have risen to about 31 per cent (assuming no significant change in definition). In turn, this will imply an urban population of roughly 370 million. The associated urban growth rate for the 2001-2011 decade will be around 2.7 per cent per year.

However, looking to the longer run one has to be much more tentative. For one thing, surprises may occur. Also, as noted, the range of uncertainty becomes much greater the further one looks ahead. It is important not to be complacent. In particular, it is important *not* to forget the role of family planning and the path of future fertility. For example, while urbanisation is both inevitable and a good thing, rapid urban population growth is not. And, as Samuel Preston (1979) among

---

8. Dyson, Tim (2008). "India's Demographic Transition and its Consequences for Development", in Uma Kapila (ed.) *Indian Economy Since Independence*, 19th edition. New Delhi: Academic Foundation.

others has noted, it is family planning that holds out the best hope of reducing urban population growth.

According to Dyson, all demographic growth in the period to 2026 will occur at ages above 15 years. There will be little change in the number of children aged less than 15 in 2026, and possibly a modest decline. By mid-century, the country's population will have surpassed that of China—it may do this around the year 2030—and it may well be approaching 1.6 billion. More than half of the demographic growth during 2001-2026 will occur in the main northern states i.e., Bihar, MP, Rajasthan and UP. The population of these four states will increase by around 45-55 per cent over this period, but those of most of the other states will grow by only about 20-30 per cent.

Turning to fertility and mortality, it seems reasonable to consider that by 2026 the total fertility rate for the country as a whole will be approximately two births per woman. It also seems plausible to suggest that women will continue to move towards a family building pattern in which they marry young, have two births in quick succession and then get sterilised while still at a relatively young age. The average life expectation for both sexes combined in 2026 may well be about 69 years (perhaps with a 3 year advantage in favour of females). There is considerable scope for future mortality gains—e.g., through higher levels of immunisation, and better control and treatment of diarrhoeal and respiratory infections.

India's future demographic evolution will also have significant implications for the economy, education and the environment. Economic growth may be enhanced by the 'demographic bonus' deriving from the projected diminishing age dependency ratio in the study's central projection in the period to about the year 2031. Benefits will arise if there are consequential increases in savings and investment. But such increases cannot be taken for granted. As Mari Bhat argued, there is nothing automatic about such potentially positive relationships (Bhat, 2001). It is virtually certain that the country's working age population is going to grow faster than the total population, and it may be roughly 50 per cent bigger in 2026 compared to 2001. However, among others, maintaining that economic growth during the 1990s was not very employment-friendly. In terms of job generation, they contend, the situation appears to have deteriorated, and this is reflected in increased unemployment. Without rapid economic growth and gains in the employment intensity of output, these authors argue that there could be a significant rise in unemployment.

So far as broader environmental issues are concerned, future demographic growth has obvious implications for food production. For example, average cereal yields must rise significantly. And in achieving this end, there is little choice other than to increase chemical fertiliser applications substantially (Hanchate and Dyson, 2004). Future population growth will also have a major impact upon the country's demand for water—which is a resource that will have to be used much more efficiently, for example in agriculture (Vira *et al.*, 2004). Population growth will also have significant implications for the use of common pool resources like fodder and forest products (Vira and Vira, 2004). And, with continuing rapid urban growth in many states, issues relating to urban environmental quality are likely to become more and more important (Vira, 2004).

The addition of several hundred million more people by 2051 is likely to have major administrative ramifications, and quite possibly political implications as well. It seems plausible to suggest that, over the long run, further population growth will help to produce an increasingly differentiated administrative hierarchy and contribute to the increasing decentralisation of governance. The next few decades will surely see the creation of many more districts, and an increasing number of states.

Finally, as Robert Cassen has remarked, a great challenge for India's future rests in limiting divergence. The experience of recent decades suggests strongly that *the poor states are mostly growing slowly economically and fast demographically; and, conversely, the country's better-off states are mostly growing fast economically and slowly demographically*. In both cases, processes of *cumulative causality* apply. That is, faster demographic change would bring about faster economic change, and vice versa.

A recent study involving the Population Foundation of India and the Population Reference Bureau rightly raises the question as to whether India will be the one and only country ever to contain two billion people (Nanda and Haub, 2007). Such a concern cannot be taken lightly.

Many people, would probably agree with a recent statement by Montek Singh Ahluwalia (2008) that China's population policy was too drastic (*much* too drastic). And in any case, such a drastic policy would have been impossible in a democratic society, one where there is attention to due process, such as applies in India. It is inevitable that in such an open society, policies evolve more slowly and therefore, fertility change is slower as a result. That said, many people would also agree with him that a faster rate of fertility decline in the past, would, other things equal, have produced a contemporary population that is better off.

Anyone who neglects the role of India's family planning programme today are closing their eyes to an important instrument of past—and future—change. Clearly, it is far from immaterial whether the country ends up with an eventual population of 1.5 or 2.0 billion. And both of these outcomes are possible. The occurrence of rapid economic growth at present should not distract from this fact. Continuing attention to the provision of high quality family planning and reproductive health care services will benefit the poor—and especially women; there is a massive amount of good demographic evidence to this effect (e.g. see Merrick, 2001). Faster, rather than slower, fertility decline will make it easier to bring education of better quality to all people. It will reduce urban population increase, and growth of the labour force—making it easier to provide better living conditions in the urban sector and better employment prospects. It will reduce pressure on environmental resources, and it may also enhance economic growth.

Questions

1. How is rapid increasing in population of India an impediment in its the economic development? What steps have been taken by the government to control population growth. *[B.A. (P) 2009]*
2. Write short on causes and problems of urbanisation. *[B.A. (P) 2009]*
3. Discuss the two way relationship between population growth and economic development with reference to Indian economy. *[B.Com 2008]*
4. How does rapid growth of population retard economic development? Suggest measures to make government's population control programme more effective. *[B.A. (P) 2008]*
5. Write a brief note on:
   Recent trends in population of India *[B.A. (P) 2007]*
   Urbanisation: Causes and Problems *[B.A. (P) 2008]*
6. Discuss the recent trends in population growth in India. Critically analyse the population policy in India. *[B.A. (P) 2007]*
7. What is the relationship between population growth and economic growth? Why has the population policy failed to check population growth in India? *[B.A. (P) 2006]*

8. Write a note on Trends in Urbanisation in India. *[B.A. (P) 2003; B.Com. (P) 2005, 2006]*
9. Discuss the growth of population during 1901-2001. *[B.Com. (P) 2005; B.A. 2006]*
10. Account for the rapid rise in India's population. What are the main reasons for the failure of Government policies in this regard? *[B.A. (P) 2005]*
11. "Rapid population growth is both a cause and consequence of slow economic growth in India". Discuss. *[B.A. (P) 2005]*
12. Write short note on urbanisation— its meaning, positive and negative aspects. *[B.Com. (P) 2005]*
13. Elaborate the theory of demographic transition. What measures had been taken by the Government of India to control population growth in India? *[B.Com. (P) 2005]*
14. Examine changes in the rate of growth of population since 1951. In this light, make an assessment of the Government of India population policy. *[B.Com. (P) 2005]*
15. Critically examine the link between population growth and economic development in India. *[B.Com. (P) 2005]*
16. How is the rapidly increasing population an impediment in the economic development of India?. *[B.Com. (P) 2004]*
17. How far is growing population slowing down India's economic development? What population policy would you suggest to solve the problem of population in India? *[B.A. (P) 2003]*
18. Examine the nature of population problem in India. How far is it true to say that increasing population is a limitation on economic development? *[B.Com. (P) 2003]*
19. What is the effect of population growth on economic development? What steps have been taken by this government to solve the problem of population growth? *[B.A. (P) 2001]*
20. Write a short note on "Theory of Demographic Transition". *[B.Com. (P) 2001]*
21. Examine the nature of population problem in India. How far is it true to say that India is over populated? *[B.Com. (P) 2001]*
22. What is the relationship between population growth and economic growth? How far is high rate of population growth an obstacle to India's economic development? *[B.A. (P) 2000]*
23. Examine the demographic trend in India since 1951. State the factors which are essential to control the rapid growth of population. *[B.Com. (P) 2000]*

5

Employment and Unemployment

Trends, Structure, Policy and Perspective

TO understand employment and unemployment, we have to understand the concepts of: (i) labour force, (ii) work force and (iii) labour force participation rate.

Labour Force

By the internationally accepted definitions, all persons who are working (have a job) and though not working, are seeking and are available for work, are deemed to be in the labour force. Correspondingly, all those who are not working and are neither seeking nor available for work are considered outside the labour force and hence, do not figure in employment or unemployment statistics.[1] Labour force is thus the sum of employed and unemployed.

The growth rate of labour force is determined partly by the age structure of the population and the age and sex specific labour force participation rate.

Work Force

Employment is conventionally measured as engagement of labour force/time in some productive activities for pay, profit, self-consumption. The productive activity could be a physical or mental activity. Persons with a job but not currently at work are also a part of work force.

To put it simply,

1. Dantwala, M.L. "Understanding Poverty and Unemployment", in Uma Kapila (ed.), *Indian Economy Since Independence*, 1999-2000 edition, p. 865.

Work force = Labour force – Unemployed

Labour Force Participation Rate

The LFPR is obtained by dividing the number of persons in the labour force with the total population.

Work Force Participation Rate

WPR, on the other hand, is obtained by dividing the number of persons in the workforce with total population.

Unemployment Rate

Unemployment rate is the proportion of labour force that is unemployed. The unemployment rate is obtained by dividing the number of those unemployed with the total number of persons in the labour force.[2]

Labour Force and Work Force Participation Rates

Male participation remained higher both in labour and work Force, throughout the period between 1983 and 2004-05. Female participation *per se* in rural areas was much higher than in urban areas. Urban male participation rates (both labour force and work Force) were higher than rural male participation in 1999-2000 and 2004-05 (Table 5.1).

TABLE – 5.1

LABOUR FORCE AND WORK FORCE PARTICIPATION

RATES (CDS BASIS) (PER CENT)

	1983	*1993-94*	*1999-2000*	*2004-05*
Labour Force Participation Rates (LFPR)				
Rural Male	52.7	53.4	51.5	53.1
Rural Female	21.9	23.2	22.0	23.7
Urban Male	52.7	53.2	52.8	56.1
Urban Female	12.1	13.2	12.3	15.0
Work Force Participation Rates (WFPR)				
Rural Male	48.2	50.4	47.8	48.8
Rural Female	19.8	21.9	20.4	21.6
Urban Male	47.3	49.6	49.0	51.9
Urban Female	10.6	12.0	11.1	13.3

Source: Various rounds of NSSO survey on employment and unemployment/Planning Commission. LFPR/WFPR represents no. of persons/person days in the labour force/work force per 1000 persons/person days.

2. Planning Commission, *Tenth Five Year Plan*, ch. 5, p. 143.

In urban India, in 2004-05, "trade, hotel and restaurant" sector had engaged about 28 per cent of the male workers while "manufacturing" and "other services" sectors accounted for nearly 24 and 21 per cent, respectively, of the usually employed males. On the other hand, for urban females, "services" sector accounted for the highest proportion (36 per cent) of the total usually employed, followed by "manufacturing" (28 per cent) and "agriculture" (18 per cent). Work opportunities for women in urban services and manufacturing sector probably exist but there is need for facilitating and improving their WPR through better education, skill development and removal of gender associated hurdles like lack of crèches, etc.

Causes of Low Participation Rate

Low labour force participation rate in the Indian economy can be attributed to the following factors:

1. Age-structure of the population. Those under 15 years constitute about 33.80 per cent of the total population. In developed countries, below-15 age groups forms only around 20 per cent of the population. As long as children below working age form such a high proportion of the population as at present, the labour force participation rate will remain low.

2. In the developed countries, a high proportion of working age women is economically active—this proportion varies between 40 and 50 per cent, whereas in India it is around 23 per cent only. Low female participation rate in turn can be attributed to various institutional, economic, technical and social factors.

Unemployment is measured through labour force surveys that elicit the 'activity' status of the respondent for a given reference period. First, the respondent is identified as not working. Second, for those not working, the typical question in the form is: are you available for work, and have you made some effort to find work during the last x days. Those who answer in the affirmative are the unemployed while those who answer in the negative are the people who have opted out of the labour force. The labour force is the sum of the employed and the unemployed and the rate of unemployment is the proportion of labour force that is unemployed. The reference period could vary from a week to four weeks to a year (Wadhwa and Ramaswami, 2007).[3]

3. Wadhwa, Wilima and Bharat Ramaswami (2007). "Unemployment, The Measurement of", in Kaushik Basu (ed.) *The Oxford Companion to Economics in India*. New Delhi: Oxford University Press.

Measurement of Employment and Unemployment

In India, employment-unemployment surveys are conducted by the National Sample Survey (NSS) Organisation. Beginning with the 27th round in 1972-73, labour force surveys have been conducted every five years using standardised concepts and procedures based on the recommendations of the Committee of Experts (Planning Commission, 1970).

The concepts/procedures presently being used in India for the classification are:

- Usual Principal Status (UPS)
- Usual Principal and Subsidiary Status (UPSS)
- Current Weekly Status (CWS)
- Current Daily Status (CDS)

Usual Principal Status: The labour force, in this context, is typically measured through the usual principal activity status (UPS) which reflects the status of an individual during a reference period of one year. Thus, a person is classified as belonging to labour force, if she had been either working or looking for work during longer part of the 365 days preceding the survey. The UPS measure excludes from the labour force all those who are employed and/or unemployed for a total of less than six months. Therefore, persons who work intermittently, either because of the pattern of work in the household farm/enterprise or due to economic compulsions and other reasons, would not be included in the labour force unless their days at work and unemployment totalled half of the reference year.[4]

Usual Principal and Subsidiary Status: The usual principal and subsidiary status (UPSS) concept was introduced to widen the UPS concept to include even those who were outside the labour force on the basis of the majority time criterion but had been employed during some part of the year on an usual basis. In the NSS 61st Round Survey (NSSO, 2006a), all those who were either unemployed or out of labour force but had worked for at least 30 days over the reference year were treated as subsidiary status workers and hence, included in the labour force. UPSS is, thus, a hybrid concept incorporating both the major time criterion and priority to work status.

---

4. Government of India (2009). *The Challenge of Employment in India: An Informal Economy Perspective*, Report of the National Commission for Enterprises in the Unorganised Sector, Chairman: Arjun K. Sengupta.

The UPSS measure was used on the ground that it was stable and inclusive. It is related to a picture emerging from a long reference period, and even those working for 30 days or more, but not working for the major part of the year, were included.

Current Weekly Status: A person is classified to be in labour force as per CWS if s/he has either worked or is seeking and/or available for work at least for one hour during the reference period of one week preceding the date of survey.

Current Daily Status: The Dantwala Committee proposed the use of current daily status (CDS) rates for studying intensity of work. These are computed on the basis of the information on employment and unemployment recorded for the 14 half days of the reference week. The employment status during the seven days is recorded in terms of half or full intensities. An hour or more but less than four hours is taken as half intensity and four hours or more is taken as full intensity. An advantage of this approach is that it is based on more complete information.

The Eleventh Five Year Plan has largely used the current daily status (CDS) basis of estimation of employment and unemployment in the country. It has also been observed that the estimates based on daily status is the most inclusive rate of 'unemployment' giving the average level of unemployment on a day during the survey year. It captures the unemployed days of the chronically unemployed, the unemployed days of usually employed who become intermittently unemployed during the reference week and unemployed days of those classified as employed according to the criterion of current weekly status.

Long-term Trends in Employment Situation: 1983 through 2005

Table 5.2 presents a comparison of the trends in employment and labour force over two relatively longer periods—1983 to 1993-94 and 1993-94 to 2004-05. It is evident that population growth decelerated in Period II as compared with Period I and this led to a deceleration in labour force growth also. However, the growth of the work force, that is, total employment, also decelerated in Period II. Employment grew more slowly than the labour force in Period II which raised the unemployment rate from 6.1 per cent in 1993-94 to 8.3 per cent in 2004-05. Measured in absolute terms, the average annual increase in employment opportunities during Period II was 6.45 million, which is lower than the annual increase of 7.09 million in Period I.

The inadequate increase in aggregate employment in Period II is associated with a sharp drop in the pace of creation of work opportunities in agriculture. Agriculture should not be expected to create additional employment but, rather, to reduce the extent of underemployment and thereby, increase incomes and wages of those employed in agriculture while surplus labour shifts to the non agriculture sector. However, the increase in employment in the non-agricultural sectors was disappointing.

Table 5.2 shows the annual increase in the work force by category of employment in Period I compared with Period II. There has been a sustained increase in employment opportunities since 1993-94, although at a slower rate than in the earlier period. A notable feature is the sharp increase in the number of jobs created at regular salaried wage—from 0.98 million per year in Period I to 1.68 million per year in Period II. This is a direct consequence of the step-up in the expansion of the manufacturing and services sectors. However, the pace of opening up of employment opportunities for casual wage labour getting released from the agriculture sector has slowed down sharply in Period II. The annual increase in this category was 2.40 million in Period I but which declined to 0.54 million in Period II (Table 5.2), mainly reflecting the lower absorption in agriculture which was not offset by an expansion in other sectors.

TABLE – 5.2

ANNUAL INCREASE IN WORK FORCE BY CATEGORY OF EMPLOYMENT

(CDS BASIS) (MILLION)

Category of Employment	*1983 to 1993-94*	*1993-94 to 2004-05*
Self-employed	3.71 (52.39)	4.23 (65.57)
Salaried Wage	0.98 (13.83)	1.68 (26.02)
Casual Wage	2.40 (33.78)	0.54 (8.41)
Work Force	7.09 (100.00)	6.45 (100.00)

Note : Figures in parentheses are percentages.

Source : Planning Commission (2008). *Eleventh Five Year Plan 2007-2012*, Vol. 1, Ch.4.

As shown in Table 5.3, the dependence of the work force on agriculture and allied sectors declined from 61 per cent in 1993-94 to 52 per cent in 2004-05, that is, a decline of 9 percentage points as compared with a decline of only 4 percentage points in the period 1983 to 1993-94. Thus, work opportunities diversified away from agriculture at a faster pace during the latter period 1993-94 to 2004-05.

TABLE – 5.3

SECTOR-WISE SHARE OF EMPLOYMENT BY CURRENT DAILY STATUS

(CDS BASIS) (PER CENT)

Industry	*1983*	*1993-94*	*1999-2000*	*2004-05*	*2006-07*
Agriculture	65.42	61.03	56.64	52.06	50.19
Mining and Quarrying	0.66	0.78	0.67	0.63	0.61
Manufacturing	11.27	11.10	12.13	12.90	13.33
Electricity, Water, etc.	0.34	0.41	0.34	0.35	0.33
Construction	2.56	3.63	4.44	5.57	6.10
Trade, Hotel and Restaurant	6.98	8.26	11.20	12.62	13.18
Transport, Storage and Comm.	2.88	3.22	4.06	4.61	5.06
Financial, Insurance, Real Estate and Business Services	0.78	1.08	1.36	2.00	2.22
Community, Social and Personal Services	9.10	10.50	9.16	9.24	8.97
Total	100.00	100.00	100.00	100.00	100.00

Source: Planning Commission (2008). *Eleventh Five Year Plan 2007-2012*, Vol. 1, Ch.4.

Employment in Organised and Unorganised Sector

A critical issue in assessing employment behaviour of the economy is the growth of employment in the organised sector *vis-à-vis* the unorganised sector. Public debate on this issue is usually conducted on the basis that unorganised sector employment is generally of low quality while organised sector employment is of high quality. The focus of attention is on whether employment has increased in the organised sector. The inadequacy of growth in the organised sector has traditionally been illustrated using data on employment by units registered with the Directorate General of Employment and Training, which are typically large units in the organised sector. These data are presented in Table 5.4 and they clearly show that whereas organised sector employment increased at the annual rate of 1.2 per cent per year in the period 1983-1994, it actually declined at 0.3 per cent per year in the period after 1994. This decline is shown to occur primarily on account of a decline in employment in public sector units. Employment growth in the private sector units has accelerated in the second period but the acceleration is clearly insufficient to offset the decline in public sector employment.[5]

TABLE – 5.4

GROWTH IN ORGANISED EMPLOYMENT

(PER CENT PER ANNUM)

Sector	*1983-1994*	*1994-2005*
Public Sector	1.53	-0.70
Private Sector	0.44	0.58
Total Organised	1.20	-0.31

The National Commission for Enterprises in the Unorganised Sector has made an important distinction between organised or formal and unorganised or informal employment as follows:

> Unorganised workers consist of those working in the unorganised enterprises or households, excluding regular workers with social security benefits, and the workers in the formal sector without any employment/social security benefits provided by the employers.

The employees with informal jobs generally do not enjoy *employment security* (no protection against arbitrary dismissal) *work security* (no protection against accidents and illness at the work place) and *social security* (maternity and health care benefits, pension, etc.) and these characteristics can be used for identifying informal employment (NCEUS, 2009).

Using the definition given above, the Commission has prepared direct estimates of employment in the unorganised sector. The total employment (principal plus subsidiary) in the Indian economy was 456 million, of which *informal sector* accounted for 393.2 million. This direct estimation shows that the unorganised sector constituted 86 per cent of total workers in 2004-05 (as was the case in 1999-2000 as well). Of the 393.2 million unorganised sector workers, agriculture accounted for 251.7 million and the rest 141.5 million are employed in the non agriculture sector (NCEUS, 2009).

The agriculture sector consists almost entirely of informal workers who are mainly the self-employed (65 per cent) and the casual workers (35 per cent).

---

5. Planning Commission (2008). *Eleventh Five Year Plan 2007-2012*, Vol. I, Ch. 4.

The total employment in the economy has increased from 396 million to 456 million between the two NSS rounds in 1999-2000 and 2004-05. The change in the organised or formal employment has been marginal (i.e., 33.6 million to 35.0 million). Therefore, the increase in total employment has been of an informal kind i.e., 58 million (from 362.8 to 420.7 million) or 16 per cent.

What this means in simple terms is that the entire increase in the employment over this period has largely been of informal in nature i.e., without any job or social security. This constitutes what can be termed as informalisation of the formal sector, where any employment increase consists of regular workers without social security benefits and casual or contract workers again without the benefits that should accrue to formal workers.

What Explains Lack of Growth in Formal Sector Employment?

The organised industrial sector has seen overall growth in gross value added and worker productivity with little growth in employment. It therefore, follows that growth is principally due to the rising capital intensity of the industrial sector. Explanations therefore, focus on why the organised or formal industrial sector has witnessed rising capital intensity.

The NCEUS Report 2009 show that in organised manufacturing, the public sector shed 0.86 million workers while the private sector shed 0.68 million workers between 1996-97 and 2003-04.

I the case of the private sector, while different arguments have been advanced for the 1980s and for the 1990s and beyond, a common argument (often described as central) that is made for both periods is that entrepreneurs have been encouraged to take a capital-intensive route due to excessive labour market rigidity and institutional features of formal labour markets.

Three features are singled out in this context *viz*.:

(i) Inability of large firms (employing more than 100 workers) to retrench workers without securing government permission (under Chapter VB of the Industrial Dispute Act, introduced in 1976 and amended in 1982); (ii) Inability of firms to acquire a flexible labour force through contract arrangements, since the relevant Act restricts contract labour only to designated "non-perennial" activities; and (iii) The industrial relations environment constituted by the Trade Union

Act, 1926, the Industrial Dispute Act, and a plethora of other laws which significantly raises the transaction cost for employers.

To summarise, the recent experience with employment growth presents a mixed picture. If we focus on the most recent period, 1999-2000 to 2004-05, there appears to be an acceleration in employment growth compared with the preceding period which is consistent with expectations, given the acceleration in GDP growth. However, looking at longer term trends, this acceleration in employment growth disappears and in any case, the rate of unemployment has increased throughout. Concerns about the quality of employment appear valid although different sources of data are not easily reconciled. However, it does appear that total employment provided by the organised sector has expanded in the period 1999-2000 to 2004-05 and this is entirely because of the growth of informal employment in the organised sector.

These trends highlight the major challenges of employment in the Eleventh Plan which can be summarised as follows:

- How to ensure faster growth in employment than in the labour force so as to reduce unemployment?
- How to ensure faster growth in the organised sector than the unorganised sector so that the share of organised sector employment increases?
- How to ensure growth in formal employment in the organised sector and not just the informal employment?

Nature and Types of Unemployment

The broad categories of unemployment in India are:

(1) Rural unemployment

(2) Urban unemployment and

(3) Unemployment among the youth.

(1) Rural Unemployment

India is a country of villages as more than 70 per cent of its population lives in rural areas. For rural workers, agriculture is virtually the sole occupation. However, agriculture is not able to provide gainful employment to all those who seek it. Thus, there is unemployment in rural areas which takes broadly three forms *viz.*,

(i) Open and chronic unemployment,

(ii) Seasonal unemployment and

(iii) Disguised unemployment.

(i) *Open and chronic unemployment.* In the agricultural sector we have a large group of landless labourers who seek wage employment on farms. There are also very small cultivators who seek additional income by working as labourers in their spare time. But due to heavy pressure of population on India's still underdeveloped agricultural sector, many people fail to get employment and hence remain chronically unemployed. Since they openly search for employment, they come in the category of open unemployment.

(ii) *Seasonal unemployment.* Agriculture, the major economic activity in villages, is a seasonal phenomenon. There are seasons like sowing and harvesting of crops when all are busy and employment is high. But there are also slack seasons such as the period between sowing of crops and their harvesting when most people have nothing much to do and are thus unemployed. Many rural industries such as sugar mills, rice shellers, cotton ginning units, are based on processing of agricultural produce. They too provide only seasonal employment. Hence, the rural economy largely has seasonal employment.

(iii) *Disguised unemployment.* In India, on account of increasing pressure of population on land, productivity per person has been declining. A situation has arisen where the marginal productivity of a large number of workers is zero, i.e., their work does not make any addition to production. Even if they are removed from agriculture, total production will not fall. Such workers, who are apparently employed, but whose productivity is zero are called disguisedly unemployed. Increased pressure of population in rural areas, with no alternative employment opportunities available, is the major cause of disguised unemployment.

(2) Urban Unemployment

Nature of unemployment in urban India is different from that in rural India. Broadly speaking, urban unemployment may be classified into—

1. Industrial unemployment
2. Educated unemployment
3. Technological unemployment
4. Unemployment among the young and educated common to both urban and rural areas.

1. *Industrial unemployment.* The exact size of industrial unemployment is not known because of the non-availability of necessary data. However, unemployment in the industrial sector has increased over the last 20 years as it is observed that employment elasticity has significantly declined in manufacturing during 1970s and 1980s. From 0.59 during the period 1983 to 1987-88, it declined to 0.38 in the period 1983 to 1993-94 and further to 0.33 in the period 1993-94 to 1999-2000.

TABLE – 5.5

SECTORAL EMPLOYMENT ELASTICITIES ON CDS BASIS

	Employment Elasticity		
Sectors	*1983 to 1987-88*	*1983 to 1993-94*	*1993-94 to 1999-2000*
Agriculture	0.87	0.70	0.01
Mining and Quarrying	1.25	0.59	-0.41
Manufacturing	0.59	0.38	0.33
Electricity, Gas and Water Supply	0.30	0.63	-0.52
Construction	2.81	0.86	0.82
Trade, Hotels and Restaurant	0.87	0.68	0.62
Transport, Storage and Communication	0.47	0.55	0.63
Financing, Insurance, Real Estate and Business Services	0.49	0.45	0.64
Community, Social and Personal Services	0.52	0.68	-0.25
All	0.68	0.52	0.16

Note : Elasticity may change after adjustment of workers of repair services.
Source : NSSO (for estimating employment growth rates) and NAS (for estimating GDP growth rates).

Other factors which have contributed to increase in industrial unemployment are: Population in urban areas has grown faster than in rural areas because of migration on a big scale from villages to cities. The industrial growth in India has been modest and thus, could not absorb all those who migrated to cities with the hope of getting some job. The decline of cottage and cottage and small industry in the countryside has further contributed to migration of labour from the countryside to urban centres. Industrial concentration in big cities attracts work force in a big way—much more than what the industries can absorb at any point of time.

2. *Unemployment among the young and educated:* With the Expansion of educational facilities in the urban areas, both at the school and the university levels, and growing consciousness about the social esteem that education brings with it, the enrolment in educational institutions has increased rapidly. The universities are turning out lakhs of graduates each year who enter the job market. But the pattern of education is not job-oriented. Hence, education does not promote job worthiness of a person. Consequently, many fail to find employment and add to the category of unemployed.

Unemployment is typically higher among the youth and the educated who look for better quality of jobs, and this phenomenon is illustrated in Tables 5.6 and 5.7. Table 5.6 shows that unemployment among the age group 15–29 years for both males and females and in urban and rural areas is significantly higher than the average level of unemployment of all persons (11th Plan).

TABLE – 5.6

UNEMPLOYMENT RATE AMONG YOUTH
(AGE GROUP 15–29 YEARS)

(%) (CDS BASIS)

Year	*Rural Areas*		*Urban Areas*	
	Male	*Female*	*Male*	*Female*
1993–94	9.0	7.6	13.7	21.2
1999–2000	11.1	10.6	14.7	19.1
2004–05	12.0	12.7	13.7	21.5

Source: NSSO Report No. 515(61/10/1).

Thus, educated unemployment is no longer confined to urban areas only as it is commonly believed.

There are distinct differences in the job preference of educated workers. In rural areas, the majority of them (62 per cent in the case of males and 58 per cent in the female) are self-employed; while in urban areas, the large majority work for wages. This difference may be partly due to the fact that a higher proportion of rural educated are from families with relatively large landholdings and engaged in cultivating own farms. The fact that they have alternative incomes perhaps also increases their 'reservation price' in respect of wage employment.

TABLE – 5.7

UNEMPLOYMENT RATES FOR PERSONS OF AGE 15 YEARS AND ABOVE BY LEVEL OF EDUCATION ON CURRENT WEEKLY STATUS (CWS) BASIS

(PER CENT)

General Level of Education	*Rural Male*			*Rural Female*			*Urban Male*			*Urban Female*		
	1993-94	*1999-2000*	*2004-05*	*1993-94*	*1999-2000*	*2004-05*	*1993-94*	*1999-2000*	*2004-05*	*1993-94*	*1999-2000*	*2004-05*
Not Literate	1.8	3.0	2.7	2.2	2.7	2.5	2.2	3.1	2.8	2.2	2.0	2.5
Literate and Up to Primary	1.9	3.0	3.0	2.6	2.6	3.1	3.5	4.1	3.7	4.8	3.6	4.0
Secondary and Above	8.3	7.3	6.5	19.8	16.9	18.2	7.0	6.9	6.2	19.6	15.8	17.9
All	3.1	3.9	3.8	2.9	3.7	4.2	5.2	5.6	5.2	7.9	7.3	9.0

Source: NSSO Report No. 515(61/10/1).

Those educated people who have regular wage/salary employment get much higher incomes than their less educated counterparts both in rural areas and urban areas.

There are indications that as the opportunities for wage salary employment are becoming scarcer relative to supply of job seekers, more and more of the educated persons tend to seek to go into self employment. The increased incidence of self-employment in rural areas probably reflects the growing number of educated people in farming households. In urban areas, on the other hand, it probably reflects a genuine shift to self-employment.

The government has also introduced special programmes to promote self-employment among educated youth and provide them with technical and financial assistance for the purpose. More importantly, several state governments have sought to accommodate unemployed educated youth by creating temporary jobs in the public sector. Though jobs are created initially on 'ad hoc temporary' basis, pressures for granting permanent jobs and parity of emoluments with regular staff are generated and sooner or later, the governments find it expedient to concede the demands.

The growth of jobs for the educated, as for the rest of the labour force has been mainly in the unorganised sector. The large gap between organised and unorganised sector wages makes the former 'coveted'. As a consequence, 'market' for public sector jobs had developed and by all accounts become widespread. Educated people, seeking such jobs, are willing to pay substantial amounts and those responsible for providing them have come to actively seek such payments. The clamour for reservations can also be seen as a strategy on the part of the backward classes to get a fairer share of the jobs than they may get if 'merit' were the sole basis of selection.

With liberalisation, we may expect a rapid growth in job opportunities for the educated in the organised private sector. These jobs are currently cornered by the 'elite' among the educated (i.e., those who have the opportunity to get into better staffed, better equipped, more expensive and very likely English medium institutions). If they expand and public sector openings get scarcer, the tension between the educated elite in the urban areas and those who are kept out of this bonanza (mostly from the urban underclass and the rural areas) can be expected to increase.

According to Vaidyanathan, "This tension can be eased only if economic growth is rapid, if education imparts skills which are needed in the economy and the educated overcome the strong cultural aversion for non-white collar work. A massive expansion of vocational education at the matriculate level and above is desirable".[6]

3. *Technological unemployment*: With the application of modern technology in industry, transport and other sectors, many people who have been working with old techniques become unfit for job and thus rendered unemployed. For example, motorised transport rendered those engaged in manually driven hand carts, *tangas* etc., unemployed. Computerisation of most activities has rendered surplus many workers who have no knowledge of this technology. This problem is being solved to some extent by retraining of technologically unemployed workers.

Unemployment is India's major problem. Every plan sought to remove unemployment by creating additional avenues of employment, yet each of them ended with much greater number of unemployed than what it started with. This is because the addition to the labour force during every plan has been invariably more than the number of employment opportunities created during the plan. The same story was repeated in every successive plan.

Causes of Unemployment

(i) *Jobless growth*: Economic growth is usually expected to generate employment. However, in India most of the time, growth has been jobless. For 30 years from 1950-51 to 1980-81, GDP growth rate was as low as 3.6 per cent per annum. At this rate of economic growth, many jobs could not be created. GDP growth accelerated to 5.6 per cent per annum in the 1980s and stayed at this level in the 1990s. At this higher rate of GDP growth, one would normally expect that many new employment opportunities would be forthcoming. But this was not to be. As already stated, during the last two decades there was a steep decline in employment-elasticity in almost all the major sectors. In the manufacturing sector, over the past two decades employment elasticity declined from 0.59 to 0.33. Considering all sectors together, employment elasticity came down from 0.68 in 1983 to 1987-88 to 0.16 over the period 1993-94 to 1999-2000. With liberalisation and opening up of the economy during the past six years, there is increased emphasis

6. Vaidyanatha, A. (2000). "Employment Situation: Some Emerging Perspectives", in Uma Kapila (ed.). *Indian Economy Since Independence* 1999-2000 edition.

on efficiency. Thus, more and more labour displacing production techniques have been favoured and as a result, growth has been jobless.

Available evidence suggests that the higher growth in the post reform period did not translate into the same rate of improvement in the quantity or quality of employment, but there have been changes in modes of employment. Overall, an important change in the mode of employment has been an increase in the share of self-employed (from 54.72 per cent in 1993-94 to 56.61 per cent in 2004-05). When the working poor are unable to find wage employment, they resort to some work by creating their own employment in such types as street vending, taking up home-based work or assisting earning family members. The formal sector, has witnessed declining share of wages in the organised manufacturing sector. Except a top but thin layer of managerial and supervisory jobs in the corporate segment of the manufacturing and service sector whose impressive gains and annual growth in salaries are news for celebration in the elite media, the picture that emerges for an overwhelming majority of Indians is one of extremely slow improvement or even deterioration in the quality of work (NCEUS, 2009).

(ii) *Increase in labour force*: The country has entered the second stage of demographic transition. The rate of population growth rose to 2.2 per cent per annum during the 1960s, and as a consequence, rate of increase in labour force also rose to 1.9 per cent per annum. During the period 1983 to 1993-94, both demographic and social factors have further raised the rate of growth of labour force. Social factors affecting the labour supply are as much important as demographic factors. Since Independence, education among women has changed their attitude towards employment. Many of them now compete with men for jobs in the labour market. The economy has, however, failed to respond to these challenges and the net result is continuous increase in unemployment backlog.

(iii) *Inappropriate technology*: According to W.A. Lewis[7], in all those countries where unskilled labour is available in excess supply, great care is needed in exercising choice in respect of techniques because monetary wage fails to reflect the real cost of labour. When labour is in excess supply at prevailing monetary rates of return, capital would not be considered productive, if it does the same work which labour also does with an equal amount of efficiency. Lewis asserts that investment in such a situation in capital equipment may be profitable

7. Lewis, W.A. (1955). *The Theory of Economic Growth*. London. p. 356.

to individual capitalists, but it is certainly not beneficial to the society, because it increases unemployment and not production.

In India, while capital is a scarce factor, labour is available in abundant quantity. Under these circumstances, if market forces operate freely and efficiently, the country would have labour-intensive techniques of production. However, not only in industries, but also in agriculture, producers are increasingly substituting capital for labour. In the western countries, where capital is in abundant supply, use of automatic machines and other sophisticated equipment is both rational and justified while in India, on account of abundance of labour, this policy results in large unemployment.

(iv) *Defective educational system*: According to Gunnar Myrdal[8], India's educational policy does not aim at development of human resources. It merely produces clerks and lower cadre executives for the government and private concerns. With the expansion in the number of institutions which impart this kind of education, increase in unemployment is inevitable. It is so because education in arts, commerce and science will not ensure employment on account of its limited utility for productive purposes. Myrdal considers all those who receive merely this kind of education not only as inadequately educated but also wrongly educated. Any educational system which fails to develop human resources properly will not be able to provide employment to all those who have received it.

(v) *Slow growth of agriculture*: A major cause of rural unemployment is the extremely low rate of growth of agriculture. With its small scattered land holdings, inadequate capital equipment, outmoded production techniques, agriculture has been the slowest growing sector that has been pulling down the overall growth rate of the economy. Excessive pressure of population on land has led to increase in disguised unemployment.

(vi) *Rural-urban migration*: Another factor that has contributed to the unemployment problem is the increasing migration of people from the rural to the urban areas. Due to excessive pressure of population of land, the rural people do not find much gainful work in agriculture. On the other hand, expanding industrial and commercial activity in urban areas offers more productive avenues of employment. Therefore, people migrate from villages to the towns and cities to seek work that they expect to give more income and better living. But with the growing influx of the migrant labour in cities, many people fail to secure gainful

8. Mydral, Gunnar (1968). *Asian Drama*, Vol. II. New York. p. 1647.

employment, as trade and industry cannot absorb all those who keep on coming and adding to labour force. Thus, those who fail to secure jobs add to the number of unemployed persons in the urban areas.

Adverse Effects of Unemployment

Unemployment is a great menance. Some of the adverse effects of unemployment are:

- Unemployment prevents nations' output from rising to its full potential. Since labour is an important factor of production, unemployed labour means unused human resources and consequently less than full production.
- Unemployment increases poverty. Unemployment and poverty go together. When some people are unemployed and hence unable to contribute to production and income, they become dependent upon others. Sharing other people's income in low income groups depresses overall consumption levels and pushes people below the poverty line.
- Socially, unemployment is extremely demoralising and gives rise to social problems. Unemployed people failing to get any legitimate means of livelihood, take recourse to anti-social activities such as gambling, theft, robbery, etc. This creates law and order problems for the country.
- Politically, unemployment has a destablising effect on the country's governance and may create problems like terrorism and militant movements for destabilising the country.
- Exploitation of labour. Unemployment is a situation where supply of labour is in excess of its demand. This excess labour supply creates a competition among the labourers who may offer their services at wage rates lower than those prevailing in the market. The employers may thus offer only lower wages and demand longer hours of work and thus exploit the poor workers.

Employment Policy

In Indian plans, the generation of employment was viewed as a part of the process of development and not as a goal in conflict with, or to be pursued independently of economic development. The Second Five Year Plan viewed full employment as a goal to be achieved in the long run in which it was conceived to be in harmony with, rather than conflicting with the policy of stepping up the rate of development. Some conflict between the two was seen in the short period of five years during which the plan aimed at preventing deterioration in the employment situation. On the question of choice of techniques, it was recognised that in 'an economy with relative abundance of labour, a bias in favour of comparatively labour-intensive techniques is both natural and desirable'. At the same time, the choice was seen to be rather limited, dictated as it was by technological facts of production. This was seen to be particularly so in the case of heavy industries where it was recognised that there was no choice as 'no one would suggest that considerations of size and technology should be set aside to emphasise employment'. In the production of consumer goods, alternative techniques could be available but generally low productivity and low surplus generation capacity of labour-intensive techniques made the choice in their favour difficult. Yet, recognising that the use of capital intensive techniques involved a 'double cost', displacement of labour which had in any case to be maintained, on the one hand, and a greater draft on scarce capital, on the other; use of labour using techniques with efforts to improve productivity levels was favoured for consumer goods industries.

The overall approach to employment, during the early years of development planning, emphasised utilisation of labour for development, as against the solution of the 'unemployment' problem as such. Unemployment, in any case, was not expected to emerge as a major problem.

Employment generation, thus, was treated as an integral part of the development proccss; and unemployment not too serious a problem warranting special or independent treatment either in plan modelling or in plan programmes.

The rising magnitude of unemployment and high incidence of poverty gave rise to doubts about the efficacy of growth as such to tackle these problems. Employment was regarded as the most important challenge to be met in the Fifth Five Year Plan (1974-1979) but its solution was sought primarily in the pattern of growth envisaged in the plan. By the late 1970s, however, a view that growth alone cannot solve these problems and that special programmes need to be introduced to deal with them, had emerged strongly. A number of special programmes for the generation of self-employment and short-term wage employment were consequently initiated during the late 1970s and particularly during the 1980s, with alleviation of poverty as their central objective.

The approach, combining growth with special programmes for employment generation, continued during the 1980s. The Indian economy grew at a relatively higher rate of about 5.5 per cent during this period but the growth of employment was lower than in earlier decades, at around 1.8 per cent per annum. This was in spite of the fact that the special employment programmes, on a relatively large scale, had been in operation during this period. Arguments have recently been, therefore, advanced to the effect that it is neither higher growth alone nor the special programmes but an employment-oriented growth strategy which can provide an effective solution to the problem of unemployment.

Employment Perspective

What are the prospects for growth and quality of employment in India in the near future? The fact that a high economic growth rate has not been able to generate high employment growth, and it has, in fact, been accompanied by a slowdown in employment growth in recent years, has led many economists and others concerned to describe the recent experience as one of 'jobless growth'. A brief look at the performance of different sectors as attempted earlier, however, shows that but for the almost negligible employment growth in agriculture, growth in the non-agricultural sector has not really been jobless. Yet employment elasticities have declined in most sectors, though in some sectors like construction, trade and transport, they continue to be relatively high. And a faster growth of these sectors will lead to an increase in overall employment growth. Their share in employment, however, is still small as compared to manufacturing which has shown a relatively low employment growth, and low and declining employment elasticity. Yet manufacturing still has an employment elasticity of around 0.3 per cent and there are indications to suggest that it may improve. For example, its export-oriented sub-sectors have recently experienced higher employment growth and employment elasticity. During the 1990s, employment in export-oriented industries grew at 3.36 per cent per annum and showed an employment elasticity of 0.48 (Goldar, 2003). A faster growth of manufactured exports, which now constitute over 75 per cent of total exports, as compared to 58 per cent in 1980, therefore, promises to be an important factor in reversing the declining trend in employment growth.

Employment growth is a function of growth of GDP and employment elasticity. The Indian economy has sustained a relatively high growth of over 6 per cent for about two decades and is expected to grow at that, if not a higher, rate in the coming years. There are indications towards a reversal of the declining trend in employment elasticities, particularly in manufacturing, and expectations of a growth structure in which sectors with higher employment elasticity will grow faster. Thus, overall employment elasticity is likely to increase from the low of 0.15 experienced during 1994-2000. There is, therefore, a strong likelihood of the growth rate of employment getting restored to over 2 per cent during the first decade of this century. In fact, the evidence from the limited sample survey of the NSSO suggests a reversal of the trend already during 2000-2004 when employment growth is estimated to be around 2.70 per cent. This, however, is still to be validated by the results of the larger sample survey (GoI, 2005b).

The recent experience, however, suggests that most of the new employment opportunities are likely to be generated in the unorganised sector and will be characterised by poor conditions of work and lack of employment and social security. Even within the organised sector, an increasing number of workers are being employed in a 'flexible' manner on casual or contract basis, without the social security benefits available to regular workers. Also, the problem of the 'working poor', namely of those fully engaged in work but earning less than poverty line income, will persist. Thus, the challenge of quality of work, in terms of earnings and social security, will continue. Tightening of the labour market with increase in the demand for labour may lead to improved earnings over time, but a vast majority of workers will continue to have no social protection against the risks of work-related hazards, unemployment, sickness, maternity and old age. A measure of security against these risks is currently available to workers in the organised sector. With a decline in its share and increase in that of the unorganised sector, the share of unprotected workers will increase. Provision of a minimum social protection to this large mass of workers is, therefore, likely to emerge as a much greater challenge than that of expanding employment opportunities. It will require special attention of the state and society at large in coming years, as the market-driven high growth, even if accompanied by an expansion in employment opportunities, may not by itself be adequate to address the issue of social protection.

The generation of productive and gainful employment, with decent working conditions, on a sufficient scale to absorb our growing labour force must form a critical element in the strategy for achieving inclusive growth. Past record in this respect is definitely inadequate and the problem is heightened by the fact that the relatively higher rate of growth achieved during the last decade or so is not seen to generate a sufficient volume of good quality employment (11th Plan).

The Eleventh Plan attempts to diagnose the reasons for past failings observed in the employment situation and to reverse at least some of the adverse employment outcomes associated with the pattern of economic growth in the recent past.

Weaknesses in Past Performance

The basic weakness in our employment performance is the failure of the Indian economy to create a sufficient volume of additional high quality employment to absorb the new entrants into the labour force while also facilitating the absorption of surplus labour that currently exists in the agricultural sector, into higher wage, non-agricultural employment. A successful transition to inclusive growth requires migration of such surplus workers to other areas for productive and gainful employment in the organised or unorganised sector. Women agricultural workers in families where the male head has migrated, also require special attention given the need for credit and other inputs if they are self-employed in agriculture or for wage employment if they do not have land.

The approach to the Eleventh Plan had identified the following specific weaknesses on the employment front which illustrate the general failing just discussed.

- The rate of unemployment has increased from 6.1 per cent in 1993-94 to 7.3 per cent in 1999-2000, and further to 8.3 per cent in 2004-05.
- Unemployment among agricultural labour households has risen from 9.5 per cent in 1993-94 to 15.3 per cent in 2004-05.
- Under-employment appears to be on the rise, as evident from a widening of the gap between the usual status and the current daily status measures of creation of incremental employment opportunities between the periods 1994-2000 and 2000-2005.
- While non-agricultural employment expanded at a robust annual rate of 4.7 per cent during the period 1999-2000 to 2004-05, this growth was largely in the unorganised sector.
- Despite fairly healthy GDP growth, employment in the organised sector actually declined, leading to frustration among the educated youth who have rising expectations.
- Although real wages of casual labour in agriculture continue to rise during 2000-2005, growth has decelerated strongly, as

compared to the previous quinquennium (1994-2000), almost certainly reflecting poor performance in agriculture. However, over the longer periods 1983 to 1993-94 (Period I) and 1993-1994 to 2004-05 (Period II), the decline is moderate for rural male agricultural casual labour, from 2.75 per cent to 2.18 per cent per annum.

- Growth of average real wage rates in non-agriculture employment in the period 1999-2000 to 2004-05 has been negligible. Seen over the longer period of two decades (Period I and Period II), the wages have steadily increased at over 2 per cent per annum.
- In respect of entire rural male casual labour, the growth in real wages accelerated from 2.55 per cent (Period I) to 2.78 per cent per annum (Period II).
- Real wages stagnated or declined even for workers in the organised industry although managerial and technical staff did secure large increase.
- Wage share in the organised industrial sector has halved after the 1980s and is now among the lowest in the world.

"It is only through a massive effort at employment creation, of the right quality, and decent conditions of work for all sections of population and at all locations that a fair redistribution of benefits from growth can be achieved. This indeed is a stupendous task. Alternative policy measures focusing on different sectors and occupations, and the specific requirements of different target groups are needed to create employment on a sustainable basis" (11th Plan).

The National Commission for Enterprises in the Unorganised Sector in their final report have highlighted the two fundamental faults of a market-led economy—the persistent reproduction of unemployment and accelerating arbitrary growth of inequality and their concomitant of poverty. It is such an understanding of the capitalist growth that led Keynes and later the post-Keynesians to advocate targeted public investment for employment creation rather than aggregate demand expansion through monetary and fiscal policy, except perhaps in the condition of depression (NCEUS, 2009).

According to the Commission (NCEUS), we need to reverse the priority of development agenda from growth first to one of employment first. According to Okun's law, every 1 per cent fall in unemployment would raise GDP by 2.5 per cent. As per the calculations of Minsky for USA, the decreasing unemployment to 2.5 per cent from the level of 5 per cent 'would create 3-5 times the GDP required to raise all households above the poverty line'. Accordingly, the higher employment goals would more than pay for poverty removal. Skills and mobility will certainly help but only if investment is forthcoming for absorption of the surplus skilled labour. Otherwise, all that would happen is the ever lengthening queue of employment seekers (NCEUS, 2009).

In the context of the global economic meltdown and its adverse impact on Indian economy, it is unlikely that we would achieve and sustain a growth rate of 9 per cent in 2008-09 and beyond. Given that the long-term growth rate in the past has been around 6 per cent, a somewhat optimistic prediction would be 7 per cent while a conservative lower bound of the growth rate could therefore be taken as 5 per cent. As such, the Commission has made projections assuming growth rates of 9 per cent, 7 per cent and 5 per cent.

The main findings of the Commission with regard to the likely employment generation may be summed up as in the following three major points: (i) At 7 per cent growth rate, unemployment (MCWS) will more or less remain the same even at the end of 12th Plan. A higher growth at 9 per cent will almost eliminate it (but will still leave the task of providing adequate employment to the under-employed and the part-time employed). A lower growth rate of 5 per cent will increase unemployment. (ii) The share of the informal sector in the total employment will continue to remain around 86 per cent. (iii) There will be increasing informalisation of employment in the economy reflecting the informal nature of the additional employment generated in the formal sector. Therefore, the problem of quality of employment will continue to loom large in the Indian economy.

Employment Projections for the Eleventh and Twelfth Plans

The Approach Paper for the Eleventh Plan had projected an addition of 52 million to labour force in the Plan period and had called for the creation of 70 million employment opportunities. However, the projections of labour growth have been revisited in view of the latest population projections made available by the National Commission on Population and work done by the Eleventh Plan Working Group on Labour Force and Employment Projections. The projected increase in labour force during the Eleventh Plan period is now estimated at 45 million (11th Plan).

Population growth is expected to decelerate through this period with a corresponding deceleration in labour force growth to 1.6 per cent per year. However, although the labour force growth is projected to decelerate, the absolute increase in the labour force is very large. In fact, India's demographic profile is such that the expansion in the labour force in India will be larger than in the industrialised countries, and even China. The demographic dividend could be a source of global competitive advantage if it is combined with successful efforts at skill upgradation and at expansion of employment opportunities.

Sectoral Employment Perspectives

There is hardly any scope for employment creation in agriculture which is characterised by underemployment. Even doubling of the rate of agricultural growth during the 11th Plan will be possible without any increase in employment.

Since the main employment issue in the agriculture sector is the increase in farm labour income, and not the creation of a larger number of employed workers, it would be appropriate to work towards a strategy in which there is higher growth in non-services employment opportunities in rural areas which can provide additional income for the rural work force by providing additional non-agricultural employment.

Employment in Manufacturing, Construction and Services

The Eleventh Plan should aim at significantly stepping up growth in employment in other sectors, countering the long-term trends observed in the past. Employment in manufacturing should grow at 4 per cent per annum against the trend of growth in the preceding 11 years (1994-2005) of 3.3 per cent per annum. Employment in construction should grow at 8.2 per cent per annum against the trend of 5.9 per cent growth, and in the transport and communication sector at 7.6 per cent against the long-term trend of 5.3 per cent.

These growth rates in employment in individual sectors are achievable provided they are supported by programmes for skill development, which will ensure availability of the relevant skills without which the growth of employment will probably choke. It is also necessary to ensure a wider provision of social security and welfare of unorganised workers, particularly in sectors such as construction and transport.

The sectors with prospects for high growth in output, creation of new establishments and for creation of new employment opportunities (direct as also indirect) are: IT-enabled services; Telecom services; Tourism; Transport services; Health care; Education and training; Real estate and ownership of dwellings; Banking and financial services; Insurance; Retail services; Media and entertainment services.

The Services Sector

The services sector is currently the fastest growing sector of the economy, and employment growth in the sector has remained more than 5 per cent per annum since the 1990s as compared with the aggregate employment growth at less than 2 per cent. This sector has the unique opportunity to grow due to its labour cost advantage, reflecting one of the lowest salary and wage levels in the world coupled with a rising share of working age population. However, two types of initiatives are required: (i) fostering the establishment of a viable size for delivery of services based on labour-intensive occupations. Only in establishments of a reasonable size (in contrast to the average enterprise size of 1.2 workers, as it exists today), with a reasonable level of occupational specialisation and corresponding productivity and wage levels, is this feasible; and (ii) a massive skill development effort, for vocational training of the new entrants to the labour force.

Planning initiatives in health, nutrition, care of children, care of the aged, education, skill development and expansion of social security services will create a large potential for employment for delivery of these services. Quantum jumps in the requirement of personnel, their skill and in their composition—by gender, by social group and by location in favour of the backward regions—will arise from:

- A massive increase in Central funding of education which is a four-fold increase over the Tenth Plan in constant price;
- Emphasis on the next phase of SSA on improvement in the quality of education;
- Reaching these services to the districts having a concentration of SC, ST and minorities;
- Rapid expansion in the mid-day meal (MDM) scheme to cover 60 million additional children at the upper primary level by 2008-09; and
- Enrolling one crore children in vocational education-skill development streams.

(i) Expansion of IT Services in Rural Areas

Village kiosks will require expansion of IT personnel deployment across the rural areas of the country, in particular to facilitate the expansion of an IT-enabled governance set-up. Such improvements are essential for keeping pace with the demand for public services that will guide the diversification of the economy away from agriculture and towards the secondary and tertiary sectors, duly supported by: (i) investments in industrial infrastructure, (ii) creation of institutional infrastructure in the rural areas, and (iii) for fostering integration of rural markets with the rest of the economy. These would require manifold expansion in a variety of matching services to be delivered by the local governments and by the village *panchayats*, and that would be feasible only if the governance set-up at the local level is overhauled and handled in an IT-friendly mode.

Employment and Labour Policy

The employment strategy for the Eleventh Plan must ensure rapid growth of employment while also ensuring an improvement in the quality of employment. While self-employment will remain an important employment category in the foreseeable future—it accounted for 58 per cent of all employment in 2004-05—there is need to increase the share of regular employees in total employment.

The above analysis implies that the success of labour policy should be seen in terms of the number of regular wage employment opportunities based on some form of a written contract between the employer and the employee, that is, an increase in the number of 'formal' jobs. The potential for creation of formal employment can be fully utilised by making appropriate changes in rules and procedures. It is often said that one of the obstacles to growth of formal employment in the organised sector is the prevalence of excessively rigid labour laws which discourage such employment.

- Encourage the corporate sector to move into more labour intensive sectors.
- Facilitate the expansion of employment and output of the unorganised enterprises that operate in the labour-intensive sectors.

At present, the incentives and subsidies are so designed as to strongly penalise entrepreneurs for crossing a threshold size from a micro/small to a medium/large unit. The excise and other taxation policies need to be reviewed in this perspective.

Changes in policies also need to be examined in regard to:

- Linking incentives with the outcomes measured in terms of employment. For example, incentives are given to a wide range of production activities primarily with the objective of promoting employment and income of workers engaged in such activities. However, such incentives are hardly ever calibrated against the benefits realised in terms of employment and wages.
- Regular wage employment, that is, formal employment, merits fiscal incentives. Such incentives already exist at a limited scale for the larger establishments, but are so designed as to make it difficult for medium and small establishments to benefit from these.

Changing labour laws is a sensitive issue and it is necessary to build a consensus. However, there are several changes short of hire and fire which should not present problems. These include:

- The locations and production activities that have a high potential for employment creation merit a differential treatment.
- Employment of women must be encouraged ensuring, *inter alia*, the special needs that they may have by virtue of change in working hours (night shifts, for example) or the requirements of the family, for example, child care.
- Contract labour in the domestic tariff area merits encouragement, provided commensurate steps are taken to increase social security.
- Monitoring the implementation of labour laws, that is, the reporting system should be simplified and be permitted in an IT-friendly mode.

Public Employment Programme for the Unorganised Workers: The Case of NREGA

Programmes to create direct employment opportunities for wage workers through public works have in the past focused on generation of supplementary employment opportunities, especially during lean periods. They have been considered as an important component of the anti-poverty strategy. These programmes are expected to create durable assets for the community and thus, enhance further economic activities. Wage employment programmes also push up demand for labour and thus exert an upward pressure on the market wage rates by attracting people to public works programmes, thereby reducing supply of cheap labour, often at wages that would not even meet their bare basic needs.

Consistent with the approach for an employment-centred development strategy that would level up the informal economy, public employment programmes should be an integral part of planning and policy. Apart from the advantages that would accrue to the unemployed, underemployed and the poorly employed, such programmes will also have a positive macro-economic impact via the increase in effective demand from the hitherto poor and vulnerable segments of the population. Viewed in this perspective, the enactment of the National Rural Employment Guarantee Act (NREGA) is a historic step in the Indian context.

National Rural Employment Guarantee Act

The National Rural Employment Guarantee Act, 2005 (NREGA) is a major step in the direction of providing security of employment to rural workers by providing at least one hundred days of guaranteed wage employment in every year to every household whose adult members volunteer to undertake unskilled manual work. The Act marks a historic step towards recognising and ensuring work as a right of the people. The programme was launched in February 2006 in 200 districts and has been extended to all the districts in 2008. It aims to provide employment through public works, which lead to development of infrastructure, land development, irrigation and construction. The main aim is to empower labour by making employment a right by which the rural workers can demand employment. From a development policy perspective, the NREGA can also be viewed as a distributive employment strategy, thereby, heralding a new deal for the country's poor and a foundation for inclusive development.

The Commission (NCEUS) has viewed NREGA as an important component of an employment-based growth strategy.

Past experiences show that India's poverty alleviation strategy, including the National Rural Employment Programme (NREP), Rural Labour Employment Guarantee Programme (RLEGP), Jawahar Rozgar Yojana (JRY), Employment Assurance Scheme (EAS), Sampoorna Grameen Rozgar Yojana (SGRY) etc., leaned towards wage employment programmes. With specific reference to NREGA, the argument has been to treat it as a component of a full employment strategy for India (Bhaduri, 2005; IHD, 2009). By ensuring employment for a minimum number of days at minimum wages, the thrust was on 'employment first, with growth as an outcome', rather than the vice versa (Bhaduri, 2005). It is also argued that this path towards full employment alone can ensure the 'economic content of participatory democracy', and allow for "development with dignity" (ibid).

The path towards full employment lies in strengthening the sectors where the poor are located and stabilising their incomes, improving their asset base, constructing basic socio-economic infrastructure at the local level, enabling access to paid work opportunities and exerting an upward pressure on market wages (IHD, 2009). NREGA as a programme is expected to create conditions for realisation of the above outcomes.

An Overview of the Scheme

NREGA has been envisaged from the perspective of 'right to employment' and guarantees 100 days employment at a minimum fixed wage rate, but more importantly it bestows an entitlement. The Act has also identified roles and responsibilities for the Central and state governments, district and block administrations and the *panchayats*. The onus of guaranteeing 100 days of employment rests with the Government and the applicant can demand for unemployment allowance in case he/she does not get work. Apart from creation of work opportunities, the Act also provides for basic facilities at the worksite namely *viz.*, crèche, safe drinking water and medical aid.

The salient features revolve around recognition of the right to work and dignity to work. These include:

- A right-based framework, with employment on demand.
- At least one hundred days of guaranteed wage employment in a financial year to every household whose adult members volunteer to do unskilled manual work.
- Wage payment within 15 days.
- Payment of unemployment allowance in case of non-provision of employment within 15 days (unemployment allowance to be at least one fourth of the minimum wage for the first 30 days, and at least one half of the minimum wages thereafter).
- Work within 5 kilometres of residence (if provided outside 5km, 10 per cent extra wage to meet additional transportation and living expenses).
- Minimum wages to be paid by the state governments.
- Priority for ensuring one-third of workers is women.

- Mandatory basic worksite facilities—drinking water, shade, medical aid and crèche if more than five children below age 6 are present.
- Ban on the use of contractors and machinery and allocation of funds in the ratio of 60:40 for unskilled and skilled/material components of the work ensure the primacy of labour intensive nature of work.
- Equal wages for men and women.
- Devolution of powers to the Panchayati Raj Institutions.
- Mechanisms of accountability and transparency.
- Creation of durable assets to strengthen the livelihood resource base of the rural poor.

The Performance

The performance of the NREGA varies significantly across the states. There are some states where NREGA has managed to achieve its key outcomes very well and which have indeed innovated in many respects. In others, performance has been unimpressive and lacklustre. Given that the overall framework for the NREGA is similar across the states, clearly, the variations in performance depend on factors such as the political and administrative will of the governments, historical background of the state as well as the nature of civil society and public actions around the NREGP. But this also suggests that the state governments which have the responsibility of framing the rules as well as overseeing the actual implementation of the scheme on the ground can "own" the scheme and give it a fillip. There is a lot of scope for state governments to innovate and adapt the scheme according to the local requirements. State-specific experiences are important sources for innovations which in turn provide valuable lessons for replication. The relative success of the scheme in some regions, and failure in others highlights the need to properly understand the reasons for inter and intra state variations and to replicate and adopt features of implementation of the better performing states. Below we highlight some of the experiences from the states.

Success Stories

The performance of the scheme in the state of Andhra Pradesh has been laudable because of strong political will and also because the state has had a rural worker and community mobilisation movement. In addition, Andhra Pradesh has successfully employed computerisation and e-governance mechanisms for monitoring the scheme. For example, funds are being transferred electronically; every jobs seeker has got a bank account and wages are paid through bank or post office account; the whole process from job application to registration is computerised.[9]

In Rajasthan, which has the history of drought relief based public employment and active civil society, the success of NREGA is more impressive compared to other north Indian states.

In Kerala, the NREGA implementation pivots around the Kutumbashree (self-help groups of poor women). These women are not only involved in identifying the public work projects, but also overseeing the implementation. Besides, Kerala has also used banks and post offices for wage payment. All these have resulted in high participation rate of women and an overall efficient system.

Remaining Gaps

In some states, the scheme has been plagued with teething problems and is yet to take off. Jharkhand faced problems in implementation because of the non-constitution of Panchayati Raj Institutions (PRIs) in the state (Dreze and Bhatia, 2006). Bihar has problems related to shortage of staff, poor infrastructure, low administrative capacity of the state, etc.[10]

Poor awareness levels of workers regarding the scheme and the entitlements can also be cited as a reason for its inability to take off in some regions. In the GBPSSI Study of six states, Rajasthan emerges favourably in this regard, with 90 per cent of workers knowing about the provision of 100 days of work. More than half of the respondents were aware of the minimum wages and the 15 days period within which wage payment should take place. This can be attributed, as already mentioned, to the state's active tradition of public mobilisation, state initiated awareness drives and presence of workers' organisations such as the MKSS. In comparison, the remaining five states where the survey was conducted, less that 50 per cent of the workers exhibited knowledge of the most basic provision of the scheme of employment for 100 days. Further, the demand based nature through which employment is offered under NREGA has still got a long way to go in terms of being operationalised, with 71 per cent of the respondents in the study being unaware that an application had to be submitted in order to gain work.

---

9. Institute of Human Development (2009). "NREGS in India: Impacts and Implimentation Experiences", Report of the conference held on September 16-18, 2008, New Delhi.
10. Ibid

However, within the existing framework and limitations, many of the problems can be substantially overcome if the political and administrative leadership at the state and local levels plays a more proactive role in implementing the objectives of the NREGA.

The Commission (NCEUS) regards the NREGA as an important component of the full employment strategy for India. In their assessment, the impact of the NREGA in the first three years of its implementation have, on the whole, been positive but given the size and the several inter-related objectives of the scheme, it needs to be carefully nurtured and strengthened, especially in the lagging areas and regions.

Indian Labour Laws and Labour Markets

Indian labour market is characterised by a sharp dichotomy. A large number of establishments in the unorganised sector remain outside any regulation, while the organised sector has been regulated fairly stringently. It can be reasonably argued that the organised sector has provided too much of job security for too long, while the unorganised sector has provided too little to too many.

Various studies indicate that Indian labour laws are highly protective of labour, and labour markets are relatively inflexible. These laws apply only to the organised sector. Consequently, these laws have restricted labour mobility, have led to capital-intensive methods in the organised sector and adversely affected the sector's long-run demand for labour. Labour being a subject in the concurrent list, state-level labour regulations are also an important determinant of industrial performance. Evidence suggests that states, which have enacted more pro-worker regulations, have lost out on industrial production in general.

Perhaps there are lessons to be learnt from China in the area of labour reforms. China, with a history of extreme employment security, has drastically reformed its labour relations and created a new labour market, in which workers are highly mobile. Although there have been mass layoffs and open unemployment, high rates of industrial growth especially in the coastal regions helped their redeployment. In spite of hardship, workers in China seem to have benefited from wage growth, additional job creation and new opportunities for self-employment.

Questions

1. Discuss the nature and causes of unemployment problem in India. What steps have been taken by the government to remove unemployment in rural areas? *[B.A. (P) 2008]*
2. Write short note on:
   Rural Unemployment in India. *[B.Com 2008]*
3. Examine the nature of unemployment problem in India. Critically explain the policy of the government to remove unemployment. *[B.Com 2007]*
4. What is the nature of unemployment in India? What steps have been taken to tackle the problem of unemployment in rural sector? *[B.A. (P) 2007]*
5. Critically examine the nature of poverty and unemployment in the rural sector in India. Discuss the major poverty alleviation and employment generation programmes that have been undertaken by the government for this sector, in recent years. *[B.Com. (P) 2006]*
6. "Poverty and unemployment are the two problems in India." Any effective programme to reduce poverty means more employment opportunities. Do you agree? *[B.Com. (P) 2006]*
7. What is the nature of unemployment problem in India? Briefly review the policy of the government to solve this problem. *[B.A. (P) External+Correspondence, 2006]*
8. Distinguish between unemployment and underemployment. Why does underdevelopment obtain? What measures would you suggest to remove it? *[B.A. (P) 2005]*
9. Write short note on 'Causes of Rural Unemployment in India'. *[B.A. (P) 2005]*
10. Examine the nature of unemployment in India. What measures do you suggest to solve the problem of rural unemployment? *[B.A. (P) 2004]*
11. Explain the nature and causes of rural and urban unemployment in India. What steps have been taken by government to reduce urban unemployment. *[B.A. (P) 2004]*
12. Discuss the nature of the unemployment problem in rural and urban India. In this context, make an assessment of the success or failure of economic policy in India. *[B.Com. (P), Correspondence, 2004]*
13. Write a short note on 'National Employment Programme'. *[B.Com. (P) 2001]*

6

Economic Planning in India

State of Indian Economy at Independence

AT the time of Independence, Indian economy was caught up in a vicious circle of poverty characterised by one of the lowest per capita consumption and income levels among the countries of the world. Low income levels resulted in low levels of saving and capital formation and, therefore, low productivity and low level of income and this vicious circle perpetuated poverty in the country. Further, the size of the market being limited because of low incomes, entrepreneurs had little incentive for making investments in diversified fields and therefore, the productivity in the economy continued to be low thereby perpetuating low incomes and mass poverty.

Judged in terms of per capita incomes and standard of well-being, the Indian economy remained more or less stagnant during the colonial regime. Quoting from the First Five Year Plan document: "This is primarily because the basic conditions under which an economy can continuously expand have been lacking."

Indian economy at the time of Independence was overwhelmingly rural and agricultural in character with nearly 85 per cent of the population living in villages and deriving their livelihood from agricultural and related pursuits using traditional, low productivity techniques. The backwardness of Indian economy is reflected in its unbalanced occupational structure with 70 per cent of working population engaged in agriculture. Even with this large proportion of population engaged in agriculture, the country was not self-sufficient in food and raw materials for industry. The average availability of food was not only deficient in quantity and quality but also precarious as exhibited in recurrent famines. Illiteracy was as high as 84 per cent; majority of children (60 per cent) in the 6-11 age group did not attend school. Mass communicable diseases were widespread and in the absence of a good public health service, mortality rates were very high (27 per thousand). Thus, the economy was faced with the problems of mass poverty, ignorance and diseases which were aggravated by the unequal distribution of resources between groups and regions.

Evolution of Planning: Strategy and Priorities

Just after the attainment of Independence, the Government of India set up the Planning Commission in 1950 to make an assessment of the material, capital and human resources of the country and to formulate a plan for its most effective and balanced utilisation of the country's resources.

The launching of the First Five Year Plan in April 1951 initiated a process of development aimed not merely at raising the standards of living of the people but also opening out to them new opportunities for a richer and more varied life. This was sought to be achieved by planning for growth and social justice.

The First Five Year Plan contains one of the clearest early formulations of the need for planning and of the State's role in it. Planning, it pointed out, involves "acceptance of a clearly defined set of objectives in terms of which to frame overall policies..., formulation of a strategy for promoting the realisation of the ends defined..., and working out a rational solution to problems—an attempt to coordinate means and ends."

Certainly, achieving higher living standards for the Indian people was seen to be a major goal after Independence. A great deal of thought and discussion in planning for independence focused on the need for rapid economic growth and rising living standards. Nehru and Gandhi had, indeed, differed on what economic policy should be, but the two leaders agreed on the centrality of economic developmental goals as a top priority after Independence.

The Nehruvian view—derived predominantly from Fabian socialism—endorsed the need for rapid development led by state economic activity and planning. The first few years after Independence were naturally focused predominantly on establishing institutions.[1]

The Planning Era

With the formulation of the First Five Year Plan, India embarked upon the programme of planned economic development of the country.

1. Krueger, Anne O. (ed.) (2002). *Economic Policy Reforms and the Indian Economy*, ch. 1 pp. 10-11.

The First Five Year Plan covered the period 1951-1956 followed by the Second Plan (1956-1961) and the Third Plan (1961-1966). After a *Plan Holiday* following the severe impact of exogenous shocks such as hostilities with Pakistan and unprecedented drought for two successive years 1965-66 and 1966-67, the country resumed the Fourth Plan in 1969 covering the period 1969-1974. Then came the Fifth Five Year Plan (1974-1979) which did not complete its five years because of the change of party in power. With the coming into power of the Janta Party Government, the Sixth Five Year Plan was launched in 1978 covering the period 1978-1983. Again, with the change in Government in 1980, the new Sixth Five Year Plan was started, covering the period 1980-1985 and followed by the Seventh Plan (1985-1990) which was completed by March-end, 1990. The Eighth Five Year Plan, to begin from April 1990 covering the period 1990-1995 could not be finalised and again, we had two years of annual plans. After a gap of two years, the Eighth Plan was launched in April 1992, covering the period 1992-1997 followed by the Ninth Plan in April 1997, covering the period 1997 to 2002 and the Tenth Five Year Plan covering the period 2002-2007. The Eleventh Five Year Plan has been launched in April 2007 covering the period 2007-2012.

Strategy and Priorities

The First Plan provided an incisive general analysis of the nature of the country's development problem and various options for mobilising resources and achieving development with more equal distribution. There was special emphasis on the role of mass mobilisation of idle rural labour and land reform. But on balance, the Plan rejected radical solutions (especially in respect of redistribution of existing wealth and incomes). The Plan projected, rather optimistically, that savings and investment as a proportion of national income would rise from an estimated 5-6 per cent in the early 1950s to 20 per cent by 1968-69 and stabilise at that level thereafter. Aggregate income was expected to double in approximately 20 years and per capita income in 27 years.

The successful completion of the modest first Plan was followed by a very ambitious Second Five Year Plan. The Plan's author, P.C. Mahalanobis, provided an analytical foundation for it with a closed economy growth model with two sectors, one of which produced consumer goods and the other investment goods.

The fundamental insight of this model was that the greater the proportion of investment devoted to increasing the capacity of the investment-goods sector, the faster the long-run growth in consumption and investment. In the strategy based on this model, rapid long-run growth was to be achieved without much sacrifice of short-run consumption by concentrating scarce investment in expanding capital goods-producing (and intermediate-goods-producing) heavy industry. Current consumption demand was to be met by employing abundant labour resources to manufacture consumer goods using labour-intensive methods that required little capital.[2]

The Second Plan underlined the political constraints on any radical solutions to redressing inequalities and re-emphasised rapid growth and diversification of economic activity through industrialisation as essential for achieving and maintaining full employment at a rising level of productivity. It went on to define a coherent overall strategy whose central elements included stepping up the rate of investment (but at a more moderate pace than envisaged in the first plan) and a conscious policy of developing an indigenous heavy industry base (comprising metallurgical, chemical and machine building industries) to lay the foundation for accelerated self-reliant growth, with a leading role for the public sector. Accordingly, the 1956 Industrial Policy Resolution emphasised that the State must play a progressive role in the development of industries and as the Resolution puts it, "The adoption of socialist pattern of society as the national objective, as well as the need for planned and rapid development, require that all industries of basic and strategic importance, or in the nature of public utility services, should be in the public sector. Other industries which are essential and require investment on a scale which only the State, in present circumstances, could provide, have also to be in the public sector. The State has, therefore, to assume direct responsibility for the future development of industries over a wider area." The encouragement of labour-intensive forms of producing mass consumer goods was seen to be a potentially important way of reconciling the conflict between emphasis on heavy industry (which would generate faster growth of income and employment in the long run) and the need to generate adequate jobs for the currently unemployed and underemployed in the transitional period.

The dominant growth orientation articulated in the Mahalanobis strategy of the Second Plan continued into the Third Plan. Thus, the economic growth was expected to take place through modern industrialisation. The industrialisation in turn, was expected to be a replica

2. Srinivasan, T.N. and S.D. Tendulkar (2003). *Reintegrating India with the World Economy*, Ch. 1, Oxford University Press.

of the same process that had taken place in the historical past in the advanced countries. However, the relatively greater emphasis on the long term growth in an import-substitution oriented strategy required a modification in the industrialisation process. This consisted of a great emphasis on the creation of domestic capacity in the direction of producing capital goods to produce more capital goods. In this strategy, the public sector was expected to play a dual role of: (a) promoting the growth of infrastructural facilities and the creation of capacity in the basic and heavy industries and (b) reducing the concentration of economic power through the expansion of public ownership of means of production.

An attempt was made with a reasonable success in implementing the long-term growth maximising Mahalanobis strategy during the Second and the Third Five Year Plans. There was, as a result, a considerable acceleration in public sector investment in infrastructure (roads, railways, major and medium irrigation) and indirectly productive investments in universal intermediates like steel, coal, power and heavy electrical machinery. Although the encouragement to the cottage, village and small scale industries as a means of providing employment as well as expanding the supplies of consumer goods were conceived as part of this strategy, very little was achieved in this regard. Similar was the fate in regard to the policies towards the reduction of inequalities.

As rightly pointed out by Kaushik Basu[3] (2004), "The actual policy regime that India followed in its early days of independence was a mixture of the two competing (and almost contradictory) visions. A Soviet-style planning system was developed, but without the state having a monopoly of control over the resources. Capitalism was allowed to flourish, but a large bureaucracy was nurtured. Huge investments were made in basic industries, but at the same time several sectors were protected as belonging to the small-scale sector. Capitalism was criticised but it was also relied upon. Socialism was never practiced, but the rhetoric of socialism was the norm. A burgeoning bureaucracy became the surrogate for socialism."

Objectives of Planning

The guiding principles of Indian Planning are provided by the objectives of growth, modernisation, self-reliance and social justice. Social justice implied reduction of inequalities, unemployment and removal of poverty. Within this framework, each five year plan involves

3. Basu, Kaushik (2004). *India's Emerging Economy: Performance and Prospects in the 1990 and Beyond*, Ch.1, Oxford University Press.

such directional changes to take into account new constraints and new possibilities.

Upto the Seventh Five Year Plan, broadly the main objectives were: (1) economic growth (approximately 5 per cent per annum increase in the net national product), (2) self-reliance, (3) removal of unemployment, (4) reduction of income inequalities, (5) elimination of poverty and (6) modernisation. Some of these objectives were elaborately discussed in the Second and Third Five Year Plans. In the subsequent plans, they were simply reiterated. Various plans, however, did not place equal emphasis on these objectives. Whereas earlier plans laid stress on rapid economic growth more than any other objective, the Fifth and Sixth Plans attached great importanc to self-reliance, generation of employment and removal of poverty. The objective of modernisation was explicitly mentioned as one of the objectives of Planning in the Sixth Plan Document. In the Seventh Plan, the objective of modernisation was stressed. In the 1990s, there was a move towards liberalisation of economic policies. The Eighth Plan document states, "Eighth Plan is a Plan for managing the transition from centrally planned economy to market led economy." The inward-looking development model was abandoned during the Eighth Plan and focus shifted from import substitution towards export promotion.

The trade and foreign investment liberalisation measures during the Eighth Plan intended to expose domestic firms to international competition. The Eighth Plan emphasised on efficiency and growth for alleviating poverty.

Thus, as the Ninth Plan document puts it, "The focus of the Ninth Plan can be described as Growth with Social Justice and Equity." India's economy will have to harmonise the roles of state, market and cooperatives. The principal task of the Ninth Plan will be to usher in a new era of peple-oriented planning in which not only the Governments at the Centre and the states, but the people at large, particularly the poor, can become effective instruments of a participatory planning process. There is a need to promote people's participatory bodies like Panchayati Raj institutions, cooperatives and self-groups (SHGs).

The recognition of the complementarity of the state and private sector initiatives in the development process does not mean an abdication of the role of the state in economic matters. It is the responsibility of the state to ensure that the historically disadvantaged section of the society is empowered to take advantage of the opportunities created by the growth process.

The Eleventh Plan commending the achievements states, "While there are significant economic achievements that India can celebrate in its 60th year of Independence, it is still far from redeeming the pledge which Pandit Jawaharlal Nehru made on the eve of Independence: '[...] for ending of poverty, ignorance, disease and inequality of opportunity'. The Eleventh Plan provides an opportunity to act decisively to consolidate the gains that have been made in the Tenth Plan and also to correct the deficiencies that have been observed."

This broad vision of the Eleventh Plan includes several inter-related components: rapid growth that reduces poverty and creates employment opportunities, access to essential services in health and education especially for the poor, equality of opportunity, empowerment through education and skill development, employment opportunities underpinned by the National Rural Employment Guarantee, environmental sustainability, recognition of women's agency and good governance.

Assessment of Performance with Reference to the Objectives

We may now briefly discuss the achievements of planning in the light of the objectives laid down in various plans.

Economic Growth

Rapid economic growth has been one of the basic objectives of planning. The basic measure of economic growth is the continuous increase in real national income and per capita income. Each plan set for itself a target for raising national income and per capita income. The target ranged from 2.2 per cent per annum in the First Five Year Plan to 9 per cent in the Eleventh Five Year Plan. The actual achievement during the plans has been anywhere between 2.8 per cent in Sixth Five Year Plan and 8.7 per cent in the Ist Year of the Eleventh Five Year Plan (Table 6.1).

While India's planning strategy in the 1960s clearly emphasised rapid growth, it did not succeed in generating growth at the level targeted. It can also be argued that it did not pay sufficient attention to examining why growth targets were not being achieved and whether changes in economic policies were needed to achieve the stated objectives. There was constant focus on the need for higher levels of investment, especially in the public sector, but not enough attention was paid to factors affecting the efficiency of investment.[4]

---

4 Montek S. Ahluwalia (2007). "Planning", in Kaushik Basu (ed.) *The Oxford Companion to Economics in India*. Oxford University Press.

TABLE – 6.1

GROWTH PERFORMANCE IN THE FIVE YEAR PLANS
(PER CENT PER ANNUM)

		Target	*Actual*
1.	First Plan (1951-1956)	2.1	3.7
2.	Second Plan (1956-1961)	4.5	4.2
3.	Third Plan (1961-1966)	5.6	2.8
4.	Three Annual Plans (1966-1969)	–	3.9
5.	Fourth Plan (1969-1974)	5.7	3.4
6.	Fifth Plan (1974-1979)	4.4	5.0
7.	Sixth Plan (1980-1985)	5.2	5.4
8.	Seventh Plan (1985-1990)	5.0	5.5
9.	Two Annual Plans (1990-1992)	–	3.2
10.	Eighth Plan (1992-1997)	5.6	6.6
11.	Ninth Plan (1997-2002)	6.5	5.5
12.	Tenth Plan (2002-2007)	8.0	7.9
13.	Eleventh Plan-1st Year (2007-08)		8.7

Source : Tenth Five Year Plan Vol.1 (2002) p. 24 (Table 2.1).
Economic Survey 2008-09.

The first three decades of economic planning witnessed an extremely modest rate of growth of GDP of 3.4 per cent per annum. During the period 1981-2005, the economy moved away from what Raj Krishna called *the Hindu Rate of Growth* of 3.5 per cent and recorded a growth rate of 5.7 per cent.

The Fifth, Sixth and Seventh Plan achieved more than 5 per cent growth rate of GDP. The Sixth Five Year Plan registered 5.4 per cent per annum increase in GDP against the targeted GDP growth rate of 5.2 per cent per annum. The Plan had proposed to pay particular attention to certain aspects of the economy for achieving the growth target. These were: (1) improving the efficiency level of existing capital stock utilisation, (2) raising the investment rate, (3) changing the investment pattern to make it more rational from the point of view of growth, and (4) keeping deficit in balance of payments within certain limits so as to prevent emergence of foreign exchange crisis. The actual growth rate exceeded the target set for the Sixth Plan. This was mainly due to good agricultural performance and a rapid growth in the services sector.

Agricultural output during the Plan period increased at the rate of 4.3 per cent per annum against the target rate of agricultural growth of 3.8 per cent per annum. The level of investment is generally considered a major determinant of growth and in this, the Sixth Plan expectations were fulfilled. However, the saving rate failed to reach the target. The shortfall in the aggregate saving was largely due to the failure of the public sector to generate the desired surplus.

The Seventh Plan also exceeded the target of 5 per cent and achieved 6 per cent growth rate per annum. The Seventh Plan aimed at 5 per cent per annum increase in GDP. This rate was a little higher than the rate of growth realised during the past decade. According to the Planning Commission, this rate was also in line with the growth rate achieved in the Sixth Plan. However, considering the resource constraint and the actual performance of the economy during the first three years of the plan, realisation of this target did not look very easy. In the first three years of the Seventh Plan, GDP had increased at a modest rate of 3.8 per cent per annum. However, during 1988-89 and 1989-90 due to bumper harvests the growth rate picked up sharply and the average annual increase in GDP during the whole of the Seventh Plan period turned out to be 6.0 per cent per annum against the target of 5 per cent per annum. Thus, the overall rate of growth exceeded the target. In isolation this may look quite impressive. However, when we examine as to how the overall rate of growth of 6 per cent per annum was realised during the Seventh Plan period, the situation appears to be less encouraging. The country did not register a steady rate of growth during the Seventh Plan period. There were marked variations in the rate of growth registered in different years of the plan.

The growth process of the 1980, in spite of an improvement in the average GDP growth rate has been widely criticised. One major criticism of this growth process which involved high fiscal deficit was that it was unsustainable as it put pressure on balance of payments and also led to inflation. Another major criticism was that it involved inefficient utilisation of resources.

The year of 1990-91 was not bad in terms of growth though in this year the economic crisis which deepened in 1991-92 had already begun. In 1990-91, GDP registered 5.4 per cent increase. This could not be sustained in 1991-92 as in this year adverse effects of the economic crisis arrested the overall growth process. The rate of growth of GDP in this year was only 0.8 per cent and both agricultural and industrial sectors registered negative growth rates of 2.8 and 0.1 per cent respectively.

The Eighth Plan began in a difficult situation. In the first two years of this Plan, the rate of increase in GDP was rather modest—5.5 per cent per annum. However, in the remaining three years annual rate of increase in GDP was 7.0 per cent or more with the result that the average rate of increase in GDP in the Eighth Plan turned out to be 6.7 per cent per annum—higher than the target of 5.6 per cent per annum. This satisfactory performance on the growth front made proponents of economic liberalisation in the country unduly optimistic. In the official circles also, the decision makers contended that the liberalisation package had put the Indian economy on the high growth path.

The Ninth Plan however could not achieve growth rate of 6.5 per cent because of poor performance of agricultural growth in three out of five years and also low industrial growth.

After a lacklustre performance in the Ninth Plan period (1997-98 to 2001-02); when gross domestic product (GDP) grew at only 5.5 per cent per annum, the economy accelerated in the Tenth Plan period (2002-03 to 2006-07) to record an average growth of 7.7 per cent, the highest in any Plan period so far. Besides, there was acceleration even within the Tenth Plan period and the growth rate in the last four years of the Plan has averaged 8.7 per cent, making India one of the fastest growing economies in the world.

One may argue that there is an element of cyclicality in the high growth. However, as the 11th Plan document states, India's growth performance goes beyond mere cyclicality. It is underpinned by a number of factors which are real sources of strength and will serve us well in the years ahead. Savings and investment rates have increased significantly. The industrial sector has responded well to economic reforms and has shown that it is capable of competing in the global economy. Perceptions about India among global investors are very favourable. These developments suggest that the economy is now at a point when it can achieve sustained economic expansion that has the potential to bring significant improvement in the lives of our people.

However, the composition of growth in recent years has also presented some problems. Agriculture has grown very slowly from the Ninth Plan onwards and this has widened the rural-urban divide and also contributed to the severe distress in rural areas in some regions. Also, economic growth across regions has not been balanced, with some of the most backward areas yet to experience any significant growth.

The National Development Council (NDC), in approving the Approach to the Eleventh Plan, endorsed a target of 9 per cent GDP growth for the country as a whole. This growth is to be achieved in an environment in which the economy is much more integrated into the global economy, an integration that has yielded many benefits but also poses many challenges. If this is achieved, it would mean that per capita GDP would grow at about 7.6 per cent per year to double in less than 10 years. However, the target is not just faster growth but also inclusive growth, that is, a growth process which yields broad-based benefits and ensures equality of opportunity for all.

Modernisation

The objective of modernisation was explicitly mentioned as one of the objectives of Planning in the Sixth Plan Document. It states, "The term 'modernisation' connotes a variety of structural and institutional changes in the framework of economic activity. A shift in the sectoral composition of production, diversification of activities, an advancement of technology and institutional innovations have all been part of the drive to change a feudal and colonial economy into a modern and independent entity."

Progress towards Modernisation

The composition of national income has changed steadily over the planning period. The share of agriculture in GDP has declined from 50 per cent in 1951 to 25 per cent in 2001 and 18.5 per cent in 2006-2007 increasing the share of mining, manufacturing, construction, productive infrastructure and other services to around 80 per cent in 2006-07.

Industry

The main component in the drive for structural diversification has been the effort to promote industrial growth and diversification. This effort commenced effectively with the Second Plan which, along with the Industrial Policy Resolution of 1956, articulated explicitly the objective of rapid industrialisation. Apart from rapid growth, this strategy involved certain other key components *viz.*, a shift in the industrial structure towards industries producing basic materials and capital goods and the growth of the public sector in industry.

The organisation of industry has also undergone a major change with the development of the public sector. Between 1960-61 and 1977-1978, the share of the public sector in the value added in mining and organised manufacturing grew from 8.1 per cent to 28.9 per cent. The development of the public sector has been the principal element in our drive for industrial diversification and in industries like steel, non ferrous metals, petroleum, fertilisers, petrochemicals and heavy engineering, public sector units play a dominant role.

The industrial policy of the Government accepted the important role of the private sector and an elaborate network of institution has been established to support it and to regulate its activities. A major component of the support system is the network of development banking institutions which have been established to finance private investment in industry. This aspect has been well emphasised in the Tenth Plan and the Eleventh Plan.

Agriculture

The tasks of modernisation and structural change in agriculture were even more difficult and discouraging at the start of the planning era. The outmoded land tenure system, the primitive technology of cultivation and lack of an infrastructure for raising productivity proved formidable barriers to agricultural advance. The fact that these barriers have been overcome to an extent is one of the major successes of our planning effort. Zamindari and other intermediary tenures have been almost eliminated. The technology of cultivation has changed substantially with the spread of high-yielding varieties and the extension of irrigation, a change which was facilitated by the elaborate network of agricultural research and extension set up during the planning era. One further change of consequence is the establishment of a system of support prices, procurement and public distribution. Significant progress has been made not only in the production of major food grains but also in horticultural crops like apples and animal products like eggs, milk and fish.

Some aspects of modernisation in agriculture have been discussed in ch. 12. The growth in irrigation is a common feature which runs through the plans though the pace of expansion in recent years is far higher than before. The use of the new technology based on high yielding varieties and fertilisers spread rapidly only after 1965. This difference is reflected in the larger contribution of productivity gain to production growth in the period after 1964-65.

Several changes have taken place in agricultural credit and marketing. The system of cooperative credit has spread, lessening the dependence of the cultivator on exploitative money-lending and trading practices. Institutional term finance for agriculture has grown with the reorientation of the banking system and the establishment of Land Development Banks, Regional Rural Banks and apex institutions like the Agriculture Refinance and Development Corporation. In agricultural marketing, the dominant role of the Food Corporation of India in food grain trade and the growth of marketing and processing cooperatives have helped both farmers and consumers. In the case of milk, cooperatives and urban milk supply schemes have captured a substantial part of the market. These and other changes in the field of credit and marketing have altered the very unequal relationship between the farmer and the trader and, by doing so, have stimulated agricultural progress (for details, see ch. 13 & 14).

Financial Sector

The mobilisation of savings and their use in preferred directions is a crucial element in any development effort. Thus, primitive processes of accumulation in which households and small enterprises invest their savings directly in their own activities or in currency hoards have given way to more complex forms in which, through financial intermediaries and capital markets, households savings can be channelled into a much wider variety of activities.

The pattern of utilisation of savings has been influenced by several innovations like the development banks for industry and agriculture and the system of cooperative credit.

Planning implies state intervention in economic matters which involves not just a few big projects but also a large number of small works and programmes directed at individuals. At Independence, we inherited a patchy administrative structure oriented towards maintenance of law and order and revenue administration. Over the planning period, an elaborate development administration has been built up from the village, through the block and district to the secretariat level. Though there are deficiencies in this structure in terms of motivation, probity and efficiency, it atleast provides a point of contact between the government and the household or the enterprise. A further change has been introduced by the establishment of Panchayati Raj which, in many states, plays an important role in development administration.

Over 50 years of planning, the structure of the Indian economy, the technology of production in agriculture and industry and the institutional framework within which economic activities are conducted have changed substantially. The bedrock on which these changes are based lies in the tremendous growth in human skills and, because of this firm base, the forces of modernisation and technological advance are firmly entrenched in all sectors of the economy even though the pace of diffusion varies from one sector to another and from one region to another. The major problems at present lie not in any lack of institutions or persons for the tasks at hand but in their effectiveness.

Self-Reliance

At the time of the First Plan, India was dependent on foreign countries at least in three respects. First, despite the fact that Indian economy was essentially agrarian, the output of food grains was not adequate and the country imported big quantities of food grains from USA and some other countries. Second, on account of virtual non existence of basic industries, transport equipment, machine tools, heavy engineering goods, electrical plant and machinees and many other capital goods had to be acquired from developed countries. Third, saving rate being very low, foreign aid had to be obtained in order to step up the investment rate in the country.

When trade is between two equal partners on purely commercial terms, it is beneficial to both. But when trade is between a developed country and an underdeveloped country, the developed country very often takes advantage of its strong bargaining position by charging higher prices, exploiting the underdeveloped country. Therefore, if some underdeveloped country seriously desires to keep its growth activity free from political pressures of other countries, it has no choice but to become completely self-reliant in food and capital equipment. Further, it has also to minimise its dependence in respect of aid from other countries and the institutions like the IMF and the World Bank.

Self-reliance is very often confused with self-sufficiency. Self sufficiency implies that a country produces all goods and services it requires within the country without having to import them. Self-reliance on the other hand, implies that a country has sufficient foreign exchange reserves to pay for its imports. Thus, while self-sufficiency rules out imports, self-reliance allows a country to import provided it has the capacity to pay for it. In the days of globalisation, no country can be self-sufficient but a country can be self-reliant by paying for everything it imports.

Self-reliance did not receive high priority in the first two plans and was not listed as one of the objectives of planning. The emphasis was on self-sufficiency in food grains in the First Plan and the Second Plan adopted import substitution based industrialisation so that India became self-sufficient in capital goods and basic and heavy industries.

The concept of self-reliance adopted in the Third Plan was to do away with the need for external assistance. It stated that the balance of payment difficulties that the country is facing are not short-term or temporary; they will continue for several years to come. External assistance is essential for this period but the aim must be to make the economy more and more self-reliant so that it is able to support within a period of 10 to 12 years an adequate scale of investment from its own production and savings. Normal inflow of foreign capital may continue but reliance on special forms of external assistance has to be reduced progressively and eliminated.[5]

Although the Third Plan was considered an important landmark in the country's advance towards self-reliance, in practice the country could neither reduce its balance of payment deficit nor its dependence on external assistance. Infact, external assistance accounted for 26 per cent of the total plan outlay during the Third Plan as compared to 22.5 per cent during the Second Plan. During the period of Annual Plans 1966-1969, external assistance provided 36.4 per cent of the total plan outlay.

The Fourth Plan concretised the goal of self-reliance and laid down the time phasing for its realisation. It stated, "dependence on foreign aid will be greatly reduced in the course of the Fourth Plan. It is planned to do away with concessional imports of foodgrains under PL 480 by 1971. Foreign aid net of debt charges and interest payments will be reduced to about half by the end of the Fourth Plan compared to the current level." It further added, national self-reliance and growth with stability can be attained only if additional effort is put forward at every level; Planned increase in the production of food grains, raw materials and manufactured goods are calculated to make it possible to limit the growth of other inputs to manageable proportion. A sustained increase of exports by about seven per cent a year is another essential element of strategy in the Fourth Plan to secure balance on foreign account and approach speedily towards the goal of self-reliance.

Under the *Fifth Plan*, a high priority was accorded to export promotion and a number of new measures were adopted to boost up exports. Import control also received particular attention. The Planning Commission once again hopefully stated that, "By 1985-86 we would

5. Planning Commission, *Third Five Year Plan* (1956-1961), p.115.

be in a position to meet the maximum of our foreign exchange requirements, including debt service charges, from our own resources, thus obviating the need for any significant inflow of concessional aid."

The external assistance as a percentage of plan outlay was 12.2 per cent in the Fifth plan which was more or less at the same level as in the Fourth Plan.

The *Sixth Plan* considered removal of poverty and achievement of self-reliance as its two main objectives. The strategy of the Sixth Plan assumed a considerable degree of import substitution in a number of industries, namely, steel, cement, fertilisers, crude oil and capital equipment of all brands including electronics. The Plan was against indiscriminate import substitution as such a policy was bound to be counter-productive. *The Plan emphasised efficient import substitution so as to improve India's balance of payment as well as national income.*

Elaborating on the successes achieved in the area of self-reliance, the *Seventh Plan* states, "The pursuit of self-reliance with growth now requires a faster growth of export earnings." Throughout Seventh Plan period, the balance of payment situation remained grim. The ratio of current account deficit to GDP was 2.4 per cent, much higher than the projected figure of 1.6 per cent in the plan document. In 1990-91, the difficult balance of payments situation acquired a crisis proportion when in June 1991, India's foreign exchange reserves declined to a level sufficient only to meet 13 days import requirements. Thus, during the Eighth Plan period, Government of India undertook various stabilisation measures and structural reforms. These have certainly reduced the strain on balance of payments.

The Ninth Plan (1997-2002) stated, self-reliance as one of the four important dimension of state policy. "India has embarked on a process of gradual and phased opening of its economy to take advantage of new opportunities in trade and investment. While this process needs to be continued and taken forward, it should be from a position of strength and not through either external compulsions or a lack of alternatives. In this sense, 'Self-reliance' must remain an important component of development policy and strategy."

Detailing the concept of economic self-reliance, the draft of Ninth Plan stated: "The first, and perhaps most important, component of self-reliance is to ensure balance of payments sustainability and avoidance of excessive external debt. This end can be best served by a focus on expanding the export base of the nation. In a market-based system, micro-level decision making by private economic agents can collectively lead to excessive draft on the foreign exchange resources of the nation and growing external debt. It is the responsibility of the government to create the conditions by which such tendencies can be corrected by the agents themselves. A framework of prudent macro-management and greater reliance on non-debt creating external flows for financing balance of payments needs are aspects of such conditions."[6]

Elucidating further the recourse to external assistance to finance development, the Ninth Plan categorically states, "Accelerating the growth of the economy will require a significant step up in the availability of investible resources. Self-reliance demands that most of these resources should be generated domestically and recourse to external sources be resorted to the extent dictated by a sustainable proportion of external liabilities." Again, it mentions: "Self-reliance in food is a basic element in any strategy of self-reliance."

On the question of technological self-reliance, the Ninth Plan stated in a very forthright manner: "A critical element of self-reliance is self-reliance in technology. While it is desirable to access the best and most appropriate technologies from wherever they are available, in the long-run it is necessary that domestic capacity is developed in respect of all critical technologies needed by the country."

It is now generally agreed that in the field of self-reliance, there have been significant achievements. The country is now almost self sufficient in food. With the growth of iron and steel, machine tools and heavy engineering industries, the country has made considerable advancement towards self-reliance in capital equipment. Our dependence on foreign aid is negligiable. Although international prices of petroleum products are highly volatile and any unexpected spurt in them can cause severe strain on the country's balance of payments, India has built up huge foreign exchange reserves on which it can fall back

The most significant achievement has been the fact that the Indian economy today has achieved a greater degree of resilience to cope with disturbances in the international economy.

Social Justice

The objective of social justice as articulated in the plans has two major dimensions. The first dimension is an improvement in the living standards of the poorest groups in society and second is a reduction in

---

6. Ninth Five Year Plan 1997-2002 (1998) Vol.1, p.10.

inequalities in asset distribution. Poverty alleviation and raising average standard of living have been the central aims of economic planning in India.

Poverty Alleviation

According to Vyas and Bhargava, the frontal attack on poverty was pursued in three successive phases. In the first phase, lasting from the beginning of the 1950s till the end of the 1960s, the major emphasis was on redistribution of land and improving the plight of poor tenants; on abolition of functionless intermediaries, on tenancy reforms culminating in the principle of 'land to the tiller', on imposing ceilings on large holdings and redistributing it among the landless agricultural labourers and marginal farmers.

However, by the time these structural reforms were introduced in different states, usually after lengthy legislative and legal procedures, the wealthier sections of rural society had consolidated their position and a middle peasantry was making its presence felt. The latter did not align itself with the poor farmers but identified its interests with those of the rich peasantry. Unfortunately, the launching of redistributive measures coincided with a growing deficit in food grains. Soon after, the government had to assign a higher priority to the "grow more food" campaign and more or less abandon far-reaching structural changes. The net result was that redistributive land reforms could make a dent only on very large holdings and that too in a few states. It could directly benefit very few marginal farmers or landless labourers. Similarly, tenancy reforms benefitted mainly the middle sized tenants. The position of the small tenants deteriorated in many areas where the land was resumed by the landowners on the plea of 'self-cultivation', thus reducing small tenants to the status of tenant-at-will.

By the late 1960s, the second phase of PAP started with measures that promised to address directly and exclusively the poor in the rural areas. This target group-oriented approach started with the programme for backward regions, graduated to the programme for the development of small and marginal farmers, landless labourers etc., and finally culminated in the Integrated Rural Development Programme and National Rural Employment Programme. Serious efforts for poverty alleviation were initiated only during this phase. The distinguishing feature of the poverty alleviation programme during this phase was the emphasis on creating employment opportunities and distributing renewable assets among the poor. This was in sharp contrast to the intentions in the earlier phase, i.e., redistributing existing, non renewable assets. Similarly, heavy emphasis was placed during this phase of PAP on transfer of income to the poor in indirect ways, e.g., through food subsidies and 'dual pricing' of essential commodities. Recourse was taken to soft, non-confrontationist measures.

In the third—the latest—phase starting from the beginning of the 1990s, emphasis has shifted to measures aimed at accelerating economic growth and on creating an environment for ensuring a 'spread effect'. In keeping with Indian traditions, lip-service is continued to be paid to structural change, as much as to target group-oriented programmes, but the dominant thought is to create more wealth and to enable the poor to benefit from the secondary effects of growth which, it is presumed, will percolate down and reach the poor.

Although over time relative emphasis has shifted from structural interventions, to a target group-oriented approach, to market-oriented policies, all states have acted in all these phases, more or less, in unison. If one finds different achievements in terms of poverty alleviation in various states, it is not because the major thrust of the programmes were dissimilar or the strategies were unique. Such differences have to be explained in terms of the initial social and economic conditions, specific geographical and demographic features, the pace and composition of economic growth, the relative emphasis placed on different poverty alleviation programmes, and the processes of and competence in programme formulation and implementation.[7]

Poverty and Unemployment

The problem of poverty and unemployment is considered as the biggest challenge to development planning in India. High poverty levels are synonymous with poor quality of life, deprivation, malnutrition, illiteracy and low human resource development. The slogan of poverty eradication has been adopted by all political parties in one form or another and there is a national agreement for the goal of poverty alleviation. The national consenses on poverty alleviation provided the necessary condition for launching various schemes and programmes aimed at achieving this objective. But the persistence of poverty during all these years suggests that the national consenses on objectives did not and could not provide sufficient conditions for poverty alleviation.

7. Vyas, V.S. and Pradip Bhargava, *Public Intervention for Poverty Alleviation: An Overview,* in Uma Kapila (ed), *op. cit.*

Employment Objective

Right from the beginning of planning, Employment objective has been listed amongst the basic objectives of planning. For instance the First Plan stated, "It is no longer possible to think of development as a process merely of increasing the available supplies of material goods; it is necessary to ensure that simultaneously, a steady advance is made towards the realisation of the wider objectives such as full employment and removal of inequalities. Maximum production, full employment, the attainment of economic equality and social justice which constitute the accepted objectives of planning under present day conditions are not so many different ideas but a series of related aims which the country must work for. None of these objectives can be pursued to the exclusion of the other".[8]

The employment objective as can be seen from various plan documents has two components: (i) The provision of employment to all job seekers which is identified as the immediate aim and (ii) gradual transfer of people from low productive jobs to high productive jobs which is a long term goal. Each plan has tried to find jobs during the plan period so as to absorb part of the backlog of unemployment and increase in labour force in that period. The approach to the problem of unemployment has been changing as can be seen from various plan documents (for detailed discussion see ch. 5).

To sum up the discussion on objectives of planning, it may be stated that the basic objectives of planning have remained the same i.e. growth and social justice. Thus there have been only directional changes to take into account new constraints and possibilities. What the Eleventh Plan calles "Inclusive Growth" is nothing but growth with social justice.

*Economic Inequalities**

Among the basic objectives of planning listed in the various Plan documents is the objective of reducing economic inequalities. However, the importance attached to the distributional objective relative to the goal of accelerating economic growth has varied over time. It was very low in the first phase of the Indian growth process from 1950-51 to the mid-sixties. In the later period, an attempt has been made to increase its importance in the successive Plan documents.

---

8. Planning Commission, *First Five Year Plan, 1951-56*, ch. 2, p. 28.

* The discussion in this section is based on S.D.Tendulkar's paper "Economic Inequalities and Poverty in India", in Uma Kapila (ed.), *Indian Economy Since Independence 1999-2000 edition.*

According to Professor Tendulkar, the objective of reducing economic inequalities in the Indian context has been specified in four different forms:

(a) reduction in the concentration of economic power;

(b) reduction in the (relative) disparities in earnings;

(c) reduction in the (relative) disparities in income and consumer expenditure; and

(d) reduction or eradication of absolute poverty.

In this connection, the discussion has centred on three inter-related issues, namely: (i) extension of public ownership of means of production, (ii) reduction of concentration in the private corporate sector, and (iii) reduction in concentration of assets in the household sector.

In his concluding observations, Prof. Tendulkar states, "The Indian scene on economic inequality and poverty is marked by a significant divergence between intentions and performance. while no attempt has been made to explain this divergence, it can be mainly attributed to certain structural features. At the top of this list is the deficiency of reproducible tangible capital and natural resources relative to labour which gets reflected in the low level of productivity and per capita income and high density of population and explains the complex nature of conflicts involved in resolving trade-offs between growth and equity in a democratic environment. The skew ownership distribution of privately owned means of production accentuates the social impact of the deficiency of capital and natural resources relative to labour. The unequal access to and the inequitable working of the economic and social institutions may be mentioned as the third structural feature."

"On the distributional front, the focus has shifted from relative inequality to absolute poverty, from the poverty of the nation as a whole to the poverty, of a large section of the population in a nation."[9]

Economic Reforms

The Background

After pursuing an inward-looking development strategy with the state assuming an important role for more than four decades, India decided to take a historic step of changing tracks in 1991. It embarked

9. S.D. Tendulkar, *op. cit.*

on a comprehensive reform of the economy to widen and deepen its integration with the world economy as a part of structural adjustment. There seems to be a general consensus on the desirability of reforms to dismantle the bureaucratic regulatory apparatus evolved over the years that may have outlived its utility. However, there has been considerable debate on the contents of the reform package, their sequencing and the pace, their implementation and their impact.

After a period of relatively robust economic performance in the late 1980s, the Indian economy entered into a period of unprecedented liquidity crisis during 1990-91. This crisis was a combined effect of a number of events coinciding. These included collapse of the Soviet Union that had emerged as India's major trading partner. The Gulf War that erupted in January 1991 worsened the balance of payments crisis, not only with rising oil prices but also by causing a virtual stoppage of remittances from Indian workers in the Gulf. These events coupled with political uncertainty prevailing in the country led international credit rating agencies to lower India's rating both for short and long-term borrowings. The erosion of international confidence in the Indian economy not only made borrowings in international markets difficult but also led to outflow of deposits of non-resident Indians with Indian banks. These developments together brought the country to the verge of default with respect to external payments liability which could be averted by resorting to borrowings from the IMF under the standby arrangements and CCF and by mortgaging gold to the Bank of England. This was complemented by emergency measures to restrict imports.

The Macroeconomic Crisis

The macroeconomic crisis was precipitated mainly by the growth of the public spending through the 1980s that increased the budget deficit as a proportion of our GNP, although external shocks played a contributory role.

The state of our public finances had indeed reached crisis proportions by the end of the 1980s. The public debt-to-GNP ratio increased through the 1980s, going up to almost 60 per cent at the end of the decade, implying a doubling of the ratio at the end of the previous decade. As is now well-known, the proximate reasons for this situation were the failure of the public sector to generate investible resources and the explosive growth of governmental current spending that saw the budget deficit as a proportion of GDP rising from 6.4 to 9 per cent during the 1980s.

According to Bhagwati and Srinivasan, the question must be addressed: Did the microeconomic inefficiencies have anything to do with this, or was "profligacy" the true, final and sole cause of the macroeconomic crisis? To them, it was the former.

The failure of the public sector enterprises to generate profits (and hence their contribution to the macro crisis) is a microeconomic efficiency failure. Because these enterprises have dominated the provision of infrastructure and critical intermediates, their inefficiency has led to downstream inefficiencies in a multiplier fashion. Then again, the restrictive trade and industrial licensing framework, for instance, led to serious loss of efficiency by reducing the scale of output, eliminating effective competition, creating bottlenecks. The result was to reduce the returns from our investments and our growth rate. In turn, surely the revenues raised from the economy, for any given tax rates, were adversely affected, the political ability to raise tax rates in a situation of slowly-growing incomes was impaired, and the necessity to undertake budgetary expenditures to support the creation of public sector jobs and for consumption were also increased—all factors contributing to the budget deficit crisis.

The rise in foreign borrowing was a major component of the fiscal crisis, reflecting in turn the excess of domestic expenditure over income. Thus, as evident from the external public sector debt (and not just the domestic public sector debt) increased greatly as a proportion of GNP during the 1980s, rising to 21 per cent by 1987-88. This increase in external indebtedness meant that debt service as a proportion of exports increased more than three-fold to 32 per cent in 1996-97 from 1980-1981.

The macro imbalance, fueled by the budget deficit and financed by the external borrowings and the decumulation of reserves, was accompanied by accelerated inflation to double-digit levels.

Given the magnitude of the fiscal and balance of payment problems, there can be no question about the need for structural adjustment. But there were questions about its context as well as viewing it primarily as a means of liberalisation and opening of the economy.

Rationale for the Reforms

As is now well-understood, India faced a macroeconomic crisis that required immediate attention when Prime Minister Rao took office. This crisis had to be attended to forthwith. But, as in many South American countries in the 1980s, the macroeconomic crisis became also the occasion for undertaking substantial microeconomic (or what are sometimes called "structural") reforms that had been long overdue.

In fact, these structural reforms were necessary because we had evidently failed to generate adequate rates of growth of income and of per capita income. Not merely did India's weak performance in this regard fall below her own expectations as defined in the earlier Plans, it also put India behind many other developing countries, and way behind the super performers in the Far East.

"Indeed, it is necessary to appreciate that we had become marginalised in the world economy. Not merely were our growth, and hence all else such as poverty alleviation, unsatisfactory, the multiplying success stories were to be found elsewhere. Increasingly, many of our economic policies were also seen as wittingly foolish, impossible to explain as sensible. Among these were our maze of senseless bureaucratic controls on production and investment. Perhaps the most compelling reason for reforms was then to clean the house and to restore India eventually to the position of respect in the world economy and polity that she enjoyed during the years of Prime Minister Nehru's stewardship."[10]

Macroeconomic Reforms

By the time the crisis of 1991 occurred, there was considerable support among key figures in and out of government for the view that a thorough going reform was necessary to pull the economy out of the morass it had gotten into.

The reform package outlined by Manmohan Singh in 1991 had three distinct components:

(1) Fiscal stabilisation to check the growing fiscal deficit and contain it at a much lower level in such a manner that public investments in basic social and economic infrastructure could be substantially stepped up without generating inflationary pressures;

(2) Internal liberalisation to increase competitive pressures, leaving enterprises free to make their production and investment decisions in the light of market conditions and enlarging the scope and freedom for private enterprise;

---

10. Bhagwati, Jagdish and T.N. Srinivasan (1993). *India's Economic Reforms*, Paper submitted to Finance Ministry.

(3) Integration with the global economy by removing controls on foreign trade and exchange rates, lowering tariffs and rationalising their structure and substantially relaxing regulations regarding external capital flows and a proactive policy for attracting foreign direct investment. This package, it was claimed, would release powerful growth impulses and lift the economy to a high growth trajectory comparable to that of east Asia. This view prevailed and has come to be accepted by successive governments since.[11]

The policy changes brought into force since July 1991 fall broadly into two categories. The first set of measures is part of what is normally known as stabilisation policy. The second set of measures come under the category of structural reform policies. As Rangarajan[12] rightly points out, while the stabilisation policies were intended to correct the lapses and put the house in order in the short-term, the structural reform policies were intended to accelerate economic growth over the medium term. Structural reform policies cannot succeed unless a degree of stabilisation has been brought about. But stabilisation by itself will not be adequate unless structural reforms are undertaken to avoid the recurrence of the problems faced in the recent period.

Structural Reforms

Structural reforms were broadly in the area of industrial licensing and regulation, foreign trade and investment and the financial sector. There is considerable unanimity among the economists about the need to reduce and, as far as possible, eliminate barriers to the entry and expansion of firms. The policy of licensing as has been practised in the past has had no particular merit and in fact, the Approach Document of the Eighth Plan submitted in May 1990 had also said: "A return to the regime of direct, indiscriminate and detailed controls in industry is clearly out of question. Past experience has shown that such a control system is not effective in achieving the desired objective. Also the system is widely abused and leads to corruption, delays and inefficiency." In relation to foreign trade policy, the aim was to liberalise the regime with respect to imports and try to bring about a closer link between exports and imports.

---

11. Vaidyanathan, A. (2003). *India's Economic Reforms and Development.* New Delhi: Academic Foundation. pp. 17-18.
12. Rangarajan, C. "The New Economic Policy and the Role of the State", in Uma Kapila (ed.), *Indian Economy Since Independence,* 2002-03 edition.

As regards import duties, the policy has been gradual even though it is accepted by all that the tariff rate in India is perhaps the highest even among the developing countries. A progressive reduction becomes essential in order to avoid a high-cost economy. As regards foreign investment, the new policy measures certainly make a break with the past. In an era in which capital is mobile and moving across borders in a big way and where technology transfer is through investment, we cannot afford to close our country to the flow of foreign investment. In fact, the flow of foreign investment into the country has been meagre. If retained earnings are excluded, the flow is almost negligible. The relaxations that we have made in relation to foreign investment are yet very modest as compared with the concessions offered by many developing countries. Many of the fears expressed in this context are in the nature of putting the cart before the horse. We must take action when and if it becomes apparent that the flow of foreign investment is excessive and it is undermining the domestic economy.

Finally, in relation to the financial sector it has to be noted that while there has been a considerable widening and deepening of the Indian financial system, many inefficiencies have crept into the system during the past 15 years. An administered interest rate structure had put the whole system in a straitjacket. The extent of cross-subsidisation in lending rates has undermined the profitability of the banking system. Equally, due to various pressures, the quality of loan assets has also deteriorated. With low profitability, the banking system in particular has not been in a position to provide adequately for loan losses. The capital of the Indian banking system is woefully inadequate. Thus, a reform of the financial system to provide greater autonomy to the institutions both in terms of the interest rate structure and operational matters had become necessary.

Implementation of the Agenda

The implementation of the agenda of the reforms has covered the following:

Trade Policy Reforms: A major reform of trade policy regime has been effected since 1991. The import licensing system has been dismantled. All non-tariff barriers (NTBs) have been phased out from all tradables except consumer goods. In spite of stiff resistance from rich industrialists on cutting tariffs, all finance ministers starting from Manmohan Singh in 1991, P. Chidambaram, Yashwant Sinha, Jaswant Singh and again P. Chidambaram forcefully fought on the subject of tariff and the tariffs have indeed been substantially done away with.

Besides, India has also undertaken a major commitment to liberalise its trade regime under WTO Agreement.

Tariffs have come down from a peak rate of 150 per cent in 1990 to a peak non-agricultural rate of 10 per cent in 2007-08. Agricultural tariffs remain relatively high and stable, isolating this segment of the economy from both the benefits and costs of globalisation. The reduction in tariffs on non-agricultural products has played an important role in the convergence of Indian to global inflation rates and needs to continue.

Removal of QRs

The process of removal of import restrictions, which began in 1991, has been completed in a phased manner with removal of restrictions on 715 items (Exim Policy 2001-02). Out of these 715, 342 are textile products, 147 are agricultural products including alcoholic beverages and 226 are other manufactured products including automobiles.

Industrial Policy Reforms: Although some liberalisation and streamlining of the industrial policy had been effected in the mid-1980s, the New Industrial Policy (NIP) announced on July 24, 1991 and subsequent amendments brought far-reaching changes in the policy regime governing industrial investments. The NIP dismantled the industrial licensing (or approval) system that regulated the industrial investments in the country by abolishing the requirement of obtaining an industrial licence from the government in all except 14 specified industries. These specified industries need to be regulated in view of environmental hazards, national security or social well-being considerations.

NIP has thrown open new industries and services to private including foreign private sector by pruning the list of 'Industries Reserved for the Public Sector'. Only six industries, which are now reserved for exclusive development by public sector, include those considered sensitive from national security point of view. Thus, a large number of industries and services including infrastructure such as telecommunication, roads, ports, power generation, petroleum refining have become accessible to the private sector. NIP accords a much more liberal attitude to foreign direct investments (FDI) than ever in post Independence India. The policy allows automatic approval system for priority industries by the Reserve Bank of India within two weeks subject to their fulfilling specified equity norms. A more favourable treatment is also accorded to non-resident Indian (NRI) investors who are allowed up to 100 per cent ownership priority industries.

A Foreign Investment Promotion Board (FIPB) has been set up to consider all other proposals that do not qualify for automatic clearance. However, to bring transparency into the working of FIPB, elaborate guidelines and time frame of six weeks in normal cases are also specified. FIPB is authorised to negotiate with foreign investors in person to expedite the clearances. FIPB is empowered to approve up to 100 per cent foreign ownership in cases involving transfer of high technology, projects producing predominantly for exports, energy and infrastructural projects, consultancy or trading companies. The restrictions on investments by large industrial houses and foreign controlled companies under the MRTP Act were also abolished.

A phased programme of disinvestment of public ownership in public sector corporations has been launched. A Disinvestment Commission followed by Department of Disinvestment was set up to make recommendations on the phasing of the disinvestments.

The outward investments by Indian enterprises were also liberalised and proposals fulfilling certain norms could now be granted automatic approval.

Exchange Rate Reforms: The rupee was devalued twice in July 1991 leading to a 20 per cent depreciation in its value. The partial convertibility of rupee on the trade account was announced in the 1992-1993 budget that was subsequently broadened to full convertibility on current account by August 1994.

Capital Market: The Capital Issues Control Act was repealed and the Securities and Exchange Board of India (SEBI) was set up as a watchdog for regulating the functioning of the capital market. SEBI has focused on regulatory reform of the capital market as well as on market modernisation. Online trading and dematerialised trading have been introduced. Companies have been allowed to buy back their own shares subject to the regulations laid down by SEBI.

In September 1992, the government announced guidelines for investments by foreign institutional investors (FIIs) in the Indian capital market. FIIs were now welcome to invest in all types of securities traded on the primary and secondary market with full repatriation benefits and without restrictions on either volume of trading or lock-in-period.

Financial Sector: In January 1993, a package of financial sector reforms was announced that included permission to new private sector banks including foreign joint ventures. The government has also established a policy regime for functioning of private non-banking finance companies (NBFCs) and agencies for rating their credit worthiness.

Thus, the government since 1991 has undertaken a comprehensive reform of the economy. In addition to the above measures, there has been an emphasis in the government budget-making to restricting budget deficits.

Macroeconomic Impact of Reforms

The compound rate of growth for the second half of 1980s was 5.8 per cent per annum. Compared to that for the post-reform period excluding 1991-92 as year of exceptional crisis, the average for 1992-1998 comes to 6.5 per cent per annum. The average rate for the 1993-1994 to 1998-99 period (based on the new series of GDP) comes to 6.8 per cent. Similarly, the trend rate for the post-reform period estimated at 6.9 per cent is higher than 5.5 per cent applicable for the 1980s. The post-reform growth, therefore, has been at least 1.1 percentage points higher than the average rate achieved during the pre reform period.[13]

Industrial Revival: Liberalisation policy helped Indian industry to come out of the recession. Liberalisation is expected to bring efficiency and productivity gains in the industry.

FDI Inflows: Liberalisation of FDI policy regime has been an important aspect of the reforms. Compared to approvals of FDI in 1991, the approvals of FDI inflows since the liberalisation of policy in 1991 reveal a dramatic jump.

While the magnitudes of inflows have recorded impressive growth, they are still at a small level compared to the country's potential. Furthermore, one of the objectives of the current reforms of policies is to remove impediments for export-oriented manufacture in general and to attract MNEs to locate efficiency-seeking FDI in the country. These investments could help India in expanding manufactured exports by using her as an export platform. The majority of the recent approvals of FDI, however, aim to exploit India's sizeable and expanding domestic market. The efficiency seeking or export-oriented FDI have yet to start flowing to the country in a considerable manner.

---

13. Kumar, Nagesh (2001-02). "Economic Reforms and their Macroeconomic Impact", in Uma Kapila (ed.), *op.cit.*

Fiscal Adjustment and Stabilisation

A key aspect of the structural adjustment programmes is to restrict the fiscal deficits of the governments. Table 6.2 summarises the trends in budget deficit of the Central government in the late 1980s and 1990s. In the second half of 1980s, the fiscal imbalance worsened with average fiscal deficit rising to 8.2 per cent of GDP compared to 6.3 per cent in the early 1980s (*Economic Survey,* 1992-93). Compared to this, the average fiscal deficit in the post-reform period has been 5.7 per cent of GDP. This suggests that the government has succeeded in managing the fiscal situation quite well.

TABLE – 6.2

TRENDS IN CENTRAL GOVERNMENT DEFICIT AS PERCENTAGE OF GDP

Year	*Revenue Deficit*	*Fiscal Deficit*
Averages		
1985-1991	2.6	8.2
1992-1999	2.9	5.7
2000-01	4.1	5.7
2001-02	4.4	6.2
2002-03	4.4	5.9
2003-04 (Prov.)	3.6	4.6
2004-05 (BE)	2.5	4.4

Source: *Economic Survey* 2004-05, 1992-93 and RBI (1999).

However, the extent of fiscal deficits tends to mask the method adopted by the government to balance the budget and its implications.

Firstly, the revenue deficit which represents the gap between revenue receipts and revenue expenditure has increased in the post-reform period (at 2.9 per cent) on average compared to an average of 2.6 during the second half of 1980s. This implies that the government has been unable to contain its current expenditure. Therefore, fiscal deficit has been contained either by reducing capital investment or by raising capital receipts such as borrowings or disinvestment of public sector holdings of the government. A rising level of revenue deficit has thus been sustained with government borrowings of the scale of the revenue deficit to finance its consumption expenditure rather than producing a revenue surplus to finance capital expenditure in social sectors (and defence) which do not yield a future income flow to the exchequer. Deepak

Nayyar[14] among other analysts, has argued that such a fiscal regime "is not sustainable in medium-term for it is bound to fuel inflationary pressures or strain the balance of payments, and thus disrupt the process of growth".

Secondly, fiscal adjustment has been achieved by squeezing public investment rather than government consumption. Capital expenditure as a proportion of total government expenditure has declined steadily from 30.18 per cent in 1990-91 to 21.8 per cent in 1998-99. As a proportion of GDP, capital expenditure has come down from 5.5 per cent to 3.6 per cent during the same period.

Finally, it has been shown that the burden of adjustment has been unequal in that it has led to declining expenditures on social sectors such as education, health and poverty alleviation. Panchamukhi and Mahendra Dev have observed a decline in social sector spending especially during the early post-reform period. Hence, concerns have been raised regarding the levels of human development.

Prices: An important focus of the stabilisation programme is to bring the rate of inflation under check. The rate of change in wholesale and consumer prices suggest that the overall trend in prices has been on decline since 1992. One striking trend is the growing divergence between the rate of inflation based on wholesale prices and that for consumer price index since 1993-94. Until 1993-94, the two rates generally converged. Since 1995-96, the consumer price index based rate of inflation has exceeded that of one based on wholesale prices by a wide margin. The diverging trend in the wholesale and consumer prices has been explained in terms of the change in the weighting scheme for the two indices. The consumer price index has a 57.0 per cent weight of the food group compared to just 27.5 per cent in WPI. The divergence between the two indices therefore, reflects substantial increases in food prices in the 1990s. Besides, a spurt in prices of housing, medical care and personal care has also contributed to the rise in CPI. *The rise in food prices and other goods of mass consumption at a faster rate than prices of other goods also indicates that sharing of burden of adjustment by different sections of society has been uneven and weaker sections may have been affected more.*

---

14. Nayyar, Deepak (1996). "Economic Liberalisation in India: Analytics, Experience and Lessons" *R.C. Dutt Lectures on Political Economy*, 1993. New Delhi: Orient Longman.

Political Resistance to Reform

Political resistance to the reform measures was to be expected from diverse sources, for diverse reasons and with varying force. Industrialists and exporters had most reason to welcome the new economic policy. But their enthusiasm has waned over time and given place to demand for a variety of protective measures.[15]

The 'middle class' with access to higher professional education constitute perhaps the most enthusiastic supporters of the new economic policy. Most of the large and growing number of non-resident Indians (NRIs) and those employed in the burgeoning software industry belong to this group. Globalisation has vastly improved the opportunities and earning potential of this class both within and outside the country. One has only to see the veritable explosion in salaries of executives and professional personnels in recent years. Some of the most ardent and passionate advocates of free markets, globalisation and capital account convertibility belong to this class.

The strongest opposition comes from farmers and from workers in the organised sector including, especially those employed in the public sector. Farmers have fiercely, and so far successfully, resisted any increase in the price of inputs in the name of reducing subsidies. Their argument is that farmers are unable to recover costs at current level of input and output prices and that farm prices are too low to enable them to have a 'decent' income. Subsidising inputs and pegging output prices higher than warranted by the balance between supply and demand is neither fiscally feasible nor a viable way of raising farmers' incomes to a higher level and even less so for ensuring their progressive improvement. Moreover, since there is much scope for increasing the productivity of water and fertilisers, higher prices do not necessarily mean an increase in unit costs. On the other hand, by encouraging excessive use of scarce resources, low input prices damage the environment and endanger long-term sustainability of agriculture.

Labour in the organised sector is the other locus of strong and organised resistance to the reform: Organised sector (registered factories, financial institutions, government agencies, public sector undertakings) constitute barely 10 per cent of the country's work force (and 20 per cent of the non-agricultural work force). Trade unions, though largely confined to this segment of the economy, have played, and continue to play a key role in protecting the interests of their

15. Vaidyanathan, A. (2003). *op.cit.*, ch.1, pp. 45-49.

members and in influencing state policy. They comprise an important section of the better-off segments of the population (most of them belong in the top quartile of the population in terms of per capita income) and get the lion's share of the benefits of subsidised or free facilities and services (higher education, health care, public transport, electricity, water) provided by the state.

Unions in the organised sector have had considerable success in securing better wages, working conditions and other benefits for workers in this sector and also legislative protection against lay-off and retrenchment. Several of the activities, especially in the public sector, being crucial to the orderly governance and smooth functioning of economy and society, those employed in them are strategically positioned to resist lay-offs, redeployment, restraint on salaries and benefits.

All this is threatened by proposals to permit flexibility in hiring and firing, retrenchment and redeployment of excess work force, privatisation of public undertakings, allowing market forces a greater role in determining wages; and measures to check leakages and corruption. As consumers, they also stand to lose by increased user charges for public services and possibly having to pay more taxes. The fierce resistance of trade unions to reforms—especially in the public sector—is hardly surprising.

Concerns Regarding Social and Political Implications of Reform

There are also wider concerns about the larger social and political implications of the reform. These include several apprehensions:

- that trade liberalisation and domestic regulation and disbanding protection for small industry would have huge and widespread adverse effects on employment and incomes;
- that in the name of fiscal consolidation, expenditures are being squeezed and the compression is at the expense of pro-poor programmes (like basic social services, social welfare, security and poverty alleviation);
- that in the name of providing incentive for enterprise and professional skills, inequalities are allowed to increase;
- that the policy of open door for foreign capital and agreeing to the jurisdiction of international organisations (like World Trade Organization) created under unequal treaties in an

unequal world dominated by the developed countries reduces the country's autonomy and makes it vulnerable to external pressure and interference;

- an added dimension is the increasing concern about the consequences of pursuing current patterns of development for the environment and sustainability.

Impact of the New Economic Policy on the Vulnerable Sections

Is there anything in the new economic policy which is inherently anti-poor?

The poor are affected most when growth is low and when prices rise. The slowdown in growth in 1991-92 and the sharp increases in prices in the same year are sometimes cited as consequences of implementing the new economic policy. This is not a correct assessment. There was a decline in agricultural production in 1991-92 and it is well known that the performance of agriculture from year to year is mostly a function of the weather. The collapse of industrial production in 1991-92 can be traced in a large measure to the high degree of import compression that was brought about which would have been inevitable in any case whether or not we shifted to a new policy orientation. Has the attempt to contain fiscal deficit affected, anyway, the poor more? While there has been some attempt to reduce fertiliser subsidy as part of the efforts to moderate the fiscal deficit, the food subsidies have been maintained. There is a dilemma here which we have to resolve. Unless we make the public distribution system more focused and directed towards only the weaker sections and low-income groups, keeping the issue price unaltered or changed moderately despite an increase in procurement prices will not be sustainable over a long time.

One aspect of the new economic policy which has created certain misgivings among the organised labour relates to the several suggestions that have been made with respect to non-viable public sector units. While the approach should be to reorganise the loss-making public sector units in such a way as to improve their viability, quite clearly, there are cases in which their viability will depend on some reduction in the labour force. The Government is again going slow in this area because of the anxiety not to create a difficult situation for labour. That is why various alternative schemes have been thought of, such as the sale of the company to the labour if they are willing to accept it, setting up a national renewal fund to provide compensation for people who may be rendered jobless, etc.

The public sector units being compelled to carry on with all the labour force, irrespective of whether or not the units are viable, is also a situation that is not sustainable over a long time. Hence, a solution which is also reasonable and acceptable to labour will have to be found.

As rightly pointed out by Rangarajan, "Redundancies and closures occurring as a consequence of modernisation and technological upgradation are not a new phenomenon. This has occurred in a big way in centres like Ahmedabad and Kanpur where there has been a concentration of the textile industry. It must be recognised that restructuring of the workforce becomes necessary for efficient growth which alone can lead to sustainable employment growth in the medium and long term. At the same time, workers rendered unemployed in these processes cannot be left high and dry. Provision for fair and reasonable separation benefits is necessary, but more important is their redeployment, with training, if necessary, as a part of the overall strategy of expansion of employment opportunities. What, in fact, is being attempted in the new economic policy, with the instrumentality of the national renewal fund, is that the hardships of the workers affected in the unavoidable and inevitable loss of jobs are minimised by providing them a fair deal in terms of separation benefits and opportunities for their productive redeployment. The national renewal fund, constituted on a non-statutory basis, envisages the provision of resources solely for the rehabilitation of labour resulting from modernisation, technological upgradation, restructuring (including revival) or closure of industrial units. It will assist workers in this process for their retraining, redeployment and placement in new employment, besides contributing towards compensation payments, including legal dues and those under the Voluntary Retirement Scheme, under the fund called the National Renewal Grant Fund (NRGF)."

Far from adversely affecting employment elasticity, the restructured growth during the 1990s is expected to be far less capital-intensive and far more employment-friendly. First, with the removal of distortions in the factor markets, the new economic policy regime can be expected to lead to greater use of labour in the production processes as has been the experience of several labour-surplus developing countries which have succeeded in increasing their exports and overall growth of manufacturing industries. Second, the processes of deregulation and liberalisation are likely to particularly benefit the employment-intensive small and decentralised sector which, it must be recognised, had to bear a heavy burden of bureaucratic hurdles in the past. In the restructured economy these sectors, particularly the rural non-farm sector, agro-processing and agri-business in general, urban small enterprises and the services sector, all of which have shown high potential for employment generation, are likely to grow faster. Third, the overall objective of the new economic policy is to improve productivity and efficiency. In a competitive environment, both public and private sector units are expected to show improved productivity and greater expansion in output.

Commenting on economic reforms Kaushik Basu remarks, "The economy's overall post-reform growth rate has been very good. From 1994 to 1997 Indian national income grew at over 7 per cent per annum, and during the entire last decade the growth rate has been around 6.5 per cent. Specific sectors, such as the consumer durables industry, have done well. A study by K.V. Ramaswamy (2001) has shown that growth in the post-reform period has been significantly higher than in the pre-reform period, and, more important, firms have responded to the reforms by going in for technological improvements."

However, Basu believes, "Ultimately an economy has to be evaluated in terms of what happens to the poorest and the dispossessed. Everything else, such as a nation's income growth rate, is of instrumental value. Not all economists concur with this view. To many, efficiency, growth, and *aggregate* welfare are the ends that they wish to pursue. However, Amartya Sen has consistently taken a normative stand where these are merely of instrumental value. While Jagdish Bhagwati has argued vigorously for free trade and raising growth, but at the same time he has been categorical: 'As regards the *objective* of development, I should emphasise, as I always have, that growth was seen by me..., from the early 1960s, as simply an instrumental variable, as a means to an end, and the end was clearly the elimination of poverty."[16]

"India, unfortunately, still has miles to go, on matters of basic needs and development of the most disadvantaged. Over the last few decades, inequality has been rising, regional disparities have been growing, and poverty and illiteracy continue to be high."

On the overall magnitude of poverty there was, initially, a lot of very confusing data coming in and it was not clear what was happening. The most scientifically convincing study by Deaton (2001), establishes fairly clearly that poverty, after remaining steady through the early 1990s, went in for a definitive dip by 1999. Though the fall in the percentage of people below the poverty line was not as sharp as the government claimed (27.1 per cent for rural areas and 23.6 per cent for

16. Bhagwati, Jagdish (1985). *Essays in Development Economics.* Oxford University Press.

urban areas in 1999), it was sufficiently sharp (down to 30.2 per cent and 24.7 per cent in rural and urban areas, respectively) to cause the absolute number of people below the poverty line to fall. This augurs well, but it must not be forgotten that the level of poverty in India continues to be unacceptably high.

Literacy has risen from 52 per cent in 1991 to 65 per cent in 2001. This is, however, not so much a consequence of government policy as people's changing view of the value of education (caused by the greater exposure to the world out there), which has led to parents demanding better education for their children and often willing to pay for that at the expense of great personal hardship. Again, while this trend is heartening, it is tragic that a nation with so much policy devoted to higher education and scientific work still has 35 per cent of its population unable to read and write (Basu, 2004).

"On these fundamental indicators therefore there is reason to be both disappointed at where the nation stands and optimistic about the changes that have taken place,"[17] says Kaushik Basu.

The Next Round of Reforms

While much has been written and talked about the next round of reforms, what is not talked about enough but is important to develop is the institution of contracts, without which no modern market can function. This is where government is important. It must play the crucial role of the third party that helps enforce contracts. But contracts are partly a matter of culture without which it is difficult to develop crucial long-term market, such as the market for mortgage and long-term investment loans, and to take full advantage of globalisation. These, in turn, are key ingredients of fast growth. According to Kaushik Basu, "There are, fortunately, enough strengths in the Indian economy for it to be a net beneficiary of globalisation. The economy has gone past that critical level where to open up is to risk being cheated and impoverished. Though there are still innumerable important reforms to undertake, the fundamentals of the Indian economy are probably strong enough for it to be able to implement and benefit from another round of market reform and further (though gradual) opening up of the economy. Globalisation and modern markets bring with them many ills. But, on balance, and given the new strengths of the Indian economy, these changes will open up rather than close windows of opportunity for India."

---

17. Basu, Kaushik (ed.) (2004). *India's Emerging Economy: Performance and Prospects in the 1990s and Beyond*. Oxford University Press.

Questions

1. What were the main objectives of economic planning in India? How far have we been able to achieve those objectives?
[B.A. (P) 2006, 2007, 2008]

2. What are the objectives of economic planning in India? Discuss what are the causes and consequences of their slow progress.
[B.Com. (P) 2006, 2008]

3. What are the main objectives of economic planning in India? To what extent have they been realised?
[B.A. (P) External+Correspondence, 2006]

4. What has been the strategy of growth adopted in our earlier Five Year Plans? How far has it been successful?
[B.A. (P) 2005]

5. What are the main objectives of planning in India? Are these objectives mutually incompatible? *[B.A. (P) 2005]*

6. What do you understand by Self-Reliance with reference to planning in India? Examine to what extent India could achieve this objective? *[B.A. (P) 2004]*

7. What are the main objectives of economic planning in India? How far have the objectives of economic growth and poverty removal been achieved? *[B.Com. (P) 2004]*

8. Write a short note on 'Role of State in Economic Development'.
[B.Com. (P) 2003]

9. Differentiate between 'objectives' and 'strategy' of Indian Economic Planning. What are the various sources of finance for Indian Plans? *[B.Com. (P) 2003]*

10. Write a short note on 'Objectives of India's Plans'.
[B.A. (P) 2000; B.Com. (P) 2000]

11. Write a short note on 'self-reliance and economic development in India'. *[B.Com. (P) 2001]*

7

Saving and Investment in Indian Economy

AMONG the many factors of underdevelopment, lack of capital formation is considered to be a factor of prime importance. How can an underdeveloped economy achieve a high rate of investment or capital formation?

The process of capital formation is a function of three variables:

(i) An increase in the volume of real domestic saving so that the resources that would have been used for consumption are released for investment.

(ii) The creation of adequate banking and financial institutions to mobilise the savings of the community.

(iii) The emergence of an entrepreneural class which can utilise the community's saving into channels of productive investment or the assumption of the entrepreneural functions by the state in critical areas.

The planners in India believed that the low level of saving was the principal bottleneck, and for achieving a higher rate of growth as also to develop a self-reliant economy, rate of saving will have to be pushed up. In case domestic savings are not sufficient, we may invite foreign capital to supplement domestic savings. But in the ultimate analysis, foreign savings have to be paid back with interest. It thus implied transfering a part of the burden of development to the future generation. In short, it was argued that development did require sacrifice in the form of restraining consumption so as to force a higher rate of saving.

Trends in Saving: 1950-51 to 1995-96

Gross domestic saving (GDS) rate broke out of a low rate of 10.4 per cent of GDP in 1950-51 and witnessed an upward trend, *albeit* with occasional oscillations, to 19.0 per cent in 1975-76. A review of the first 25 years makes it possible to discern two periods. During the first period up to 1967-68, the financial infrastructure of the Indian economy was set up by the Reserve Bank and the Government of India. The State Bank of India was brought under public sector, the insurance companies got nationalised under the Life Insurance Corporation and premier financial institutions like the Unit Trust of India (UTI), the Industrial Development Bank of India and the Agricultural Refinance and Development Corporation were established. During this phase of setting up of financial infrastructure, a fillip to household financial saving was imparted. The nationalisation of 14 major commercial banks and ushering in of Green Revolution more or less coincided with the second period from 1968-69 to 1975-76. The financial infrastructure was expanded and geared up to mobilise potential savings from hitherto untapped rural and semi-urban areas. The onset of Green Revolution increased rural saving propensity and this, coupled with the better accessibility to banks, enabled channelising of saving in bank deposits. After the mid-seventies, there was a sudden acceleration of the GDS rate to 23.2 per cent in 1978-79 attributable to some special factors. Some commentators termed it as the 'high saving phase'. Household saving improved in terms of both financial and physical assets. However, the GDS rate plunged to a low of 18.2 per cent in the mid-eighties. Subsequently, there was a steady rise in the late eighties, followed by rebounding of the GDS rate to the highest historical rate of 25.6 per cent in 1995-96.

Sectoral Components of Gross Domestic Saving

It would be of interest to understand the behaviour of three sectors which contribute to saving.

Private savings consist of household savings, including direct investment by households, and corporate sector savings. Public sector savings consist of the savings of the government departments (Centre and states) and public sector corporations.

Saving of Household Sector

The household savings has gone up from 8.4 per cent during 1950-1951 to 1967-68 to 19.2 per cent during 1993-94 to 1995-96.

Three factors are responsible for this favourable trend:

(a) The rapid branch expansion after bank nationalisation in 1969 and the setting up of the regional rural banks thereafter helped considerably in mobilising savings from the areas which earlier did not have banking facilities.

(b) The inherent desire to acquire physical assets like a house or durable consumer goods promoted households to undertake financial savings for a long period till they accumulated to the level sufficient for the purchase of the physical asset. The government schemes of allowing individuals to purchase physical assets and then pay in instalments spread over a long period also introduced a higher propensity to save.

(c) To have a regular source of income for the old age or to supplement current income, households invest in some pension schemes.

Private Corporate Saving

Private corporate savings had stagnated over the first three periods but accelerated over the latter three periods. This stagnation and the relative poor saving performance compared to household and public sectors were attributable to the corporate sector being caught in a low profitability cycle. The tendency on the part of the corporate sector to rely more on borrowed funds and less on owned funds led to increased interest outgo, resulting in poor saving performance of the sector. Traditional industries like tea, jute, cotton textiles, cement and some other units of engineering became a drag on profitability. However, in the liberalised environment of the eighties and the nineties, the corporate saving rate increased. A striking feature of this acceleration phase of the private corporate saving has been a rise in the share of financial joint stock companies from 2.1 per in the period 1979-80 to 1984-85 to 10.6 per cent in the period 1993-94 to 1995-96. This has been the result of the development of new financial institutions and mutual funds in the private corporate sector. Private corporate sector saving rate crossed the public sector saving rate for the first time in 1988-89 and has remained higher ever since. In the liberalised environment, with increased internal and foreign competition, as well as foreign direct investment in various sectors, the profits of private corporate sector have registered a high growth, leading to increased saving (Table 7.1).

TABLE – 7.1

NOMINAL GROSS DOMESTIC SAVING RATE AND ITS COMPONENTS

(As Percentage of GDP at Current Market Prices)

Period	*1950-51 to 1967-68*	*1968-69 to 1975-76*	*1976-77 to 1978-79*	*1979-80 to 1984-85*	*1985-86 to 1992-93*	*1993-94 to 1995-96*
1. Household Saving	8.4 (70.9)	11.7 (72.2)	15.8 (72.2)	14.3 (72.2)	17.1 (79.4)	19.2 (78.5)
1.1 Household Financial Saving	2.5 (20.1)	3.6 (22.1)	6.1 (27.8)	6.5 (33.1)	8.4 (38.8)	10.7 (43.8)
1.2 Household Physical Saving	6.0 (50.7)	8.1 (50.1)	9.7 (44.4)	7.8 (39.1)	8.8 (40.6)	8.5 (34.6)
2. Private Corporate Saving	1.3 (10.7)	1.5 (9.4)	1.4 (6.6)	1.7 (8.6)	2.4 (10.9)	3.9 (15.8)
3. Public Sector Saving	2.2 (18.4)	3.0 (18.4)	4.6 (21.2)	3.8 (19.2)	2.0 (9.7)	1.4 (5.7)
3.1 Public Authorities	1.8	2.0	3.1	1.8	-1.1	-1.8
3.2 Non-Departmental Enterprises	0.4	1.0	1.5	2.0	3.1	3.2
4. Gross Domestic Saving	11.9	16.2	21.8	19.8	21.5	24.5

Note : Figures in brackets are percentage shares in gross domestic savings.
Source : Partha Ray and Bose, RBI occasional Papers, Vol-18, Sep.1997.

Public Sector Saving

During the first three periods (1950-51) to (1978-79), public sector savings peaked to a level of 4.6 per cent of GDP during 1976-77 as against 2.2 per cent during 1950-1968. Two factors contribued to this situation: First, rate of inflation was reasonably controlled and secondly, as a result of greater tax effort, public sector saving improved. This period is marked by increasing saving rate of public administration from 1.8 per cent to 3.1 per cent of GDP, although the savings of the non departmental enterprises picked up very slowly from 0.4 per cent to 1.5 per cent of GDP.

In the subsequent three periods (1979-80 to 1995-96), there is a continuous and noticeable decline in public sector savings from 3.8 per cent to 1.4 per cent of GDP. This was largely the result of continuous deficit budgets and increasing dependence on borrowings to meet growing non-Plan expenditure. Along with this, to meet the demands of various lobbies, there was a sharp increase in subsidies. As a consequence of the increase in government administration, increase in subsidies and interest payments due to rising debt burdens, the savings of public authorities became negative to the tune of 1.1 per cent during 1985-1993 and 1.8 per cent of GDP during 1993-1996. As against it, the savings of non-departmental enterprises showed a continuous improvement from 1.5 per cent during 1976-1979 to 3.3 per cent during 1993-1996, but this was not enough to compensate for the erosion of the savings of public administration. The net result of these two opposing tendencies was a decline in the savings of the public sector from 4.6 per cent of GDP to 1.4 per cent in 1993-1996.

Capital Formation

The Indian planners in the fifties recognised that the material shortage of capital in relation to labour was the principal constraint to growth process. It was envisioned that increased capital formation would usher in a 'virtuous circle' of growth. In order to obviate the structural limitations of converting saving to productive investment, the *modus operandi* was an active state policy of investment.

Trends in Capital Formation (1950-51 to 1995-96)

A comparative analysis of aggregate investment (Gross capital formation adjusted for errors and omissions) as well as gross capital formation across the various periods, as presented in Table 7.3, brings out the following features. First, there has been an increase in investment rate over time although the tempo has dampened in the last three periods. This resulted directly from the shift in emphasis of the plan objectives from quantitative targeting of investment rate to the need for efficient use of available investment. Reorientation of the strategy was essential, as commensurate growth had not fructified despite achievement of the envisaged high investment rates in the 'high saving phase'. Secondly, there has been a decline in the share of construction in gross capital formation and a rise in machinery and equipment over the various phases. Thirdly, while household and public sectors contributed heavily to capital formation in the first three periods, private corporate investment has been rising in the last three periods. The setting up of infrastructure in the initial phase faciliated later corporate investment. Finally, except for the 'high saving phase', domestic saving has been below the aggregate investment, reflecting the need for inflow of foreign resources. However, for the rest of the period the net capital inflow from abroad was required to sustain the investment levels, although the level was contained below 2.0 per cent, barring the period, 1985-86 to 1992-93.

Recent Trends in Saving and Investment

The domestic saving as a percentage of GDP in the nineties was the highest at 24.4 per cent in 1996-97. However, it declined to 23.2 per cent in 1999-2000. In 2000-01, the saving rate was 23.4 per cent. The acceleration in saving rate, observed from 1994-95 onwards, underscores the positive impact of the financial sector reforms in mobilising savings. The bulk of the savings continued to be sourced from the household sector; the saving of this sector as a percentage of GDP, hovering around 17-19 per cent in the nineties and since 2000 it has been 23-24 per cent. The composition of the household sector's saving has been generally in favour of financial assets as compared to physical assets. The greater preference for financial assets as against physical assets could be attributed to the higher rates of return on financial saving, growing financial intermediation and preference of households for less risky assets like bank deposits, contractual saving and small saving instruments. The private corporate sector saving recorded an increasing trend in the nineties reaching a peak level of 4.8 per cent in 1995-96. Since then, however, it has declined reaching 3.9 per cent in 2002-03. Since 2003-04, private corporate sector saving has been increasing and reached 7.8 per cent in 2006-07. Both components of private savings (households and corporate sector) have risen as a per cent of GDP in the Ninth Plan and also in the Tenth Plan. Corporate savings have been especially buoyant in the Tenth Plan, reflecting the very strong output and financial performance of the private sector in recent years. On the other hand, the public sector saving rate, which peaked at 2.1 per cent of GDP in the Eighth Plan (1992-93 to 1996-97) declined to 1.0 per cent in 1997-98 and became negative (-0.9 per cent) in 1999-2000 and -1.7 in 2000-01.[1]

The marked deterioration in public savings in the Ninth Plan period, was on account of the impact of the Fifth Pay Commission which led to an increase in government salaries. Departmental savings deteriorated from -0.9 per cent of GDP in the Eighth Plan to -4.1 per cent of GDP in the Ninth Plan. There was a marginal improvement in the savings of public sector undertakings from 3 per cent of GDP in the Eighth Plan to 3.3 per cent in the Ninth Plan, but the deterioration in departmental savings in the Ninth Plan meant that total public sector savings deteriorated from 2.1 per cent of GDP in the Eighth Plan to -0.8 per cent of GDP, a turnaround of 3 percentage points.

Both components of public sector savings showed an improvement in the Tenth Plan. Reduction in the dis-savings of government

1. RBI Bulletin, June 2002.

administration has been due to three main reasons: first, the impact of the Fifth Pay Commission's recommendations worked itself out in the system; second, the implementation of the Fiscal Responsibility and Budget Management (FRBM) Act, and the fiscal and revenue deficit targets for 2008-09 established thereby helped introduce an element of discipline; and third, the buoyancy in tax revenues arising out of the high growth rate recorded in the Tenth Plan combined with improvements in tax administration contributed to improved savings.

TABLE – 7.2

COMPOSITION OF SAVING

(% of GDP)

Period/ Years	*Private Sector*			*Public Sector*			
	House-hold Sector	*Private Corporate Sector*	*Total Private Sector*	*Government Adminis-tration*	*Public Sector Under-taking*	*Total Public Sector*	*Gross Domestic Savings*
Eighth Plan (1992-93 to 1996-97)	17.0	4.0	21.0	(-) 0.9	3.0	2.1	23.1
Ninth Plan (1997-98 to 2001-02)	20.5	4.0	24.5	(-) 4.1	3.3	(-) 0.8	23.6
2002-03	23.2	3.9	27.0	(-) 4.7	4.0	(-) 0.6	26.4
2003-04	24.4	4.4	28.7	(-) 3.1	4.2	1.1	29.8
2004-05	23.0	6.6	29.6	(-) 2.0	4.2	2.2	31.8
2005-06	24.2	7.5	31.7	(-) 1.4	4.0	2.6	34.3
2006-07	23.8	7.8	31.6	(-) 0.8	4.0	3.2	34.8
Tenth Plan (2002–03 to 2006–07)	23.7	6.3	30.0	(-) 2.2	4.1	1.9	31.9
Eleventh Plan	23.0	7.3	30.3	0.5	4.0	4.5	34.8

Note: Ratios for Eleventh Plan are at constant 2006–07 price; Ratios for earlier years' Plans are at current price; 2005–06: Provisional Estimates; 2006–07: Quick Estimates.

The projections for the Eleventh Plan assume that the private sector savings effort will continue to be strong with some further improvement and that this will be combined with a very strong improvement in public sector savings. The scale of the public sector effort can be seen from the fact that the Eleventh Plan projects a combined public sector savings rate of 4.5 per cent of GDP compared with an achieved level of only 1.9 per cent in the Tenth Plan. The projected turnaround of 2.6 percentage points of GDP in public sector savings requires a massive effort on the part of both the PSEs and the departments, mainly, the latter. It is important to note that this favourable outcome assumes that the award of the Sixth Pay Commission will not present severe difficulties. Hopefully, since the Fifth Pay Commission had indexed salaries fully to inflation, the pay increases should be only moderate. Pay revision should also increase private savings. If some of the subsidies financed by the government can be moderated, the savings target of public administration is realisable. It is also assumed that PSEs will maintain their savings performance of the Tenth Plan.

In tandem with the saving rates, investment rates (GDCF) too started picking up from 1994-95 recording a peak level of 25.8 per cent in 1995-96 and 35.9 per cent in 2006-07.

As shown in Table 7.3, the investment rate averaged 24.4 per cent in the Eighth Plan period and was almost unchanged in the Ninth Plan period. Thereafter, it rose to an average of 32.1 per cent in the Tenth Plan with the last year of the Plan showing an acceleration to 35.9 per cent. This rate of investment should normally be adequate to attain 9 per cent growth, but in our circumstances, because of prolonged underinvestment in infrastructure and the consequent need to enhance investment in this area, the Eleventh Plan aims at a further increase in the rate of investment in succeeding years to reach 38 per cent at the end of the Plan period, yielding an average of around 37 per cent in the entire Plan period.

An important structural change in the investment behaviour of the economy in the recent past is the change in relative shares of public and private investment. Although the rate of total investment as a percentage of GDP was almost the same in the Eighth Plan as in the Ninth Plan, the composition shifted in favour of private investment. Public sector investment as a percentage of GDP declined from 8.5 per cent in the Eighth Plan to 7 per cent in the Ninth Plan. This meant that the share of public sector investment in total investment declined from 34.7 per cent in the Eighth Plan to 29 per cent in the Ninth Plan. This trend of a declining rate of public investment as a percentage of GDP continued in the first two years of the Tenth Plan but then began to be corrected in the rest of the Plan period. Private sector investment continued to be buoyant throughout the Tenth Plan period so the share of public investment in total investment in the Tenth Plan fell to 22 per cent.

TABLE – 7.3

INVESTMENT, SAVINGS AND GROWTH RATES

(% of GDP)

Year	*Investment Rate*	*Savings Rate*	*Growth Rate*
Eighth Plan (1992-93 to 1996-97)	24.4	23.1	6.5
Ninth Plan (1997-98 to 2001-02)	24.3	23.6	5.5
2002-03	25.2	26.4	3.8
2003-04	28.2	29.8	8.5
2004-05	32.2	31.8	7.5
2005-06	35.5	34.3	9.5
2006-07	35.9	34.8	9.7
Tenth Plan (2002-03 to 2006-07)	32.1	31.9	7.7
Eleventh Plan Targets	36.7	34.8	9.0
2007-08	39.1	37.7	9.0
2008-09	NA	NA	8.7

Note: Ratios for Eleventh Plan are at constant 2006–07 price; Ratios for earlier years' Plans are at current price; 2005–06: Provisional Estimates; 2006–07: Quick Estimates.

The rapid increase in private sector investment in the aggregate investment is in large part a reflection of the impact of the reforms initiated in the 1990s, which reduced restrictions on private investment and created a more favourable investment climate. It reflects the fact that the private sector has responded positively with an improvement in the investment climate. This is clearly a welcome development and should be encouraged in the Eleventh Plan. It must be emphasised that a higher share of public investment can be justified only if there is a demonstrable improvement in the efficiency of public investment. However, it can be argued that the infrastructure gaps are so large that an increase in public investment in infrastructure will actually crowd in private investment. These objectives are reflected in the projections for the Eleventh Plan.

The private sector, which includes farming, micro, small and medium enterprises (MSMEs), and the larger private corporate sector, accounts for over 77 per cent of the total investment in the economy and an even larger share in employment and output. Expansion in this sector will have to play a critical role in achieving the objective of faster and more inclusive growth. The MSMEs, in particular, have a vital role to play in making the growth regionally balanced, and in generating widely dispersed off-farm employment, some of it in rural areas. The Eleventh Plan, therefore, aims at an increase in investment in the private sector to

28.7 per cent from an average of 25.1 per cent in the Tenth Plan. This is best done by creating an environment in which entrepreneurship can flourish at all levels. New entrepreneurs should be able to enter and expand. In order to compete with incumbents, there must be strong competitive pressures which promote efficiency, government policies must be investor-friendly, transaction costs should be low and infrastructure services of good quality should be readily available, especially to small and medium enterprises. Many elements of this environment are already in place. Licensing controls and discretionary approvals have already been greatly reduced, but remnants of the control regime remain that still need drastic overhaul, if not elimination, especially at the state government level. Quantitative controls, where they exist, should give way to fiscal measures and increased reliance on competitive markets, subject to effective and transparent regulation. The burden of multiple inspections by government agencies must be removed and tax regimes rationalised. Since MSMEs are expected to create the bulk of new employment, it is particularly important to make the financial system more efficient in meeting the needs of our expanding private sector, and to ensure financial inclusiveness.

While encouraging private investment, the Eleventh Plan also aims at a substantial increase in public investment in critical areas such as agriculture, irrigation and water management, and in social and economic infrastructure. Public investment in infrastructure is projected to increase from 4.1 per cent in 2006-07 to 6.8 per cent in 2011-12. Since this increase must be accommodated with the overall increase in public investment from 7.8 per cent in 2006-07 to 8.6 per cent in 2011-2012, it implies that public investment will shift from the non infrastructure to infrastructure sector.

Saving, Investment and Growth

Is the growth rate of the Indian economy compatible with its saving and investment rate?

Saving and investment in India have risen since 1951 from just 9 per cent 1950-51 to around 23 to 24 per cent in 1999-2000. However, the growth rate has been modest. This can be due to: (i) savings have possibly not been mobilised effectively for investment purposes and (ii) which is more important, is the low efficiency of investment.

Savings preference of households can be an important constraining factor on growth. Substantial portion of household savings is in the form of physical assets which are not productive in some cases.

Slow growth combined with a rather high level of investment implies low efficiency of investment. The extensive bureaucratic controls over production, investment and trade stifled efficiency and growth until the 1970s. The low productive efficiency of investment is reflected by increasing capital-output ratios. The incremental capital output ratio (ICOR) rose continuously in the period 1950-51 to 1980-1981. The decade of eighties which shows a significantly higher growth rate also shows a significantly lower ICOR. The ratio declined from 6 per cent in 1970s to 4.1 per cent in 1980s.

There has been some improvement in the general efficiency of the use of resources and an improvement in the quality of investment in the eighties. This along with the liberalisation measures adopted in the industrial policy framework are responsible for a higher growth in 80s.

In the nineties after a swift recovery from the 1991 crisis, economic growth accelerated to an average of 6.5 per cent in the eighth plan period (1992-93 to 1996-97), which is significantly better than 5.6 per cent in the 1980s.

GDP growth rate in the Ninth Plan registered 5.5 per cent growth inspite of almost the same saving investment rates as during the Eighth Plan period. The period 2003-04 to 2008-09 recorded high growth rates of 7 to 9 per cent accompanied by increasing saving and investment rates (Table 7.3) The economic reforms since 1991 are aimed at enhancing efficiency and growth in the economy. The liberalisation process and deregulation process has removed entry barriers and has brought in increased competition from domestic sources. At the same time, liberalisation of the import regime, tariff reduction, convertibility of rupee and liberalisation of foreign investment policy has brought in external competition. These measures will result to efficiency gains.

Overall, an increase in savings rate and investment rate in the coming years coupled with efficiency gains can generate a growth rate of 8 to 10 per cent in the future.

Questions

1. India has achieved high rate of savings yet the rate of growth is very slow. Explain. *[B.A. (P) 1999]*
2. What are the main sources of domestic savings in India? Is the present level of savings in India adequate? *[B.A. (P) 1992]*
3. Why has the growth of domestic product remained low in spite of substantial increase in investment. *[B.A. (P) 2009]*
4. Briefly examine the trends in saving and investment in India.

8

Financing the Plans

Pattern of Plan Financing

THE main sources of funds for financing development expenditures contemplated in the plans are grouped under the following heads:

1. Balance from current revenue of government;
2. Surpluses of public enterprises;
3. Borrowings;
4. Additional resource mobilisation;
5. External assistance; and
6. Deficit financing.

The balance from current revenue (BCR) is the excess of Government's revenues over non-plan current expenditure

Surpluses of public sector enterprises is the internal and extra budgetary resources of public sector undertakings.

Borrowings consist of market borrowings, small savings, state provident funds, term loans, from financial institutions and miscellaneous capital receipts.

Additional resource mobilisation (ARM) is an important item and it represents resources generated from additional efforts made by the Government or the public enterprises. In case of Government, ARM represents what it can raise by intensifying tax collection efforts and cutting down on expenditure. In case of PSEs, ARM represents what they can raise by revising their price upwards or by cutting costs or improving operational efficiency.

Net external assistance is net inflow of budgetary resources from abroad. All the other five items are domestic sources of plan financing. Net external assistance includes both external loans and grants.

Deficit financing is Government's borrowing from Reserve Bank of India. In most of the five year plans, deficit financing and other borrowings have been higher than the original estimates.

Balances from current revenue, surpluses of PSEs and additional resource mobilisation constitute public savings. These are the least inflationary instruments for raising resources for public expenditure. Deficit financing is the most inflationary source of plan financing.

The pattern of plan financing as originally contemplated and as it emerged in reality since the First Five Year Plan is set out in Table 8.1.

Looking at the pattern of financing, one finds that plan financing in India depended primarily on domestic sources. External assistance has constituted no more than 12 per cent of the total outlay in the recent Plans (4th, 5th, 6th, 7th and 8th Plan). While in the Fourth and the Fifth Plan, external assistance contributed about 12 per cent to plan finances, in Sixth Plan 7.7 per cent, in Seventh Plan 9 per cent and in the 8th Plan the net inflow from abroad although projected at 6.6 per cent, turned out to be little less than 4 per cent.

The most important sources of financing are "additional resource mobilisation" (ARM) and domestic borrowings. The term ARM represents the resources which the government and the public enterprises at the Centre and in the states (the federating units of the Indian Union) are expected to raise over and above the surplus which their budgets are likely to generate. This surplus is worked out after projecting the current revenues and non-Plan current expenditure in the five years of a given Plan period, assuming normal growth in both revenues and expenditures. The growth rates of revenues of government are derived on the basis of past trends and/or their elasticities with respect to major determinants (e.g., with respect to GDP in the case of income-tax). Similarly, in the case of public enterprises, the growth is worked out on the basis of the existing structure of prices and costs. The ARM figures are based on an assessment of what the governments at the Centre and in the states and the public enterprises run by them can raise through additional efforts such as by raising the tax rates or intensifying collection efforts and cutting down non-Plan expenditures. In the case of public enterprises, ARM represents what they can raise by revising their prices upwards or by cutting costs and improving their operational efficiency.

TABLE – 8.1

FINANCING OF PLAN OUTLAY IN PUBLIC SECTOR DURING FIVE YEAR PLANS

Figs. in (00 Crore)
(In bracket percentage)

	First Plan (1951-1956)		Second Plan (1956-1961)		Third Plan (1961-1966)		Fourth Plan (1969-1974)	
	Original	Actuals Estimates	Original	Actuals Estimates	Original	Actual Estimates	Original	Actual Estimates
Balance from Current Revenues	5.7 (27.55)	6.8 (32.50)	3.5 (7.29)	-5 (-1.09)	5.5 (7.33)	-4.2 (-4.90)	16.7 (10.52)	-2.4 (-1.46)
Public Enterprises CPSEs including Railways	1.7 (8.22)	1.2 (5.87)	1.5 (3.13)	1.6 (3.26)	5.5 (7.33)	4.4 (5.07)	22.3 (14.03)	14.3 (8.86)
Borrowings	5.2 (25.04)	6.9 (35.20)	14.5 (30.21)	14.4 (30.84)	19.4 (25.87)	21.1 (24.62)	55.4 (34.84)	68.3 (42.26)
Additional Resource Mobilisation	—	2.6 (13.27)	8.5 (17.71)	10.5 (22.48)	17.1 (22.80)	28.9 (33.72)	32.0 (20.11)	42.8 (26.49)
External Assistance (net)	5.2 (25.18)	1.9 (9.69)	8.0 (16.67)	10.5 (22.48)	22.0 (29.33)	24.2 (28.23)	26.1 (16.42)	20.9 (12.93)
Deficit Financing	2.9 (14.02)	3.3 (16.84)	12.0 (25.00)	9.5 (20.34)	5.5 (7.33)	11.3 (13.19)	8.5 (5.35)	20.6 (12.75)
Aggregate Resources	20.0 (100.00)	19.7 (100.00)	48.0 (100.00)	46.0 (100.00)	75.0 (100.00)	85.7 (100.00)	159.0 (100.00)	161.6 (100.00)

(contd...)

(....contd....)

	Fifth Plan (1974-1979)		Sixth Plan (1980-1985)		Seventh Plan (1985-1990)		Eighth Plan (1992-1997)		Ninth Plan (1997-2002)	
	Original	*Actuals Estimates*	*Original*	*Actual Estimates*	*Original*	*Actual Estimates*	*Original*	*Actual estimates*	*Original*	*Actual estimates*
Domestic Budgetary resources										
Current Revenues	49.0	66.4	144.8	18.9	-52.5	-125.0	-350.0	-462.5	-1406.0	-2637.5
	(12.47)	(16.30)	(14.85)	(1.71)	(-2.92)	(-7.00)	(8.06)	(12.01)	-	-
Public Enterprises CPSEs including Railways	8.5	25.8	94.0	58.1	354.9	140.8	1481.4	1012.6	3404.0	2809.0
	(2.20)	(6.35)	(9.64)	(5.24)	(19.72)	(7.89)	(34.13)	(26.34)	-	-
Borrowings	105.0	115.1	323.8	385.7	604.1	1012.0	2022.5	2237.0	4601.7	6712.2
	(28.61)	(30.52)	(37.32)	(41.45)	(40.59)	(56.68)	(46.59)	(58.19)	-	-
Additional Resource Mobilisation	146.9	103.0	213.0	329.7	447.0	313.1	-	-	-	-
	(37.97)	(25.30)	(21.85)	(29.75)	(24.83)	(17.58)	-	-	-	-
External Assistance (Net)	58.3	52.1	109.3	85.3	180.0	161.0	287.0	381.1	600.0	1745.2
	(15.07)	(12.79)	(11.21)	(7.70)	(10.00)	(9.03)	(6.61)	(9.93)	-	-
Deficit Financing	13.5	35.6	50.0	156.8	140.0	282.0	200.0	290.0	-	-
	(3.49)	(8.74)	(5.13)	(14.15)	(7.78)	(15.82)	(5.01)	(7.55)	-	-
Aggregate Resources	393.0	407.1	975.0	1108.2	1800.0	1786.7	3990.9	3845.0	8592.0	7058.0
	(100.00)	(100.00)	(100.00)	(100.00)	(100.00)	(100)	(100)	(100)	-	-

Source : Planning Commission, January 2001, *Indian Planning Experience: A Statistical Profile*, p.39, Table 4.1.

Borrowings, currently the biggest single item of domestic resources for the Plans, are made up of market borrowings, small savings, state provident funds, term loans from financial institutions and miscellaneous capital receipts. Market borrowings come mainly from the subscription primarily by the commercial banks. The commercial banks are required compulsorily to keep a fraction of their deposits in government securities to maintain what is called the statutory liquidity ratio and this has been a major instrument for channelising the flow of household savings into the public sector. The other sources of borrowings are the small savings schemes designed to garner the savings of the households in the form of deposits with post offices which are spread all over the country reaching the far corners of rural areas, state provident funds and deposits of other financial institutions like the Life Insurance Corporation of India, General Insurance Corporation of India and so on.

Borrowings constituted 40 per cent to 63 per cent of plan finances (42 per cent in the 4th Plan, 30.5 per cent in the 5th Plan, 41.5 per cent in the 6th Plan, 58 per cent in the 7th Plan and for the 8th Plan against the projected figure of 46.5 per cent the actual turned out to be 63.1 per cent of the total finances). Amaresh Baghchi[1] points out that as a result of the large shortfalls in budgetary savings and inadequate surpluses of PSUs, the financing of public sector plan outlay had to depend heavily on borrowings. Total domestic borrowings contributed anything between 40 and 60 per cent to plan finances in recent years (6th, 7th and 8th Plan) as compared to about one-fifth to one-fourth in most of the earlier Plans. Inadequacy of current revenues to meet even current expenditures has resulted in the use of borrowed funds to meet current expenditures, leading close to what is called an internal debt trap. The main factor responsible for the falling contribution of the Central budget to the financing of the plans is the mounting burden of non-Plan expenditure in the form of interest payments and subsidies on food and fertilisers.

Total debt servicing consisting of interest payments and repayment of debt was 112.8 per cent of total revenue receipts in 1993-94 (RE). If we include, on the receipt side, the receipts from the sale of the equity of Central Public Sector Enterprises (CPSEs) and recovery of loans, the total debt servicing then constitutes 100.7 per cent of total receipts.

---

1. Baghchi, Amaresh, *Fiscal Policy for Financing Development: The Indian Experience*, in Uma Kapila (ed.) *op. cit.*

The Central government has resorted to a fiscal system of high fiscal deficits on a consistent basis over the last 20 years. The second half of the 1980s was exceptional in the attainment of much higher fiscal deficits than other periods and this resulted in the crisis of 1990-91. The consequences of such a sustained high fiscal deficit are many.

With increasing levels of borrowing financing activities which have zero or low yields, interest payments increase inexorably. Thus, non productive committed current expenditures rise giving rise to higher and higher revenue deficits. This leads to yet higher and higher borrowing levels.

Second, because of debt service payments forming a higher proportion of both revenues and expenditures all other activities of the government suffer, since wages and salaries, interest payments, defence expenditures, pensions, food subsidies are all committed expenditures with little or no flexibility. The main sufferer in this process is government capital expenditure in both social and infrastructure facilities.

Third, high debt service payments also preclude increase in or even maintenance of current real levels of expenditures in social services. The continued high levels of public borrowings also have an effect on the rest of the economy through prevalence of high interest rates. Because of the necessity to finance government deficits, the Reserve Bank of India has to keep the level of both CRR (Current Reserve Ratio) and SLR (Statutory Liquidity Ratio) high on the deposits in commercial banks. This leads to the necessity for banks to have higher margins on their commercial activities, thereby subjecting the rest of the economy to high interest rates.

The consequence of a sustained high fiscal deficit over 20 years can be seen in Table 8.2. Debt service payments of the Central government have risen sharply from about 30 per cent of tax revenues in 1980-1985 to about 70 per cent now. According to Rakesh Mohanm the day is not far off when the tax revenues will equal debt service payments. As a proportion of total revenue receipts, debt service has increased from about 24 per cent in 1980-1985 to about 50 per cent now. As a proportion of GDP, debt service payments have increased from about 2.2 per cent in 1980-1985 to about 5 per cent now. Another consequence of rising debt service is that the revenue deficit has increased from about 17 per cent as a proportion of fiscal deficit in 1980-1985 to about 50 per cent now. In other words, half of current borrowing goes to finance current expenditure. By definition current expenditure yields no economic returns in the future and hence, debt service payments will continue to rise in the foreseeable future unless a significant correction is made in this situation.

TABLE – 8.2

BURDEN OF RISING DEBT SERVICE OF CENTRAL GOVERNMENT (1980-2000)

	1980-1985	*1985-1990*	*1990-1995*	*1995-1999*	*1997-98*	*1998-99 (RE)*	*1999-2000 (BE)*
As:							
% of Tax Revenue	30.1	40.5	58.9	65.9	68.6	70.5	71.7
% of Revenue Receipts	23.5	30.4	43.7	47.6	49.0	49.0	50.8
% of Total Revenue	14.3	18.4	26.4	29.3	28.3	27.7	31.0
% of Total Expenditure	13.3	16.5	24.6	28.3	28.3	27.4	31.0
% of GDP	2.2	3.4	4.4	4.6	4.6	4.8	4.9
Revenue Deficit/ Fiscal Deficit	17.0	32.0	48.0	50.0			

Source: Govt. of India, Budget Documents various years.

The Approach Paper to the Tenth Plan stated that the fiscal situation of Central government has deteriorated continuously in 1990s and especially during the Ninth Plan. The combined balance of current revenues of the Centre and the states declined from a negative Rs. 13,324 crore in 1996-97 or 1 per cent of GDP to negative Rs. 92,969 crore or 4.8 per cent of GDP in 1999-2000. This has occurred because of a substantial increase in interest payments and the increased wages and salaries on account of the Fifth Pay Commission award and equally importantly because the revenue receipts of Centre as a proportion of GDP have declined from 11.3 per cent in 1989-90 to 9.3 per cent in 2000-01. The shortfall between the revenue receipts and expenditure (non-Plan) has been increasing and is around 3.6 per cent of the GDP. The Central government has bridged this gap through consistently high public borrowings including borrowing from small savings—the most expensive source of capital receipts for the Government.

As a result, debt service payments of the Central government have risen inexorably from about 30 per cent of tax revenue in 1980-1985 to about 70 per cent at present. A rise in debt service burden has meant that revenue deficit, which was 17 per cent as a proportion of fiscal deficit in 1980-1985, has now increased to about 50 per cent. In other words, nearly half of the current borrowings go to financing current expenditure.

Fiscal Reform

What is to be done? The key objective of fiscal reform has to be a reduction in debt service payments. This has to be achieved by a progressive reduction in public debt and through higher revenues. The possibility of achieving higher revenues through increased rates of taxes is both undesirable and infeasible. Higher tax revenues can be achieved only through buoyancy and expansion of the tax base. Thus, the main instruments for achieving a sustained increase in overall revenues are: (i) expansion of the tax base; (ii) widespread and bold imposition of user charges on all non-merit goods; and (iii) widespread and bold privatisation.

Fiscal Responsibility and Budget Management (FRBM)

While interest rates have fallen, and have generally been below nominal GDP growth, persistent revenue deficits have been financed by new debt. This has led to an escalation of the debt/GDP ratio. In particular, the fiscal deterioration has been particularly marked in the eight-year period from 1996-97 to 2004-05, where the liabilities/GDP ratio worsened by 12.2 percentage points.

The persistent fiscal deficits, and the steadily growing Debt/GDP ratio, constitute the most important challenges affecting India's growth prospects. In response to this challenge, Parliament passed the Fiscal Responsibility and Budget Management (FRBM) Act, which was notified on August 26, 2003. A central requirement of the FRBM concerns the revenue deficit in 2007-08. It requires that government undertake:

> Appropriate measures to reduce the fiscal deficit and revenue deficit so as to eliminate revenue deficit by 31st March 2008 and thereafter build up adequate revenue surplus.

Financing the Tenth Plan (MTA) and Eleventh Plan Projections[2]

Table 8.3 compares the structure of financing projected in the Eleventh Plan for the Centre and States, combined with that actually realised in the Tenth Plan. The most notable feature is that the Eleventh

2. Planning Commission (2008). *Eleventh Five Year Plan 2007-2012*, June 25.

Plan projections show relatively modest dependence on borrowings amounting to 38.9 per cent of the total Plan resources compared with 73.9 per cent in the Tenth Plan realisation. This outcome is the consequence of tighter fiscal discipline imposed by the fiscal responsibility framework, both at the Centre and the states, and an optimistic revenue outlook driven by the buoyancies in revenue collections during the last three years of the Tenth Plan reflecting the robust performance of the economy. This is reflected in the projected massive improvement in BCR which was negative in the Tenth Plan and is projected as a large positive figure for both the Centre and the states.

The financing plan outlined above will pose major challenges. The total resources for the Central and state Plans taken together have to increase from an average of 9.46 per cent of GDP in the Tenth Plan to an average of 13.54 per cent of GDP in the Eleventh Plan. It may be noted that while the total size of the Plan is projected at 13.54 per cent of GDP, the total public investment in the economy is projected to be lower at 8.6 per cent. This difference reflects the fact that a great deal of Plan expenditure finances current expenditure on various items of public service delivery which are not counted as investment. The increase of 4.08 per cent of GDP in total resources for the Plan has to be achieved while keeping borrowing within the FRBM requirement of reducing the fiscal deficit of the Centre and states to 3 per cent on each account. Taking account of the resources mobilised by the public sector, the combined BCR of the Centre and the states has to increase by more than the projected increase in Plan resources.

The Centre's BCR, realised in the Tenth Plan, averaged (-)0.84 per cent of GDP. It is projected to average 2.31 per cent of GDP over the Eleventh Plan, that is, an improvement of 3.15 percentage points of GDP. Similarly, the BCR of the states is also expected to improve substantially from (-) 0.18 per cent of GDP as realised in the Tenth Plan to 1.41 per cent of GDP in the Eleventh Plan. The projected improvement required in the combined BCR of the Centre and states taken together is therefore 4.74 percentage points of GDP. It must be emphasised that achievement of these BCR targets is a key element in the financing of the Plan.

The assumption of strong growth in tax revenues of the Centre and the states built into the projections is not unreasonable. Tax revenues recorded in the recent past has shown high buoyancy facilitated by tax reforms and also significant improvements in the efficiency of tax administration. These efforts will continue in the Eleventh Plan period and should contribute to achieving the targeted tax-to-GDP ratios.

TABLE – 8.3

COMPARISON OF TENTH PLAN REALISATION WITH ELEVENTH PLAN PROJECTION OF RESOURCES

(Rs. crore at 2006-07 price)

	Sources of Funding	Tenth Plan Realisation			Eleventh Plan Projection		
		Centre	States & UTs	Total	Centre	States & UTs	Total
1	Balance from Current Revenues	-127166 (-13.4)	-31722 (-4.5)	-158888 (-9.6)	653989 (30.3)	385050 (25.9)	1039039 (28.5)
2	Borrowings including Net MCR	850382 (89.9)	371779 (52.5)	1222161 (73.9)	767722 (35.6)	649423 (43.6)	1417145 (38.9)
3	Net Inflow from Abroad	16121 (1.7)	–	16121 (1.0)	–	–	–
4	Centre's GBS (1+2+3)	739337 (78.2)	–	739337 (44.7)	1421711 (65.9)	– –	1421711 (39.0)
5	Resources of PSEs	458530 (48.5)	119003 (16.8)	577533 (34.9)	1059711 (49.1)	128824 (8.7)	1188535 (32.6)
6	State's Own Resources (1+2+5)		459060 (64.9)	459060 (27.8)	– –	1163296 (78.2)	1163296 (31.9)
7	Central Assistance to States & UTs	-252539 (-26.7)	248677 (35.1)	-3862 (-0.2)	-324851 (-15.1)	324851 (21.8)	– –
8	Resources of the Public Sector Plan (1+2+3+5+7)	945328	707737	1653065	2156571	1488147	3644718

Note: Figures in parentheses are percentages of Resources of the Public Sector Plan.
Source: Planning Commission.

There are several factors which could make it difficult to contain expenditures to the projected level. There are inevitable uncertainties associated with the impact of the Sixth Pay Commission's recommendations. Equally, if not, more important is the upward pressure of subsidies, particularly on fertiliser and petroleum, and also on food. Petroleum subsidies have not so far been factored into the plan resources calculations since they have been financed by the issue of bonds not included in fiscal deficit accounting, and some portion being borne by the oil companies themselves. However, this practice cannot be sustained indefinitely. Reform of the subsidy regime has to be urgently taken up to keep the total subsidy, including the present off-budget subsidy, to within the ceiling of 0.93 per cent of GDP in 2011-12 that the resources projections have built in.[3]

Questions

1. Examine the relative importance of foreign aid and deficit financing in financing of the Five Year Plans in India. *[B.A. (P) 2009]*
2. Write a brief note on: Sources of finance of five year plans. *[B. Com 2007; B.A. (P) 2008]*
3. Examine the role of deficit financing as a source of financing the plans in India. *[B.A. (P) 2007]*
4. Examine relative importance of foreign aid and deficit financing in financing of five year plans in India. *[B.A. (P) 2005]*
5. Analyse the various methods of financing of five year plans in India. *[B.Com. (P) 2005]*
6. Write a note on 'deficit financing'. *[B.A. (P) 2000, 2003]*
7. Differentiate between 'objectives' and 'strategy' of Indian Economic Planning. What are the various sources of finance for Indian Plans? *[B.Com. (P) 2003]*
8. What are the various sources of finances for Indian Plans? *[B.Com. (P) 2003]*
9. What are the various sources of financing Indian Plans? Assess the role of market borrowings in recent years. *[B.A. (P) 2001]*
10. Write a short note on sources of financing India's Plans. *[B.Com. (P) 2001]*

3. Ibid.

9

Fiscal Federalism

Centre-State Fiscal Relations

INDIA has 29 states governed by their own elected parliaments. It has 7 union territories which come under the jurisdiction of the Central government. Fiscal relations between the Centre and states are shaped by the Seventh Schedule in the Indian Constitution which describes the legislative, executive and judicial powers of the Centre and state through the Union, State and Concurrent lists. The division of revenue and expenditure powers between the Centre and states is specified by: (a) the Union List, which states the powers that are exclusively under the purview of the Central government and (b) the State List, which gives those powers exclusively under the state government. All residual powers rest with the Centre.

In 1992, the 72nd and 73rd Constitutional Amendments introduced a third tier of fiscal authority, giving constitutional validity to existing rural and urban local governments.

Till that time, local governments acted as agencies of the state governments. Panchayati Raj institutions in the villages informally provided basic community and judicial services while in urban areas municipal authorities fulfilled this purpose. The constitutional amendments of 1992 gave these institutions an elective status and gave them powers to impose taxes—usually property taxes in urban areas. Education, housing and land use, development of industrial and commercial estates, and electricity distribution are some of the functions that have been decentralised in urban areas.[1]

1. Dhillon, Amrita (2007). "Fiscal Federalism" in Kaushik Basu (ed.) *The Oxford Companion to Economics in India*. New Delhi: Oxford University Press.

Fiscal Federalism[2]

Fiscal federalism is the economic counterpart to political federalism. Fiscal federalism is concerned with the assignment, on the one hand of functions to different levels of government and on the other with appropriate fiscal instruments for carrying out these functions. It is generally believed that the Central government must provide national public goods that render services to the entire population of the country. A typical example cited is defence. Local governments are expected to provide goods and services whose consumption is limited to their own jurisdictions. The argument here is that output of such goods and services can be tailored to meet the preferences and circumstances of the people in that jurisdiction. Such a process of de-centralisation enhances the economic welfare above that which could result from the more uniform levels of such services that are likely under a centralised regime. Apart from the provision of national public goods, the Central government is to be vested with the responsibilities for economic stabilisation and for income re-distribution. While income redistribution to some extent is possible even within sub-national government jurisdictions, a truly re-distribution effort is possible only at the national level. An equally important question in fiscal federalism is the determination of the specific fiscal instruments that would enable the different levels of government to carry out their functions. This is the 'tax-assignment problem' which is discussed very much in the literature. The traditional issues in fiscal federalism have been how to determine the assignment of taxes and responsibilities to different levels of government. Recognising the possibility of imbalance between resources and responsibilities, many countries have a system of inter governmental transfers. In fact, inter-governmental transfers constitute a distinctive economic policy instrument in fiscal federalism. For example, inter-governmental transfers as a percentage of provincial or state revenues have been 41 per cent in Australia, 40 per cent in India and 20 per cent in Canada in recent years. Correcting vertical and horizontal imbalances has been a major concern with which fiscal federalism has wrestled with. While actual designs of fiscal transfer systems differ across federations, these constitute experiments in search of satisfying the twin objectives of equity and efficiency in a multi-tiered system of government.

2. Rangarajan, C. (2009). " Fiscal Federalism: Some Current Concerns" in *India: Monetary Policy, Financial Stability and Other Essays*. New Delhi: Academic Foundation.

Fiscal Transfers

The roots of fiscal federalism in India go back to the Government of India Acts of 1919 and 1935. While the Act of 1919 provided for a separation of revenue heads between the Centre and the provinces, the 1935 Act allowed for the sharing of Centre's revenues and for the provision of grants-in-aid to provinces. The Indian Constitution carried these provisions a step forward by providing for a Finance Commission to determine the distribution between the Union and the states of the net proceeds of taxes and the grants-in-aid to be provided to the states which are in need of assistance. While the Constitutional provisions relating to the functions of the Finance Commissions have remained unchanged, one notable change in the framework of federal fiscal arrangements was brought out by the 80th Amendment which broadened the ambit of the sharable Central taxes. The enlargement of the sharable pool to cover all Central taxes except those listed in Articles 268 and 269 and earmarked cesses and surcharges, has enabled states to share in the overall buoyancy of taxes. It has also provided greater stability to resource transfers as fluctuations in individual taxes are evened out. With the 73rd and 74th Amendments to the Constitution which have provided constitutional support to the process of decentralisation, the Finance Commissions are also required to suggest measures to augment the resources for the *panchayats* and municipalities.

The Indian Constitution lays down the functions as well as taxing powers of the Centre and states.

Most taxes with a broad tax base are assigned to the Centre—for example income and wealth tax from non-agricultural sources, corporation tax, customs duties and excise duties. Sales taxes, land revenue, alcohol excises and agricultural income taxes are with the state government. Out of these, the sales tax is the most significant source of revenue for states. On the expenditure side, the Centre spends on defence and infrastructure while state governments spend mainly on internal security, law and order, and social and economic services. Among social services, the largest proportion goes to education, public health and family.[3]

There is a well-documented vertical imbalance between the Centre and states: in 2002-03, the state governments on average raised about 38 per cent of total revenues but accounted for 58 per cent of the expenditures. This imbalance has grown worse over the years: in 1955-

3. Dhillon, Amrita (2007). *op cit*.

1956 these figures were 41 per cent and 59 per cent, respectively. The imbalance was a direct result of the types of taxes that were assigned to the Centre and the bias in favour of the Centre which was an artefact of the colonial system and the subsequent emphasis on planned development and reducing inequalities between states. The Constitution recognised this imbalance and provided for the assignment of revenues between the Centre and states as well as for the sharing of revenues from the proceeds of certain centrally levied taxes. In addition to this, the Constitution provides for grants from the Centre to the states. The President of India appoints the Finance Commission, an independent body, to determine the shares of Centre and states in shared Central revenues and their allocation between states. Under the provisions of the Constitution, 13 Finance Commissions have been constituted so far. The specific terms of reference of each of the Finance Commissions have varied, although all the Commissions have been entrusted with the primary task of: (i) determining the share in net tax revenue of the Centre, and (ii) determining the principles of grants-in-aid to the states. The Thirteenth Finance Commission will be submitting its report during this year. The Finance Commission also recommends grants to states in need on the basis of the formula that weights different states according to their population, income, area, infrastructure, tax effort and fiscal discipline. After the 72nd and 73rd Amendments to the Constitution, State Finance Commissions were set up analogous to the Finance Commission at national level.

As a consequence of the skewed distribution of taxing and expenditure powers, state governments typically run a deficit that is financed by Central transfers (there are corresponding deficits noted at local government level). On average in 2000-01, states' own revenue to current spending was 49 per cent. State governments can rely on both tax and non-tax revenue sources. The latter comprise interest receipts from loans issued by the state government, dividends and profits from public sector undertakings owned by states, and revenue from state lotteries. In 2000-01, states' share of Central taxes was approximately 27 per cent while grants to states accounted for 11 per cent of total revenues. Hence, states' dependence on Central transfers is very high and causes many problems of fiscal indiscipline and low tax effort.

The issues relating to the correction of vertical and horizontal imbalances have been addressed by every Finance Commission, taking into account the prevailing set of circumstances. Central transfers to states are not, however, confined to the recommendations of the Finance Commissions. There are other channels such as those through the

Planning Commission as well the discretionary grants of the Central government.

The traditional concerns of fiscal federalism such as the assignment of taxes and responsibilities as well as the correction of vertical and horizontal imbalances continue to remain important. However, it is necessary to take note of the changes in the environment in which governments operate. Fiscal federalism must enable national and sub national governments to operate in such a way that it leads to efficiency in the use of resources. This improvement in efficiency must be reflected not only in the services provided by the various levels of government but also in creating an environment in which all economic agents use resources efficiently.[4]

The notion of efficiency is implicit in an equalisation approach since transfers are related to some standard revenue effort. But some times efficiency indicators are used more directly in the devolution formulae. The two previous commissions who have explicitly introduced some efficiency factors have focused on tax effort and improvement in revenue account balance. There is also the issue of backward looking *vis-à-vis* forward looking indicators of efficiency. Only in the case of medium term reform facility, incentives are linked to performance. However, there are several inherent difficulties in including forward looking indicators in the distribution formula.

An important issue in the context of transfers under the Finance Commission pertains to the relative role of tax devolution and grants. Tax devolution has a built-in flexibility as it can increase automatically if the Central taxes are more buoyant. Conversely, there is risk if their buoyancy falls short of expectations. Grants are ensured as these are fixed in nominal terms. It is easier to target grants towards states or sectors. The flexibility in the case of devolution is limited by the criteria used. Yet states have often expressed a preference for devolution because by definition it is unconditional and comes to the states as a matter of right. Within the subset of grants, grants could be made conditional or purpose specific, although Article 275 grants have generally been unconditional. However, if a move is made towards equalisation of services through grants, conditional grants are inescapable.

Beginning with the Eighth Finance Commission, two changes occurred. First, there was a move towards unifying the formulae for the

4. Rangarajan, C. (2009). *op cit*.

inter se distribution of both income tax and Union excise duties and, secondly, a portion of the Union excise duties was kept aside for distribution according to 'assessed deficits' of states after the devolution of Central taxes.

The Eleventh and the Twelfth Finance Commissions have also used a unified formula for horizontal devolution. In determining the criteria and the weightage to be accorded to these criteria, both the Eleventh and the Twelfth Finance Commission's claim to have followed two basic principles of 'equity' and 'fiscal efficiency'. The principle of equity implies that, as a result of revenue-sharing the resource deficiencies across the states are evened out. Thus, this principle makes up for resource deficiencies. According to the Eleventh Finance Commission, this tends to create a vested interest in continuing with resource deficiency. Accordingly, it included criteria for rewarding efficiency also. The criteria and the relative weights adopted by the Eleventh and the Twelfth Finance Commissions are given in Table 9.1.

TABLE – 9.1

CRITERIA AND RELATIVE WEIGHTS FOR DETERMINING *INTER SE* SHARE OF STATES

Criterion	*Relative Weight (Per cent)*	
	EFC	*TFC*
1. Population	10.0	25.0
2. Income (Distance Method)	62.5	50.0
3. Area	7.5	10.0
4. Index of Infrastructure	7.5	—
5. Tax Effort	5.0	7.5
6. Fiscal Discipline	7.5	7.5
Total	100.0	100.0

Source: Report of the Eleventh Finance Commission (for 2000-2005), July 2000, Table 6.2, p. 58; and Report of the Twelfth Finance Commission (for 2005-2010), Table 7.2, p. 133.

Population has always been one of the criteria for determining the share of states in tax proceeds—only the weights have kept changing. Area was introduced by the Tenth Finance Commission. The logic is that states which have a large area and low density of population have to incur heavy expenditure for providing basic administrative infrastructure. The cost is very high compared to a state with an area of similar size but a high density of population. From a weight of 5 per cent in Tenth Finance Commission, the weight of area has been hiked to 7.5 per cent by the Eleventh Finance Commissions and further to 10 per cent by the Twelfth Finance Commission.

As can be seen from Table 9.1, the largest weightage of 62.5 and 50 per cent has been given to the income-distance criterion by the Eleventh and Twelfth Finance Commissions respectively. While computing distance-based shares of states, the Ninth and Tenth Finance Commissions followed the practice of measuring the distance of the per capita income of state from that of the highest per capita income state. The Eleventh Finance Commission has changed this practice somewhat. Instead of taking a single high income state as the 'respective' highest income state, it has taken a three-state average of Punjab, Maharashtra and Goa as the benchmark from which distances are measure.

Grants-in-Aid

The principles for grants-in-aid to the revenues of the states have evolved over the last five decades through recommendations of the various Finance Commissions. What came to be accepted is that the grants-in-aid may be given to the states to cover the assessed deficit on non-plan revenue account, after devolution of taxes and duties. Secondly, grants-in-aid may be recommended for the upgradation of the standards of administration of the states. The idea is to correct the disparities in the availability of administrative and social services between the developed and the less developed states so that a citizen, irrespective of the state boundary where the lives, is provided with certain basic minimum standards of such services. And lastly, grants-in-aid may be recommended by the Finance Commission to provide assistance to a state to meet expenditure on account of any special problems peculiar to the state.

In a significant departure from previous Finance Commissions with reference to grants-in-aid, the Twelfth Finance Commission has raised the share of grants in total transfers to nearly 19 per cent from 13.5 per cent recommended by the Eleventh Finance Commission. The share of taxes has correspondingly declined from 86.5 per cent to 81.1 per cent as can be seen from Table 9.2.

This increase in the share of grants has been explained on the basis of their greater certainty and their capacity to be targeted better.

TABLE – 9.2

PER CENT SHARE OF TAXES AND GRANTS-IN-AID IN TOTAL TRANSFERS

Commission	*Period*	*Grants-in-Aid*	*Taxes*
Tenth	1995-2000	8.96	91.04
Eleventh	2000-2005	13.47	86.53
Twelfth	2005-2010	18.87	81.13

Source: Report of the Twelfth Finance Commission (2005-2010) Tale 10.1, p. 175.

The Twelfth Finance Commission has also recommended grants to states for the upgradation of services in the social sectors of education and health and additional grants-in-aid for certain common and specific needs of the states.

In contrast to the Eleventh Finance Commission recommendations, the Twelfth Finance Commission has recommended an additional separate grant at Rs. 20,000 crore for the maintenance of roads and buildings. Additional grants-in-aid have been recommended for maintenance of forests and heritage conservation as well as for taking care of state specific needs.

Calamity Relief

Natural calamities of one type or the other have been occurring at a rather regular frequency in the country. For meeting the expenditure on these calamities, the approach up to the Eighth Finance Commission was to provide a margin to the states under, what came to be known as, 'margin money scheme'. The Ninth Finance Commission adopted an entirely different approach and created a Calamity Relief Fund (CRF) for each state to which the Centre and the state were to contribute in a ratio of 75:25. The Tenth Finance Commission continued this scheme. It also recommended the setting up of a separate Central Fund—the National Fund for Calamity Relief (NFCR)—under the Ministry of Agriculture, to provide assistance to the states affected by natural calamity of rare severity. It held the view that if a calamity of rare severity occurs, it should be dealt with as a national calamity, requiring additional assistance and support from the Centre, beyond what is envisaged under the CRF scheme.

The Twelfth Finance Commission has recommended the continuation of the scheme of Calamity Relief Fund with contributions from the Centre and the states in the ratio of 75:25 as before. The amount of CRF for 2005-2010 has been worked out at Rs. 21,333.33 crore. The Twelfth Finance Commission has also agreed to the suggestion made by the states to continue the National Calamity Contingency Fund (NCCF) with a core corpus of Rs. 500 crore. The definition of natural calamity has been widened to include landslides, avalanches, cloud bursts and pest attacks as well.

Transfers from the Centre to state governments have been criticised for displaying a political bias. This criticism is especially directed towards *discretionary* transfers although even formula-based transfers have been suspect. The proportion of discretionary transfers has been increasing over time. There are three major channels through which the Centre transfers funds to state governments. These are:

(i) Tax devolution and grants through the Finance Commissions (approximately 65 per cent of total transfers in 2000-01).

(ii) Grants and loans given by the Planning Commission (approximately 32 per cent of total transfers in 2000-01).

(iii) Transfers for various Central sector and Centrally sponsored schemes by various Central ministries (approximately 4.32 per cent of total transfers in 2000-01).

From 1969, plan transfers (that is transfers determined by the Planning Commission) have been effected on the basis of a formula called the 'Gadgil Formula' after the first chairman of the National Development Council. The formula is based on population, per capita income, and its deviation from an average of all states as well as from the highest per capita income, fiscal performance and 'special problems'. The decision-making body is the National Development Council which is chaired by the Prime Minister, and contains all cabinet ministers at the Centre, Chief Ministers of the states and members of the Planning Commission. These are called transfers on account of state plan schemes. Although these transfers are based on a consensus formula, discretionary elements can enter into the determination of these grants for two reasons. First, while each state proposes its plan size to the Planning Commission, the final approval of the size rests with the Commission. Hence, there is some scope for negotiation and 'persuasion'. Second, the formula explicitly sets aside 7.5 per cent of the grants on account of special problems of states. This allows for some subjectivity to creep into the determination of grants for state plan schemes. In addition to grants, the Planning Commission also gives assistance in the form of loans. Major states get 70 per cent of all transfers by the Planning Commission at present and out of this 70 per cent is in the form of loans and the rest is in the form of grants.

Central plan schemes are funded entirely by the Centre, the states merely exercising an agency role in executing these programmes. Centrally sponsored programmes involve some element of cost sharing between the centre and the concerned state. In principle, discretionary grants are meant to provide flexibility and responsiveness to states' contingencies. However, they have often been criticised for the political bias displayed in the disbursement of such grants. Indeed, the scope for politics to play a role in disbursement has only been increasing as the discretionary component of grants has grown at the expense of formula based grants.

The transfers given to states through Central plan schemes and centrally sponsored schemes have attracted the sharpest criticism because these are essentially completely discretionary. In financial year 1996-97, states' share of Central taxes accounted for 23.3 per cent of states' total revenues, while grants on account of state plan schemes, Centrally sponsored schemes and Central plan schemes (that is items (ii) and (iii) jointly amounted to 15.9 per cent of states' total revenues (averaged over 15 major states).

Political favouritism in discretionary grants may work through different channels. There may be favouritism by the incumbent party at the Centre which is interested in furthering its re-election prospects, both at Central and state levels. The lobbying model (for example, Rao and Singh, 2002)[5] predicts that states with higher representation in the central parliament get more transfers—hence that the degree of alignment should matter.

While there is emerging consensus in the recent literature on the political economy of transfers that politics matters, there is no such consensus as yet on the exact mechanisms through which it matters. Recent developments in Indian politics like the emergence of coalition governments at Central level and regional parties in many states mean that the nature of transfers may change in the future.

The other notable feature of Indian fiscal federalism is the interstate inequalities in revenue capacity and per capita expenditures. This is a natural consequence of the huge differences in per capita incomes between states, which are, moreover, increasing over time: in 1980-81

5. Rao, M.G. and Nirvikar Singh (2002). "The Political Economy of Centre-State Fiscal Transfers in India", *mimeo*, University of California at Santa Cruz.

the per capita income of Punjab, the richest state was about three times that of Bihar, the poorest state, while in 1998-99 the per capita income in Punjab was five times that of Bihar. Hence, differences in the ability to raise revenue have also increased over time. Per capita expenditures were 44 per cent higher than the all-India average in the high income states while they were 36 per cent lower than the average in low income states in 2000-01. Part of the rationale for transfers by the Centre to states was to reduce the horizontal imbalance. The empirical evidence on the issue of whether Finance Commission transfers have resulted in lower inequality is ambiguous at best.[6]

The economic policy environment in India has undergone a fundamental change. Transition to an increasingly market based development and opening up of the economy to face global competition will require policy changes, creation of market institutions and a responsive decentralised system of governance. The reform agenda of both the Centre and states should be calibrated in a coordinated manner in the spirit of cooperative federalism. At the same time, it is necessary to recognise that governmental units in the federation have also a competitive relationship. It is important to nurture this competition to secure efficiency gains. Thus, we need both coordination and competition and this makes the challenge formidable.[7]

Problems of Federal Finance in India

(i) *Gap between needs and resources of state government*: The Constitution provides for division of financial powers between the Centre and the states. However, the revenue-raising capacity of the states is restricted because of the nature of taxes assigned to them. Since land is limited, the scope for increasing land revenue is also limited. Similarly, taxes on agricultural income, excise duties on intoxicants, taxes on motor vehicles, entertainments, etc., are also comparatively less elastic than the taxes assigned to the Centre. Sales tax is the only tax levied by the states which has substantial elasticity. Because of the economic progress registered by the country in the last three decades, the base of income tax, Union excise duties, customs duties and other important Central taxes has expanded considerably. This has given immense powers to the Central government to increase its resources with the passage of time. This structure of financial relations between the Centre and the state governments—less elastic sources of revenue for

6. Dhillon, Amrita (2007). *op cit.*
7. Rangarajan, C. (2009). *op cit.*

the states and more elastic sources of revenue for the Centre—places the states at a distinct disadvantage. While demands on the states' resources are increasing rapidly because of the pressure of development services, especially in the field of social welfare, their income has failed to increase correspondingly. Accordingly, vertical imbalances have accentuated over the years and the dependence of the state governments on the Centre has considerably increased. This has made them vulnerable to increasing pressures from the Central government to tow its line. Where the state government belongs to a different political party, these pressures give rise to open conflict seriously jeopardising the effectiveness of the policy measures introduced by the concerned State government.

(ii) *Reduced importance of the Finance Commissions.* Transfers through the Finance Commission (which is a statutory body) contribute only about one-third of total transfers from the Centre to states. This means that about two-thirds of the transfers are channelled through the Planning Commission or the Central government directly. For a considerable period of planning, the Planning Commission was not guided by any objective criteria to determine the share of different states in its assistance and this introduced an aura of arbitrariness in the whole transfer mechanism. Since the Centre contributed a large amount of resources in the form of discretionary grants to the states, it acquired considerable powers to affect the decision making processes at the state level. This led to erosion of autonomy of the states.

(iii) *Failure to tackle the problem of regional imbalances to any satisfactory extent.* The process of resource transfers through the Planning Commission and the Finance Commission has failed in correcting the "horizontal imbalance" among the federating units and disparities in their per capita incomes are growing. We have already noted that plan assistance is provided 70 per cent in the form of loans and 30 per cent in the form of grants. Since the ratio is a fixed one and does not discriminate between advanced and backward states, it amounts to discrimination against backward states. Since advanced states have a relatively better economic position, they should be granted a greater percentage of resources in the form of loans while backward states should receive a larger percentage in the form of grants. Non compliance to this common sense logic has resulted in a paradoxical situation where the comparatively richer states received a higher per capita grant than poorer states.

As far as transfers through Finance Commissions are concerned, all Finance Commissions sought to give due importance to backward states. However, there was no clear-cut bias in favour of backward states. The ultimate result was that advanced states cornered a major share of the actual devolution of resources from the Centre to the states in the awards of many Finance Commissions.

All Finance Commissions gave undue importance to budgetary needs while deciding the allocation of grants-in-aid. They did not realise that advanced states could also incur large budgetary deficits (even deliberately at times) and qualify for larger grants-in-aid as compared to poorer states.

The third constituent of resource transfer, viz., discretionary grants is not guided by any distinct philosophy of helping the poorer states to a greater extent. It is guided more by political considerations than by anything else. In any case, discretionary grants also do not seem to have helped the backward states more *vis-à-vis* the advanced states.

Suggestions for Improvement

(i) The scope of the Finance Commission should be enlarged considerably since it is a statutory body. This would reduce the interference of the Centre in the financial management of the states and the 'arbitrariness of discretionary grants' that accompanies such interference. In addition, it would reduce the atmosphere of suspicion and distrust in the states over the role of the Centre in federal finance system.

(ii) Some states have demanded the setting up of a permanent Finance Commission instead of one constituted in five years. This is sought to be justified on the following considerations: (i) a permanent Finance Commmission would reduce the scope for the Central government to make discretionary transferes in an ad hoc manner to the states; and (ii) when a Finance Commission is appointed, it has to start on a clean slate, collect the material required for its work from the state governments and the Central government, and then initiate such studies and analysis as it requires. A permanent Finance Commission (as the Australian Grants Commission in Australia) would be able to keep under review various aspects of the finances of the Centre and the state governments, special features of particular states, and the factors which affect their finances.

The Eighth Finance Commission and the Tenth Finance Commission advocated the setting up of a permanent Finance Commission Division in the Ministry of Finance, appropriately staffed, and with adequate technical expertise under a senior officer.

(iii) Adequate steps should be undertaken to narrow down inter-state disparities by adopting a set of criteria distinctly biased in favour of backward states. This can be ensured by giving more weightage to backwardness reflected through various economic and social indicators like per capita income, level of literacy, road length, administrative services, hospital beds, etc.

(iv) It is necessary to enlarge the very quantum of resources transfered from the Centre to the states. Many states have clamoured for long to include corporation tax, customs dusties and such other 'elastic sources' of revenue in the divisible pool. In this context, the Tenth Finance Commission made a path-breaking recommendation. It favoured a system of vertical resource sharing in which all Central taxes are pooled and a proportion devolved to the states. The main beenfit of this scheme is that the states will be able "to share the aggregate buoyancy of Central taxes". On its part, the Central government will be able to pursue tax reforms without the need to consider whether a tax is shareable with the states or not. Moreover, according to the Commission, this arrangement has distinct advantages in the context of the current economic reforms.

Thirteenth Finance Commission

The Thirteenth Finance Commission was constituted on November 14, 2007 with Vijay K. Kelkar as its chairman. The Commission is expected to make available its report by October 30, 2009. The recommendations of the commission will cover the period from April 1, 2010 to March 31, 2015.

(i) To look into the principles governing grants-in-aid of the revenues of the states out of the Consolidated Fund of India.

(ii) To look into the resources needed to augment the Consolidated Fund of a state to supplement the resources of *panchayats* and municipalities.

(iii) To review the finances of the Union and the states and recommend steps for maintaining a stable and sustainable fiscal environment consistent with equitable growth.

(iv) To take stock of the existing arrangement for financing disaster management with the reference to the National

Calamity Contingency Fund, the Calamity Relief Fund and the funds envisaged in the Disaster Management Act, 2005.

(v) To review the likely impact of the implementation of the Goods and Services Act with effect from April 1, 2010, including on foreign trade.

(vi) To consider the need for improving the quality of public expenditure to attain better outcomes.

Questions

1. Write short note on Recommendations of the 12th Finance Commission. *[B.A. (P) 2009]*
2. What are the sources of revenue of the Union Government and the State Governments in India? What are the bases on which financial resources are transferred from the Union Government to the State Government?
3. Discuss the federal nature of public finance in India. In this context explain the role of Finance Commission.

Part - II

Sectoral Analysis of Indian Economy

Chapters :

10

Agriculture

The Problem of Productivity

Importance of Agriculture in National Economy

AGRICULTURE is the mainstay of Indian economy because of its high share in employment and livelihood creation. The importance of agriculture in our economy can be judged from the following facts:

Agriculture as a Source of Employment

Data provided by the Census of India reveals that whereas in 1961, 75.9 per cent of total workforce was engaged in agriculture (the absolute number being 143.2 million workers), in 1981 the percentage was 69 and further fell to 63.8 in 1993-94 and 59.9 in 1999-2000. In absolute terms, agriculture provided employment to 238.68 million persons in 1993-94. In 1999-2000 also, although the percentage had declined from 63.8 to 59.9, the number of persons employed remained 237.8 million.

In the advanced countries like the United Kingdom and United States, only 2 to 3 per cent of the working population is engaged in agriculture; in France, the proportion is about 7 per cent; and in even Australia and New Zealand which have well developed agriculture, only about 6 to 8 per cent of working population are engaged in agriculture. It is only in backward and less developed countries that the working population engaged in agriculture is quite high.

Contribution to National Income

In 1951, agriculture contributed 56.5 per cent to India's national income. The economic development since Independence resulted in declining contribution of agriculture to national income. The share declined from 56.5 per cent in 1950 51 to 52.1 per cent in 1960-61, 45.7 per cent in 1970-71, 39.6 per cent in.1980-81, 33 per cent in 1990-

1991, 26.3 per cent in 2001-02 and less than 17 in 2008-09 (RE) (CSO, 2009).[1] The significance of this share of agriculture in national income becomes clear when we compare it with USA, UK and many other advanced countries where this sector contributes only between 2 to 5 per cent of their national income.

Linkage between Agriculture and Other Sectors

The linkages between agriculture and industrial sectors, widely recognised in the literature, focus on the role of agriculture as:

(i) Supplier of wage goods to the industrial sector,

(ii) Provider of raw materials to agro-based industries which have a weight of 21.2 per cent in the Index of Industrial Production (base: 1980-81=100) and weight of 17.6 per cent in the index with base 1993-94=100, and

(iii) Generator of agricultural income that enables rural demand for industrial products to take place. Empirical tests show that a unit increase in agricultural output would have a positive effect on both industrial production and national income. Rangarajan (1982) estimated that a 1 per cent increase in agricultural output tends to raise industrial production by 0.5 per cent and augment national income by 0.7 per cent. The experience in the eighties and nineties also lends support to this. During the eighties, the trend growth rate of 3.2 per cent in agricultural production appeared to have had contributed to accelerated industrial production. The decelerated growth rate in agricultural production seems to have impacted on growth of industrial production in the nineties.

(iv) Agriculture is the main support for India's transport system, since railways and roadways secure bulk of their business from the movement of agricultural goods. Internal trade is mostly in agricultural products.

Agricultural growth has direct impact on poverty eradication, containing inflation, raising agricultural wages and employment generation.

To quote the *Economic Survey* 2008-09, "The performance of the agricultural sector influences the growth of the Indian economy. Agriculture (including allied activities) accounted for 17.8 per cent of

---

1. Central Statistical Organisation, May 31, 2006.

the Gross Domestic Product (GDP-at constant prices) in 2007-08 as compared to 21.7 per cent in 2003-04. Notwithstanding the fact that the share of this sector in GDP has been declining over the years, its role remains critical as it accounts for about 52 per cent of the employment in the country. Apart from being the provider of food and fodder, its importance also stems from the raw materials that it provides to industry. The prosperity of the rural economy is also closely linked to agriculture and allied activities. Agricultural sector contributed 12.2 per cent of national exports in 2007-08. The rural sector (including agriculture) is being increasingly seen as a potential source of domestic demand; a recognition, that is shaping the marketing strategies of entrepreneurs wishing to widen the demand for goods and services."

Productivity in Indian Agriculture

Low Levels of Productivity

Productivity is generally considered from two angles—(i) productivity of land, and (ii) productivity of labour engaged in agriculture. There has been a slow and steady rise in productivity during 1950-51 to 1997-98 for most of the crops. GDP per hectare was Rs. 875 in 1950-51 which rose to Rs.1023 in 1960-61, Rs.1204 in 1970-1971 and further to Rs.1401 in 1979-80 (figures are at 1970-71 prices). Thus, output per hectare rose by 60 per cent over the period 1950-51 to 1979-80. However, productivity per worker has remained almost stagnant over the period as would be clear from the fact that GDP per worker which was Rs.1019 in 1950-51 fell to Rs. 988 in 1960-61, rose to Rs.1013 in 1970-71 and to Rs.1025 in 1979-80 (figures are at 1970-71 prices).[2]

A comparison of productivity levels in Indian agriculture with the levels in other countries shows how low the productivity in Indian agriculture is. Productivity of wheat in India is about 35 per cent of the productivity in France. It is 66 per cent (i.e., less than two-thirds) of the productivity in comparison to another underdeveloped country, China. As far as rice is concerned, productivity in India is 46 per cent of the productivity in China and Japan (i.e., less than half). The productivity of cotton in India is one-third of the productivity in China. Even in comparison to Pakistan, productivity of cotton in India is just 61 per cent. As far as groundnut is concerned, productivity in India is 34 per cent of the productivity in USA, 40 per cent of the productivity in China and 51 per cent of the productivity in Argentina. Similar

2. Rao, J. Mohan (1994). "Agricultural Development under State Planning", in Terrence J. Byers (ed.), *Development Planning in India*, Table 3, p. 260. New Delhi: Oxford University Press.

TABLE – 10.1

INTERNATIONAL COMPARISION OF YIELD SELECTED COUNTRIES 2004-05 (METRIC TONNES/HA.)

Rice/Paddy		*Wheat*		*Maize*		*Cotton*		*Major Oilseeds*	
Country	*Yield*	*Country*	*Yield*	*Country*	*Yield*	*Country*	*Yield*	*Country*	*Yield*
Egypt	9.8	China	4.25	U.S.A.	9.15	China	11.10	Argentina	2.51
India	2.9	France	7.58	France	7.56	U.S.A.	9.58	Brazil	2.48
Japan	6.42	India	2.71	India	1.18	Uzbekistan	7.98	China	2.05
Myanmar	2.43	Iran	2.06	Germany	6.69	India	4.64	India	0.86
Korea	6.73	Pakistan	2.37	Philippines	2.1	Brazil	10.96	Germany	4.07
Thailand	2.63	U.K.	7.77	China	4.9	Pakistan	7.60	U.S.A.	2.61
U.S.A.	7.83	Australia	1.64					Nigeria	1.04
World	**3.96**	**World**	**2.87**	**World**	**3.38**	**World**	**7.33**	**World**	**1.86**

Source : Ministry of Agriculture and Cooperation.
Economic Survey 2006-07.

conclusions hold for most of the other crops.[3] The low levels of productivity in Indian agriculture point to the possibilities of increasing productivity by adopting appropriate strategies and policies.

International comparisons reveal a wide gulf in India's performance between achievements in output and productivity. While India compares favourably in terms of total output, it compares poorly in terms of yield per hectare. For example, India has 60 million hectares of land under irrigation compared with just 47 million in China, but its food grain production is barely 40 per cent of China's cutput. Broadly, Table 10.1 shows India's relative world ranking in production and yields of a range of agricultural commodities.

Causes of Low Productivity

The causes of low productivity can be divided into the following three categories: (i) general, (ii) institutional, and (iii) technical.

General Causes

Pressure of Population on Land: With increasing pressure of population on land, per capita cultivated land has declined from 0.444 hectares in 1921 to 0.296 hectares in 1961 and further to 0.219 hectares in 1991. Increasing pressure of population on land is partly responsible for the sub-division and fragmentation of holdings resulting in low productivity.

Institutional Causes

Land Tenure System: A very important reason of low agricultural productivity has been the exploitative land tenure system in the form of *zamindari* system. Highly exploitative in character, this system drained out the very capacity, willingness and enthusiasm of the cultivators to increase production and productivity. Legislations passed for abolition of intermediaries in the post-Independence period did not break the stranglehold of the *zamindars* on the rural economy. They only changed their garb and became large landowners. Exploitative practices continued. Regulation of rent, security of tenure, ownership rights of tenants, etc., did not make the position of tenants better. Tenancy of most of the tenants continues to be insecure and they have to pay exorbitant rates of rent.

Uneconomic Holdings: According to the National Sample Survey, 52 per cent holdings in 1961-62 had a size of less than 2 hectares. In 1990-

3. Tata Services Ltd., *Statistical Outline of India*, 1998-99.

1991, 78 per cent of total holdings fell under this category. Most of these holdings are not only extremely small, they are also fragmented into a number of tiny plots so that cultivation on them can be carried out only by labour-intensive techniques. This results in low productivity. Until the excessive labour employed in agriculture is transferred to alternative jobs and the holdings are consolidated (or cooperative farming initiated), modern techniques of agriculture cannot be adopted and the possibilities of increasing agricultural productivity will remain limited.

Inedequate Credit and Marketing Facilities: The farmers need credit for various purposes llike purchase of seeds, fertiliser, irrigation pumps, etc. Since not many banks and other institutions give him loans, he has to depend on money lenders, who charge exorbitant interest, and indulge in many other unscrupulous practices. The farmer remains under perpetual debt. Thus, he is not able to make much investment on improvements in land. This keeps the productivity very low.

Technological Factors

Outmoded Agricultural Techniques: Most of the Indian farmers continue to use outmoded agricultural techniques. Wooden ploughs and bullocks are still used by a majority of farmers. Use of fertilisers and new high-yielding varieties of seeds is extremely limited. In brief, Indian agriculture is traditional and therefore, productivity is low.

Lack of Fertilisers: Chemical fertilisers like nitrogenous, phosphate and potassic fertilisers (NPK) which provide high nutrition to plants were not used in the early years of Independence. The use of fertilisers has sharply increased after mid 1970s, but it is still confined to smaller area covered by the 'Green Revolution'. Over a wider area even now cowdung and farm yard manure is used which keeps productivity low.

Poor Quality of Seeds: Mostly the Indian farmers use seeds which are not of a good quality. Consequently the plants that grow out of those sees do not give high yield. The emergence of high yielding varieties of seeds (HYV) has made substantial contribution to improvements in agricultural productivity. But the use of HYV seed is limited to irrigated areas only. Hence, most of the farmers still use low quality seeds which accounts for low productivity.

Lack of Pesticides: Indian farmers lose a substantial part of their crops to pests and insects which eat away the plants. The use of pesticides and insecticides is still limited to a few areas and larger farms. Thus, over a wider area, crops suffer much damage due to pests and insects resulting in lower output and low productivity.

Inedequate Irrigation Facilities: Adequate and assured water suply at the appropriate time is necessary for high crop yield. But in India, most of the land area still depends on rainfall, which is mostly uncertain, inadequate and sometimes unseasonal. Only about 36 per cent of total area on which crops are raised is covered by irrigation. This contributes to low productivity in agriculture.

Irrigation plays an important role in Indian agriculture. Currently, nearly 45 per cent of the 175 million ha of the country's cropped area is irrigated.

Irrigated area has nearly trebled since the early 1950s—from around 24 million ha in 1953-54 to nearly 75 million ha in 1998-99. According to one recent estimate, nearly three-fourths of the increment in total crop output between the early 1970s and early 1990s came from expansion of irrigated area and increase in per hectare yields on irrigated land. Unirrigated crop areas have actually declined and the rate of yield improvement on these areas has been far slower overall, compared to irrigated areas (Vaidyanathan, 2007).[4]

This shows that even now about 55 per cent of the gross cropped area continues to depend on rains. Rainfall is often insufficient, uncertain and irregular. Accordingly, productivity is bound to be low in all those areas which lack irrigation facilities, and are totally dependent on rains. Even in areas having irrigation facilities, potential is not wholly utilised because of defective management. The costs of irrigation are also increasing continuously and the small farmer is, therefore, unable to make use of available irrigation facilities.

Measures to Improve Agricultural Productivity

The causes of low productivity discussed suggest the measures also which need to be taken up to improve agricultural productivity. These are as follows:

1. **Reduction in the Pressure of Population on Land :** If some people could be withdrawn from agriculture by providing them alternative avenues of employment outside agriculture, the pressure of population on land would be reduced. This would facilitate introduction of new technology and thereby increase productivity.

---

4. Vaidyanathan, A. (2007). "Irrigation" in Kaushik Basu (ed.) *The Oxford Companion to Economics in India*. New Delhi: Oxford University Press.

2. **Consolidation of Small Fragmented Pieces of Land** which will make unit of cultivation more efficient and viable. (Details discussed in the ch. 11 on Land Reforms).

3. **Speedy Implimentation of Land Reforms.** (For details see ch. 11).

4. **Use of Modern Technology :** New technology consistsing of a package of HYV seeds, chemical fertilisers, water, pesticides will contribute to significant increase in production and productivity of various crops. (For details see ch. 12).

5. **Reform in Marketing :** Apart from the fact that productivity in agriculture is low, it is also a fact that due to defective marketing system, the price per unit of output that a farmer gets is also very low. This is because in unorganised agricultural markets, there is a long chain of middlemen who do not allow farmers to get a full price of the produce. Reforms in the marketing system will enable the farmer to get a reasonable price for his output and thereby increase his income out of which he will be able to invest in his land which will raise productivity agriculture. (For details see ch. 14).

6. **Agricultural Extension Services :** To improve agricultural productivity, farmers must be made aware of scientific methods and given training for their use through demonstrations, training programmes and extension services. This would enable them to understand, accept and apply new methods.

All these measures combined will go a long way in raising agricultural productivity.

Questions

1. What are the factors responsible for low productivity of agriculture in India? What steps have been taken by the Government to improve it. *[B.A (P) 2009]*

2. What is the importance of agriculture in Indian economy? Why is the level of agricultural productivity so low? *[B.Com (P) 2008]*

3. What are the causes of the low productivity of agriculture in India? Examine the role of the new agricultural strategy in improving it. *[B.A (P) 2008]*

4. What are the causes of low productivity in agricultural sector in India? What steps have been taken to improve it? *[B.A (P) 2007]*

5. Write brief note on: Causes of low productivity of agriculture in India. *[B.Com (P) 2007]*

6. What is the importance of agriculture in Indian economy? Discuss briefly the main problems faced by Indian farmers. *[B.A. (P) 2006]*

7. Discuss the factors that are responsible for the low productivity in agriculture. What steps have been taken to improve the productivity during the Five Year Plan? *[B.A. (P) External+Correspondence, 2006; B.Com. (P) 2001]*

8. What are the causes for low productivity in Indian agriculture? Discuss the role of 'New Agricultural Strategy' to solve them. *[B.Com. (P) 2003; B.Com. (P) Correspondence, 2006]*

9. Account for the low productivity in Indian agriculture. What measures would you suggest to raise it. *[B.A. (P) 2005]*

10. Discuss the basic factors that are responsible for low productivity of Indian agriculture. What steps have been taken to increase the productivity during the Five Year Plan? *[B.A. (P) 2003]*

11

Land Reforms

AT the time of Independence, India inherited a semi-feudal agrarian structure with onerous tenure arrangements over substantial areas. The ownership and control of land was highly concentrated to a relatively few landlords and intermediaries. The principal interest of this controlling group in agriculture was to extract maximum rental from tenants, either in cash or in kind. Often tenants of land under intermediary and landlord control sublet their lands in smaller plots to working cultivators, thus smaller holdings increased. Under this arrangement, economic motivation to develop farm land for increased production or to improve the economic conditions of cultivators was lacking. At the same time, working cultivators after paying high rent had no surplus to invest in farm improvement. They had neither resources nor knowledge for increasing agricultural production. Thus, the agricultural land resource of India, along with its operators was gradually improverished because economic motivation tended toward exploitation rather than toward investment and improvement.

With increasing pressure on land, the operating land base of many working cultivators was further reduced. Land occupancy rights became increasingly insecure. Often cultivators were continuously shifted from one plot to another according to the whims of superior holders. Land was divided into small fragments, each owned or leased by cultivators whose objective was subsistence. Together then, the size and distribution of land holding, cultivation practices and product sharing, operated concertedly to hold down farm income. Over time, a large number of farms became disincentive-ridden due to size disability. A substantial portion of such cultivators sought to supplement their farm income by working as hired labourers, competitive with even poorer landless workers. Independent India thus emerged with serious imbalances in man-land relationship among the three principal groups in the agricultural sector, *viz*., proprietors, working cultivators and labourers.

Objectives of Land Reforms

It was basically to stop the exploitation of the actual tillers of the soil and pass on the ownership of land to them that land reforms were introduced in the post-Independence period in India. The government has defined the objectives of land reforms as follows:

(i) to remove such impediments to increase in agricultural production as arise from the agrarian structure inherited from the past; and

(ii) to eliminate all forms of exploitation and social injustice within the agrarian system, to provide security for the tiller of soil and assure equality of status and opportunity to all sections of the rural population.

Measures

Measures contemplated to achieve the objectives were as given below:

1. Abolition of intermediaries,
2. Tenancy reforms, and
3. Reorganisation of agriculture.

Reorganisation of Agriculture included the following policies:

(i) Ceiling on land holdings and redistribution of land,
(ii) Consolidation of holdings, and
(iii) Cooperative farming.

Abolition of Intermediaries

The process of initiating, debating, amending and finally passing the bill for *zamindari* abolition mostly took a very long time. For example, in Uttar Pradesh, the Zamindari Abolition Act took four and a half years to become law. However, it goes to the credit of the government that most of the states had passed such Acts before the end of the First Five Year Plan. This possibly reflected the popular sentiment against the *zamindars* and their exploitative practices. Once the stage of legislation was completed and the stage of implementation started, fresh difficulties had to be faced. *Zamindars* were not willing to lay down their rights and privileges and turned to courts. As was to be expected, the legal battle between the *zamindars* and the state governments took an unduly long time. When the *zamindars* ultimately lost the battle, they turned to other delaying tactics by refusing to hand over land records and other related documents.

The policy laid down in the First Plan was that *zamindars* could assume land for personal cultivation up to the ceiling limit and tenants could acquire permanent and heritable rights in land only over and above the ceiling limit. With a view to bringing about uniformity in the definition of personal cultivation as adopted in different states, the Second Five Year Plan specified that personal cultivation should have three elements: (i) risk of cultivation, (ii) personal supervision and (iii) labour.

Though the official documents claim that *zamindari* has been completely abolished, yet the fact is that it has only changed its 'garb'. The previous *zamindars* have acquired large areas for personal cultivation on which cultivation is done with the help of hired agricultural labour. They are now designated as 'big landowners' and along with the rich peasantry, have formed "a new and dominant class of rural capitalists". In the states where a ceiling has been fixed as to the amount of land a former *zamindar* can hold, the ceiling has been kept so high that very few *zamindars* have been affected. Flaws in the legislation have also enabled them to transfer their land to other members of their families and thus escape the ceiling law. For example, Daniel Thorner found that in post-reform Bihar, there existed estates of 500, 700 or even 1,000 acre and the older structure of landowner, occupancy *raiyat*, non-occupancy *raiyat*, under-*raiyat* and *bataidar* (cropsharer) continued even after the so-called *zamindari* abolition. Bihar remained a stronghold of large landholders and hierarchical property rights, where "leasing, sub-leasing and evictions are all common".

Tenancy Reforms

Under the tenancy reforms, the following three measures were undertaken: (i) Regulation of rent, (ii) Security of tenure, and (iii) Conferment of ownership rights on tenants.

Regulation of Rent

In the pre-Independence period, the rent charged by *zamindars* from the tenants was exorbitant. The British government was merely interested in its share and consequently gave unlimited powers of suppression to the *zamindars* to squeeze the tenants.

These highly exploitative rates spelt misery on the toiling tenants who could hardly make both ends meet. As a consequence, legislations were enacted after 1947 to regulate the limits of rents and reduce the burden on tenants. The First Five Year Plan stated that maximum rent should be fixed at one-fourth or one-fifth of the total produce. Except Punjab, Haryana, Jammu and Kashmir, Tamil Nadu and some areas of Andhra Pradesh, this limit has been generally observed by all the states. In Punjab and Haryana, fair rent is fixed at one-third of total produce. In Tamil Nadu, it is 40 per cent of gross produce for irrigated lands, 35 per cent where irrigation is supplemented by lift irrigation, and 33.33 per cent in other cases. In Jammu and Kashmir, landowners have been divided into two categories—(i) those holding less than 12.5 acre and (ii) those holding more than 12.5 acre. For the former, fair rent has been fixed at one-half of total produce while for the latter, it has been fixed at one-fourth of total produce for wet lands and one-third for dry lands. In some areas of Andhra Pradesh, fair rent is 30 per cent of total produce for irrigated land and 25 per cent for dry land.

However, legislations fixing maximum limit of rent have been often violated. Because of the strong socio-economic and political hold of the landowners in the countryside, they have been able to extract considerably more rent from the peasants than the rent fixed by the legislations. For example, while in Bihar the maximum limit is 25 per cent of gross produce, sharecroppers are usually required to pay 50 per cent. In Balasore district of Orissa, it was found that sharecroppers had to hand over 50 per cent of gross produce as late as in 1972. Similarly, while law had fixed the maximum rent at 25 per cent of gross produce in West Bengal, sharecroppers continue to pay 50 per cent.

Security of Tenure

To protect tenants from ejectment and grant them permanent rights in land, legislations have been passed in most of the states. Legislation for security of tenure had three essential aims: (a) Ejectments do not take place except in accordance with the provisions of the law; (b) Land may be resumed by an owner, if at all, for 'personal cultivation' only; and (c) In the event of resumption, the tenant is assured of a prescribed minimum area.

However, as pointed out by P.S. Appu, the degree of protection to tenants afforded by the law in a particular area, depends upon the following important factors:

1. Definition of the term tenant;
2. The circumstances in which landowners are allowed to resume tenanted land for cultivation;
3. Definition of the term 'personal cultivation';

4. Status of land records.

In all tenancy laws of the country, persons cultivating the lands of others on payment of rent (either in cash or kind or both) are treated as tenants. However, in some states like Uttar Pradesh and West Bengal, sharecroppers (who pay rent by division of produce) are not regarded as tenants. Thus, all laws aiming at protecting tenants do not, in any way, help them. A limited right of resumption of land by landowners for personal cultivation was granted in all states excepting Uttar Pradesh and West Bengal. In some states, landowners were permitted to resume land rights up to the ceiling limit while in others the permissible limit was below the ceiling limit. Several states also passed laws requiring the landlord to leave a certain minimum area with the tenant as and when he assumes land for personal cultivation. For example, the laws in Kerala, Gujarat, Himachal Pradesh, Maharashtra, Karnataka, Orissa and Tamil Nadu provided that one-half of the tenanted land should be left with the tenant.

The right of resumption combined with flaws in the definition of personal cultivation rendered all tenancies insecure. The landlord could eject any tenant on the plea of personal cultivation. It was on account of this fact that the Fourth Five Year Plan recommended that all tenancies should be declared non-resumable and permanent (except in cases of landholders who are serving in the defence forces or suffering from a specified disability) and penalty should be imposed for wrongful evictions.

Another serious problem that had to be faced related to 'voluntary surrenders'. Many landlords compelled their tenants to give up the tenancies on their own accord. In this manner they succeeded in circumventing the tenancy laws because no laws can help the tenants if they give up their right voluntarily. Experience has shown that most of the 'voluntary' surrenders were anything but voluntary. In fact, landlords applied various kinds of threats and pressures on the tenants to surrender their land. Because of their weak socio-economic conditions and abject poverty, the tenants easily succumbed to these pressures. It was on account of this reason that the Fourth Plan recommended that "voluntary surrenders' should be regulated by the state in such a way that landowners are prohibited from taking possession of surrendered land which could be given over to other eligible tenants selected by the government. This means that all surrenders should be in favour of the government only. However, this provision has been enacted only in the states of Gujarat, Himachal Pradesh, Kerala, Orissa, Karnataka and West Bengal.

Laws relating to security of tenure can be implemented effectively only if correct and up-to-date land records are available. A person can claim that he is a tenant only if his name appears as such in the land records. However, it has been observed that in many states either no records of tenancy exist or (in areas where they exist) are incomplete and out-of-date.

Ownership Rights of Tenants

It has been repeatedly emphasised in the Plan documents that ownership rights should be conferred on tenants, that is, they should be made owners of the land they cultivate. Accordingly, some states have passed legislations to confer right of ownership on tenants. However, while some states did not adopt legislations for conferment of ownership right, in some other states the laws fall short of expectation. On tenancy reform, Appu found that it "...has not put an end to absentee ownership of land nor has it led to the disappearance of tenancies. It has only resulted in tenancies being pushed underground...". Summing up the performance on this front, he wrote:

"...Taking country as a whole, by 1992 ownership rights had been conferred on (or tenancy rights had been protected of) some 11 million tenants on 14.4 million acre of land. That constituted no more than 4 per cent of the operated area. It is interesting to note that the seven states of Assam, Gujarat, Himachal Pradesh, Karnataka, Kerala, Maharashtra and West Bengal account for 97 per cent of the beneficiaries. Practically, no benefits accrued to the tenants in the other states. Even in these seven states tenancy reform led to the large scale eviction of tenants. Except in West Bengal, sharecroppers by and large remained beyond the pale of tenancy reform everywhere. Only in West Bengal and Kerala did those in the lowest rungs of the peasant society received solid benefits on the implementation of tenancy reform. The rights of some 14 lakh share-croppers were protected in West Bengal and in Kerala some 2.84 lakh rural poor, mostly agricultural labourers, became owners of tiny homesteads. As a result of tenancy reform there has been a sharp fall in the area of land under tenancy. From over one-half of the operated area on the eve of the reform, the area under tenancy has come down to about 15 per cent of the operated area now. The tenants acquired ownership rights or were made secure in only about 4 per cent of the operated area. Thus the reform led to the rural poor losing access to some 30 per cent of the operated area."[1]

1. Ray, S.K. "Reforms in Land System in Post Independent India", in Uma Kapila (ed.) *op. cit.*

Reorganisation of Agriculture

Ceiling on Land Holdings and Redistribution of Land

An important aspect of land reform measures has been ceiling on land holdings. Justifying ceiling on holdings, Gadgil observed "among all resources the supply of land is the most limited and the claimant for its possession are extremely numerous. It is therefore obviously unjust to allow the exploitation of any large surface of land by single individual, unless other overwhelming reasons make this highly desirable. Moreover, in the context of current socio-political climate, redistribution of land would rather appear to be imperative."

Ceiling on land holdings were designed to offset the extremely uneven distribution of agricultural land. The policy implications of this measure were: (i) to meet the land hunger of working cultivators, (ii) to reduce disparity in agricultural incomes, in ownership and in the use of land, and (iii) to increase employment opportunity in the rural sector.

Legislation for ceiling was enacted in two phases. The first phase upto 1972 and the second phase after 1972. In the first phase, individual land holding was treated as the unit of application. After 1972, it was decided to have family as the basis of holding. Further ceiling limit was also reduced to bring about a more equitable distribution of this scarce asset. Also the exemption list was reduced in the new ceiling laws.

The performance regarding the implementation of ceiling on agricultural holdings has turned out to be more disappointing. Appu observed:

"...As a result of the implementation of the old and the new laws, by 1992 only about 2 million hectares of surplus land could be distributed to some 4.76 million beneficiaries. Thus, the efforts spread over a period of three and a half decades to enforce ceilings and take over surplus land led to the redistribution of less than 2 per cent of the operated area. If we look into the performance of individual states, we find that the area distributed as a percentage of the total area operated is 17.4 for Jammu and Kashmir, 6.3 in West Bengal and 5 in Assam. In all the other states only less than one per cent of the operated area could be distributed. Obviously, the imposition of ceilings and the redistribution of surplus land made no impact on the agrarian structure in most states."[2]

2. S.K. Ray, *op. cit.*

On balance, there seems to be some reasons to conclude that agrarian reorganisation in India has failed to make any considerable impact on the socio-economic conditions of the working cultivators. Indeed, the record so far is so depressing and frustrating that even an able administrator like Appu, who championed and spent a considerable part of his career in administering land reform programmes noted:

"Thus the programmes of land reform implemented since Independence did not lead to any significant re-distribution of land, or, the removal of all the obstacles to increasing agricultural production. Of the three programmes considered in this study, the laws for the abolition of intermediary interests were implemented fairly well. But in the case of tenancy reform and ceilings on holdings, the policies adopted were ambivalent and there were large gaps between policy and legislation and between legislation and implementation. We have seen that as result of the implementation of the tenancy laws, tenants became owners of or acquired rights in only about 4 per cent of the operated area. The enforcement of ceilings led to the redistribution of less than 2 per cent of the operated area. Thus these two measures taken together led to the redistribution of only about 6 per cent of the operated area."[3]

Consolidation of Holdings

The national policy on land reforms right from its inception has continued to press the need for consolidation of holdings. Consolidation means bringing together the scattered holdings of a farmer in one compact block. The Sixth Five Year Plan states, "Consolidation is achieved by first pooling all land in the village into one compact block and then dividing it into compact blocks among all the farmers in the village. Most of the States in the country have enacted legislation to undertake consolidation of holdings. It is estimated that by now, nearly 45 million hectares of land, i.e., about 1/4th of the consolidable land has been consolidated all over the country. However, the implementation has been extremely patchy and sporadic. Only in Punjab, Haryana and Western Uttar Pradesh, the work is complete. Even a beginning has not been made in the Southern States and Rajasthan. In the Eastern States, some work has begun only in Orissa and Bihar."

Major difficulties coming in the way of consolidation are the unwillingness of the farmers to join consolidation because of strong attachment to their ancestral land as well as the fear that they may not get in return inferior quality of land after consolidation. The Fifth Plan

3. S.K. Ray, *op. cit.*

stated, "A major weakness of the programme was that the consolidation was done without taking effective steps to ensure security of tenure to tenants, particularly share-croppers. As a result, consolidation of holdings has often led to the large-scale ejectment of insecure tenants."

Co-operative Farming

In the initial phase of planning, Government of India accepted cooperative farming as the official policy in the scheme of agarian reorganisation. The Congress Agarian Reforms Committee in its Report (1949) came to the conclusion : "Without various co-operative moulds —co-operative better farming for family farms and co-operative joint farming for holdings below basic—the efficiency of agriculture cannot be substantially increased."

However, the story of co-operative farming in India is a story of complete failure. Co-operative farming was used as a convenient device to by-pass land reforms—(to escape ceiling on land holdings as no ceiling was applied to co-operative farms) and also to use it for receiving preferential treatment in the provision of credit, irrigation, HYV seeds etc.

Emerging Perspectives and Policy Issues

Appu observes, it is against the background of the last four decades experience that the need to reformulate the land policy of India should be considered. Even persons emotionally attached with land reform programmes agree that the scope for improving implementation through legislative measures is now very limited. They point out, the socio economic and political environment in which these programmes were introduced have changed so dramatically, that it would be almost impossible to carry out the reforms. Appu described the changed environment as follows:

"...If the political will in favour of meaningful land reform was weak at independence and weaker still later on, it is non-existent today. Land reform has practically disappeared from the agenda of most political parties This, in my view, is the inevitable consequence of the great changes that have taken place in the social and economic fields. With the abolition of intermediary interests the erstwhile superior tenants belonging mostly to upper and middle castes acquired a higher social status. Rise in agricultural productivity, rising land values and higher incomes from cultivation have added to their economic strength. Substantial landowners who wield great authority in rural India are bitterly opposed to ceilings on agricultural holdings. They are able to have their way because no serious efforts have been made to organise the landless and the land poor, and enlist their support in favour of reforms. As for tenancy reform is concerned, there is a certain commonality of interest between all landowners—large, medium, small and even marginal. They are all passionately attached to their land and all of them are opposed to conferring benefits on insecure tenants. In the first round of land reform only the intermediaries were adversely affected. They were few in number and were weak politically. they had also made themselves obnoxious by aligning themselves with the colonial power. So it was easy enough to abolish intermediary interests. And it was done without hurting them much. But injuring the interests of the present class of landowners is an entirely different proposition. No political party that wishes to win elections and come to power can afford to do that. At the time of independence this class of landowners did not wield much political and economic power, and with a modicum of political will the reforms could have been implemented. But now it has become almost impossible to carry out the reforms."[4]

Land Reforms: Tenth Five Year Plan (MTA)[5]

The Tenth Plan had indicated that demographic factors, changes in the agricultural technology and the increasing importance of market forces had considerably weakened the case for a land reform programme that concentrated on the abolition of intermediaries and reduction in land ceilings to generate ceiling surplus land for redistribution. The Plan suggested that there was need to implement the ceiling laws with greater vigour, re-examine the issues of tenancy, address the question of tribal land alienation and incorporate more gender friendly laws in the context of feminisation of agricultural operations.

Land Ceiling

The prevailing agricultural structure is in sharp contrast to the conditions that obtained immediately after Independence. The number of large holdings has declined and the average size of landholding of 80 per cent of the cultivators is less than 2 hectares. Therefore, the case for reduction in land ceilings is weak. Measures need to be taken to detect concealed lands and acquire them for distribution to the rural poor. Up to March 31, 2003, only 2.12 million hectares of ceiling

---

4. Appu, P.S. (1995), *Land Reforms in India: A Survey of Policy, Legislation and Implementation, Land Reforms Unit*, Lal Bahadur Shastri National Academy of Administration, Mussoorie, U.P. (mimeo), pp 232 233.
5. Planning Commission (2005). Mid-term Appraisal of the *Tenth Five Year Plan* (2005).

surplus land had been redistributed. This accounts for just 1.5 per cent of the total cultivable land in the country. Given the poor record in detection and distribution of ceiling surplus land, it is unlikely that large tracts of land would become available for distribution to the poor. A new initiative could be to restrict the land owned by non-resident Indians (NRIs). The land ceiling for households which do not depend on land as their primary source of livelihood also need to be reduced. This would release some land for distribution. Further, where irrigation facilitates two to three crops a year, existing ceilings on land ownership could be reviewed.

Tenancy Reforms

The country's tenancy laws are highly restrictive. They were enacted in the context of exploitation of the peasantry. The current situation, however, is very different. The economic and political hold of large landowning classes has been considerably weakened. The deepening of democracy through successive elections and setting up of PRIs has strengthened the bargaining power of the rural poor. Research studies indicate that restrictive tenancy laws have prevented optimum allocation of land resources and denied the rural poor access to land. They have also led to concealed tenancy, which is widespread. In such cases, the tenant has no protection. The fear of reverse tenancy is also unfounded as small and marginal farmers account for over 80 per cent of the total leased land in the country. In any case, the existing ceiling laws can be leveraged to prevent reverse tenancy by stipulating that operational holdings could not exceed those prescribed under the ceiling laws.

There is a need to re-examine the tenancy laws in the country in the light of the fact that tenancy is widespread. Prohibition of tenancy by law in many states, especially the poorer states of Uttar Pradesh, Bihar and Orissa, has only driven the practice underground. This has adversely affected the interests of the rural poor. It is necessary to recognise tenancy and register the tenants and provide them security of tenure. The tenurial right need not be heritable but may be given for a fixed period. The success of "Operation Barga" in West Bengal, under which heritable and cultivable land rights were provided to shareholders, should encourage other states to bring about tenancy reform, which would generate greater employment and enhanced output, and thus reduce poverty.

Land Rights for Women

The Tenth Plan had highlighted the need for an active policy to provide land rights to women. In many states, agricultural land does not devolve on women if male heirs are present. In almost all states, tenancy is not inheritable by women. Some progress has been made in states like Rajasthan and Madhya Pradesh, which have decided that issues relating to property, including landed property, would be dealt with in accordance with the appropriate personal laws. Many other states have yet to take action in this regard. Women are playing an increasing role in agricultural operations due to migration of male members in search of employment and various other factors. In the absence of secure land rights in their names, they are excluded from institutional support that is provided only to the owners of land. It is, therefore, necessary to make inheritance rights in land more gender equal.

Computerisation of Land Records

Updating of land records is vital for land management. To bring land records up-to-date and facilitate quick retrieval of land records, the government has been implementing two schemes—computerisation of land records and strengthening of revenue administration. The progress in some states has been commendable while the process of computerisation needs to be accelerated in others. Even in states which have taken steps for computerisation of land records, online availability of land records continues to be an area of concern. This has been accomplished only in Karnataka and partly in Tamil Nadu and Gujarat. Updating of land records is also necessary to eliminate unnecessary litigation.

However, in the Approach Paper to the 11th Five Year Plan, the need to implement unfinished land reforms has been emphasised.

The National Commission on Farmers has placed the unfinished agenda in land reform first in its list of five factors central to the present agrarian crisis, and states "the first and foremost task of the National Policy for Farmers should be in the area of land reform with particular reference to tenancy laws, distribution of ceiling surplus land, attention to common property and wasteland resources and the consolidation of holdings. Following the conferment of land rights to women under the Hindu Succession Amendment Act (2005), the provision of appropriate support services to women farmers has become urgent. Joint Pattas are essential for women to get access to credit. Also, there should be stringent restrictions on the diversion of prime farmland for non-farm purposes."

Since migration and feminisation are increasing trends, land reforms that make tenancy legal and give well defined rights to tenants and to women are now more necessary than ever not only to reduce distress but also to increase agricultural growth. Facilitating leasing of land for cultivation is necessary to prevent cultivated land from turning fallow due to migration of owners to urban areas. Lack of recognised tenancy rights makes it difficult for *de facto* tenants to get credit from formal sources. Tenants without legal rights do not have proper incentive to develop the land and this explains part of the yield gap. Similarly, a woman without property title is unable to get credit when the male member is away. Giving access to land and homesteads not only reduces poverty but is the most powerful way to bring dignity in the lives of today's excluded. This, along with the more general need to record land titles properly where these are weak, is also one way to deal effectively with encroachment and non-participation that plague watershed and wasteland development programmes.

Causes for Slow Progress of Land Reforms

The Task Force on Agrarian Relations set up by the Planning Commission for the purpose of appraising the progress and problems of land reforms headed by P.S. Appu made a critical study of the land reform programme in India and enumerated the following causes of the slow progress of land reforms in India.

(i) *Lack of Political Will*: Considering the character of the political power structure obtaining in the country, it was only natural that the required political will was not forthcoming.

(ii) *Absence of Pressure from Below*: Except in a few scattered and localised pockets, practically all over the country the poor peasants and agricultural workers are passive, unorganised and inarticulate. In the circumstances, it is small wonder that there has been no insistent pressure from below, a prerequisite for the effective implementation of land reform laws.

(iii) *Administrative Organisation—Inadequate Policy Instrument*: The administrative organisation has proved to be an inadequate instrument for the speedy and efficient implementation of land reforms.

(iv) *Legal Hurdles*: Legislations relating to the land reforms were full of loopholes. Some loopholes were deliberately built in, while others were the result of poor drafting. Practically, in every State protracted litigation has delayed and often frustrated the implementation of land reform laws.

(v) *Absence of Correct Updated Land Records*: A programme that aims at the redistribution of income and wealth in the rural areas cannot succeed unless the beneficiaries can produce evidence of their rights. The position regarding records of tenancies, particularly in the matter of entries relating to the rights of share-croppers is not satisfactory anywhere in the country, and no records exist in some areas.

The problem is largely administrative. The absence of up-to-date land records is a serious obstacle in the implementation of land reforms.

Questions

1. Briefly discuss the various land reform measures undertaken by the government. What are the causes of unsatisfactory progress of land reforms in India? *[B.A. (P) 2009]*
2. Describe the land reform measures undertaken by Indian Government after Independence. How far have these reforms contributed to agricultural growth? *[B.A. (P) 2001; B.A. (P) External+Correspondence, 2006]*
3. Critically analyse the various land reform measures undertaken by the government after Independence. *[B.Com. (P) 2005]*
4. Write short note on 'Objectives of Land Reforms in India'. *[B.A. (P) 2005]*
5. Explain the need and scope for ceiling legislation in agriculture in India. Critically examine progress. *[B.Com. (P), Correspondence, 2004]*
6. What do you mean by land reforms? Is land reform necessary to improve agricultural productivity? *[B.A. (P) 2003]*

12

New Technology in Indian Agriculture and the Green Revolution

The New Technology

IT was becoming clear by the mid-sixties that there was no alternative to technological change in agriculture for achieving self sufficiency in food grains. Even those countries in Asia which could carry out radical land reforms and build up an adequate infrastructure for agriculture had taken to the path of modernising agriculture. Japan took the lead in this direction and China followed suit even after successfully experimenting with structural changes and mobilisation of a growing labour force for capital construction in agriculture.

Characteristics of New Technology

The distinguishing characteristic of the new technology lies in the substitution of traditional robust but low-yielding varieties of seed by the so-called high-yielding variety. These seeds have the physiological attribute of being able to turn large amounts of soil nutrients into grain rather than leaf growth. This enables the plant to produce higher yields, especially so if the supply of nutrients in the soil can be increased. This in turn creates the demand for chemical fertilisers to supplement the natural fertility of the soil. Because these contain nutrients in concentrated form, they have to be applied with adequate supplies of water to enable the plant to absorb them without damaging itself. A lack of adequate water supply not only reduces the yield but may do so substantially.

Better Agricultural Practices

This seed-fertiliser-water package in turn calls for better agricultural practices for the effective utilisation of the technology.

First, the plant requires the fertiliser-water input at particular stages of growth to give the best yields.

Secondly, as fertilisers can be absorbed by weeds as well as by the plant, effective weeding is required to prevent waste of expensive fertiliser.

Thirdly, while the HYV seeds give higher yields, they are more prone to damage from excessive watering. For example, shorter stemmed dwarf varieties are more liable to be flooded. They, thus, require more effective water control and better drainage. The need is for controlled and adequate water supplies.

Fourthly, being relatively new and non-acclimatised strains, they are more prone to local pests and diseases than established indigenous varieties and therefore, require a supply of germicides and pesticides.

Two further physiological characteristics of the new seeds are that they are quicker maturing than the traditional varieties and they are non photosensitive. On the one hand, these two characteristics give rise to a shorter harvesting period, thus making it possible for farmers to practise multiple cropping, enabling them to use more intensively a given amount of land. Fertilisers, by enabling more production per acre to be achieved, and the quicker maturing HYV seeds, by making it possible to practice double cropping during the year, both act as land saving innovations. Hence, their attraction to a land-hungry south Asia. On the other hand, as the crop may be ready for harvesting during the monsoon season at a time when the cloud-cover has not yet dispersed, a possibility of loss of output due to a lack of drying and storage facilities is also opened up.[1]

Thus, the basic technological characteristic of the new technology is the application of a number of inputs which are complementary to each other. The application of these joint inputs yields much larger volumes of output of food grains as a result, largely by increasing yield per acre. However, in order to assess the impact of the technology on Indian agriculture, we have to also take into account some of the economic characteristics of that technology. In an economy where labour

1. Choudhary, Pramit (1978). *The Indian Economy: Poverty and Development*, ch. 5, pp. 121-123. New Delhi: Vikas.

is relatively plentiful, it has low opportunity cost. Most agricultural holdings in India use either family labour or fairly low-paid agricultural labour, neither of which, generally speaking, can command high levels of alternative earnings. For traditional agriculture, the most expensive input, other than land, is bullock-power. The new inputs are mostly of manufactured origin, such as fertilisers, pesticides or pumps, and are more expensive. In non-rainfed agriculture, there are also costs attached to irrigation, in the form either of the capital costs of sinking a well or installing a pump or running costs in the form of purchase of diesel fuel or payment of water rates.

Economic Aspects of New Technology

The new practices, therefore, are much more expensive to the farmer. This has three implications. First, the extent to which the various inputs are applied in practice depends not on some technologically efficient dosage but on an economically optimum one. This depends in turn on the relative prices of inputs and outputs facing the producer. Minhas and Srinivasan have shown that fertiliser application is subject to diminishing returns, the economically optimum dose being smaller than the technical optimum. As technologically some of the inputs are complementary, the extent to which the application of a particular input can be profitably pushed depends also on the availability of, and the ability to purchase, other inputs. For example, the degree of fertiliser application that is profitable will depend on the availability of water and on the ability of a farmer to purchase the use of both inputs.

Secondly, the new technology is only worthwhile in terms of private benefits, e.g., if the farmer receives yields which are not only larger than traditional varieties but are substantially so, to make up for the additional variable costs of cultivation. This in turn requires, thirdly, a more intensive use of the fixed factor, e.g., land. The new technology opens up the possibility of multiple cropping; the economic imperative drives the farmer to it. This is compounded by the fact that while the new technology yields larger outputs, it is also more subject to risks. We have noted that the HYV seeds are prone to damage from flooding, water scarcity and pests. Moreover, because the farmer is a newcomer to these practices, he is also ignorant of how to respond if something goes wrong. Additionally, where he is involved in substantial cash outlays in order to utilise the new technology, he bears a liquidity risk. This is reinforced by the fact that very often, the farmer may have to resort to borrowing in order to meet the additional costs of cultivation. A crop failure saddles him with the burden of debt.

These economic aspects of the new technology are as important as its technological characteristics to our understanding of the impact of the 'green revolution' upon the agrarian economy, especially in relation to the problems of mechanisation and of unequal incidence of acceptance and use between large and small farmers. That impact can best be studied in terms of the effects of the new technology on output, employment and the regional and interpersonal distribution of gain arising from the adoption of that technology.

Three Phases of Green Revolution

Gulati and Fan (2008)[2] identify three phases of the green revolution.

The First Phase, 1966-1972

To end its dependence on P.L. 480, India, prompted by the minister of agriculture at that time, C. Subramaniam adopted a new agricultural strategy to boost grain production accompanied by remunerative support price for farmers. In January 1965, the Agricultural Prices Commission was set up to recommend a MSP, followed by the Food Corporation of India (FCI) to take charge of the logistics of procuring major agricultural commodities (Gulati, 2003). In the same year, India took a bold step by allowing the introduction of new high-yielding seed varieties (HYV) of wheat from Mexico. In 1966, India ordered the import of 18,000 tonnes of HYV wheat seeds that were distributed in the highly irrigated areas of Punjab, Haryana and western Uttar Pradesh where the past investments in irrigation had paid rich dividends.

The new seeds could yield more than double the existing levels and thus had the potential to dramatically increase wheat production and food grain supply. Under the new agricultural policy, the spread of HYVs was supported by public investments in fertilisers, power, irrigation and credit.

The total amount of food grains harvested increased from 74 mt in 1966-67 to 105 mt in 1971-72, and that year India became self sufficient, with grain imports declining to nearly zero.

These outcomes would not have been possible without the favourable pricing policy that provided farmers with adequate incentives, the dynamism of the national research system that proceeded to indigenise the new seeds to tackle their shortcomings (Gulati, 2003), and the availability of inputs including canal water, fertilisers, power

2. Gulati, A. and Shenggen Fan (ed.) (2008). *The Dragon and the Elephant—Agricultural and Rural Reforms in China and India*, ch.2. New Delhi: Oxford University Press.

and credit. In view of the strategic importance of these critical inputs, it was the responsibility of the government to ensure that farmers had affordable access to them. Subsidies thus, became an instrument of agricultural policy in the late 1960s and acquired greater importance in the 1970s. The role of credit began to be important after 1969 following the nationalisation of banks.

Improved agricultural production resulting from modern input and technologies "trickled down" to the poor and led to a rise in farmer income, while output growth and increased grain supplies caused a decline in real food grain prices, benefiting the poor. Thus, rural poverty declined significantly in this phase, from 64 per cent in 1967 to 56 per cent in 1973. Several government anti-poverty programmes were also introduced during the Fourth Five Year Plan in the early 1970s.

Debacle and the Second Phase, 1973-1980

After the nationalisation of the banks, Prime Minister Indira Gandhi took other steps to extend the role of the state in key areas of economic management. In agriculture, private wholesale traders came under attack because, due to their speculative motives, they were regarded as responsible for fluctuations in food grain prices and supplies. Thus, in 1973-74 the government took over the wholesale trade in wheat, which proved a disaster and therefore, it was soon abandoned. Wheat procurement was hindered by limited supply resulting from droughts in several states in 1972-73.

Following two consecutive droughts in 1972-73, food grain production decreased by 7.7 per cent, and India slid back into the trap of food grain imports of an average of about 4 mt a year from the United States between 1973 and 1976.

After the oil shock, the government increased fertiliser subsidies to prevent a drop in consumption following the rise in fertiliser prices. In 1977, the retention price scheme was introduced for urea, the predominant fertiliser in Indian agriculture. During the 1970s, other input subsidies grew in importance within the state budget, and the subsidy bill excluding fertilisers grew from Rs. 10 billion at constant prices to Rs. 33.2 billion, or from 0.5 per cent to 4.0 per cent of agricultural GDP between 1973 and 1980.

Also during this period, groundwater irrigation increased in importance, with its share rising from 0.55 per cent to 19.5 per cent between 1960 and 1975 on account of private investment in tube-wells by farmers who reinvested the income from the earlier burst in food grain production. As a result, power subsidies for water pumping grew dramatically, reaching 44 per cent of the total input subsidy at the start of the 1980s (Gulati and Narayanan, 2002a).

The extension of HYV technology from wheat to rice, favoured by the growth of tube wells, spread the green revolution to new areas, marking a new phase in the expansion of domestic production. From 1972-73 to 1979-80, production as well as yields of food grains showed remarkable growth, at 3.1 per cent and 2.5 per cent, respectively, and rural poverty declined from roughly 56 per cent to 50 per cent.

The Third Phase, 1981-1990

In the 1980s, India consolidated its status as a food self-sufficient country. Rice production soared to 63.8 mt in 1986, up from 37.0 mt in 1964. Wheat output grew, too, from 12 to 47 mt in 1986, a year in which India had her first 25.4 mt of grain buffer stocks. When in 1987 the "worst drought of the century" struck the country, food needs could be easily met without any loss of lives (Gulati, 2003).

During this phase, the HYV technology spread eastward to states like West Bengal and Bihar, which experienced surpluses in rice, with output over the 1980s growing at 5.0 and 3.7 per cent, respectively. However, in the rest of the country the green revolution ran out of steam by 1985 once the new seed varieties had been widely adopted in the main producing regions. Yields for rice and wheat that had grown, respectively, by 3.5 per cent and 4.5 per cent per annum between 1967-1968 and 1984-85 slowed down to 2.3 and 2.4 per cent per year between 1985-86 and 1999-2000 (IFPRI, 2004). With the HYV technology exhausting its impact in the mid-1980s, input subsidies were steadily increased to continue sustaining food grain production growth. By 1991, input subsidies had grown to 7.2 per cent of agricultural GDP as compared to 4.4 per cent in 1980 and 2.0 per cent of total GDP from 1.5 per cent in 1980 (Gulati and Narayanan, 2002a).

Throughout the green revolution, Indian agriculture laboured under a strictly regulated policy regime characterised by wide restrictions on production through licensing requirements and barriers to entry, as well as controls on pricing, movement and private trading of agricultural produce. On the external front, too, the sector was burdened with various tariff and non-tariff barriers to agricultural trade flows.

The high level of protection accorded to industry produced high industrial prices and adverse terms of trade (ToT) for agriculture, reducing the relative profitability of the primary sector. Agriculture was overall net taxed (disproteced) on account of the overvalued rupee, which produced an anti-export environment for agriculture. The objectives of this framework were broadly dictated by the dominant strategy of the pre-reform era, that is, food self-sufficiency resulting from domestic supplies, aiming to: (1) ensure inexpensive food for consumers, (2) protect farmers' incomes from price fluctuations, and (3) keep the balance of payments in check (Gulati and Fan, 2008).

Reform Period, 1991 to the Present

Starting in 1991, India adopted a series of sweeping macroeconomic and structural reforms in industry, the exchange rate, and foreign trade and investments.

These policy changes led to a higher rate of economic growth, with GDP recording an impressive 6.5 per cent per year growth between 1991-92 and 1996-97 compared to 5.2 per cent in the 1980s.

Overall, the reforms helped accomplish the shift from a closed to a more liberalised and open system. This is reflected in the change of indicators such as FDI inflows and the ratio of trade to GDP.

Although the reforms were implemented in off-farm activities, they affected agriculture in at least two important ways (Landes and Gulati, 2003). First, the higher rate of economic growth and the consequent rise in per capita incomes resulting from the 1991-1993 reforms had a significant impact on food demand. Higher per capita incomes, growing at 4.5 per cent per annum in this phase as opposed to 3.6 per cent in the 1980s (WDI, 2004), led to the diversification of food demand into non food grain crops such as fruits and vegetables, as well as meat—mainly poultry—and dairy products. Second, the lowering of industrial protection significantly improved the incentive framework for the sector through improvement in the domestic ToT between agricultural and industrial prices, which rose from 0.9 to 1.2 between 1991 and 2000 (Gulati and Fan, 2008).

Improved ToT for agriculture in turn resulted in an increase in the profitability of the primary sector relative to industry and led to an increase in private investments, which are now double the public investment in agriculture. These were increasingly directed to the production of horticultural produce, poultry, fish, milk and eggs in response to booming consumer demand for these high-value agricultural products, leading to a remarkable growth in output of these commodities during the 1990s relative to the previous decade.

As a result of these developments, agricultural GDP went up from 3 per cent in the 1980s to 4.1 per cent in the aftermath of reforms between 1991 and 1996.

Deceleration in Agriculture Growth—1997-98 to 2004-05

Growth of agricultural GDP decelerated from over 3.5 per cent per year during 1981-82 and 1996-97 to only around 2 per cent during 1997-1998 and 2004-05 (Table 12.1). This deceleration, although most marked in rainfed areas, occurred in almost all the states and covered almost all the major sub-sectors, including those such as horticulture, livestock and fisheries where growth was expected to be high. Consequently, growth of agricultural GDP has been well below the target of 4 per cent in both Ninth and Tenth Plans. In fact, Tenth Plan growth averaged even less than that during Ninth Plan because, as was noted in the Mid-term Appraisal of the Tenth Plan (MTA), growth fell below 1 per cent during its first three years (2002-03 to 2004-05).

States with high percentage of rainfed areas have suffered heavy decline in growth during the period 1995-96 to 2004-05. Also, the instability in output growth is more in states with high percentage of rainfed areas.

There had been a declining trend of acreage for most of the crops during the period 1995-96 to 2004-05, except that for wheat, the acreage of which registered a modest growth of 0.11 per cent per annum. In the decade prior to 1995-96, the area under oilseeds, cotton and sugarcane registered impressive growth but this trend also reversed in later decadal interval. Given the near stagnant net sown area of 140 million hectares and gross cropped area of about 190 million hectares, there was increase in area under certain crops at the expense of declining area under other crops. In the subsequent decade, the scope of increase in area vanished across the crop segments. This trend clearly indicated constraints in availability of land for agriculture due to competing pressure on land demand for non-agriculture sector and rapid urbanisation witnessed in the recent years.

There was sharp decline in the growth rate of productivity of all the crops in the decade of 1995-96 to 2004-05. The productivity growth of rice and wheat, the anchors of Green Revolution in the past, decelerated to 0.82 per cent per annum and 0.56 per cent per annum respectively from 2.40 per cent per annum and 2.61 per cent per annum respectively in the previous decade. The productivity of pulses during 1995-96 to 2004-05 had a declining (negative) trend of 0.07 per cent, reflecting the absence of any technological breakthrough reaching at farmer's end. Only cotton and maize registered productivity growth rate in excess of 2 per cent during 1995-96 to 2004-05. The healthy performance of cotton and maize, the semi-arid crops grown generally outside the traditional green revolution regions, is due to combined response to the technology, delivery and post-harvest linkages (Planning Commission, December 2006).

TABLE – 12.1

AVERAGE GDP GROWTH RATES—OVERALL AND IN AGRICULTURE
(PER CENT PER YEAR AT 1999-2000 PRICES)

Period		*Total Economy*	*Agriculture and Allied Sectors*	*Crops and Livestock*
1. Pre-green Revolution 1951-52 to 1967-68		3.69	2.54	2.65
2. Green Revolution Period 1968-69 to 1980-81		3.52	2.44	2.72
3. Wider Technology Dissemination Period 1981-82 to 1990-91		5.40	3.52	3.65
4. Early Reforms Period 1991-92 to 1996-97		5.69	3.66	3.68
5. Ninth Plan 1997-98 to 2001-02		5.52	2.50	2.49
6. Tenth Plan Period 2002-03 to 2006-07		7.77	2.47	2.51
of which	2002-03 to 2004-05	6.60	0.89	0.89
	2005-06 to 2006-07	9.51	4.84	4.96

Source: *Eleventh Five Year Plan 2007-2012*, Vol. III, 2008.

Agricultural Growth during 2005-06–2007-08

According to Economic Survey 2008-09,[3] with an average growth of over 4.9 per cent over three years (2005-06 to 2007-08), the agriculture sector (including allied activities) lent credible support to the overall growth in GDP. However, in 2008-09, the growth originating from agriculture and allied activities declined to 1.6 per cent (as per the revised estimates). While this is lower than the 4.9 and 4.0 per cent growth witnessed in 2007-08 and 2006-07 respectively, the performance in 2008-09 needs to be viewed in the light of the high base of the

3. Government of India, *Economic Survey 2008-09*, ch. 7.

previous years. Agricultural growth is characterised by sharp fluctuations and remains vulnerable to the vagaries of nature.

Instability in Output

Although the growth rate in food grains output seems to have improved because of the impact of new technology, the growth performance has by no means been smooth. The instability or the year-to-year variation in food grains output has increased in the post-green revolution period. Even within the post-green revolution period, the instability in the last decade (1978-79 to 1988-89) was higher than in the preceding decade. The rural poor, particularly in the drought-prone areas and in the remote areas of the country, continue to suffer from fluctuations in employment and income and inadequate availability of food grains in years of drought.

However, this increase in instability cannot be attributed to new technology. Rather, the instability arises from the adverse agro-climatic conditions in which the technology is used. The new seed-fertiliser technology has raised the response of output to water. Thus, for a given variability in rainfall or moisture conditions, the instability in output would be greater. However, when the new technology is applied under assured irrigated conditions, the increase in output would be on a stable path. This is exactly what has happened in the case of wheat where the new technology has made the maximum impact. The rise in instability is significant for crops like rice, oilseeds and pulses. This is explained by the increasing application of new seed-fertiliser technology for these crops in rainfed areas and under uncertain irrigation in the recent period. This suggests the need for stabilising consumption through larger procurement of food grains when harvests are good and their liberal release through public distribution system for the vulnerable groups in years of drought.

Regional Disparities and Intra-Personal Disparities

Perhaps the most widely debated issue about green revolution is the growing disparities in income between different regions and classes of farmers. The experience after the mid-seventies covering nearly a decade and half reveals trends which are typical of a diffusion process. These trends are: the spread of green revolution to new areas, the increasing adoption of new technology by the small farmers, the decline in the relative prices of food grains and the rise in real wages in agriculture in the less developed regions where new technology is spreading.

In the early phase of green revolution, large farmers, owing to better access to capital resources, stepped up yields per acre at a faster rate than small farmers. Because of this, in areas experiencing technological change, the inverse relationship between farm size and output per acre began to disappear. In course of time, however, the supply of institutional credit for the less developed regions and small farmers improved significantly. As a result of this and also because of improved extension services, the use of new seed-fertiliser technology among small farms caught up with that among large farms. And, because of the continued advantage that small farmers have in respect of cropping intensity, the inverse relationship between farm size and output per net operated acre has started reappearing. However, labour input per acre continued to decline sharply with the increase in the size of holding.

Insofar as large farmers have resumed land for self-cultivation from share-croppers because of the profitability of new technology, it has led to lower labour absorption and reduced incomes for erstwhile tenants. However, in quite a few places, cost-sharing on new inputs between landowners and sharecroppers has become popular resulting in the sharing of benefits from new technology by the landowners as well as tenants.

Even in the early phase of green revolution, the emerging disparities between different regions were more conspicuous than the disparities between different classes of farmers within regions experiencing technological change. The uneven regional growth was mainly responsible for low absorption of labour within agriculture. In a large number of states, especially in those regions where there was abundant availability of labour, the growth of output was too slow to generate adequate employment opportunities. In high growth regions, labour was not plentiful and wage rates were high. The sudden rise in the demand for labour in these areas induced mechanisation and labour-saving practices in general. This happened despite the use of migrant labour from the less developed regions for certain operations. The net result was a significant decline in the elasticity of employment with respect to agricultural output for the country as a whole. At the same time, the inter-state disparities in the growth of output and in output per worker continued to increase from the early seventies through the early eighties. However, the inter-state disparities in agricultural wages started declining since the mid-seventies. The decline in disparities in real wages is even more significant. This is because the decline in the relative prices of food grains had a greater impact on the purchasing power of wage earners in low wage areas. For example, the disparities in real wages in agriculture between Punjab, on the one hand and Bihar, on the other, started coming down since the mid-seventies. The real wages in Punjab having risen significantly in the early phase of green revolution, virtually stagnated after the mid-seventies whereas the real wages in Bihar started rising. The causes for the decline in inter-state disparities in real wages are: the out-migration of labour from the less developed regions to the high wage areas; mechanisation of agricultural operations in the developed regions; the decline in the relative prices of food grains; the increase in employment generated in the less developed regions under the poverty alleviation programmes; and the recent pick-up in agricultural growth in these regions. An encouraging consequence of these developments is that the disparity between male-female wage rate has started declining in several states. The use of new technology may have improved the bargaining power of female labour for operations such as transplanting and interculturing on account of the rise in seasonal demand for such labour.

Low income groups, both in the rural and urban areas, would derive greater benefit from the decline in the relative prices of food grains, because they spend a larger proportion of their income on food grains than the upper income groups. Agricultural price policy has been able to ensure that the productivity gains from technological change are shared both by the consumers and producers. However, consumers seem to have benefited relatively more than the producers from the productivity gains, particularly in the case of rice and *jowar*. The demand for wheat has been more favourable than for other cereals. So the decline in the relative price of wheat was only about 25 per cent, while the productivity gains amounted to nearly 45 per cent of output growth.

The indirect contribution of green revolution to equity through food security and the decline in the relative prices of food grains has perhaps been more significant than its direct impact by way of labour absorption in agriculture. Because of slow growth of employment in agriculture, the employment and income generated under poverty alleviation programmes had to be stepped up by using surplus stocks of food grains. From about 20 million man-days of employment generated annually in the mid-sixties, the employment generated under such programmes in the country as a whole amounted to 850 million man-days in 1988-89. These employment programmes together with the income generated under the Integrated Rural Development Programme (IRDP) seem to make up for about half the deficiency in employment generation in agriculture in the post-green revolution period. The relative contribution of these poverty alleviation programmes to employment generation is more significant in the poorer regions where agricultural growth has been below the national average. These programmes have been made possible because of the increased availability of food grains from internal procurement.

New Technology and Environmental Degradation

Pollution of environment due to the intensive use of chemical fertilisers and pesticides has become a major problem in the developed countries. In India, environmental degradation in the rural areas has arisen not so much from the high level of chemical inputs used as from deforestation and extension of cultivation to ecologically fragile areas. Land-saving technological changes by reducing pressure for extension of cultivation and by augmenting biomass, contribute to the conservation of fragile areas and regeneration of forests.

Across different states in India, the extension of area under cultivation and the denudation of forests seem to be high where the progress of yield-increasing technology is slow. In such regions, the levels of agricultural income and wages are low and poverty levels are high. Similarly, the pressure from animals such as goats and sheep on forests and common lands has been increasing in regions where growth in crop production is slow. This is because the rural poor supplement their incomes by rearing these animals (Rao, forthcoming; Mellor, 1988). Apart from yield-increasing technology for crops, the use of new technologies in forestry and animal husbandry to raise the yields from trees and animals and to improve management practices are likely to contribute significantly to the protection of environment. The emerging biotechnologies are opening up opportunities for environmentally sound management of agriculture.[4]

Limits to Growth

There are some tentative indications about the limits to growth of Indian agriculture. First, the extensive margin of cultivation has already reached a plateau in Indian agriculture. Since the beginning of Green Revolution in 1967-68, the area under all crops increased only at a rate of 0.4 per cent per annum as against 1.3 per cent during the period prior to Green Revolution (1950-51 to 1966-67). In the case of food grains, there was hardly any growth since the beginning of Green Revolution.

---

4. Rao, C.H.H. and Ashok Gulati (2001). "Indian Agriculture: Emerging Perspectives and Policy Issues", in Uma Kapila (ed.), *Indian Economy Since Independence*. New Delhi: Academic Foundation.

However, agricultural production has increased by 2.9 per cent per annum. It is improvement in yields (2.0 per cent per annum) that made the production growth possible.

Further, state-wise trends indicate that the largest slump occurred in those areas/states that are predominantly rainfed.

Major Factors Affecting the Growth Potential

A number of factors are constraining the growth potential of the sector.[5]

i) Lack of Long-Term Policy Perspective

On the policy front, there was lack of long-term strategy for agricultural development. One will be surprised to find that only recently the Government has come out with a national agricultural policy. From the very beginning of the planning process in India, especially from the Second Five Year Plan with the sectoral priorities of Mahalanobis model favouring industry, the emphasis has been placed on industry relative to agriculture. The policies followed for agricultural development suffers from a number of weaknesses. First, agricultural sector has suffered from a typical anti-agricultural bias due to the nature of policies followed in other sectors like industry, trade, exchange rate, etc. (Gulati, 1998). Agricultural policies provided little incentives for the farmers, as the agricultural prices were depressed (Indian farmers received lower price than international prices). As there were numerous controls and restrictions, the sector was disprotected *vis-a-vis* other sectors of the economy. The restrictions on agricultural exports were believed to be one of the prime reasons for the disprotection of the sector as compared to the industrial sector. Second, the nature of the policies was inward-looking as it was driven less by comparative advantage. In general, agricultural policies gave little emphasis on agricultural exports as a means of stimulating domestic production (Jeromi, 1997). Third, it has excessive price-based focus than non-price factors like water, infrastructure, research and development (R&D), extension services, etc., which are important determinants of agricultural production in India. These weaknesses of agricultural policies, *inter alia*, affected the faster growth of the sector and in creating a sound infrastructure base for future growth.

5. Jeromi, P.D. (2002). "Is Indian Agriculture Approaching the Limits to Growth" in Raj Kapila and Uma Kapila (eds.) *Economic Developments in India*, Vol. 58, New Delhi. Academic Foundation.

ii) Investment in Agriculture and Subsidies

An unfortunate trend over the past two decades has been that expenditure control efforts have led to cutbacks in agricultural investment and extension, but not in subsidies. Budgetary subsidies to agriculture have increased from around 3 per cent of agriculture GDP in 1976-1980 to about 7 per cent in 2001-2003. During the same period, public investment in agriculture declined from over 4 per cent of agriculture GDP to 2 per cent. Most of the subsidies are on fertiliser, power and irrigation water, and these have actually contributed to the degradation of natural resources. Further, a considerable amount of Plan expenditure on agriculture is not on investment but on subsidies.

It is imperative to reduce these subsidies for stepping up public investment in agriculture. However, there is considerable political resistance and, in a democratic polity like India, the process of change towards rational pricing of inputs is bound to be slow. In these days of globalisation and easy flow of information, it is becoming difficult to convince the Indian farmers about the need to reduce such subsidies when their counterparts in the 'market economies' like the United States, European Community and Japan enjoy much higher levels of subsidies. It is not easy to convince the farmers in India that our resources are scarcer and their alternative uses in agriculture are more productive.

Nonetheless, an important policy gain of recent years is the turnaround in public investment in later years of the Tenth Plan, reversing years of decline. Overall capital formation in the sector is now 12 per cent of agricultural GDP, which is the highest in 25 years. This must have contributed to the recent upturn in growth. But incremental capital-output ratio has risen from about 2.5 to around 4. Unless efficiency of investment is restored, investment would need to increase much further, to about 16 per cent of agricultural GDP, to achieve the 4 per cent agricultural growth target.

In formulating future policy toward public investment in agriculture and rural development, three areas should get priority: rural roads, electricity (including rural electrification), and major and medium irrigation projects (Panagariya, 2008). Rural roads that feed into major highways connect farmers to the market place, and electricity is the critical input in both agricultural and non-agricultural economic activities. The provision of these two critical amenities can go a long way toward allowing farmers to exploit their private entrepreneurial talents. Major and medium irrigation projects provide a key public input into agriculture. Luckily, all three items are on the agenda of

Bharat Nirman, a four-year business plan of the Central government for rural infrastructure extending from 2005-06 to 2008-09 (Panagariya, 2008).

TABLE – 12.2

INVESTMENT IN AGRICULTURE

(as % of GDP from Agriculture)

Year	*GCF in Agriculture*		
	Public Sector	*Private Sector*	*Total*
1980-81 to 1984-85	5.0	5.5	10.5
1985-86 to 1989-90	3.5	5.2	8.7
1990-91 to 1994-95	2.4	5.9	8.4
1995-96 to 1999-2000	2.0	5.9	7.9
2000-01	1.8	7.8	9.6
2001-02	2.0	9.1	11.1
2002-03	2.0	9.8	11.8
2003-04	2.1	8.0	10.2
2004-05	2.8	8.3	11.1
2005-06	3.2	8.5	11.7
2006-07	3.7	8.9	12.5

Source: Government of India (2008). *Eleventh Five Year Plan*, Volume III.

iii) Lagging Research and Development Efforts

Another important factor limiting the growth potential of the sector is the lack of breakthrough in research and development after the green revolution. Perhaps, it may be one of the reasons for the decline of productivity in the nineties. India compares poorly with the productivity levels in major producing countries. Though India is one among the major producers of agricultural commodities in the world, the yield levels, here, for a number of commodities like paddy, wheat, groundnut, cotton, jute, etc., were far lower than the yield levels in major producing countries and in case of some crops, it was even lower than the world average.

India is considered as having the largest public agricultural research establishments in the world. Indian Council of Agricultural Research

(ICAR) and agricultural universities constitute the main part of governmental agencies. However, agricultural research in India suffers from several weaknesses like: i) uneven progress of varietal improvement across crops and regions; ii) neglect of crop systems research; iii) unimpressive results of local adaptive research; iv) inadequacy of collaborative multi-disciplinary research; v) weak interaction between researchers, extension workers and farmers; vi) excessive centralisation of planning and monitoring; vii) lack of accountability for performance, etc. (Vaidyanathan, 2000). Compared to other countries, India's efforts in research and development, in terms of provision of resources, is insufficient. India is investing only around 0.3 per cent of GDP in agriculture for agricultural research, as against 0.7 per cent in the developing countries and 2-3 per cent in case of developed countries.

Since there is hardly any scope for further expansion of area under cultivation, the future production prospects depends largely on the improvements in the yield levels. Here what we need is to break the yield barrier and bridge the gap between the potential and actual yield through research and development (R&D) efforts. ICAR studies reveals that there is vast unexplored technological potential for improvement in the yield of crops. In this context, Swaminathan (1999) noted that the "low yield phenomena" in India should be considered as a "yield reservoir" and it should be treated as an asset for future development of the sector. Therefore, it is imperative for the country to build up a sound agricultural research system, which is responsive to the changing needs and circumstances. As the agricultural growth reduces rural poverty directly, and it fosters the conditions for pro-poor growth in the non-farm sectors, it is imperative to overcome the limits to growth by increase in productivity of the sector.

iv) Technology Generation and Dissemination

With availability of land and water fixed, the goal of 4 per cent growth in agriculture can be achieved only by increasing productivity per unit of these scarce natural resources through effective use of improved technology. The research system has so far focused mainly on breeding varieties that increase the yield potential of individual crops by enabling more intensive use of inputs. But although such research did increase potential yields substantially in the past, it puts less emphasis on the efficient and sustainable use of soil nutrients and water and is no longer leading to adequate outcomes. Analysis of new varieties released of major crops (rice, wheat, maize, groundnut, mustard and sugarcane) shows significant deceleration of the growth of yield potential, with negligible increase over the last decade. This technology fatigue has to be addressed urgently by changing research priorities suitably.

There is a large potential for raising output with effective dissemination of existing technology. This must be the main source of 11th Plan yield growth since overcoming technology fatigue, although first priority, will take time. Moreover, since yield gaps vary considerably from crop-to-crop and from region-to-region, the 11th Plan strategy must focus on specific requirements of each agro-climatic region and will require much stronger linkages between research, extension and farmers.

v) Rising Soil Degradation and Over-exploitation of Groundwater

Large-scale soil degradation and over-exploitation of groundwater are other important factors putting limits on growth of the sector. Around 40 per cent of India's total geographical area are officially estimated as degraded (some other estimates put the figure at 50 per cent).

The emergence of rice-wheat crops system in states like Punjab and Haryana, on account of continuous increase in procurement prices, has resulted in over-exploitation of natural resource base. An ICAR study found that soil health is deteriorating in Punjab and Haryana and this is a major cause of decline or stagnation in productivity of cereals, particularly of rice and wheat. In case of groundwater, the study found that the rapid increase in the number of tube wells during the last three decades in the region has resulted in over-exploitation of groundwater. This decline forces the farmers to lower the pumps further deeper in the wells, which results in the use of irrigation with saline water.

The total irrigation potential in the country has increased from 81.1 million hectares in 1991-92 to 102.08 million hectares up to the end of the Tenth Five Year Plan (2006-07). Of the total potential created, however, only 87.2 million hectares is actually utilised. Even after full utilisation of the irrigation potential, nearly 45 per cent of the net cultivated area will have to depend on rainfall. As the present agricultural development strategy in India is centred mainly on the irrigated areas and the yield levels of crops in many irrigated areas are plateauing, there is a growing realisation that agricultural production cannot be increased beyond a point.

vi) Degradation of Natural Resources

The pressing need to accelerate agriculture growth should not be at the cost of sustainability of our natural resource base, which is starkly limited. This is compounded by degradation of soil and overexploitation of groundwater. Deforestation has affected both soils and water. Nearly 2/3rds of our farmlands are in some way either degraded or sick and only about 1/3rds are in good health. Rapid expansion of groundwater use for irrigation was a key factor in the relatively rapid growth of agriculture between the mid-1960s and late-1980s. But further expansion should be strictly monitored, especially in regions where aquifer levels have dropped causing concern about future sustainability. Action on these environmental fronts cannot wait, especially in the face of a possibly looming adverse climate change due to global warming.

Rural Distress in Post-reform India

A recent nationwide survey (NSS 59th Round, Report 498, 2005) brings out the grave agrarian situation in terms of farmer indebtedness. Almost 50 per cent of the farming households are indebted, but the proportion is much higher in states like Andhra Pradesh (82.0 per cent), Tamil Nadu (74.5 per cent), Punjab (65.4 per cent) and Kerala (64.4 per cent), which are also states with relatively higher investment. More than 50 per cent of the borrowing is for investment in agriculture, but it is much higher in Andhra Pradesh (77 per cent), Karnataka (73 per cent) and Maharashtra (83 per cent). Institutional sources account for about 50 per cent on an average, but it is much lower at 30 per cent in states like Andhra Pradesh, where the remaining 70 per cent comes from informal sources (IDR, 2008).[6]

There has been a steep increase in the costs of farming across the country, which is substantially due to the reforms. The fertiliser price index increased from 99 in 1990-91 to 228 in 1998-99 at a compound annual growth rate of 11 per cent (Acharya, 2004). And one estimate, across the crops and country, suggests that fertilisers presently account for 29 per cent of farmers' inputs costs (Acharya, 2004). There have also been increases in the water charges in many states. One of the often cited reasons for agricultural trade liberalisation is that it provides access to higher prices in the global markets. However, there has actually been a decline in global prices of some of the agricultural commodities such as rice and cotton for which India enjoyed comparative advantage. Before 1998-99, the Indian domestic lint prices

6. Radhakrishna, R. (2008). *India Development Report 2008*, ch. 3, *op.cit.*

were lower than world prices and India was an exporter of cotton. With the removal of QRs and with the recent fall in the global cotton prices, India has turned into an importer of cotton, which has depressed domestic prices of cotton and has been the cause of serious losses to cotton farmers. According to one estimate, most of the global agricultural commodity prices in 2002 were lower than those in 1994, and particularly cotton prices were 30 per cent lower. Farm business income (FBI), the difference between the value of output produced and the costs actually paid out, which was on the rise in the 1980s, started declining in the 1990s. The growth of FBI per hectare decelerated from 3.21 per cent in 1980s to 1.02 per cent in the 1990s. The growth of real FBI per cultivator declined from 1.78 per cent in 1980s to 0.03 in 1990s and in actual terms also, it seems to have declined in the states of Andhra Pradesh, Bihar, Gujarat, Karnataka, Maharashtra, Orissa and Rajasthan.

There is the steep rise in cost of living in rural areas as indicated by the CPI for agricultural labour (CPIAL) while the farmers' income languishes. This is a familiar scissors crisis in agriculture often resulting in pauperisation of the peasantry. This has also resulted in widening of disparities between agricultural and non-agricultural incomes (Table 12.3). The disparities have doubled over the last two and a half decades, leaving agriculture way behind (IDR, 2008).

TABLE – 12.3

PER WORKER INCOME IN AGRICULTURE AND NON-AGRICULTURE SECTORS IN INDIA

(1993-94 prices)

Period	*Income Per Worker (rupees)*		*Ratio of Non-agriculture to Agriculture*	*Growth Rates in the Last Decade (per cent)*	
	Agriculture	*Non-agriculture*		*Agriculture*	*Non-agriculture*
1978-99 to 1983-84	9961	28,430	2.85	-	-
1988-89 to 1993-94	11,179	39,355	3.52	1.16	3.31
1998-99 to 2003-04	11,496	59,961	5.22	0.28	4.30

Source: Chand (2006).

Opening up of the economy has led to certain cash crops like cotton and pepper among others being exposed to greater price volatility. Excess international supply of cotton at a lower price is also because of direct and indirect subsidies, leading to dumping by the USA. Domestic policies in India have led to the removal of QRs and the subsequent reduction of import tariff from 35 per cent in 2001-02 to 5 per cent in 2002-03 has increased our vulnerability to the volatility of international prices.

Farmers' Suicides

The available evidence tends to show that the farming community is passing through a particularly high stress situation during this high growth reform period. Though the specific and immediate triggers may vary from region to region, the overall macroeconomic context is the one of structural adjustment and trade liberalisation. The evidence available from the states emphasises the reform induced stress. In Andhra Pradesh, declining public investment in irrigation and unavailability of credit from institutional sources meant heavy investment in digging of borewells by borrowing from informal sources at a higher interest burden. This search for water led to a fall in the water table and the expected returns from agriculture did not come about, resulting in debt burden that threatened the individual's self-respect. An enterprising hard working farmer is now identified as someone who is reneging on contracts—he cannot repay his loans. It is the government sponsored mission on oilseeds that led to shifts in cropping pattern shifts in expectation of higher returns. The worst affected are the marginal, small and even medium farmers who do not get the MSP because of their dependence on traders for credit at high rates of interest, along with a system where they are tied up with sale of output to the trader at prices lower than the MSP. A study by Bhushan and Reddy (2004), based on a survey of suicide households, indicates that the households had taken to mono-cropping of input-intensive, nonfood, commercial crops and even leased in land, but the crops failed due to inadequate water (IDR, 2008).

By and large, the incidence of suicides has been higher among small-marginal farmers, farmers moving from subsistence agriculture to the high value crops with a strong motivation to improve their social and economic status. They are indeed risk-taking small agricultural entrepreneurs whose success would be the basic premise for the transformation of rural India towards better and equitable incomes and livelihoods. To sum up, 'farmers' distress is not due to lack of agricultural growth but paradoxically due to enterprising qualities of farmers who pursue growth and even achieve it in good measure. But, drought-prone environment and non-caring policy regime turn those who bring growth into victims' (Rao and Gopalappa, 2004).

Small-marginal farmers in dry regions are the most vulnerable but least cared for in the economic reforms framework. It is policy neglect that has been forcing these farmers to shoulder all the costs and risks of high investment, including land and water resource development (with borrowed capital at unurious interest rates). They have lifted the states' agriculture to relatively better productivity agriculture at a cost that they can ill afford.

These costs are the costs of transition of agriculture in the state from subsistence levels to higher productivity. These costs are necessarily social costs, which should not be compounded on to the shoulders of the distressed peasantry. The state has to own up to the responsibility for these social costs of investment in the development of land and water (including groundwater) resources, provision of adequate economic support by way of institutional credit, extension, supply of quality inputs and remunerative prices as well as social sector support of ensuring quality education and health facilities in the countryside. There is incontrovertible evidence that agricultural growth driven by improved productivity of small-marginal farmers would result in much more equitable distribution of income, augmentation of effective demand with its spread effects on non-farm sector, and would be more sustainable as well. The essential condition is the need for a policy shift from the mindless neo-liberal market centred reforms to building of economic and social supprt systems to make small-marginal farming, especially in dry regions, viable, and to ensure that these farmers are protected against exposure to distress due to vagaries of domestic and global market forces (Reddy and Mishra, 2008).[7]

National Policy for Farmers, 2007

Based on the recommendations of the National Commission on Farmers and in consultation with the concerned Central Ministries/departments and the states, the Government of India has adopted the National Policy for Farmers, 2007. Major policy provisions include provisions for asset reforms, water use efficiency, use of technology, inputs and services like soil health, good quality seeds, disease free planting material, support services for women, credit, insurance etc. Provisions have also been made for National Agricultural Bio-security System, setting up of farm schools in the fields of outstanding farmers

7. Reddy, D. Narasimha and Srijit Mishra (2008). "Crisis in Agriculture and Rural Distress in Post Reform India", *India Development Report, op.cit.*

to promote farmer to farmer learning and to strengthen extension services and expanding food security basket to include nutritious crops like *bajra*, *jowar*, *ragi* and millets mostly grown in dry land areas. A comprehensive National Social Security Scheme for the farmers for ensuring livelihood security by taking care of insurance needs on account of illness and old age is included.

Towards Sustainable and Inclusive Growth[8]

The Eleventh Plan seeks to increase public investment further, from 3 per cent of agricultural GDP to about 4 per cent. But it also needs to do much more to ensure that future growth is more efficient, sustainable and inclusive.

- With availability of land and water fixed, growth in agriculture can be achieved only by increasing productivity per unit of these scarce natural resources through effective use of improved technology. The research system has so far focused mainly on breeding varieties that increase the yield potential of individual crops by enabling more intensive use of inputs. Although such research did increase potential yields substantially in the past, it put less emphasis on efficient and sustainable use of soil nutrients and water, or on identifying location-specific farming systems with proper mix of crops and livestock, especially for rainfed areas. Besides, the potential yields of new varieties being released seem to have plateaued suggesting that the current system is no longer leading to adequate outcomes. This 'technology fatigue' has to be countered by changing research priorities suitably.

- At the same time, frontline trials of various research departments provide clear evidence of large gaps between what can be attained at the farmer's field with adoption of available technology as compared to what is obtained with existing practices. Exploiting this potential must be the main source of yield growth in the Eleventh Plan because overcoming technology fatigue will take time. Moreover, since yield gaps vary considerably from crop-to-crop and from region-to-region, the strategy must enable specific plans for each agro-climatic region.

---

8. Kapila, Uma (2009). "Output and Productivity Growth in Indian Agriculture" in K.L. Krishna and Uma Kapila (eds.) *Readings in Indian Agriculture and Industry*. New Delhi: Academic Foundation.

TABLE – 12.4

LEVEL OF AGGREGATE PRODUCTIVITY AND GROWTH IN NSDP AGRICULTURE IN VARIOUS STATES

State	*Trend Growth Rate in NSDP Agri. at 1993-94 Prices*	
	1984-85 to 1995-96	*1995-96 to 2004-05*
Rajasthan	5.52	0.30
Chhattisgarh		-0.91
Madhya Pradesh (Old)	3.63	-0.23
Madhya Pradesh (New)		-0.05
Maharashtra	6.66	0.10
Orissa	-1.18	0.11
Gujarat	5.09	0.48
Karnataka	3.92	0.03
All India	3.62	1.85
Bihar (New)		2.82
Bihar (Old)	-1.71	3.51
Jharkhand		5.39
Andhra Pradesh	3.18	2.69
Uttar Pradesh (New)		1.91
Uttar Pradesh (Old)	2.82	1.87
Assam	1.65	0.95
Tamil Nadu	4.95	-1.36
Himachal Pradesh	1.64	3.51
Haryana	4.60	1.98
Jammu & Kashmir	2.18	3.25
Uttaranchal		1.36
West Bengal	4.63	2.67
Punjab	4.00	2.16
Kerala	3.60	-3.54

Source: Ramesh Chand *et al.* (2007).

According to a study by Vaidyanathan and Sivasubramaniyan (2004), "inter-state differences in output per unit of total crop area yields are strongly correlated to the irrigation ratio, gross irrigated area (gia)/gross cropped area (gca). Higher yields go with higher more productive use of water (yield/mm of consumptive use) both overall and on unirrigated land."

Low level of input use and low productivity in most of the states offer some ray of hope to revive agricultural growth, but this according to Chand would certainly require simultaneous efforts on several fronts. These include: (a) stepping up investments and putting in place suitable institutional mechanisms to exploit irrigation potential that exists in most of the states; (b) increasing power supply to the sector; (c) promoting fertiliser use by expanding the distribution network and improving credit facilities for farmers; (d) establishing competitive seed markets and ensuring attractive prices for seeds; (e) improvement in terms of trade for agriculture; and (f) measures to mitigate risk in farming.

Challenges and Outlook

The agriculture sector faces challenges on various fronts. On the supply side, the yield of most crops has not improved significantly and in some cases, fluctuated downwards. The scope for increase in the net sown area is limited and farm size has been shrinking. In the case of certain crops like sugarcane, extreme variability in the acreage and production over the years has been a matter of concern. On the other hand, in the case of pulses, production has just not kept pace with the requirement leading to a rise in prices given that its availability in the international markets is limited.

Therefore, there is clearly a need for a renewed focus on improving productivity; at the same time, to step up the growth of allied activities and non-farm activities that can help improve value addition. The current focus on developing rural infrastructure particularly rural roads needs to be maintained as it would go a long way in providing connectivity that is essential for movement of agricultural produce. The irrigation sector requires a renewed thrust both in terms of investment as also modern management. There is considerable scope for development of micro-irrigation systems and watersheds and in the use of a participatory approach for achieving the same.

On the whole, while the challenges faced by agriculture are numerous, the possibilities for new investment, the use of new technologies that could generate incomes in the rural sector are also immense (Economic Survey 2008-09).

Questions

1. What is the importance of agriculture in the Indian economy? Why is the level of agricultural productivity so slow? *[B.Com. (P) 2008]*
2. What are the causes of the low productivity of agriculture in India? Examine the role of the new agricultural strategy in improving it. *[B.A. (P) 2008]*
3. What are the causes of low productivity in agricultural sector in India? What steps have been taken to improve it? *[B.A. (P) 2007]*
4. Write short note on: Causes of low prodcutivity in agriculture in India. *[B.Com. (P) 2007]*
5. What is the importance of agriculture in Indian economy? Discuss briefly the problems faced by Indian farmers. *[B.A. (P) 2006]*
6. Account for the low productivity in Indian agriculture. What measures would you suggest to raise it? *[B.A. (P) 2005]*
7. Write short note on 'Institutional *versus* technological changes in agriculture'. *[B.Com. (P) 2006]*
8. Explain the importance of agriculture in Indian economy. Do you agree with the view that the Green Revolution had only a limited impact on Indian agriculture? *[B.Com. (P) 1997; B.A. (P) 2005]*
9. What is meant by Green Revolution? What are main limitations and criticism of green revolution? *[B.Com. (P) 2005]*
10. What is meant by the green revolution? Do you agree with the view that the green revolution has solved the food problem in India? Give reasons in support of your answer. *[B.Com. (P) Correspondence, 2005]*
11. Describe the main features of Green Revolution. How far has it been able to solve India's food problem? *[B.A. (P) 2001, 2004]*
12. What is new Agricultural strategy? What have been the social and economic consequences of Green Revolution in India? *[B.Com (P) 2004]*
13. What is 'Green Revolution'? How far has it been able to solve India's food problem? *[B.A. (P) 2003]*
14. "Green Revolution has increased the production level substantially. At the same time it has led to substantial increase in interregional and interpersonal inequalities". Discuss *[B.Com. (P) 2000]*
15. What is Green Revolution? Discuss its impact on productivity and distribution of income in Indian agriculture. *[B.A. (P) 2000]*

13

Agricultural Credit

Credit Requirements of Cultivators

THERE are two types of credit requirements of the farmers. First, the purpose for which the credit is required, and then the period for which it is required i.e., short-term, medium-term or long-term.

The credit requirement of the farmer can be for the purchase of additional piece of land or to make some permanent improvements in the land as digging or deepening of wells or fencing on the land, or to acquire costly agricultural implements, etc. Such requirements are for medium-term or long-term i.e., for one year or for over five years. There is also the short-term requirement of funds for buying seeds, fertilisers, cattle-feed, etc. During bad crop years, the farmers require short-term funds for household expenses. The short-term loans are generally repaid after the harvest.

The credit requirements can be for productive purposes or unproductive. Productive purposes include loans to buy seeds, fertilisers, implements, etc., or even to pay taxes to the Government and for carrying out permanent improvements on land. The productive credit helps the farmer in agricultural operations. But the farmer also borrows for unproductive purposes, such as for marriage, birth or death, or for litigation, etc.

Sources of Agricultural Finance

There are mainly two sources of finance available to the farmers: institutional and non-institutional. The institutional sources include the Government, the Co-operatives, and the Commercial Banks including the Regional Rural Banks (RRBs). The non-institutional sources include moneylenders, traders and commission agents, relatives and landlords.

TABLE – 13.1

INSTITUTIONAL AND NON-INSTITUTIONAL SOURCES OF FINANCE

(Percentages)

	1951-52	*1961-62*	*1981-82*	*1991-92*	*2002*
A. Institutional	**7.3**	**18.7**	**63.2**	**66.3**	**61.1**
Government	3.1	15.5	4.6	1.1	4.6
Coop. Soc./Banks etc.	3.3	2.6	29.8	30.0	30.2
Commercial Banks	0.9	0.6	28.8	35.2	26.3
B. Non-Institutional	**92.7**	**81.3**	**36.8**	**30.6**	**38.9**
Moneylender	69.7	49.2	16.1	17.5	26.8
Landlords and Others	23.0	32.1	20.7	13.1	12.1
Total (A+B)	**100.0**	**100.0**	**100.0**	**100.0**	**100.0**

In 1951-52, the institutional sources of finance, including the Government, accounted for only 7 per cent whereas the non-institutional sources accounted for 93 per cent of the total credit. This share of non-institutional sources declined sharply to about 39 per cent in 1991, moneylenders accounting for only 16 per cent. The share of institutional credit, on the other hand, has gone up to 61 per cent, the co-operatives accounting for 30.2 per cent and commercial banks for 26.3 per cent. Thus, the emphasis now is on strengthening the co-operatives and expanding the commercial banks' network to meet the increasing demand for agricultural credit.

Institutional Sources of Finance

State governments also provide "Taccavi loans" to farmers and extend financial support to State Co-operative Banks (SCBs) and Land Development Banks (LDBs).

The Primary Agricultural Credit Societies (PACs) provide mainly short- and medium-term loans and Land Development Banks (LDBs) provide long-term loans to the farmers.

The commercial banks, including RRBs, provide short-term as well as long-term loans for agriculture and allied activities.

At the national level, the National Bank for Agriculture and Rural Development (NABARD) is the apex institution for agricultural finance and also provides refinance assistance to the agencies mentioned above.

The Reserve Bank of India plays a crucial role by giving overall directions for rural credit and provides financial support to the National Bank (NABARD).

Co-operative Societies

Co-operative credit is the cheapest and the best source of finance for agriculture. The rate of interest is low. The Government has come to rely on co-operatives as the most appropriate institutional arrangement for catering to the financial requirements of the farmers. Directly helped by the Government, the co-operative societies have made spectacular progress in the last two decades: notably in Tamil Nadu, Andhra Pradesh, Karnataka, Punjab and Himachal Pradesh. The primary credit societies cover over 85 per cent of the villages, and account for 36 per cent of the rural population. The credit provided by the co-operatives is 30 per cent of the total requirements for agriculture and this was only 3 per cent in 1951-52. However, the stranglehold of moneylenders on the peasants is not completely eliminated as all the financial requirements of farmers are not met by the co-operatives. Moreover, there are vast areas and regions in West Bengal, Bihar, Orissa and Rajasthan where the co-operative movement has not spread adequately.

Commercial Banks

The commercial banks were not concerned with the provision of short-term and medium-term credit for agricultural purposes as these were met by the co-operative credit societies and land development banks. Moreover, the uncertain character of Indian agriculture, lack of proper accounting of agricultural transactions, small amount of individual loans, inadequate security for loans, difficulty of collection from farmers—these were some of the factors which prevented the commercial banks from taking interest in agricultural finance. However, after the nationalisation of banks in 1969, the commercial banks started giving loans to farmers. Direct credit is given for short-term and medium-term periods. Indirect finance is provided by way of advances for the distribution of fertilisers and inputs, etc., and also through financing primary agricultural credit societies. The financial requirements of service units catering to warehousing, processing, marketing, transporting, and repairing of tractors, etc., form part of the bank's credit for infrastructure. The banks finance the operations of Food Corporation of India, the state governments and their agencies for food procurement. Stocking and distribution of agricultural inputs is another sector served by banks. Along with SBI group, they are implementing the 'village adoption scheme' under which the credit and other needs of farmers are fully met by banks. They have sponsored regional rural banks to extend credit to small and marginal farmers and rural artisans to save them from the clutches of the moneylenders.

Land Development Banks

The requirement of long-term finance is being satisfied by land development banks which were formerly known as land mortgage banks. These banks provide long-term credit to farmers against mortgage of their lands. The loans from the land development banks are relatively cheap and are spread over long periods of 15 to 20 years. Farmers find it convenient to borrow from these banks whenever previous debts have to be cancelled or when additional land is to be purchased or when permanent improvements, like digging of wells, have to be made. As the land development banks lend against the security of land, the big landlords take advantage of them so much so that, by and large, small peasants have not benefitted from them.

Regional Rural Banks

Set up in 1975 to give direct loans and advances to small and marginal farmers, agricultural labourers, rural artisans, etc., the 196 RRBs have been lending around Rs. 5,500 crore annually. Over 90 per cent of the loans of RRBs are given to the weaker sections.

Non-Institutional Sources of Credit

Rural Moneylenders

There are agriculturist moneylenders who combine farming with moneylending. The village shopkeeper also acts as a moneylender. Besides, there are professional moneylenders also whose only occupation is moneylending.

The farmers depend upon the moneylender for their requirements of cash. The importance of moneylenders as suppliers of cash to the cultivators is, however, declining rapidly. According to the All-India Rural Credit Survey undertaken in 1951, the moneylenders accounted for about 70 per cent of all rural credit. In 1991, they accounted for only 16 per cent of rural credit. The moneylenders are, thus, losing ground to institutional agencies. But even now however, there are many reasons for the preponderance of the village moneylenders: (i) the village moneylender is easily accessible and maintains a close and personal contact with the borrower, often having relations with the family extending over generations; (ii) his methods of business are simple and elastic; (iii) he has local knowledge and experience and therefore, can lend against land as well as against promissory notes. He knows how to protect himself against defaults; and (iv) the moneylender supplies credit for productive as well as non-productive purposes, and also for short-term and long-term requirements of the farmers.

There are, however, many malpractices which are associated with the village moneylenders. They obtain bonds and promissory notes from their debtors on false pretences, and enter in them sums larger than actually lent. They deduct exorbitant premiums. They give no receipts for repayments and often they deny such repayments. They charge high rates of interest, over 24 per cent.

Landlords, Traders and Relatives

The village cultivators generally borrow from their relatives in order to tide over temporary difficulties. These loans are generally contracted in an informal manner. This source of finance has all the defects associated with moneylenders, traders and commission agents. Interest rates are exorbitant. Often the small farmers are cheated and their lands are appropriated. The landless labourers are forced to become bonded slaves. Then, there are traders and commission agents who supply funds to farmers much before the crops mature. They, in turn, force the farmers to sell their produce at low prices and they charge a heavy commission for themselves. This source of finance is particularly important in the case of cash crops like cotton, groundnut, tobacco, etc.

There are, however, many defects in the system of private sources of agricultural finance: the use of credit for unproductive consumption purposes, high rates of interest and hence inability of farmers to meet the high interest charges and return the principal.

Have the Institutional Sources of Credit Replaced the Non-Institutional Sources in Rural India?

As a result of the efforts undertaken by the government to develop the institutional sources of credit, the role of non-institutional sources like moneylenders in agricultural credit declined considerably. The share of non-institutional sources in rural credit which was as high as 92.7 per cent in 1951 fell consistently to 68.3 per cent in 1971 and further to 30.6 per cent in 1991 (in 2002, it rose to 38.9 per cent). More significantly, the share of moneylenders fell from 71.6 per cent in 1951 to merely 17.5 per cent in 1991 (though it rose to 26.8 per cent in 2002). The share of institutional sources in rural credit rose correspondingly from only 7.3 per cent in 1951 to 31.7 per cent in 1971 and further to 66.3 per cent in 1991. However, the share of institutional sources in rural credit, according to Rakesh Mohan[1] is 61.1 per cent in 2002.

Expansion of Institutional Credit to Agriculture

There has been massive expansion of institutional credit to agriculture over the years. This would be clear from the fact that institutional credit to agriculture rose from Rs. 744 crore in 1970-71 to Rs. 9,830 crore in 1990-91 and Rs. 62,045 crore in 2001-02 (the last year of the Ninth Plan) to Rs. 2,00,000 crore during 2006-07, the final year of the Tenth Five Year Plan. This was a more than three-fold increase over five years. The share of commercial banks in total agricultural credit increased from 54 per cent in 2001-02 to around 69 per cent in 2005-06. The share of investment credit increased from 35 per cent in 2001-02 to around 41 per cent in 2004-05, despite the negative growth achieved by the long-term co-operative credit structure. As against a target of Rs. 7,36,570 crore, the total institutional credit flow to agriculture during the Tenth Five Year Plan is expected to be above Rs. 6,50,000 crore, that is, a likely compound annual growth rate (CAGR) of 26 per cent. This is much better than the CAGR of 18 per cent achieved during the Ninth Five Year Plan.[2]

The growth of credit was especially impressive during the last two years of the Tenth Plan on account of the 'Farm Credit Package' announced by the Government of India (GoI). A Special 'Farm Credit Package' as enunciated by the GoI on 18 June 2005 for doubling the credit flow to agriculture, contained various innovative propositions for credit growth. As per provisional figures available for 2005-06, the ground-level credit flow to agriculture during 2005-06 was Rs. 1,80,446 crore; 128 per cent of the target of Rs. 1,41,000 crore, and registering an annual growth of 44 per cent. While commercial banks registered a growth of 54 per cent during the year, co-operative banks recorded 25 per cent growth, followed by RRBs at 22 per cent.

However, although the total agricultural credit has increased during the Tenth Plan period, there are serious quantitative as well as qualitative concerns. The outreach of the formal institutional credit

---

1. Mohan, Rakesh (2006). "Agricultural Credit in India", *Economic and Political Weekly*, March 18, Table 2, p. 1017.
2. Planning Commission (2008). *Eleventh Five Year Plan 2007-2012*, Vol. III.

structure is very limited. The findings of the National Sample Survey Organisation (NSSO) 59th Round (2003) revealed that only 27 per cent of the total number of cultivator households received credit from formal sources while 22 per cent received credit from informal sources. The remaining households, comprising mainly small and marginal farmers, had no credit outstanding. It is unlikely that the situation has changed much since 2003.

At present, direct finance to agriculture under priority sector lending includes credit for the purchase of trucks, mini-trucks, jeeps, pick-up vans, bullock carts, and other transport equipment to assist the transport of agricultural inputs and farm produce. Direct finance also includes credit for the construction and running of cold storage facilities, warehouses and godowns.

Doorstep banking implemented through designated agent of commercial banks has now been facilitated by recent decision of the Reserve Bank of India (RBI) and provides an opportunity for farmers to interact with banks with timings suitable to the farming community. The banks are currently allowed to extend financial outreach by utilising the services of civil society organisations, farmers' clubs, NGOs, post offices, etc., as 'Business Facilitators' or as 'Business Correspondents'.

Co-operatives

The most potent means *for widening and deepening access to institutional* credit to the innumerable small and marginal farmers are the cooperative credit societies that are autonomous and democratic. The revitalisation of the co-operative credit structure in order to transform them into vibrant and viable democratic financial institutions is therefore vital. It is, therefore, extremely important, that the restructuring of co-operative credit now in progress, on the lines of the recommendations of the Vaidyanathan Committee are implemented speedily and rigorously.

Change in Relative Shares of Institutions

After the nationalisation of 14 major commercial banks in 1969, the commercial banks have consistently increased their share in institutional credit to agriculture from 38.4 per cent in 1980-81 to 65.0 per cent in 2004-05. As a result, the relative share of co-operative societies has declined from 61.6 per cent in 1980-81 to 25.0 per cent in 2004-05. RRBs have contributed about 9 to 10 per cent of agricultural credit over the years (Table 13.2).

TABLE 13.2

INSTITUTIONAL CREDIT TO AGRICULTURE: RELATIVE SHARE OF DIFFERENT INSTITUTIONS

(Per Cent)

Year	*Cooperatives*	*Scheduled Commercial Banks*	*Regional Rural Banks*	*Total Credit to Agriculture*
1970-71	100.0	-	-	744
1980-81	61.6	38.4	-	3,292
1990-91	49.0	47.6	3.4	9,830
2000-01	39.4	52.6	8.0	52,827
2001-02	38.0	54.1	7.9	62,045
2002-03	34.1	57.2	8.7	69,560
2003-04	31.0	60.3	8.7	86,981
2004-05	25.0	65.0	10.0	1,25,309

Source: (1) Rakesh Mohan, "Agriculture Credit in India", *Economic and Political Weekly*, March 18, 2006, Table 1, p. 1016; and (2) Government of India, *Economic Survey* 2005-06 (Delhi, 2006) Table 8.13, p. 165.

Weaknesses in Rural Credit System

Over the years, rural credit system has been suffering from a number of weaknesses like, limited outreach, skewness in the availability of credit in different regions, sectors and sections of the farming community, lower recovery of loans and growing non-performing assets, loss making institutions, etc.

With the rising rural income and agricultural exports, agricultural output mix is likely to undergo radical changes in the coming years which would substantially increase the demands for rural credit. The investment needs for the production of highly income elastic agricultural products such as dairying and livestock, horticulture, farm-forestry and agro forestry, which are more land-saving and capital-intensive, would rise much faster than before. Similarly, with the liberalisation of agricultural exports, the agriculture sector will be more commercialised and capital-intensive, particularly in area like horticulture, floriculture, aquaculture, agro-industries, etc. Since many of the emerging activities are land-saving in character, the income earning prospects for small and marginal farmers can be improved by providing requisite credit and technical expertise. Owing to these factors, rural credit has to expand at a rate faster than in the recent past.

National Bank for Agriculture and Rural Development (NABARD)

The most important development in the field of rural credit has been the setting up of the National Bank for Agriculture and Rural Development (NABARD) in July 1982. It took over from Reserve Bank of India all the functions that the latter performed in the field of rural credit. NABARD is now the apex bank for rural credit.

The main functions of NABARD are as follows:

(i) Works as an apex body to look after the credit requirements of the rural sector;

(ii) Oversees the functioning of the co-operative sector through its agricultural credit department;

(iii) Provides short-term credit (up to 18 months) to state co-operative banks for seasonal agricultural operations (crop loans), marketing of crops, purchase and distribution of fertilisers and working capital requirements of co-operative sugar factories;

(iv) Provides medium-term credit (18 months to 7 years) to state co-operative banks and RRBs for approved agricultural purposes, purchase of shares of processing societies and conversion of short-term crop loans into medium-term loans in areas affected by natural calamities;

(v) Provides medium and long-term credit (not exceeding 25 years) for investments in agriculture under schematic lending to state co-operative banks, land development banks, RRBs and commercial banks;

(vi) Provides long-term assistance in the form of loans to state governments (not exceeding 20 years) for contribution to share capital of co-operative credit institutions;

(vii) Has been entrusted with the responsibility of inspecting district and state co-operative banks and RRBs. The inspection of state land development banks and other feberations/co-operatives is undertaken on a voluntary basis; and

(viii) Maintains a research and development fund to be used to promote research in agriculture and rural development so that projects and programmes can be formulated and designed to suit the requirements of the different areas.

NABARD and Rural Credit

NABARD does not deal directly with farmers and other rural people. It grants assistance to them through the co-operative banks, commercial banks, RRBs etc. In 2004-05, NABARD sanctioned 161 schemes with a commitment of Rs. 8,594 crore while actual disbursement stood at Rs. 8,577 crore. Some details about NABARD's assistance to agriculture are given below:

1. Refinance: NABARD provides two types of refinance. The first is extended to RRBs and apex institutions, namely SCBs and state governments. The other type of refinance is extended to augment resources for ground level deployment of rural credit.

2. Rural Infrastructure Development Fund: RIDF-I was established in 1995-96 with a corpus of Rs. 2,000 crore with the major objective of providing funds to state governments and state owned corporations to enable them to complete various types of rural infrastructure projects. RIDF has been continued on an annual basis. RIDF-XI covered the year 2005-06. The total corpus of RIDF (RIDF-I to RIDF-XI) amounted to Rs. 50,000 crore. Cumulative sanctions and disbursements under various tranches of RIDF stood at Rs. 42,950 crore and Rs. 25,384 crore respectively as on March 31, 2005.

Loans under RIDF are given for various purposes like irrigation projects, watershed management, construction of rural roads and bridges etc. While in the initial tranches of the scheme, the accent was on sanctioning loans for various irrigation projects, in the later stage, construction of rural roads and bridges claimed the major portion of the fund. The projects, however, showed considerable time overruns. According to NABARD, the reasons for this were: (i) mismatch between physical and financial disbursements; (ii) the implementing departments (of governments) were not adequately funded by the state governments; (iii) the projects faced problems of land acquisition, forest and environmental clearance; (iv) inadequate monitoring and inability to take corrective action by government officers; and (v) lack of transparency among the key functionaries.

3. Micro Finance Innovations: In operational terms, micro credit involves small loans, up to Rs. 25,000, extended to the poor without any collateral for undertaking self-employment projects. Such loans are provided through micro finance institutions (MFIs). One of the most popular models of MFI has been the *Grameen Bank* model, developed originally in Bangladesh and replicated in various parts of the world. Under this model, non-government organisations (NGOs) form and develop self-help groups (SHGs) and provide credit to them.

Cumulative disbursement of bank loans to these SHGs stood at Rs. 6,898 crore as on March 31, 2005 with an average loan of Rs. 42,620 per SHG and Rs. 2,850 per family.

However, despite the substantial increase in the number of SHGs and expansion of micro finance, there are certain issues that need to be addressed. These issues are as follows:

1. The coverage of poor families in SHG movement is highly unsatisfactory with only about 30 to 32 per cent of poor families being covered as on March 31, 2004. Thus, micro finance institutions have tended to exclude a large number of poor families.
2. The present average amount of loan is just Rs. 2,850 per poor family which is not sufficient to enable the poor to cross the poverty live.
3. The existing savings and loan products are not sufficient to suit the requirements of the poor *viz.* consumption, housing, education etc.
4. The growth of micro finance has been uneven across regions. This would be clear from the fact that the four states of Andhra Pradesh, Karnataka, Tamil Nadu and Uttar Pradesh together accounted for almost 70 per cent of total SHGs credit linked and four-fifth of total amount of bank loan as on March 31, 2003.

However, despite the above problems, micro finance can play an effective role in achieving the long-cherished objectives of poverty alleviation and rural development by 'credit-deepening' in rural India.

4. Kisan Credit Card Scheme: The Kisan Credit Cards (KCC) scheme was introduced in 1998-99 to facilitate short-term credit to farmers. Commercial banks, cooperative banks and RRBs are implementing this scheme. Each farmer is provided with a Kisan Credit Card and a pass book for providing revolving cash credit facilities. NABARD has accelerated the pace of issue of KCCs.

5. Co-operative Development Fund: NABARD set up the Co-operative Development Fund (CDF) in 1993 with the objective of strengthening the co-operative credit institutions in the areas of organisational structure, human resource development, resource mobilisation, recovery position, etc.

The three main functions of NABARD are refinancing, institutional development and inspection of client banks, as noted by the ACRC. An evaluation of these functions shows that the refinance function has attracted relatively more attention and resources over the years. NABARD has not been able to strengthen co-operatives as the management control vests in the state governments. The latter, however, have failed to discipline the errand units.

Questions

1. Examine various sources of agricultural credit in India. *[B.Com. (P) 2005, 2008]*
2. Critically assess the performance of institutional sources in meeting the credit requirements of the agricultural sector in India. *[B.Com. (P) 2006]*
3. What are the institutional sources of agricultural finance in India? Have they succeeded in replacing the traditional money lender? *[B.Com. (P) 2004]*
4. What are the various sources of agricultural finance in India? What improvements need to be affected in existing system to make it competitive for trade in world market? *[B.A. (P) 2003]*
5. Write a short note on National Bank for Agriculture and Rural Development. *[B.A. (P) 2003; B.Com. (P) 2001]*

14

Agricultural Marketing and Price Policy

ONE of the prerequisites for agricultural development is an efficient marketing system. Unless the farmer is able to sell his produce at a remunerative price, he will have no incentive to adopt better farm practices to increase agricultural output.

WEAKNESSES OF THE EXISTING SYSTEM

Distress Sales

We must appreciate the Indian farmer's inability to wait after harvesting the crop, mainly because he has to honour his debt obligations. He has to sell off his produce immediately after the harvest. Therefore, these sales are virtually distress sales either in the village primary market or to the local moneylender. It has also been observed that many a time the moneylenders lend against the standing crop, so that they have the first right to the purchase of crops. Therefore, the farmer under debt gets only unremunerative prices. We can even say that the Indian farmer sells his produce at an unfavourable time, unfavourable place and unfavourable price.

Lack of Storage Facilities

The storage facilities available with farmers in the form of pits or *kutcha* storehouses, *kothis*, etc., are inadequate to protect their crops over a fairly long period of time from dampness and other vermins like ants, rats, etc. According to official estimates, rodents alone consume 10 to 15 per cent of India's agricultural output.

Malpractices of Middlemen in Mandis

The cultivators makes use of the services of a broker to sell his output to the big wholesaler. The *dalal* and the *arhatiya* do not bargain openly but through a code language. The *dalal* is often in collusion with *arhatiya* and therefore, the price which is settled is generally to the advantage of the *arhatiya* and not the farmer. Through the use of false weights and measures and through unnecessary deductions on the plea that his produce is of inferior quality, the farmer often loses in going to the *mandis*. The cultivators do not ordinarily get information about the ruling prices in the big markets. As a result, they have to accept whatever price is quoted to them and have to believe whatever the traders tell them.

Inadequate and Expensive Means of Transport

The distress sales are further facilitated by the fact that the means of transportation available to the farmers are inadequate and far from satisfactory. His bullock cart, though fitted with inflated tyres now, continues to be the chief source of transport. Although other mechanised means of transportation have also fairly developed over a period of time to carry agricultural produce over long distances, they are still so costly that they are beyond the reach of the small farmer.

Lack of Grading and Standardisation

The other factor that makes things difficult for the farmer is the absence of proper grading and standardisation of agricultural produce. Under the circumstances, the dishonest functionaries in the market take undue advantage. They can declare any produce as inferior and quote correspondingly lower price for such stocks.

Measures to Remove Weaknesses in Agricultural Marketing

The government has taken various steps to improve the conditions of agricultural marketing: The co-operative marketing and processing societies have been started to market the agricultural goods of the farmers. Co-operative marketing assures reasonable prices so as to remove all exploitation of the farmers by *dalals* and *arhatiyas*. A network of co-operatives at the national level, state level and at primary level operates to help farm producers to get best markets and best prices for their products.

Regulated Markets

The purpose of a regulated market is to eliminate unhealthy market practices, to reduce marketing charges and to ensure fair prices. Considerable publicity is given to market information. Food grain prices are being stabilised by the government through the recommendations of the Agricultural Prices Commission.

All the states have now passed legislation for the establishment of regulated markets. In 1951, there were more than 200 regulated markets in India. By the end of March 1998, over 7,000 agricultural markets in the country had been regulated.

A regulated market is started either for any specific commodity or for a group of commodities. Such a market is administered by a market committee, which consists of representatives of the state government, the legal bodies (as for instance, the district board), the traders, the commission agents or the *dalals* and the cultivators themselves. The committee is appointed by the government for a specific period and is entrusted with management of the market. The market committee fixes the market charges, such as the commission to be charged. It ensures that no *dalal* represents either the buyer or the seller. It prevents unauthorised deductions from the price paid to the farmer and ensures that correct weights and measures are always used. The committee hears all the complaints and settles them. In cases of dispute, it arranges for arbitration. The committee is responsible for the licensing of brokers and weighmen. It is vested with powers to punish anyone who is found guilty of dishonest and fraudulent practices.

Co-operative Marketing

Prior to 1954, there used to be separate co-operative marketing societies as distinct from the co-operative credit societies. Since 1954, however, multipurpose societies have been started with the purpose of giving credit to the farmers and marketing their surplus produce. The society collects the produce of all the members as also of the non members who are willing to sell their produce; often processes the produce and then disposes it off in the *mandi*. It does away with many of the middlemen. If the current prices are not favourable and if it is anticipated that prices may rise in the future, the society may decide to stock the commodity. As soon as the produce is sold, the society pays the farmers the balance amount due to them. An important feature of the marketing society is that it is managed by paid staff. Usually, a society covers a number of villages so that it is viable.

The various features of co-operative marketing of agricultural produce can be enumerated as follows: (i) the marketing society substitutes collective bargaining in place of individual bargaining. The farmer by himself is weak but the marketing society enjoys the bargaining power; (ii) the society advances loans to the farmers and enables them to wait for better prices. Besides, it lends to them for their other needs. Thus, co-operative marketing societies can link credit, farming, marketing and processing to the best advantage of the cultivators; (iii) the society can have its own storage and warehousing facilities, it can thus remove the damage to agricultural produce through rats, ants, dampness, etc.; (iv) the society can arrange to have quick and cheap transport and sometimes it can even have its own transport; (v) the society can encourage the farmers to produce graded and standardised products and discourage them from adulterating their produce; (vi) the society can control the flow of supplies and thus influence the prices; (vii) the society can eliminate many of the middlemen and thus remove their large-profit margins; and (viii) apart from selling the produce of the farmers, the society can supply them such essential goods as seeds, fertilisers, implements etc. Thus, the cooperative marketing society is probably the best method to reorganise rural marketing and promote planned growth of rural areas.

The network of cooperative marketing structure now comprises over 6,000 primary marketing societies, of which 3,500 are special commodity marketing societies; at the district level, there are 160 central marketing societies, covering nearly all the important *mandis* in the country; at the state level, there are 29 general purpose state level Co-operative Marketing Federations and 16 Special Commodity Marketing Federations and, at the all-India level, there are: the National Co-operative Development Corporation (NCDC), the National Agricultural Co-operative Marketing Federation (NAFED), National Cooperative Tobacco Growers Federation Ltd., the National Consumers' Cooperative Federation, and the Tribal Cooperative Marketing Development Federation of India. All these are working in the field of agricultural marketing.

Role of NAFED and NCDC

The National Agricultural Co-operative Marketing Federation of India Ltd. (NAFED) is the apex co-operative organisation at the national level; it deals in procurement, distribution, export and import of selected agricultural commodities. NAFED promotes inter-state as well as export-trade of farm produce. It exports commodities like onions, pulses, chillies, ginger, garlic and cardamom to many countries. The export of pulses, HPS groundnut, onions and potatoes is canalised through NAFED. It also undertakes movement of essential commodities from surplus areas to scarcity areas and helps ease consumer supplies. NAFED is a central nodal agency for undertaking price support operations for pulses and oilseeds and market intervention operations for horticultural items like *kinoo/malta*, onions, potatoes, grapes, black pepper and red chillies, etc. In general, NAFED has played a useful role in stabilising market prices of such commodities like onions and potatoes in principal producing areas through strategic market interventions.

The National Co-operative Development Corporation (NCDC) was set up in 1963 under an Act of Parliament with the object of planning and promoting programmes for the production, processing, storage and marketing of agricultural produce and notified commodities through cooperative societies.

The NCDC has extended its activities to the development of co-operative dairy, fisheries and minor forest produce which are basically intended to benefit the weaker sections.

NCDC has actively promoted distribution of essential consumer articles such as food grains, sugar, edible oils, controlled cloth, kerosene, salt, soft coke, etc., in rural areas through service co-operatives.

Agricultural Price Policy

Objectives

The objectives of price policy as propounded from time to time are multiple and often conflicting. The price policy was evolved in the context of relative shortage of agricultural products, particularly of food grains. Thus, we had the overriding objectives of the price policy as achieving self-sufficiency in food grains (understood as the availability of adequate food grains from domestic production) and protection of consumer from scarcity-induced speculative price rise. As V.S. Vyas points out[1], "The main function of prices, i.e., to act as signals for allocation of resources has been made subservient to income parity and food security objectives."

Apart from the consideration of income transfers, the policy is also directed to increase agricultural production by offering higher

1. Uma Kapila (ed.) *Indian Economy Since Independence*, ch. 30, 2004-05 edition.

'incentive' prices. A discriminatory price policy can be used to encourage inter-crop shifts in resource use. However, when it comes to aggregate agricultural output, greater reliance has to be placed on 'non-price' factors, e.g., generating and extending more efficient technologies. The available studies clearly bring out that aggregate supply response of agriculture is very weak. Thus, any attempt to use high prices to encourage agricultural production can bring in its wake irreparable distortions in the price structure.

These limitations of price policy are not very often recognised. Also the strength of price policy in affecting desirable shift in cropping pattern fully exploited. As Vyas remarks, "In a mixed economy like ours an important objective of the price policy could be to give directions to the cropping pattern not only on the basis of the existing demand supply situation but also to take into account a qualitatively superior crop mix, *e.g.,* to provide a price advantage to nutritionally superior crops or to the crops where the country may have comparative advantage. In fact, in this respect we seem to be regressing. In the 1970s price policy was used as an effective tool to encourage production of crops where superior technology was available" (Vyas, 1989). In recent years we have largely neglected this aspect of price policy.

Further, there has been no clarity on the priority to be assigned among these numerous objectives, or the trade-off involved in pursuing these objectives simultaneously. If we are to go by the public pronouncements, the objectives sought to be achieved by the price policy include, ensuring: (i) reasonable prices for the growers, (ii) reasonable prices for the grains released from public distribution system, and (iii) reasonable prices in the open market. A moment's reflection will show that in most of the circumstances, these aims conflict with each other. The price policy cannot resolve all conflicts in the society.

It must be recognised that price policy taken by itself is a weak instrument in giving directions to agricultural economy, more so as an instrument of income transfer. While the objective of providing an insurance cover in terms of guaranteed minimum prices to a large section of agricultural producers could be a worthy objective but until and unless required resources are available and administrative machinery is in place, mere announcement of minimum prices for a large number of commodities may not serve any purpose. It may, in fact, do more harm with an erosion of the credibility of the government. In view of this, it is suggested that the support prices should be applicable only for a limited number of crops. Crops which can be considered as price leaders or the crops, for which technological breakthrough is imminent ought to be covered under the price guarantees. The other crops to be considered for support are the crops grown under high risk environment and there also it should be a transient measure i.e., till a viable crop insurance programme is evolved.

Along with limiting the scope for price policy is the need for a discriminatory and flexible approach to price interventions. By covering a large number of commodities on the one hand and by ensuring minimum prices in the guise of procurement prices on the other, not only government's commitment has enhanced to an unmanageable extent, it has also led to serious distortions in agricultural economy.

V.S. Vyas remarks, "The time has come to take a serious look at the scope, instruments and institutions of agricultural price policy. There is a need to recognise that the price policy is a weak instrument for income transfers; our capacity to offer minimum support prices for a large number of commodities is limited; need for dovetailing agriculture and trade policies is urgent. instrument of minimum support prices has to be used sparingly; procurement operations need to be made more business like; CACP should retain its expert character rather than trying to be representative of various interests, FCI should be decentralised and debureaucratised and the states should be made major stakeholders."

According to N. Krishnaji,[2] the objectives as laid down in the terms of reference of the APC are to some extent mutually conflicting, and difficult to realise for other reasons as well. One may thus say that the APC was given an impossible task. Let us elaborate.

(a) If the sole objective is to promote agricultural growth—whether or not broad based with respect to crops and regions—through subsidies and price incentives, there is a clear possibility that the implied policy would hurt the interests of the buyers of food and agricultural raw materials. A resolution of the conflict of interests between producers and consumers—or between net sellers and net buyers, and between 'surplus' and 'deficit' areas, as some have described it in the case of food grains—thus becomes a necessary element of overall policy-making. It is a recognition of this necessity that is reflected in the expressed concern about the impact of policy on cost of living etc., and has led to the conversion of price policy into an approach which seeks

2. Krishnaji, N. "Agricultural Price Policy: A Survey with Reference to Indian Foodgrains Economy", in *Indian Economy Since Independence. op. cit.*

to integrate in some measure production objectives with those of distribution. In the case of food grains, this meant that price policy had to be combined with the operations of a public distribution system (PDS) to ensure supply of food grains at subsidised prices to at least some of the poorer sections of the population. However, to the extent that subsidising both the producer and consumer is severely limited by financial constraints, it cannot be sustained on either a short or long-term basis without being supplemented by compensating measures of taxation. All this makes the design of price policy difficult, especially by a body with no decision making powers; more importantly, the difficulty leads to politically expedient measures which exacerbate rather than resolve conflicts.

(b) The difficulty is compounded by two other obvious factors. First, if relative prices are to play an efficient allocative role and not lead to undesirable cropping pattern shifts, policies must be designed to cover all the major crops on a countrywide basis, an impossible task to accomplish. Second, since public distribution of subsidised grain cannot hope to meet the entire market demand (of both the rural and urban consumers), the impact of policies on market prices assumes importance. Thus, with the government handling only a fraction of the marketed surplus, the pricing objectives may in the end be defeated by market forces. The design of price policies with only a limited control over the market thus not only involves an appropriate combination of procurement, stock accumulation and depletion policies but must necessarily be based on a sound knowledge of the implied working of dual markets. The biggest hindrance in this respect is not lack of knowledge about production trends and demand elasticities but our virtual ignorance about the operations of private traders at the different tiers of the grain markets and their impact on prices.

(c) Finally, it must be noted that the objectives are not only conflicting—the fact that there is no indication in policy formulations whether it is only in short-run but also in the long-run, these conflicts could be left unresolved is also important—they are also incomplete and imprecise in some respects. For example, income and price stabilisation are common objectives of price policy; maintenance of some form of parity between the agricultural and industrial sectors and prevention of the erosion of purchasing power of agricultural incomes is a related concern, and all these are adequately discussed in the literature. Indeed they can be stated with some precision; unlike the vague 'protection' of producer and consumer 'interest'; but it is doubtful if multiple objectives are realisable.

Beginning in the late-1990s, the MSPs set for wheat and rice became increasingly out of step with domestic market conditions. One key factor was (and still is) that the CoP concept used in setting the price became a "full cost" measure that, in addition to variable input costs, included the rental value of land, the imputed value of family labour, and a return to management. Another was pressure to compensate farmers for the price swings associated with changes in India's rice and wheat export policy during 1995 and 1996. For rice, higher market prices resulting from the initial removal of export restraints later created pressure for higher MSPs when world prices fell. Similarly for wheat, lower market prices following the re-imposition export restraints led the government to compensate farmers with higher MSPs. With these developments, the MSPs became disconnected from domestic market conditions and— when world prices fell from a temporary spike in 1996-1997—from competitive world market prices. The tendency for MSPs to be increased has likely been compounded as MSP benefits boost land rental, labour and management costs, thus leading to higher CoP.

An important factor affecting MSP policy in the 1990s concerns the changing political dimensions of the policy when India entered an era of coalition governments and the farm lobby became more influential. During 1995-96–2001-02, just before and during the accumulation of surpluses, the government set MSPs above the CACP recommendation in four out of seven years for rice and five out of seven years for wheat (Parikh *et al.,* 2002). Another key dimension is that the MSP mechanism is one of the few levers available to Indian policy makers and there is a tendency to try to use it to achieve multiple policy goals, including both price stabilisation and income support.

The failure of price policy to successfully adapt to the new environment has had a number of impacts. First, breaking with the historical pattern, domestic wheat and rice prices have tended to strengthen relative to both world and domestic prices, and to move above domestic market clearing levels. While benefiting the relatively few producers receiving wheat and rice MSPs, higher consumer prices have undoubtedly had negative impacts. Per capita wheat and rice consumption has actually declined in recent years, as higher procurement and prices contributed to decline in consumption of open market supplies that have not been offset by subsidised distribution. A recent study of the economy-wide impacts of increasing the wheat and rice MSPs when they are above market clearing levels found that reduced consumption and investment associated with higher prices actually reduced incomes, both in aggregate and for most rural and urban income groups (Parikh *et al.*, 2002).

Second, by focusing on supporting relatively high prices only for wheat and rice in a few regions, MSP policy has not been made an effective tool for stabilising producer prices for other crops and supporting the diversification of agriculture.

Third, the budgetary cost of FCI operations under current policies has now reached about $5.5 billion. When policies support domestic prices above market clearing, much of this subsidy accrues to producers rather than consumers. Combined with the cost of subsidies on fertiliser and other inputs, the subsidy bill has burgeoned to about 43,668 crore annually, far exceeding both public and private capital formation in agriculture. Subsidy outlays are crowding out new investment needed to boost productivity and marketing efficiency.

Finally, the policy of maintaining high wheat and rice prices has contributed to emergent environmental problems, particularly associated with the intensive wheat-rice cropping system in northern India. When combined with the low cost of irrigation water—much of which is either free, stolen or subsidised—the strong price incentives for wheat and rice are contributing to the rapid deterioration of groundwater resources, and rising concern with deteriorating soil fertility in some areas.[3]

Removal of Export Restraints

Through the 1980s and early 1990s, Indian agriculture was burdened with export restrictions and overvalued exchange rates that resulted in net taxation of the sector. Exports of agricultural goods were restricted through myriad controls, including prohibitions, licences, quotas, marketing controls and minimum export prices, for the sake of domestic food security. For a number of products, the quantitative controls on exports were administered through trading enterprises in the public and co-operative sectors.[4]

Agricultural export policies began to change in 1994 and, barring the occasional reversal, have been progressively liberalised. The ministry of commerce, through the director general of foreign trade, imposes or removes export restrictions in order to promote exports while also ensuring 'adequate' domestic supplies of essential commodities at 'reasonable' prices.[5]

---

3. Landes, Rip and Ashok Gulati (2004). "Farm Sector Performance and the Reform Agenda", in K.L. Krishna and Uma Kapila (eds.) (2009), *Readings in Indian Agriculture and Industry*. New Delhi: Academic Foundation.
4. Ibid.
5. Ibid.

Developments in the Indian rice market since the removal of export restraints may be indicative of the impacts of this type of reform. Private traders were permitted to export common rice beginning in 1994-95 and, although exports remain small relative to production, India immediately became a major player, selling primarily into the lower end of the international market. Since 2000-01, however, the combination of lower world prices and firm domestic prices has made Indian rice exports less price-competitive, leading to GoI subsidies for rice exports.

Landes and Gulati maintain that rice exports have helped moderate the growth of surplus rice stocks and, together with higher MSPs and lower domestic distribution of subsidised rice, contributed to a strengthening of domestic prices. The growth in exports, along with relaxation of earlier policies limiting rice milling to small-scale enterprises, are stimulating investment in modern rice milling and grading equipment.

With these potentially positive impacts on investment and competitiveness, the removal of export restraints opens up a new set of policy issues concerning the impacts of global price changes on the domestic market. First, the removal of rice export restraints initially benefited producers and traders when it pulled domestic prices above the MSP. But when world prices retreated, the MSPs became disconnected from market realities, leading to increases in domestic and export subsidy costs. Thus, with the removal of export restraints, it becomes important to have an MSP setting mechanism (and discipline) that keeps MSPs connected with domestic and world prices.[6]

Rao and Gulati maintain, "The process of economic reforms, and the gradual opening up of Indian agriculture to world markets is likely to turn the terms of trade in favour of agriculture, creating a better incentive environment for agriculture than has been the case in preceding decades. To fully exploit this opportunity, a major reform in supply-side factors is needed as well as a clean sweep to dismantle all export controls on agricultural commodities, including foodgrains. It is these supply-side factors—technology, fertilisers, irrigation, infrastructure, and credit—that raise aggregate supply response and are the prime movers behind accelerated and sustainable growth of Indian agriculture."[7]

---

6. Ibid.
7. Rao, C.H.H. and Ashok Gulati (2001). "Indian Agriculture Emerging Perspectives and Policy", in Uma Kapila (ed.), *Indian Economy Since Independence*, *op.cit.*

Questions

1. Explain the main defects in the agricultural marketing in India. What steps have been taken to improve upon it?
[B.A. (P) 2006, 2008]
2. What are the main problems of agricultural marketing? How far have these problems been solved in India? In this context, examine the role of government procurement policy.
[B.Com. (P) Correspondence, 2005]
3. Write short note on 'Defects of agricultural marketing system in India'. *[B.A. (P) 2004]*
4. Write brief note on 'Problems of Agricultural Marketing in India'.
[B.A. (P) 2003; B.Com. (P) 2004]
5. State the main problems of agricultural marketing in India. Examine the steps taken by the Government to make marketing system more efficient. *[B.Com. (P) 2000]*

15

Agricultural Labour in India

AGRICULTURAL labour can be divided into various categories: (i) Landless labourers who are attached to the landlords; (ii) Landless labourers who though independent but work exclusively for others; (iii) Small farmers with tiny pieces of land who out of economic necessity have to devote most of their time working for others; and (iv) Farmers who although have economic holdings but some members of their family work for other farmers.

The first group of agricultural workers are also known as bonded labour. They do not normally receive wages in cash but are generally paid in kind. They have to work for their masters and cannot shift from one to another. Among the other groups, the second and the third are quite important.

According to second Agricultural Labour Enquiry (1960), more than 85 per cent of the rural workers are casual, serving any farmer who is willing to engage them and only 15 per cent of agricultural labourers are attached to specific landlords. More than half of the workers do not possess any land, and even the rest of them own only very little of land. Agricultural labourers predominantly belong to the scheduled castes, scheduled tribes and other backward classes.

According to 1981 census data as a percentage of total workers which were 224.6 million, agricultural labourers (64.4 million) constituted 26.3 per cent of the total labour force. In 1961, agricultural labourers numbered only 31 million. This indicates that there has been a sharp increase in the number of agricultural labourers. The National Commission on Rural Labour states: "During the seventies and the eighties, the rural population registered an annual growth rate of 2 per cent and 1.5 per cent, respectively. However, for the corresponding decades, the growth in the number of agricultural labourers has been at higher levels of 4.1 per cent and 3.0 per cent per annum respectively." This implies that marginal farmers have been swelling the ranks of landless labourers. On account of the increasing economic compulsions in terms of past debts, they have been forced to sell their lands.

Another finding of the National Commission on Rural Labour (NCRL) is that whereas during 1977-78, the average days worked per year by men and women of agricultural labour households in agricultural wage employment were 230 days and 184 days respectively, the corresponding figures for the year 1983 (4th Rural Labour Enquiry) were 159 days and 136 days respectively. This decline in the days of employment did produce an adverse effect on the earnings and debt conditions of agricultural labour households.

It has also been found that the proportion of wage labour to total workforce increased at the all-India level from 34.1 per cent in 1972-73 to 41.4 per cent in 1987-88. During the same period, the proportion of casual wage labour to total wage labour increased from 64.8 per cent in 1972-73 to 75.8 per cent in 1987-88. Explaining the growing trend towards casualisation of agricultural labour, NCRL states, "The technological change in agriculture, marginalisation of small farmers, eviction of tenants, destruction of traditional cottage industries, inflation etc., are some of the important factors that are operating differently in different regions of India leading to the swelling of the number of agricultural labourers."

Economic Condition of Farm Labour

Low wages and poor economic conditions of agricultural labour are due to the following factors:

1. Low Social Status

Most agricultural workers belong to the low caste and the depressed classes who have been socially handicapped and therefore, never had the courage to assert themselves.

2. Weak Bargaining Power

Agricultural workers, illiterate and ignorant, live in scattered villages. Hence, they cannot easily be organised in unions. In urban areas, workers can generally organise themselves and it is convenient for political parties to take interest in trade union activity. This is extremely difficult in case of farm labour. Accordingly, it is difficult for farm workers to bargain with the land owners and secure good wages.

3. Unemployment and Working Conditions

The nature of work in agriculture is such that a farm labourer cannot get work continuously. On an average, a farm labourer finds employment for about 200 days in a year and for the rest of the year he is idle. Apart from under-employment, there is also unemployment in rural areas. Unemployment and under-employment are two important factors responsible for low income and consequently low economic position of the agricultural workers in India.

Though bonded labour has been abolished in the country, yet news about the existence of this system in rural India keep pouring in daily from different parts of the country. According to the NSS (32nd round), there are still about 3.5 lakh bonded labourers in the country. Even where this practice has been totally abolished, there is no provision for fixation of hours of work. At the time of sowing and harvesting, the agricultural workers have to work on the farms from dawn to dusk. Since they are employed on a daily basis, there is no question of any leave or other benefits for them.

4. Lack of Alternative Jobs

Paucity of non-agricultural occupations in villages is another important factor for the low wages and poor economic condition of the farm labourers.

5. Indebtedness

Agricultural labour is heavily indebted. Normally, the farm labourers borrow from the landowners under whom they work. Since they have no security to offer, they pledge themselves to the moneylenders and rich landlords and become bonded labourers in many areas. Naturally, they are forced to accept lower wages.

Thus, partly because of factors beyond their control and partly because of their inherent bargaining weakness, the farm labourers have been getting very low wages and have, therefore, to live a miserable sub-human life.

6. Feminisation of Agricultural Labour with Low Wages

Female agricultural workers are generally forced to work harder and are paid less than their male counterparts. Such bias against female workers exists is most of the dryland areas. At many places, wages paid to female workers are even less than the minimum wages.

7. High Incidence of Child Labour

Incidence of child labour is high in India and the estimated number varies from 17.5 million to 44 million. It is estimated that one-third of the child workers in Asia are in India. The largest number of child workers are in agriculture. Child employment benefits the employer but adversely affects the poor as a class although it may supplement the income of the household supplying child labour. The poor are made worse-off as employment of children brings down the wage levels.

Measures to Improve the Lot of Agricultural Labour

Since Independence, the Centre as well as the state governments have taken some measures to improve the economic conditions of agricultural labour. They include the passing of legislation to fix minimum wages for agricultural labour, the removal of disabilities, the ceilings on holdings and the redistribution of land among the landless labourers, etc.

Abolition of Bonded Labour

The Indian Constitution has declared the practice of serfdom an offence. It has abolished agrarian slavery including forced labour by law but it will take some time before it is removed in practice.

A legislation has been passed known as the Bonded Labour System (Abolition) Act, 1976. Under this Act which extends to wide country, the bonded labour system was abolished and every bonded labourer was freed and discharged from any obligation to render bonded labour. Accordingly, all contracts for bonded labour, attachment for recovery of bonded debt, etc., were declared null and void. As a consequence of this Act, 2,82,368 bonded labourers were identified and freed in various parts of the country.

However, even after the passing of the Act complaints of bonded labour are often heard from different parts of the country. Moneylenders and large landowners are often able to force agricultural workers into bonds because of a number of factors. Firstly, many agricultural labourers are not aware of the existence of such an Act. Secondly, because of their extreme poverty and economic compulsions, some agricultural labourers voluntarily enter into bonds while in the case of some others, moneylender taking advantage of the situation compel agricultural workers to enter into bonds.

Minimum Wages Act

The Minimum Wages Act was passed in 1948, according to which every state government was asked to fix minimum wages for agricultural labour within three years. The minimum wages are fixed keeping in view the total costs and standard of living. Since conditions in various parts of the country are different and even within a state, the law allows different rates of wages to be fixed. In practice minimum wages are very difficult to enforce effectively: (i) the Act has been a dead letter in every state; (ii) the minimum wages in agriculture have not been revised over long periods; (iii) almost everywhere, the actual wages rule higher than the minimum wages during the peak season and tend to fall in slack seasons; (iv) the machinery for enforcement is hopelessly inadequate to cope with the task of effective implementation; and (v) the other difficulties in the implementation of the Act arise mainly from poverty and illiteracy of agricultural labour, absence of knowledge of the existence of legislation, scattered nature of agricultural farms, casual nature of employment, unorganised character of agricultural labour, etc.

Providing Land to Landless Labourers

The government has distributed land to landless labourers with a view to improving their economic position. The First Plan made a provision of Rs. 1.5 crore for the resettlement of landless labourers on newly reclaimed land as well as culturable wasteland. In September 1957, the National Development Council proposed that lands obtained as a result of enforcing ceiling laws and those donated in Bhoodan and Gramdan should be primarily devoted to the settlement of landless labourers. Priority in the distribution of land is accorded to landless labourers belonging to scheduled castes and scheduled tribes. Approximately 70 lakh hectares of land has been distributed among landless labourers so far. However, most of the land made available to these labourers is not fit for cultivation.

Provision of Housing Sites

Laws have peen passed in several states for providing house sites in villages to agricultural workers. A number of steps were undertaken during the Second Plan to provide house sites free or on a subsidised basis. During Fourth Plan, a scheme was introduced under which financial assistance was given to the states for provision of house sites with an area of 91 sq. metres of cover, where necessary, the cost of acquisition and development of house sites. During the Seventh Plan, the scheme has to components—provision of free house sites and construction assistance.

Special Schemes for Providing Employment

A number of schemes have been initiated for providing employment to rural poor, the important ones being the Rural Works Programme (RWP), Crash Scheme for Rural Employment (CSRE), Employment Guarantee Scheme (EGS) initiated in Maharashtra, Food for Work Programme (FWP), National Rural Employment Programme (NREP) and Rural Landless Employment Guarantee Programme (RLEGP). NREP was launched in the Sixth Five Year Plan. RLEGP was introduced in August 1998, specifically with the object of providing employment to the rural landless. This was a 100 per cent centrally funded programme. NREP and RLEGP were merged to form the Jawahar Rozgar Yojana (JRY) in 1989-90, JRY was in existence till 1998-99. With effect from April 1, 1999, JRY was restructured and streamlined and was renamed as Jawahar Gram Samridhi Yojana (JGSY). An Employment Assurance Scheme (EAS) was launched on October 2, 1993 in 1,772 identified backward blocks situated in drought-prone, desert, tribal and hill areas. Sampoorna Grameen Rozgar Yojana (SGRY) was launched with effect from September 2001 to provide wage employment in rural areas as also food security, alongwith the creation of durable community, social and economic assets. With effect from April 1, 2002, EAS and JGSY were integrated with SGRY. In November 2004, National Food for Work Programme (NFFWP) was launched in the 150 most backward districts of the country to generate additional supplementary wage employment with food security. SGRY and NFFWP will now be subsumed under the most ambitious wage employment programme 'National Rural Employment Guarantee Scheme' (NREGS) launched in February 2006.

Summing Up

Agricultural labour constitutes the poorest section of the rural population. The NCRL records that as against the general (rural) poverty ratio of 33.4 per cent in 1987-88, the poverty ratio for the rural labour households (NCRL) would be around 57 per cent. To help agricultural labourers, the Commission has emphasised on the one hand an employment-oriented strategy of development and on the other, suggested the organisation of agricultural labourers into trade unions to improve their bargaining strength.

Problems of agricultural workers can be solved by providing alternative avenues of employment through small and cottage industries and village handicraft, by improving their bargaining position, improving their working conditions by fixing hours of work and banning child labour and above all by providing social security. Since these labourers are not permanently attached to any employer, the responsibility of providing social security has to be borne by the state.

Questions

1. Write short note on problems of agricultural labour in India. *[B.A. 2009]*

2. What are the main problems faced by landless rural labour in India? In this context, discuss the various policy measures taken by the Government. *[B.Com. (P) Correspondence, 2005]*

3. Critically analyse the various land reforms measures undertaken by the Government after Independence. *[B.Com. 2005]*

4. Write a short note on 'Problems of Agricultural Labour in India'. *[B.A. (P) 2000, 2001; B.Com. (P) 2003]*

5. What are the main problems faced by the agricultural labour in India? What steps have been taken to improve their conditions? *[B.A. (P) 1999]*

16

Industrial Policy

Pre- and Post-1991

Extent and Pattern of Industrialisation during the British Rule

INDIAN manufacturers had a worldwide market prior to the Industrial Revolution and the rise of modern industry. The exports consisted chiefly of manufactures like cotton and silk fabrics, calicoes, artistic ware, silk and woollen cloth. The impact of the British rule and the industrial revolution led to the decay of Indian handicrafts. Machine-made goods started pouring into the country. The decline of handicrafts was not followed by the rise of modern industry in India because of the British policy of encouraging the import of manufactures and export of raw materials from India.

The British government in India followed the policy of discriminating protection to some selected industries since 1923. This protection was accompanied by the most favoured nation-clause for British goods. Despite this factor, some industries such as cotton textiles, sugar, paper, matches and to some extent iron and steel did make progress. But one thing was quite obvious that during the British period, no effort was made to foster the development of capital goods industries.

The Industrial Scene at Independence

The main features of the industrial scene in India on the eve of planning (1950) were as under:

(i) There was the preponderance of consumer goods industries *vis-à-vis* producer goods industries resulting in lopsided industrial development. In 1953, the ratio of consumer goods to producer goods worked out to be 62:38.

(ii) The industrial sector was extremely underdeveloped with a very weak infrastructure.

(iii) The lack of government intervention in favour of the industrial sector was considered as an important cause of under-development.

(iv) Export orientation had been against the country's interests.

(v) The structure of ownership was highly concentrated.

(vi) Technical and managerial skills were in short supply.

As a result, the national consensus was that economic sovereignty and economic independence lay in rapid industrialisation including particularly the promotion of industrial infrastructure.

Organised thinking concerning the direction of industrial development in India may be traced to the Statement of Industrial Policy, 1945; the Industrial Policy Resolution of 1948; the enactment of the Industries (Development and Regulation) Act, 1951; the First and Second Five Year Plan documents; and the Industrial Policy Resolution of 1956.

The First Five Year Plan stated that the objective of industrial planning was to make good the deficiencies in production of key industrial items. The scope and need for the development of India's industries was felt to be so great that it was necessary for the public sector to develop those industries 'in which private enterprise is unable or unwilling to put up the resources required and to run the risk involved'. The idea was that the rest of the field could be left free for private enterprise.

The Industrial Policy Resolution of 1948 had identified a small number of industries to be reserved for production by the public sector. The production of arms and ammunition, production and control of atomic energy and ownership and management of railways were to be the sole preserve of the Central government. However, coal, iron and steel, aircraft manufacturing, ship-building, manufacture of telegraph and wireless equipment (except radios) and minerals were reserved for production by Central or state government undertakings.

After the adoption of the Constitution and the socio-economic goals, the Industrial Policy was comprehensively revised and adopted in 1956.

The thinking concerning the public sector had changed during the course of the 1950s. As far as can be ascertained, the original thinking was concerned with the use of the public sector investment in industries which the private sector would find difficult to invest in. By 1956 this had changed towards an explicit preference for state ownership of industries that were termed as capturing the 'commanding heights of the economy'.

Industrial Policy Resolution of 1956

The Industrial Policy Resolution of 1948 was followed by the Industrial Policy Resolution of 1956 which had as its objective the acceleration of the rate of economic growth and the speeding up of industrialisation as a means of achieving a socialist pattern of society. In 1956, capital was scarce and the base of entrepreneurship not strong enough. Hence, the 1956 Industrial Policy Resolution gave primacy to the role of the state to assume a predominant and direct responsibility for industrial development.

Important Provisions of the 1956 Resolution were:–

(i) New Classification of Industries: The resolution laid down three categories which bear a close resemblance to the earlier classification, but were more sharply defined and were broader in coverages as to the role of the state. These categories were:-

(a) *Schedule A*: Those which were to be an exclusive responsibility of the state;

(b) *Schedule B*: Those which were to be progressively state-owned and in which the state would generally set up new enterprises, but in which private enterprise would be expected only to supplement the effort of the state; and

(c) *Schedule C*: All the remaining industries and their future development would, in general be left to the initiative and enterprise of the private sector.

Under Schedule A were listed 17 industries: arms and ammunition, atomic energy, iron and steel, heavy castings and forgings of iron and steel; heavy machinery required for iron and steel production, mining, machine tool manufactures, etc.; heavy electrical industries, coal; mineral oils, mining; iron ore and other important minerals like copper, lead and zinc; aircraft; air transport, railway transport, shipbuilding; telephone, telegraph and wireless equipment; generation and distribution of electricity.

Under Schedule B, 12 industries were listed: other mining industries, aluminium and other nonferrous metals not included in Schedule A;

machine tools, ferroy-alloys and tool steels, the chemical industry; antibiotics and other essential drugs; fertilisers; synthetic rubber, carbonisation of coal; chemical pulp; road transport and sea transport.

The Schedule C category industries consisted of the rest of the industries and had to fit into the framework of social and economic policy of the state and be subject to control in terms of the Industries (Development and Regulation) Act and other relevant legislations.

Inspite of this clear cut grouping of industries under three schedules, categories were not watertight compartments and room for exceptions could be made. In appropriate cases, private units might produce an item in category A for meeting the industry's own requirements or as by-products. Further, heavy industries in the public sector could obtain some of their requirements of higher components from the private sector while private sector in turn would rely for many of its needs on the public sector. Moreover, the state reserved the right to enter category C, which would normally be reserved for the private enterprise, when the needs of planning required or for other important reasons. Though the state was now to act as the senior partner unlike under the 1948 policy, the public and the private sector were still expected to work closely together. The basic objective was to create a mixed economy in India.

(ii) Fair and Non-discriminatory Treatment for the Private Sector: In order that the private sector may feel confident and function efficiently, the state was to facilitate and encourage the development of industries in the private sector by ensuring the development of transport, power and other services, and by appropriate fiscal and other measures. When there exist in the same industry both private and publicly owned units, it would continue to be the policy of the state to give full and non-discriminatory treatment to both of them.

(iii) Encouragement to Village and Small-scale Enterprises: The state would support cottage and village and small-scale enterprises by restricting volume of production in the large-scale sector, by differential taxation, or by direct subsidies. The state would concentrate on measures designed to improve the competitive strength of the small scale producer by constantly improving and modernising the technique of production.

(iv) Removing Regional Disparities: The Resolution stressed the necessity of reducing the regional disparities in levels of development in order that industrialisation may benefit the country as a whole. The resolution fully supported the idea that only by securing a balanced and

coordinated development of the industrial and the agricultural economy in each region, can the entire country attain higher standards of living.

(v) The Need for the Provision of Amenities for Labour: The Resolution also recognised that in a socialist democracy, labour is a partner in the common task of development and should participate in it with enthusiasm and for this, the maintenance of industrial peace is one of the essential conditions. It stressed that the living and working conditions of workers should be improved and their standard of efficiency raised.

(vi) Attitude towards Foreign Capital: The Resolution, made it amply clear, "that as a rule, the major interest in ownership and effective control, should always be in Indian hands. In all cases, however, the training of suitable Indian personnel for the purpose of eventually replacing foreign experts will be insisted upon." Thus, while recognising the need for foreign capital in the industrialisation of the economy, the government insisted upon the progressive Indianisation of foreign concerns.

To meet new challenges, from time to time, the Industrial Policy of 1956 was modified through statements in 1973, 1977 and 1980.

The Industrial Policy statement of 1973, *inter-alia*, identified high priority industries where investment from large industrial houses and foreign companies would be permitted.

The industrial policy statement of 1977 laid emphasis on decentralisation and on the role of small-scale, tiny and cottage industries.

The industrial policy statement of 1980 focused attention on the need for promoting competition in the domestic market, technological upgradation and modernisation. The policy laid the foundation for an increasingly competitive export base and for encouraging foreign investment in high-technology areas.

These policies created a climate for rapid industrial growth in the country. Thus, on the eve of the Seventh Five Year Plan, a broad-based infrastructure had been built up. Basic industries had been established. A high degree of self-reliance in a large number of items—raw materials, intermediates, finished goods—had been achieved. New growth centres of industrial activity had emerged, as also a new generation of entrepreneurs. A large number of engineers, technicians and skilled workers had also been trained.

The Seventh Plan recognised the need to consolidate on these strengths and to take initiatives to prepare Indian industry to respond effectively to the emerging challenges. A number of policy and procedural changes were introduced in 1985 and 1986 under the leadership of Rajiv Gandhi, aimed at increasing productivity, reducing costs and improving quality. The accent was on opening the domestic market to increased competition and to make our industry ready to stand on its own in the face of international competition. The public sector was freed from a number of constraints and given a larger measure of autonomy. The technological and managerial modernisation of industry was pursued as the key instrument for increasing productivity and improving our competitiveness in the world. The net result of all these changes was that Indian industry grew by an impressive average annual growth rate of 8.5 per cent in the Seventh Plan period.

Performance of the Industrial Licensing System

Until the recent industrial and trade policy reforms, the establishment and operation of an industrial enterprise in India required approvals from the Central government at almost every step. Before making an investment, an entrepreneur had to first obtain approval in principle from the Ministry of Industry. The granting of this approval resulted in the issuance of a Letter of Intent (LoI). Armed with this LoI, the entrepreneur could then tie up other requirements for setting up the project. If he needed to import a capital good, he had to obtain a capital goods import licence from the Chief Controller of Imports & Exports (CCI&E) in the Ministry of Commerce. The approval for the import, however, was given by a committee set up in the Ministry of Industry. If there was also need for a foreign technology collaboration agreement, the entrepreneur had to obtain a specific approval for this (a Foreign Collaboration– FC-approval) from a committee chaired by the Finance Secretary but serviced by the Ministry of Industry. In order to raise funds for the project, if an entrepreneur wanted to go to the capital market, he needed separate approval from the Controller of Capital Issues in the Ministry of Finance. For imports of raw material and components, separate licences had to be obtained on an annual basis from the CCI&E. In each case, an 'essentiality' and indigenous non-availability clearance had to be given by the technical wing of the Ministry of Industry (the Directorate General of Technical Development–DGTD). Once everything was tied up and the unit was about to go into production, the entrepreneur had to go back to the Ministry of Industry for an 'Industrial Licence'.

In addition to these approvals, since the enactment of the MRTP Act in 1969, the firms covered under this needed to obtain separate MRTP clearances from the Department of Company Affairs. Further, resulting from the desire to promote small-scale industries, 836 items have been reserved for production in small-scale enterprises. Since 1956, there has also been a list of industries reserved for exclusive production in the public sector. Since 1977, there has also been a ban on the location of industries in the largest 20 to 30 cities. In 1988, this ban was extended to include municipal areas of all towns and cities and to specified areas of influence around the largest 21 cities.

That this system was unsuited for directing investments has been well understood since the early 1960s. The most comprehensive description, evaluation and indictment of this system is that by Bhagwati and Desai (1970). The government appointed one committee after another in the 1960s to examine the industrial licensing system (The Swaminathan Committee, 1964; the Mahalanobis Committee, 1964; the Hazari Report, 1967; the Dutt Committee Report, 1969; and the Administrative Reform Commission, 1969). Despite the findings of most of these early committees, that the licensing mechanism was not serving its purpose of channelising investments into desired directions, there seems to have been a continuing inability of the government, until recently, to bring any substantative changes to the industrial licensing system.

It seems the promotion of a sheltered home market had a common appeal to the bureaucratic authoritarian state, urban manufacturers and multinationals that supplied technology and capital. Protection also met the state's objectives pursuing revenue and expenditure maximising activities through maximum revenue tariffs and export tariffs.

Thus, the interests of politicians, bureaucrats, multinationals as well as domestic industrial houses all coincided to keep Indian industry sheltered through the operation of the industrial control system.

The stagnation of Indian industrial production between the mid-1960s up to the late 1970s induced some serious new thinking. Towards the end of the 1970s and by the early 1980s, there emerged a growing consensus that Indian industry was exhibiting a slowdown in industrial growth due to low productivity, high costs, low quality of production and obsolete technology (Ahluwalia, 1985). Three important committees were set up in the early 1980s—the Abid Hussain Committee on trade policy, the Narasimham Committee on the shift from physical to fiscal controls and the Sengupta Committee on the public sector. These committees clearly recommended an easing up of trade policy, the substitution of physical and quantitative controls by fiscal and other means of macroeconomic management, the promotion of greater public sector autonomy in business and operating decisions and the need for measures for enhancing productivity efficiency and modernisation.

The result of such thinking was that there was some progress in the process of deregulation during the 1980s, though perhaps not as significant as is often believed. Two kinds of delicensing activity took place. First, 32 groups of industries were delicensed without any investment limit. Second, in 1988, all industries were exempted from licensing except for a specified negative list of 26 industries. This exemption from licensing was, however, subject to investment and location limitations. As has often been done in the past, this announcement also contained further restrictions which reduced significantly the effectiveness of exemption from licensing that was provided in this announcement. On the trade policy front, the key change was increasing access of exporters to inputs at international prices. However, it seems that tariff protection to industry increased significantly during the 1980s relative to previous decades.

While the industrial licensing system underwent some changes in terms of threshold levels and types of products, it formed an essential part of Government policy until the end of the 1980s.

New Industrial Policy - 1991

The 1991 policy[1] states, "The major objectives of the new industrial policy package will be to build on the gains already made, correct the distortions or weaknesses that may have crept in, maintain a sustained growth in productivity and gainful employment and attain international competitiveness. The pursuit of these objectives will be tempered by the need to preserve the environment and ensure the efficient use of available resources. All sectors of industry whether small, medium or large, belonging to the public, private or cooperative sector will be encouraged to grow and improve on their past performance. Government's policy will be continuity with change."

In pursuit of the above objectives, government took a series of initiatives in respect of the policies relating to the following areas:

---

1. Full text of the Policy in *Indian Economy Since Independence* (ed.), Uma Kapila, ch. 20, (2004-05 edition).

a. Industrial licensing
b. Foreign investment
c. Foreign technology agreements
d. Public sector policy
e. MRTP Act.

Industrial Licensing

Industrial licensing is governed by the Industries (Development and Regulation) Act, 1951. The Industrial Policy Resolution of 1956 identified the following three categories of industries: those that would be reserved for development in the public sector, those that would be permitted for development through private enterprise with or without state participation, and those in which investment initiatives would ordinarily emanate from private entrepreneurs.

Over the years, keeping in view the changing industrial scene in the country, the policy has undergone modifications. Industrial licensing policy and procedures have also been liberalised from time to time. A full realisation of the industrial potential of the country calls for a continuation of this process of change.

In the above context, industrial licensing will henceforth be abolished for all industries, except those specified, irrespective of levels of investment.

These specified industries, will continue to be subject to compulsory licensing for reasons related to security and strategic concerns, social reasons, problems related to safety and overriding environmental issues, manufacture of products of hazardous nature and articles of elitist consumption.

The exemption from licensing will be particularly helpful to the many dynamic small and medium entrepreneurs who have been unnecessarily hampered by the licensing system.

"As a whole, the Indian economy will benefit by becoming more competitive, more efficient and modern and will take its rightful place in the world of industrial progress," states the 1991 Industrial Policy.

Foreign Investment

While freeing Indian industry from official controls, opportunities for promoting foreign investment in India should also be fully exploited.

This is particularly necessary in the changing global scenario of industrial and economic cooperation marked by mobility of capital. The government will, therefore, welcome foreign investment which is in the interest of the country's industrial development.

In order to invite foreign investment in high priority industries requiring large investments and advanced technology, it has been decided to provide approval for direct foreign investment upto 51 per cent foreign equity in such industries. There shall be no bottlenecks of any kind in this process. This group of industries has generally been known as the "appendix industries" and are areas in which FERA companies have already been allowed to invest on a discretionary basis.

This change will go a long way in making Indian policy on foreign investment transparent. Such a framework will make it attractive for companies abroad to invest in India.

Foreign Technology

There is a great need for promoting an industrial environment where the acquisition of technological capability received priority. In the fast changing world of technology, the relationship between the suppliers and users of technology must be a continuous one. Such a relationship becomes difficult to achieve when the approval process includes unnecessary governmental interference on a case to case basis involving endemic delays and fostering uncertainty.

With a view to injecting the desired level of technological dynamism in Indian industry, government will provide automatic approval for technology agreements related to high priority industries within specified parameters.

Similar facilities will be available for other industries as well if such agreements do not require the expenditure of free foreign exchange. Indian companies will be free to negotiate the terms of technology transfer with their foreign counterparts according to their own commercial judgement.

Public Sector

The public sector has been central to our philosophy of development. In the pursuit of our development objectives, public ownership and control in critical sectors of the economy has played an important role in preventing the concentration of economic power, reducing regional disparities and ensuring that planned development serves the common good.

The Industrial Policy Resolution of 1956 gave the public sector a strategic role in the economy. Massive investments have been made over the past four decades to build a public sector which has a commanding role in the economy. Today, key sectors of the economy are dominated by mature public enterprises that have successfully expanded production, opened up new areas of technology and built up a reserve of technical competence in a number of areas.

After the initial exuberance of the public sector entering new areas of industrial and technical competence, a number of problems have begun to manifest themselves in many of the public enterprises. Serious problems are observed in the insufficient growth in productivity, poor project management, over manning, lack of continuous technological upgradation, and inadequate attention of R&D and human resource development.

In addition, public enterprises have shown a very low rate of return on the capital invested. This has inhibited their ability to regenerate themselves in terms of new investments as well as in technology development. The result is that many of the public enterprises have become a burden rather than being an asset to the government. The original concept of the public sector has also undergone considerable dilution.

The most striking example is the takeover of sick units from the private sector. This category of public sector units accounts for almost one-third of the total losses of central public enterprises. Another category of public enterprises, which does not fit into the original idea of the public sector being at the commanding heights of the economy, is the plethora of public enterprises which are in the consumer goods and services sectors.

It is time, therefore, that the government adopts a new approach to public enterprises. There must be a greater commitment to the support of public enterprises which are essential for the operation of the industrial economy. Measures must be taken to make these enterprises more growth oriented and technically dynamic. Units which may be faltering at present but are potentially viable must be restructured and given a new lease of life.

The priority areas for growth of public enterprises in the future will be the following: Essential infrastructure goods and services; exploration and exploitation of oil and mineral resources; technology development and building of manufacturing capabilities in areas which are crucial in the long term development of the economy and where private sector investment is inadequate; manufacture of products where strategic considerations predominate such as defence equipment.

At the same time, the public sector will not be barred from entering areas not specifically reserved for it. In view of these considerations, government will review the existing portfolio of public investments with greater realism. This review will be in respect of industries based on low technology, small scale and non-strategic areas, inefficient and unproductive areas, areas with low or nil social considerations or public purpose, and areas where the private sector has developed sufficient expertise and resources.

Government will strengthen those public enterprises which fall in the reserved areas of operation or are in high priority areas or are generating good or reasonable profits. Such enterprises will be provided a much greater degree of management autonomy through the system of memoranda of understanding.

Competition will also be induced in these areas for private sector participation. In the case of selected enterprises, part of government holdings in the equity share capital of these enterprises will be disinvested in order to provide further market discipline to the performance of public enterprises.

MRTP

The thrust of policy will be more on controlling unfair or restrictive business practices. The MRTP Act will be restructured by eliminating the legal requirement for prior governmental approval for expansion of present undertakings and establishment of new undertakings. The provisions relating to merger, amalgamation, and takeover will also be repealed. Similarly, the provisions regarding restrictions on acquisition of and transfer of share will be appropriately incorporated in the Companies Act.

Simultaneously, provisions of the MRTP Act will be strengthened in order to enable to MRTP Commission to take appropriate action in respect of the monopolistic, restrictive and unfair trade practices. The newly empowered MRTP Commission will be encouraged to investigate complaints received from industrial consumers or classes of consumers.

Decisions of the Government

In view of the considerations outlined above, government has decided to take a series of measures to unshackle the Indian industrial economy from the cobwebs of unnecessary bureaucratic control. These measures compliment the other series of measures being taken by government in the areas of trade policy, exchange rate management, fiscal policy, financial sector reform and overall macroeconomic management.

(i) Industrial licensing will be abolished for all projects except for a short list of industries related to security and strategic concerns, social reasons, hazardous chemicals, overriding environmental reasons, and items of elitis consumption. Industries reserved for the small scale sector will continue to be so reserved.

(ii) Areas where security and strategic concerns predominate, will continue to be reserved for the public sector.

(iii) In projects where imported capital goods are required, automatic clearance will be given: a) in cases where foreign exchange availability is ensured through foreign equity, or b) if the CIF value of imported capital goods required is less than 25 per cent of total value (net of taxes) of plant and equipment, upto a maximum value of Rs. 2 crore.

In other cases, imports of capital goods will require clearance from the Secretariat for Industrial Approvals (SIA) now renamed as secretariat for Industrial Assistance in the Department of Industrial Development according to availability of foreign exchange resources.

In locations other than cities of more than 1 million population, there will be no requirement of obtaining industrial approvals from the Central government except for industries subject to compulsory licensing. In respect of cities with population greater than 1 million, industries other than those of a non-polluting nature such as electronics, computer software and printing will be located outside 25 kms of the periphery, except in prior designated industrial areas.

A flexible location policy would be adopted in respect of such cities (with population greater than 1 million) which require industrial regeneration. Zoning and land use regulation and environmental legislation will continue to regulate industrial locations.

Appropriate incentives and the design of investments in infrastructure development will be used to promote the dispersal of industry particularly to rural and backward areas and to reduce congestion in cities. The system of phased manufacturing programmes run on an administrative case by case basis will not be applicable to new projects. Existing projects with such programmes will continue to be governed by them.

Existing units will be provided a new broad banding facility to enable them to produce any article without additional investment. The exemption from licensing will apply to all substantial expansions of existing units. The mandatory convertibility clause will no longer be applicable for term loans from the financial institutions for new projects.

Industrial Policy: Recent Policy Initiatives

The Government has been constantly reviewing the policy framework to bring about improvements to suit the emerging situation. Some of the major policy developments which have taken place during the year 1998-99 are outlined below:

Industrial Licensing

During the year 1998-99, three industries, *viz*., i) coal and lignite, ii) petroleum (other than crude) and its distillation products and iii) sugar were delicensed. Accordingly, there are only six industries now under compulsory licensing. Two industries, *viz*., coal and lignite and mineral oils were taken out from the list of industries reserved for the public sector. At present there are only three industries reserved for the public sector (Box 16.1). Nine items (six from 'farm implements and tools' and three from 'leather') were removed from the list of industries reserved for exclusive manufacture by the Small Scale Industry (SSI). Entries on toys now excludes electronic toys from the purview of reservation. During the year 1998-99, the number of items reserved for the SSI sector stood at 812.

BOX – 16.1

LIST OF INDUSTRIES RESERVED FOR THE PUBLIC SECTOR

1. Arms and ammunition and allied items of defence equipment, defence aircraft and warships.
2. Atomic energy.
3. Railway transport.

Location Policy

At present, there is no requirement of obtaining industrial approvals from the Central government (except for the industries under compulsory licensing) for locations not falling within 25 kms. of cities having population of more than one million. However, industries of non-polluting nature such as electronics, computer software and printing can be located within 25 kms. of the periphery of cities with more than 1 million population. Other industries are permitted only if they are located in industrial areas designated prior to July 25, 1991. Further, zoning and land use regulations as well as environmental legislation continue to regulate industrial locations.

Industrial licensing had already been substantially dismantled. Drugs and pharmaceuticals including biotechnology were delicensed in 2005. At the end of the Tenth Five Year Plan period, only the following manufacturing activities needed industrial license:

- Distillation and brewing of alcoholic drinks;
- Cigars and cigarettes of tobacco and manufactured tobacco substitutes;
- Electronic aerospace and defence equipment;
- Industrial explosives;
- Specified hazardous chemicals.

Entrepreneurs are free to select the location for setting up industry. Approval is required from the government for locating an industrial unit within 25 km of the periphery of cities having a population of more than one million according to the 1991 census, provided that is not within an industrial area designated before 24 July 1991. However, these locational restrictions are not applicable for electronics, computer software, printing industries and other non-polluting industries that may be designated from time to time.

Apart from the licensing restrictions, there are some restrictions arising from certain industries reserved for the public sector and for the small-scale sector. Reservation for the public sector is now very limited, covering only manufacturing involving certain substances relevant for atomic energy (as well as production of atomic energy and provision of railway transport). The list of items reserved for SSIs has been reduced to 114. Larger units are allowed to manufacture items reserved for the small-scale sector only if they undertake an export obligation of 50 per cent of their industrial production.

The Foreign Direct Investment (FDI) policy was also successively liberalised during the Tenth Five Year Plan. Following a comprehensive review in 2006, it was further liberalised, particularly by allowing FDI under the automatic route for manufacture of industrial explosives and hazardous chemicals and making it easier for new investments by foreign investors who had entered into joint ventures with Indian partners earlier. At the end of the Plan period, FDI upto 100 per cent was permitted in all manufacturing activities except where the foreign investor had an existing joint venture/technical collaboration/trademark agreement in the same field of activity (11th Plan).

Conclusion

The New Industrial Policy of July 1991 and subsequent liberalisation measures have changed the role of the government from that of only exercising control over industry to that of helping it to grow rapidly by cutting down bureaucratic delays, removal of entry barriers and bringing out transparency in procudures. The policy, therefore, aims at virtually ending the 'Licence-Permit Raj' which has been hampering private initiative and industrial development. The public sector's role has been limited to industries relating to defence, strategic and environmental concerns. The entire field of industry has been thrown open to the private sector.

The industrial policy reforms during the 1990s were bold in doing away with numerous barriers to entry, e.g., removal of industrial licensing for investment, opening up all but a few strategic areas which were earlier reserved for investment only by the pubic sector, preparing to replace the earlier MRTP Act with a new Competition Law which would regulate anti-competitive behaviour. Even on the policy for reservation for the small-scale sector, a beginning was made by dereserving a number of items. However, the absence of institutional and legal reforms creates barriers to exit. Delays in securing numerous permissions from state governments and environmental clearances from the Government of India are also emerging as the new barriers to entry.

Entry barriers adversely affect the investment climate of the state. One of the determinants of the investment climate for an industry is the ease with which the firms are able to enter into the business activities. *Doing Business 2007: How to Reform*—a co-publication of the World Bank and the International Finance Corporation (2007) shows that the average time spent in completing entry requirement in India is 35 days and the number of procedures is 11 compared to 35 days and 13 numbers of procedures in China.[2]

Investment climate in the country is also affected by the exit barriers. Perhaps the most important exit barrier relates to Chapter V-B of the Industrial Disputes Act, 1947 under which units with more than

2. Planning Commission (2008). *Eleventh Five Year Plan (2007-2012)*, Government of India.

100 employees cannot exit an unprofitable enterprise without the consent of the concerned state government. This consent is often difficult and time consuming to obtain.

The other important exit barrier to the industries in India is the legal provision relating to insolvency, rehabilitation, liquidation and winding up proceedings, which need to be simplified and be made time bound. The co-publication of the World Bank and the International Finance Corporation (2007) reports that resolving the insolvency cases takes upto 10 years in India against 2.4 years in China, 1.5 years in South Korea and 3 years in the US. Similarly, the recovery rate of closing business is 13 per cent in India compared to 82 per cent in South Korea.

Questions

1. Write a short note on: The New Industrial Policy, 1991. *[B.A. (P) 2007]*
2. In what respects has the role that was envisaged for the public sector changed from the industrial policy resolution of 1956 to the new industrial policy of 1990s? What was the rationale behind this change. *[B.A. (P) 2006]*
3. Critically examine the main features of the New Industrial Policy introduced in 1991. *[B.A. (P) 2001, 2005]*
4. How is the present industrial policy different from the Industrial Policy Resolution 1956? Highlight the achievements of the current policy. *[B.A. (P) 2005]*
5. Write short note on 'Industrial policy in India'. *[B.Com. (P) 2005]*
6. In what respects is the Industrial Policy of 1991 different from Industrial Policy 1956? To what extent have these change resulted in rapid growth of Indian economy. *[B.A. (P) 2004; B.Com. (P), Correspondence, 2004]*
7. Write brief note on 'Industrial Policy statement of 1991'. *[B.Com. (P) 2004]*
8. What are the main features of the Industrial Policy of 1991? *[B.A. (P) 1999; B.Com. (H) 2003]*
9. What changes have recently been introduced in the industrial Policy in India? What impact did these changes have on the role of industrial growth in the country? *[B.Com. (P) 1997]*
10. Examine the liberalisation policy of the Government of India in the context of the Industrial Policy of 1991. *[B.Com. (P) 1993]*

17

Public *versus* Private Sector

THE declared social objective of the Indian development strategy since Independence has been growth with social justice which was sought to be achieved within the democratic political framework and for which India adopted the concept of mixed economy. The expansion of the public sector was considered to be a major instrument of state policy in a mixed economy to achieve the stated objectives as embodied in the Constitution and five year plans. However, a large part of the economic activity will remain market based, decentralised in nature and in the private sector.

The Rationale

In India, the rationale for the public sector has been explicit or implicit in all plan documents as well as policy statements although the emphasis has changed in degrees depending upon the constraints faced and the emerging major issues of the time.

Tracing the chronological developments in this connection, we find that as far back as 1948, the Industrial Policy Resolution declared that "a dynamic national policy must... be directed to a continuous increase in production by all possible means, side by side with measures to secure its equitable distribution". For this purpose, while recognising that the "State must play a progressively active role in the development of industries", it was conceded that in the conditions then prevailing "the mechanism and the resources of the State may not permit it to function forth within Industry as widely as may be desirable". The First Five Year Plan that followed did not have a clear-cut strategy of development and hence, it did not contain any operational statements on the public sector.

It was in the context of the Mahalanobis strategy that the approach to the public sector got further crystallised. The long-term growth orientation in an import-substitution dominated strategy required that the domestic capacity creation be biased in the direction of producing capital goods to produce more capital goods. According to Prof. Tendulkar[1], the distinct preference for the public sector in this strategy can be traced to the following reasons.

First, the concentration of economic power that would result from the uncontrolled operation of the market forces can be reduced through the extension in the public ownership of means of production.

Secondly, private investors may demand a higher risk premium for investment in certain industries than would be socially justified. Off-shore drilling of oil is one example in this connection.

Thirdly, the scale of investment efforts in certain heavy industries may be beyond the capital-raising capacity of the private sector e.g., steel mills, heavy electrical machinery.

Fourthly, the public sector, through the appropriate price policy for its output will generate investible surpluses for further investment in the economy.

Fifthly, by production as well as distribution of certain universal intermediate inputs like coal, steel, electricity etc., the state will be able to control the composition of private economic activity in a socially desirable direction.

Finally, the public sector would assume the role of a model employer and its employment and wage policies would have a moderating influence on the corresponding policies in the private sector.

Analysing these reasons, one finds that public sector was expected to fulfil varied and sometimes conflicting objectives. The generation of investible surplus was bound to conflict with subsidies involved in keeping the prices of certain universal intermediates at low levels as well as the public sectors role as a model employer.

Objectives of Public Sector

The main objectives of public sector in India are as follows:

(i) To help in the process of economic growth.

(ii) To step-up the tempo of industrialisation.

---

1. Tendulkar, S.D. "Approach to the Public Sector in the Context of an Overall Development Strategy", in Uma Kapila (ed.), *Indian Economy Since Independence*.

(iii) To create necessary infrastructure for development.

(iv) To correct the prevailing imbalances in industrial structure.

(v) To generate resources for development.

(vi) To promote redistribution of income and wealth.

(vii) To create employment opportunities.

(viii) To promote balanced regional growth.

(ix) To save foreign exchange by promoting import substitution.

(x) To assist in the development of village and small-scale industries.

In the sixties and seventies, the public sector policy has been largely guided by the Industrial Policy Resolution of 1956 which gave the public sector a strategic role in the economy.

All industries of strategic importance and those providing base for further development were reserved for the public sector. Consequently, the number of enterprises in the public sector which was 5 in 1951 with an investment of Rs. 29 crore, increased to 47 with investment of Rs. 948 crore in 1961. Public sector expanded rapidly since then and the number of public enterprises increased to 235 in 1998-99 wherein the government had made investment of Rs. 2,73,700 crore. It may be noted that these figures relate only to the enterprises of the Central government (or Central public enterprises) and exclude those which are run by state governments and municipal bodies.

Massive investments have been made over the past five decades to build a public sector which had a commanding role in the economy. Many key sectors of the economy are today dominated by mature public enterprises that have successfully expanded production; opened up new areas of technology and built up a reserve of technical competence in a number of areas.

As a result, the country's ranking in terms of industrialisation with other developing countries is quite high. India's comparative advantages such as a large pool of well-trained workforce, technical skills in manufacturing and chemical industries primarily stem from the public sector.

PSEs have made a notable contribution to the economic growth of the country, particularly by creating a diversified industrial base.

Role and Performance of Public Sector

One may look at the role of public sector in Indian economy in terms of its share in providing employment, its share in investment, its share in national income generated and its share in savings and capital formation.

Public Sector and Employment

Since employment in the public sector is confined to the organised sector, public sector employs 70 per cent of the workers employed in organised sector of the Indian economy (Economic Survey 1999-2000).

TABLE – 17.1

PUBLIC AND PRIVATE SECTOR EMPLOYMENT IN INDIA

(in lakh)

	Public Sector	*Private Sector*	*Total*	*1 as % of 3*
	(1)	*(2)*	*(3)*	*(4)*
1971	71	121	192	55
1981	155	74	229	68
1991	190	77	267	71
1998	194	87	281	70

From Table 17.2, it may be noted that 50 per cent of the total employment (i.e., 194 lakh) in the public sector was in Government administration and community and personal services. The biggest chunk of employment in economic enterprises was in transport, storage and communications was of the order of about 31 lakh and next in importance was manufacturing (17 lakh). 5.3 lakh persons employed in agriculture and other allied activities reflect employment under Employment Guarantee Scheme rather than any productive activity in the normal sense.

The share of public sector in total employment in the organised sector (public plus private) reveals that in transport and communications, electricity, gas and water and construction, the share of the public sector is in the range of 95-98 per cent, a situation of total dominance. However, in manufacturing, the share of the public sector was about 27 per cent of the total since its entry in this area is of recent origin. With the nationalisation of coal mines and takeover of 20 major commercial banks, there has been a significant improvement in the position of the public sector. In an overall sense, the public sector is a big employer (70 per cent of total) insofar as the organised sector of the Indian economy is concerned.

TABLE – 17.2

EMPLOYMENT IN THE PUBLIC SECTOR IN 1998

		(Lakh)	*Per cent of Total*
1.	Manufacturing	16.1	8.5
2.	Transport, Storage and Communications	30.8	15.7
3.	Financing, Insurance, Real Estate and Business Services	12.9	6.6
4.	Government Administration, Community, Social and Personal Services	97.4	50.0
5.	Other Sectors	37.0	19.2
	Total	**194.2**	**100.0**

Source: *Economic Survey* 1999-2000.

Share of the Public Sector in GDP

During the last five decades, the share of the public sector in net domestic product (NDP) has shown a steady improvement. Measured at current prices, public sector accounted for 7.5 per cent NDP in 1950-1951, its share in 1995-96 had risen to 26.2 per cent. Public sector, therefore, accounts for about one-fifth of national output. This is largely due to a rapid expansion of the public sector enterprises.

Despite this fact, the private sector still occupies a dominant position in the economy. There are some sectors such as agriculture and small-scale sector in which the share of the state is almost zero.

The gross value added of the administrative departments, broadly representing Adam Smith's "duties of the sovereign", account for 8 to 9 per cent of GDP; natural monopolies such as the railways and the postal system add another 3 to 4 per cent. But the largest share of public sector gross value added, 12 to 13 per cent of GDP, comes from the non-departmental enterprises (NDEs), producing many private goods and services, but mainly from utilities and infrastructure, owned and operated by the Central, state and local governments. NDEs are further disaggregated into: (a) financial enterprises that are part of the financial sector (including the Reserve Bank of India), and (b) the non-financial enterprises, which account for much of the growth in public sector output during the last half century.[2]

Despite the privatisation accomplished upto the middle of the Tenth Five Year Plan, when the policy changed, the role of PSEs and their contribution to the GDP has not diminished. In fact, the GDP from non-departmental enterprises (NDEs) registered an increase during the first two years of the Tenth Five Year Plan.

In 2004-05, the share of CPSEs in the GDP was 6.82 per cent out of 11.85 per cent for NDEs. The number of operational CPSEs has decreased from 231 in 2001-02, the last year of the Ninth Five Year Plan, to 225 in 2005-06. What is significant is that the number of profit-making CPSEs has gone up from 120 to 157 and the number of loss-making CPSEs has decreased from 109 to 58. The profits of profit-making CPSEs have increased from Rs. 36,432 crore to Rs. 76,240 crore and the losses of loss-making ones have come down from Rs. 10,454 crore to Rs. 5,752 crore during the same period. Table 17.3 gives the macro picture of CPSEs.

Share of the Public Sector in Savings and Capital Formation

Gross domestic capital formation has increased from 10.7 per cent of GNP during the First Plan to 24.6 per cent during the Eighth Plan.

However, the share of the public sector in capital formation improved from 3.5 per cent during the First Plan (1951-1956) to 11.1 per cent in the Sixth Plan but has subsequently declined to 7.1 per cent during the Tenth Plan. The share of the public sector which accounted for one-third of capital formation during the First Plan gradually increased to about one-half during the Sixth Plan, and has thereafter declined to 22 per cent during the Tenth Plan.

2. Nagaraj, R. (2008). "Public Sector Performance since 1950", in K.L. Krishna and Uma Kapila (eds.), *Readings in Indian Agriculture and Industry*. New Delhi: Academic Foundation.

TABLE – 17.3

MACRO VIEW OF CENTRAL PUBLIC SECTOR ENTERPRISES

(Rs. Crore)

	2001-02	*2002-03*	*2003-04*	*2004-05*	*2005-06*	*April-Sept. 2005*	*April-Sept. 2006*
Number of Operating CPSEs	231	226	230	227	225		
Profit before Interest, Tax, and EP (PBITEP)	63190	72539	95039	108420	106533	64962	73169
Capital Employed	289934	417160	452336	504407	581250		
Turnover	478731	572833	630704	744307	832584	377370	468221
Net Profit	25978	32344	52985	64963	70288	27235	35465
Net Profit as % of Turnover	5.4	5.6	8.4	8.7	8.4	7.2	7.6
Profit of Profit-making CPSEs	36432	43316	61606	74433	76240		
Loss of Loss-incurring CPSEs	10454	10972	8522	9356	5952		
Profit-making CPSEs (nos.)	120	119	139	138	157		
Loss-incurring CPSEs (nos.)	109	105	89	79	58		

Source : Public Enterprise Survey 2005-06 and Mid-Year Review of CPSEs for 2006-07, Department of Public Enterprises (DPE).
Government of India, *Eleventh Five Year Plan*, Planning Commission.

However, the share of savings by the public sector has not undergone a similar change. The share of the public sector in gross domestic saving rose from 1.7 per cent of GNP during 1951-1956 to merely 4.6 per cent during the Fifth Plan but declined thereafter and touched a low of -0.8 per cent during Ninth Plan but has increased to 1.9 per cent in the Tenth Plan.

(a) It has been mainly on account of the inefficiency of the government and the public sector enterprises and their consequent failure to generate internal surplus commensurate with the increase in their capital stock.

TABLE – 17.4

SHARE OF PUBLIC AND PRIVATE SECTORS IN GROSS DOMESTIC SAVINGS AND GROSS DOMESTIC CAPITAL FORMATION

Averages for Plan Periods	*Gross Domestic Savings as % of GDP*			*Gross Investment as % of GDP*			*Public Investment as %age of Total Investment*
	Public	*Private*	*Total*	*Public*	*Private*	*Total*	
First Plan: 1951-1956	1.7	8.7	10.4	3.5	7.2	10.7	34.0
Second Plan: 1956-1961	2.0	10.4	12.4	6.6	8.8	15.4	54.6
Third Plan: 1961-1966	3.4	10.9	14.3	8.4	8.3	16.7	63.7
Fourth Plan: 1969-1974	3.0	14.4	17.4	7.2	10.9	18.1	60.3
Fifth Plan: 1974-1979	4.6	17.0	21.6	9.5	11.7	21.2	57.6
Sixth Plan: 1980-1985	3.6	16.5	20.1	11.1	10.5	21.6	52.9
Seventh Plan: 1985-1990	2.3	18.1	20.4	10.7	12.1	22.8	47.8
Eighth Plan: (1992-1997)	2.1	21.0	23.1	8.5	15.9	24.4	34.7
Ninth Plan (1997-98 to 2001-02	-0.8	24.5	23.6	7.0	17.3	24.3	29.0
Tenth Plan (2002-03 to 2006-07)	1.9	30.0	31.9	7.1	25.1	32.1	22.0
Eleventh Plan	4.5	30.3	34.8	8.0	28.7	36.7	21.9
2007-08	39.1	37.7	9.0				
2008-09	NA	NA	8.7				

Source: C.S.O. 1998, National Accounts Statistics, RBI. Compiled from RBI
Handbook of Statistics on Indian Economy (1999) and Economic Survey 1999-2000.
Eleventh Five Year Plan 2007-2012 (Vol. I).

(b) The self-defeating efforts of the government to make up the shortfall in resources through excessive borrowings from the banking sector (better known as deficit financing).

Output and Capital Formation

According to Nagaraj, with the acceleration of the domestic output growth rate after 1980-81, the public sector has contributed to the additional output growth in equal measure (Nagaraj, 1991). In spite of industrial deregulation and growing import competition, the public sector has broadly maintained its share in domestic output in producing private goods and services, and its composition has also remained roughly the same.[3]

In contrast, however, the public investment ratio, after peaking at 12.5 per cent of GDPfc in 1986-87 nearly halved to 6.4 per cent by 2001-02, taking the ratio back to the level where it was in the mid-1950s. Clearly, what took the "big planners" three decades to accomplish, the "reformers" undid in less than two decades!

Whether the fall in the share of public investment by design (market-oriented reforms), or by default (the fiscal imbalance) is a moot point. But undisputedly, the public sector has managed to deliver roughly an unchanging share of the accelerating domestic output for nearly 20 years, even when its investment share was halved—an impressive record of productivity growth by any yardstick, at least so far. Corroborating the finding, also there is a steady decline in the public sector's average capital output ratio (ACOR) in constant prices, from 7.0 in 1981-82 to about 4.4 in 2001-02. This holds true for most (1-digit) sectors of the economy as well (EPWRF, 2004).

It is arguable that the decline in ACOR could mean a shift in public investment to less capital-intensive activities. But this is not the case. In fact, the share of infrastructure (sum of mining, electricity, gas and water, and transport and communication) in public sector gross capital formation—representing capital-intensive industries—has increased from 33.3 per cent in 1973-74 to over 53.5 per cent in 2001-02; the manufacturing sector's share has declined. Infrastructure's share in public sector output narrowly fluctuated around 30 per cent; the manufacturing sector's share has tumbled from 23.7 in 1974-75 to 5.5 per cent in 2001-02. Thus, there is little basis to suggest a shift in public investment into less capital-intensive sectors; on the contrary, the investment composition has moved in the desired direction of

3. Nagaraj (2008). *op.cit.*

infrastructure that is capital-intensive, away from (much contested) manufacturing.

Thus, the public sector has shown remarkable progress that has gone virtually unnoticed. What could account for the improvement? It suggests a decline in what Harvey Leibenstein called X-inefficiency (in production and in organisation), and a deceleration in investment and employment. There is evidence of both (Nagaraj, 2008).

Fall in Public Sector Employment Growth

A bloated workforce, often employed on non-economic considerations, is widely cited as a source of public sector inefficiency. But the evidence suggests that despite such pressures, the growth rate in public employment has declined drastically: from about 6 per cent per year in the mid-1970s to a negative 1 per cent in 2002-03 in public sector enterprises owned and managed by the Central government (central PSEs, for short), in quasi public sector, and in the public sector as a whole as well. Without denying the need for further rationalisation of the workforce, what can certainly be claimed is that public sector employment growth has got drastically reduced in spite of the compulsions to the contrary, contributing to the improved productivity.

Improvement in Efficiency of Thermal Power Plants

Gross inefficiency in thermal power plants, producing the bulk of the nation's electricity generation, is also a widely cited reason for poor productivity. But the average plant load factor (PLF) for all the thermal power plants (a proxy for efficiency) has witnessed an uninterrupted rise from 44.3 per cent in 1979-80 to over 74.8 per cent in 2004-05. Since the electricity sector roughly accounts for about a third of total public investment, such an improvement would have surely contributed to the overall productivity growth noted above.

Although the forgoing measures of physical efficiency display impressive strides, does it show up in the financial results?

The net profits made by the CPSEs has led to the accumulation of large reserves which totalled as much as Rs. 3,53.641.62 crore for 157 profit-making enterprises at the end of the financial year 2006-07. Between 2002-03 and 2005-06, the cash and bank balances of all CPSEs rose from Rs. 53,453 crore to Rs. 1,50,680 crore. Thus, CPSEs have accumulated large amounts of investible funds, which are not being put to productive use.[4]

4. Planning Commission (2008). *Eleventh Five Year Plan* 2007-2012.

The top 10 profit-making CPSEs made a net profit of Rs. 47,371 crore in 2005-06. The ONGC (Rs. 14,431 crore), Bharat Sanchar Nigam Ltd. (BSNL) (Rs. 8,940 crore), National Thermal Power Corporation (NTPC) (Rs. 5,820 crore) were the top three profit-making CPSEs. The top 10 loss-making CPSEs accounted for a net loss of Rs. 4,552 crore, the top three loss-making units being the Fertilizer Corporation of India, Food Craft Institute (FCI) (Rs. 1,294 crore), Hindustan Fertilizer Corporation Limited, HFC (Rs. 965 crore), and Hindustan Photo Films Co. Ltd., (Rs. 561 crore). While the top 10 profit-making enterprises are diversified, the top 10 loss-making enterprises are largely concentrated in manufacturing.

Mid-year review (April-September 2006 against April-September 2005) showed that the turnover of 202 CPSEs (out of 225) for which data was available increased by 24.07 per cent and the net profit increased by 18.18 per cent.[5]

Central PSEs' Profitability

What is the correct measure of profitability? It depends upon the purpose. From the view point of a private individual, the ratio of net profits to equity capital (or net worth) may be appropriate, but it may be unsuitable to measure a PSE's contribution to the economy, for many reasons. One, PSEs usually have a high depreciation cost since they have to invest not only in plant and machinery, but also on social overhead capital, for which budgetary provisions are made. Second, a PSE's capital structure is not aimed to maximise return on shareholders' investment, but provision of goods and services that the market has not (or inadequately) succeeded in supplying—the argument of "missing market". Third, very often PSEs start with a high proportion of debt as government expects a certain interest on its loans. When the enterprise commences production it is often saddled with a high debt-equity ratio, which is usually renegotiated to make the enterprise commercially viable. Finally, for the economy, what matters is not the capital structure but return on total capital employed. Thus, gross profit to total capital employed is a better measure of public sector profitability, which we have used below (Nagaraj, 2008).

Thus measured, according to Nagaraj, profitability of the central PSEs has increased from around 8 per cent in the mid-1970s to 21 per cent in 2003-04—a respectable figure by any reasonable reckoning.

---

5. Ibid.

Such rosy estimates may conceal the effect of high mark-up, cost-based administered pricing in the performance of petroleum companies. Surely, net of the petroleum sector, the profitability is lower, but with an unmistakable rising trend, at 18 per cent return on gross capital employed in 2003-04.

Thus, the central PSEs as a source of NDNFEs' poor financial position is ruled out, leaving us mainly with the utilities and infrastructure services at the state level—that is, state electricity boards (SEBs) and road transport corporations (RTCs). In principle, public irrigation would belong to this category, as it accounts for a sizeable share of plan expenditure in most states.

According to Nagaraj, the real culprit of poor public sector saving is not the central PSEs (that have been the subject of much of reforms) but inadequate pricing of the utilities and infrastructure services, and lack of recovery of user charges for the services rendered. Perhaps a telling evidence of the problem, in the aggregate, is the movement of the public sector price deflator, relative to the GDP deflator since 1960-61. Over the last 40 years, public sector prices never exceeded the overall price level, and in 2003-04 the relative price stood at just 83 per cent of what it was in 1960-61. In other words, public sector prices have risen since 1951 at a slower rate than the overall prices in the economy over the long-run, adversely affecting its financial position. However, as these are decreasing cost industries, their prices can be expected to rise relatively slowly. But they are also capital-intensive industries, where the principle of access to these services on social considerations raises the cost of provision. Moreover, the public sector, being an instrument of public policy is often made to shoulder many social responsibilities, increasing its expenditure, which needs to be recovered from reasonably pricing the output or from the budget. With a growing fiscal imbalance, reasonable pricing is the only avenue to compensate for the services rendered.

The main finding so far according to Nagaraj are:

(1) There is a distinct improvement in the efficiency of resource use in the public sector in the aggregate since the second half of the 1980s, and a corresponding fall in the average capital output ratio.

(2) Improvement in physical efficiency, in part, may reflect a fall in public sector employment growth (however, measured).

(3) Thermal power plants in India that account for the bulk of electricity generation (and a sizeable share of public investment) show an uninterrupted rise in efficiency.

(4) These trends are, however, inadequately reflected in public sector financial performance, despite a sustained improvement in profitability of the central PSEs (even excluding the petroleum enterprises).

(5) Thus, the source of financial distress is the utilities and infrastructure services, like the SEBs, RTCs and the railways.

(6) The SEBs' revenue-cost ratio deteriorated since the 1990s; the same is true of the railways and the RTCs.

(7) That inadequate pricing of the output public sector utilities is the main reason for their deteriorating financial position is illustrated by a 17 percentage point fall in the public sector price deflator output relative to the GDP deflator over the last 40 years since 1960-61.

According to Nagaraj, the real problem is not the lack of efficiency in production, but one of pricing and collection of user charges. Hence, unless these problems are squarely addressed, public sector finances are unlikely to shape up.

Public Sector and 1991 Industrial Policy

To improve the performance of the public sector, the Government of India announced in July 1991 the new Industrial Policy which contained the following decisions pertaining to the public sector.

(i) Portfolio of public sector investments will be reviewed with a view to focus the public sector on strategic, hi-tech and essential infrastructure. Whereas some reservation for the public sector is being retained, there would be no bar for area of exclusivity to be opened up to the private sector selectively. Similarly, the public sector will be allowed entry in areas not reserved for it.

(ii) Public enterprises which are chronically sick and which are unlikely to be turned around will, for the formulation of revival/rehabilitation schemes, be referred to the Board for Industrial and Financial Reconstruction (BIFR), or other similar high level institutions created for the purpose. A social security mechanism will be created to protect the interests of workers likely to be affected by such rehabilitation packages.

(iii) In order to raise resources and encourage wider public participation, a part of the government's share-holding in the public sector would be offered to mutual funds, financial institutions, general public and workers.

(iv) Boards of public sector companies would be made more professional and given greater powers.

(v) There will be a greater thrust on performance improvement through the Memoranda of Understanding (MoU) system through which managements would be granted greater autonomy and will be held accountable. Technical expertise on the part of the Government would be upgraded to make MoU negotiations and implementation more effective.

The Industrial Policy 1991 provides a new approach to public enterprises. The new policy emphasises that measures must be taken to make these enterprises more growth oriented and technically dynamic. According to the New Industrial Policy, the priority areas for growth of public enterprises in the future will be the following: Essential infrastructure goods and services; exploration and exploitation of oil and mineral resources; technology development and building of manufacturing capabilities in areas which are crucial in the long-term development of the economy and where private sector investment is inadequate; manufacture of products where strategic considerations predominate such as defence equipment.

Government will strengthen those public enterprises which fall in the reserved areas of operation or are in high priority areas or are generating good or reasonable profits. Such enterprises will be provided a much greater degree of management autonomy through the system of memoranda of understanding.

Competition will also be induced in these areas for private sector participation. In the case of selected enterprises, part of government holdings in the equity share capital of these enterprises will be disinvested in order to provide further market discipline to the performance of public enterprises common detriment, control of monopolies and prohibition of monopolistic, restrictive and unfair trade practices.

Portfolio of public sector investments will be reviewed with a view to focus the public sector on strategic, high tech and essential infrastructure. Whereas some reservation for the public sector is being retained, there would be no bar for areas of exclusivity to be opened up to the private sector selectively.

Public enterprises which are chronically sick and which are unlikely to be turned around will, for the formulation of revival/rehabilitation schemes, be referred to the Board for Industrial and Financial Reconstruction (BIFR), or other similar high level institutions created for the purpose. A social security mechanism will be created to protect the interests of workers likely to be affected by such rehabilitation packages.

In order to raise resources and encourage wider public participation, a part of the government's shareholding in the public sector would be offered to mutual funds, financial institutions, general public and workers. Boards of public sector companies would be made more professional and given greater powers.

There will be a greater thrust on performance improvement through the memorandum of understanding (MoU) system through which managements would be granted greater autonomy and will be held accountable. Technical expertise on the part of the government would be upgraded to make the MoU negotiations and implementating more effective.

Policies toward CPSEs and their Implementation

In accordance with the mandate in the NCMP, the two main elements of the GoI policy have been devolution of full managerial and commercial autonomy to successful, profit-making companies and modernisation and restructuring of sick PSUs (as well as sell-off or closure of chronically sick CPSEs).

Pursuant to the recommendations of an ad hoc group of experts under the chairmanship of Arjun Sengupta, the government introduced a series of measures for enhancement of financial delegation to *Navratna*s, *Miniratna*s and profit-making CPSEs. These include measures for creation of and disinvestment in subsidiaries, transfer of assets to such subsidiaries and floating of fresh equity.

Under the provisions of Sick Industrial Companies (Special Provisions) Act, 1985, 62 CPSEs had already been referred to the BIFR earlier and during the Tenth Five Year Plan, 12 more were referred to them for considering revival/restructuring/closure. A total of 28 of these had been recommended for winding up. Because of the delays inherent in the process of BIFR, the government has already sought to replace it by the National Company Law Tribunal (NCLT) but the creation of NCLT has been under dispute in the Honourable Supreme Court. Hearing in the special leave petition is already over and the final judgment has been reserved.

The government constituted a Board for Reconstruction of Public Sector Enterprises (BRPSE) in December 2004, as a part time advisory body to address the task of strengthening, modernisation, revival and restructuring of CPSEs. Until February 2007, the BRPSE had considered cases of 46 CPSEs received from 14 administrative ministries/ departments and made recommendations in respect of 40 CPSEs. On the basis of the recommendations of BRPSE, the government has also approved the winding up of one CPSE, namely, Bharat Opthalmic Glass Limited. It has approved revival schemes in respect of 25 CPSEs, envisaging assistance of Rs. 1,951.30 crore in cash by way of equity/ loan/grant and Rs. 5,709 crore by way of waiver of interest/loan/ guarantee fees. Out of the 20 CPSEs for which the budgetary support has been sanctioned for revival, 13 had posted profits after tax in 2005-2006 while the remaining have continued to incur losses. The data for 2006-07 that have been made available in respect of some CPSEs show that while some like the Cement Corporation of India, Heavy Engineering Corporation, Mineral Exploration Corporation Ltd. (MECL), Bharat Compressors Ltd., have shown better financial performance than projected in the revival proposal, others such as Hindustan Antibiotics Ltd. and Andrew Yule & Company Ltd., have been below the projected levels. Thus, rehabilitation proposals have been effective in about 50 per cent of the cases. However, it must be observed here that the improvement in market situation and hand-holding by the government in terms of price preference, placing of orders on nomination basis have also contributed to the success of the revival efforts of the government.

Privatisation

There has been a significant move towards privatisation in economies across the globe. Several industrial countries have embraced it as have most of the transition economies for East Europe and large parts of the developing world. In India, privatisation or disinvestment of the public sector emerged as a major public policy option after the country embarked on a process of economic reforms in 1991.

Privatisation may be broadly defined as the transfer of various activities from the public to the private sphere. Specifically, it could mean the sale by government or state-owned enterprises (SOEs) to private economic agents. It could refer to a sale that is effected in full or in part. It can also mean a partnership between the public and private sectors through a transfer of responsibilities from the public to private sector. In terms of broad political economy, it could also simply mean a shrinking of the welfare state (Nayak, 2007).[6]

Privatisation: Indian Experience since 1991

In 1991, when the government embarked on a comprehensive process of economic reform and liberalisation, the public sector in India accounted for more than one-fifth of the country's GDP. Since a large number of public sector enterprises (PSEs) regularly showed negative profit margins, the government was keen on a programme of privatisation, calling it disinvestment instead.

In the interim budget of 1991-92, the government took a policy decision to disinvest up to 20 per cent of the equity in selected PSUs in favour of mutual funds and financial or investment institutions in the public sector. The disinvestment, which was to broad base the equity, was to improve management and enhance the availability of resources for these enterprises. The Rangarajan Committee report on the Disinvestment of Shares in PSEs in April 1993 emphasised the need for substantial disinvestment, and recommended that the percentage of equity to be divested could go up to 49 per cent for industries especially reserved for the public sector. It recommended that in exceptional cases, such as enterprises that had a dominant market share or where separate identity had to be maintained for strategic reasons, the target public ownership level could be kept at 26 per cent, that is disinvestment could take place to the tune of 74 per cent. In all other cases, it recommended 100 per cent divestment of the government stake. Holding of 51 per cent or more equity by the government was recommended only for six scheduled industries, namely: (i) coal and lignite, (ii) mineral oils, (iii) arms, ammunitions and defence equipment, (iv) atomic energy, (v) radioactive minerals, and (vi) railway transport.

In 1996, the government set up the Disinvestment Commission with a view to formulate procedures so that any decision to disinvest would be taken and implemented in a transparent manner. The revenues generated from such disinvestment were to be allocated for education and health and for creating a fund to strengthen PSEs. By August 1999, the Disinvestment Commission made recommendations on 58 PSEs. The recommendations indicated a shift from public offerings to strategic/trade sales, with transfer of management. The Commission also observed that the essence of a long-term disinvestment strategy should be not only

6. Nayak, Pulin (2007). "Privatisation", in Kaushik Basu (ed.), *The Oxford Companion to Economics in India.*

to enhance budgetary receipts, but also to minimise budgetary support to unprofitable units while ensuring their long-term viability. By 1998, government was of the view that 'in the generality of cases its shareholding in PSEs will be brought down to 26 per cent'. In PSEs involving strategic considerations, namely arms and ammunitions, atomic energy and railway transport, government was to retain majority voting.

By 2000-01, the government's policy regarding privatisation and public sector restructuring comprises the following considerations: restructure and revive potentially viable PSEs, close down PSEs that cannot be revived, bring down government equity in all strategic PSEs to 20 per cent or lower, if necessary, and fully protect the interests of workers. The entire receipt from disinvestments and privatisation was to be used for meeting expenditure in social sectors, restructuring of PSEs and meeting public debt.

The Ministry of Disinvestment was converted into a Department under the Ministry of Finance with effect from 27 May 2004 after the UPA (United Progressive Alliance) government headed by Dr. Manmohan Singh as Prime Minister assumed office. From this point on, the disinvestment programme had to be in conformity with the National Common Minimum Programme. All privatisations were from now on to be considered on a transparent and consultative case-by-case basis. It was made explicit that the UPA would retain the existing *navaratna* companies, which include the BHEL (Bharat Heavy Electricals Limited), in the public sector and that these will be permitted to raise resources from the capital market. The government constituted a 'National Investment Fund' in January 2005 into which the realisation from sale of minority shareholding of the government in profitable PSEs would be channelised. This fund would be maintained outside the Consolidated Fund of India and the income from this Fund would be used for the following purposes: (i) invest in social sector projects that promote education, health care and employment and (ii) capital investment in selected profitable and revivable PSEs that yield adequate returns, in order to enlarge their capital base to finance expansion or diversification (Nayak, 2007).

The total proceeds on account of privatisation from April 1991 to March 2006 amounted to Rs. 49,214 crore. This is just a little above the half mark figure of the target receipts of Rs. 96,800 crore for this period.

In conclusion, we may quote Minhas (1991) which is very relevant even today.[7]

"The choice between the public sector enterprises and private firms is not a simple either/or question. While there may be eminently good reasons for promoting public sector production under certain circumstances, nevertheless there is no basis whatever for the doctrine of the so-called commanding heights. The Indian economy is struggling in the deep swamps of inefficiency. Its deliverance from this inefficiency trap can be vastly facilitated if both the public sector and private firms are exposed more and more to global competition and the arbitrary bureaucratic controls for the regulation of entry and freedom of exit of firms are substantially rolled back."

There is certainly no clear superiority of private *vis-à-vis* public ownership from the standpoint of economic theory. More than ownership, it would seem that the degree of competition and the regulatory environment are more relevant to productive efficiency. The empirical evidence presents a mixed picture. As the world environment gets more competitive, it would be necessary to put the sizeable assets of the PSEs in countries like India to more productive use. Ultimately, it is this consideration that should be of relevance rather than the simplistic presumption that the public sector is necessarily inefficient or that privatisation is an all-purpose panacea (Nayak, 2007).

---

7. Minhas, B.S. (2008). "Public *versus* Private Sector Neglect of Lessons of Economics in Indian Policy Formulation", in Uma Kapila (ed.), *Indian Economy Since Independence*.

Questions

1. What are the causes of poor performance of public sector in India? Will disinvestment of government's share in these units improve their performance? *[B.A. (P) 2009]*
2. Critically examine the performance of public sector in India. Has it fulfilled the role assigned to it? *[B.Com. 2007; B.A. 2008]*
3. Write a brief note on: Disinvestment Policy. *[B.A. (P) 2007]*
4. Write short note on 'Role of public sector'. *[B.Com. (P) 1999, 2006]*
5. Examine the changing roles of private and public sectors in the economic development of India since independence. Do you consider the privatisation of public sector enterprises to be justified? Give reasons for your answer. *[B.Com. (P), Correspondence, 2004]*
6. What are the merits and demerits of public sector? How far is private sector a better choice for faster economic growth of India and why? *[B.A. (P) 2003]*
7. Examine the statement that profitability is not the only criterion to judge the performance of public sector in India. Will you favour disinvestment of government's share in these units to improve their performance? *[B.Com. (P) 2003]*
8. Critically examine the performance of public sector enterprises in India. Would you recommend disinvestment of public sector units? *[B.A. (P) 2000]*
9. What role has been assigned to the public sector in India's economic development? How far has this role been fulfilled? *[B.Com. (P) 1998]*
10. Explain the role played by the public sector enterprises in economic development of India. What are the main reasons for their poor performance? *[B.Com. (P) 1997]*

18

Small Industry

Micro and Small Enterprises

SMALL industry has been one of the major planks of India's economic development strategy since Independence. Today, small industry occupies a position of strategic importance in the Indian economic structure due to its significant contribution in terms of output, exports and employment.

In India, MSEs (till recently, known as village and small enterprises) account for almost 40 per cent of the total industrial production, 95 per cent of the industrial units (along with medium industries) and 34 per cent of the exports. They manufacture over 6000 products ranging from handloom *sarees*, carpets and soaps to pickles, *papads* and machine parts for large industries.

In 2003–04, the contribution of SSI sector alone to the GDP was 6.71 per cent. In the last decade, the growth rate of MSEs has been consistently higher than the overall growth rate of the industrial sector, crossing the 12 per cent mark in the terminal year of the Tenth Plan.

The MSEs are, however, more than just GDP earners; they are instruments of inclusive growth which touch upon the lives of the most vulnerable, the most marginalised—women, Muslims, SCs and STs—and the most skilled. Being the largest source of employment after agriculture, the MSE sector in India enables 650 lakh men, women and children living in urban slums, upcoming towns, remote villages and isolated hamlets to use indigenous knowledge, cultural wisdom, dexterous hands and entrepreneurial skills for the sustenance of their lives and livelihoods (Planning Commission, 2008).[1]

---

1. Planning Commission (2008). *Eleventh Five Year Plan 2007-2012*, Vol. III.

Role of SMEs in Global Economy: International Scenario

Worldwide, MSMEs have been recognised as engines of economic growth.

The overall contribution of small firms—formal and informal—to the GDP and employment remain about the same across low, middle and high-income group countries. As income increases, the share of the informal sector decreases and that of the formal SME sector increases. In Brazil, MSEs represent 20 per cent of the total GDP. Of the country's 4.7 million registered businesses, 96.8 per cent are MSEs and—along with the other 9.5 million informal enterprises—they employ 59 per cent of the economically active population. In Japan, SMEs employ more than 70 per cent of the wage earners, contributing over 55 per cent of value added in the manufacturing sector. In Thailand in 2003, there were 2006528 enterprises of which 99.5 per cent were SMEs. These SMEs generated products worth 38.1 per cent of GDP and in 2003 they employed 60.7 per cent of Thailand's working population.

The real importance of the SMEs, however, can be seen in China where over 68 per cent of the exports come from the SMEs. China has created more SMEs in the last 20 years than the total number of SMEs in Europe and the US combined. Their numbers have increased from about 1 million private sector SMEs in the 1990s to 40 million in 2004.

Defining MSEs—MSMED Act, 2006

There is no globally accepted definition of MSMEs. Different countries use different criterion; most of the definitions are based on investment ceiling and number of people employed. In India, the Micro, Small and Medium Enterprises Development (MSMED) Act, 2006 defines MSMEs. It introduces the concept of 'enterprise' as opposed to the earlier concept of industry. According to the Act, MSMEs are classified into the following: (i) enterprises engaged in the manufacture or production of goods pertaining to any industry specified in the first schedule to the Industries (Development and Regulation Act, 1951) and (ii) enterprises engaged in providing or rendering services. Table 18.1 defines the MSMEs in both these sectors.

The Act also provides for a statutory consultative mechanism at the national level with a balanced representation of all the sections of stakeholders and with a wide range of advisory functions. Establishment of specific funds for promotion, development and enhancement of the competitiveness of these enterprises; notification of schemes/ programmes, progressive credit policies and practices; preference to products and services of MSEs in the government procurement; more effective mechanisms for mitigating the problems of delayed payments; and a scheme for easing the closure of business by these enterprises are some features of the Act.

TABLE – 18.1

DEFINITION OF MSMEs

	Manufacturing Sector
Enterprises	Investment in plant and machinery (original cost excluding land and building and the items specified by the then ministry of small scale industries, vide its notification No. S.O.1722(E) dated 5 October 2006)
Micro Enterprises	Does not exceed Rs. 25 lakh
Small Enterprises	More than Rs. 25 lakh and less than Rs. 5 crore
Medium Enterprises	More than Rs. 5 crore and less than Rs. 10 crore
	Service Sector
Enterprises	Investment in equipments
Micro Enterprises	Does not exceed Rs. 10 lakh
Small Enterprises	More than Rs. 10 lakh and less than Rs. 2 crore
Medium Enterprises	More than Rs. 2 crore and less than Rs. 5 crore

Source : Micro, Small and Medium Enterprises Development Act, 2006.
Planning Commission (2008). *Eleventh Five Year Plan 2007-2012*.

Role of MSEs in Indian Economy

To Generate Large-scale Employment

As countries develop, the share of agriculture in providing employment and in GDP decreases. According to the Australian economist Chris Hall, the SMEs contribute about 70 per cent of net new jobs across the globe, while larger firms tend to be job destroyers.

The MSE sector in India has grown significantly since 1960, when there were only 12376 MSEs providing employment to 10 lakh people—of which, direct employment was 1.85 lakh; annual production level was Rs. 875 crore. At the beginning of the Tenth Plan, 249 lakh people in the rural and urban areas were employed in 105.21 lakh MSEs. This has increased to 295 lakh people in 128 lakh units now; an average annual growth rate of 4.4 per cent in the number of these units and 4.62 per cent in employment. If the units in the *khadi* industries, village industries and coir industries are taken into account, the employment is estimated to be over 332 lakh. With the inclusion of handlooms, handicrafts, wool and sericulture, the total job in the MSE sector in India goes up to 650 lakh. The employment intensity of the registered units indicates that an investment of Rs. 0.72 lakh is required for creating one employment in MSME sector as against Rs. 5.56 lakh in the large organised sector.

Not only do MSEs generate the highest employment per capita investment, they also go a long way in checking rural–urban migration by providing villagers and people living in isolated areas with a sustainable source of employment. Among the MSEs in India, the dispersed food products sector generates maximum employment (13.7 per cent of total employment in the MSE sector), followed by non metallic mineral products (10.9 per cent) and metal products (10.2 per cent). In chemicals and chemical products, machinery parts except electrical parts, wood products, basic metal industries, paper products and printing, hosiery and garments, repair services, and rubber and plastic products, the contribution ranges from 9 per cent to 5 per cent. In all other industries, the contribution is less than 5 per cent.

Per unit employment is highest (20) in units engaged in beverages, tobacco and tobacco products. Next come cotton textile products (17), non-metallic mineral products (14.1), basic metal industries (13.6), and electrical machinery and parts (11.2). Per unit employment is highest (10) in the metropolitan areas and lowest (5) in the rural areas. Non metallic products contribute 22.7 per cent to the employment generated in the rural areas, followed by food products (21.1 per cent), wood products, and chemicals and chemical products. As for the urban areas, food products and metal products almost equally share 22.8 per cent employment. Machinery parts except electrical, non-metallic mineral products, and chemicals and chemical products between them account for another 26.2 per cent employment. Metal products, machinery and parts except electrical, and paper products and printing (total share being 33.6 per cent) are the leading industries in metropolitan areas (Planning Commission, 2008).

To Sustain Economic Growth and Increase Exports

According to 11th Plan estimates in order to achieve the target of 10 per cent growth in the Eleventh Plan, the MSE sector needs to grow at 12 per cent.

Non-traditional products account for more than 95 per cent of the SSI exports. The performance of garments, leather, and gems and jewellery units has been remarkable in the last decade. The SSI sector dominates in export of sports goods, readymade garments, woollen garments and knitwear, plastic products, processed food and leather products. The US, Europe and West Asia are the major export destinations.

There is tremendous potential to expand the quantum of exports from traditional MSEs because they are handcrafted and hence ecofriendly and exclusive. Further, while MSEs are unable to take advantage of economies of scale, they are ideal for meeting small order quantities—a bonus in industries such as readymade garments, home furnishings, etc.

MSEs often act as ancillary industries for LSIs providing them with raw materials, vital components and backward linkages. For instance, large cycle manufacturers of Ludhiana rely heavily on the small MSEs of Malerkotla which produce cycle parts. MSEs also promote ecofriendly growth, especially in difficult terrains and the ecologically sensitive areas. In large tracts of barren desert land in Barmer and Kutch, in the scattered *dhanis* of Udaipur, in the hilly hamlets of J&K, Ladakh, Himachal and the Northeast, in the tribal hinterlands of central India, they are the only source of livelihood.

For Making Growth Inclusive

The MSE sector facilitates inclusive growth and take care of all vulnerabilities—it touches upon the lives of women, children, minorities, SCs and STs in the villages, in the urban slums and in the deprived pockets of flourishing towns and cities. For many families, it is the only source of livelihood. For others, it supplements the family income. Thus, instead of taking a welfare approach, this sector seeks to empower people to break the cycle of poverty and deprivation. It focuses on people's skills and agency.

Different segments of the MSE sector are dominated by different social groups. Women are mostly found in the unregistered sector—food processing enterprises, manufacturing enterprises and weaving—and often work part time in the family enterprises. Women and small children roll *bidis*, make *agarbattis*, do *zari* and sequin work for meagre wages. Large number of Muslims are found in the unorganised weaving sector and in powerlooms. In the Northeast, most women weave. In states like Tripura, 50 per cent of rural men and 35 per cent rural women are engaged in MSEs. In Nagaland and Mizoram, over 68 per cent of urban men are with MSEs (Planning Commission, 2008).

Globalisation and Small Industry Performance[2]

The overall performance and contribution of small industry to the Indian economy is generally described in terms of its absolute growth in units, employment, production and exports. Equally important is its relative contribution, which can be analysed in terms of small industry share in national income, total exports and total organised sector employment. Thus, the growth performance of small industry can be evaluated in two ways:

(1) To compare the growth rates of units, employment, output and exports of small industry in the 1990s with that of the 1980s.

(2) To ascertain the change in small industry's relative contribution to GDP, exports and organised sector employment in the 1990s with that of the 1980s.

This, according to Bala Subrahmanya, will reveal how the sector is coping with challenges and changes in the intensifying competitive environment emerging since 1990-91. The growth rates of small industry in terms of units, employment, output and exports for the 1980s and 1990s are presented in Table 18.2. It is clear that the growth of small industry in the transitional period of 1990s has come down not only in terms of units and employment but also output. This could be an indication that increasing competition in the globalisation period does affect the growth of Indian small industry adversely. However, the growth rate of exports has actually increased marginally. To probe the growth pattern further, growth rates are estimated for five-year periods for both the 1980s and 1990s. They also broadly correspond to India's five year plans, namely, the Sixth, Seventh, Eighth and Ninth Five Year Plans. The scenario does not differ much, except for exports (Table 18.2). The growth rates of units and employment have steadily come down. But the growth rates of output and more importantly, exports have fluctuated. In fact, the growth rate of output increased in the late 1980s compared with the early 1980s but then declined in the early 1990s and further in the late 1990s. Whereas the growth rate of exports increased steadily till the early 1990s but then declined considerably.

---

2. Subrahmanya Bala, M.H. (2009). "Small Industry and Globalisation: Implications, Performance and Prospects", in K.L. Krishna and Uma Kapila (eds.) *Readings in Indian Agriculture and Industry*. New Delhi: Academic Foundation.

TABLE – 18.2

GROWTH OF SMALL INDUSTRY: 1990s *VS* 1980s

	Period	*Units**	*Employment**	*Output**	*Exports**
I.	1980s	18.40	5.84	18.66	19.38
	1990s	5.62	4.00	15.31	20.62
II.	1980-81 to 1985-86	9.18	6.21	16.88	11.00
	1985-86 to 1990-91	7.63	5.47	20.46	28.40
	1990-91 to 1995-96	6.88	4.02	18.05	30.42
	1995-96 to 2000-01	4.37	3.99	12.62	11.56

Note: * Figures represent compound average rate of growth (CARG).

Source : SIDBI (1999), GoI (2002).
Bala Subrahmanya (2009).

The other dimension of small industry performance is its relative contribution to national income (GDP), exports and employment. The contribution of small industries is considered for three periods of time: 1980-81, 1990-91 and 2000-01 (Table 18.3). The share of small industry in national income increased in the protection period of the 1980s but declined considerably in the transitional period of the 1990s. The share of small industry in exports and its employment in relation to organised sector employment have consistently increased both in the protection period and in the transitional period. But the increase in the share of small industry in total exports was more significant in the protection period of the 1980s than in the transitional period of the 1990s. However, the increase in the relative share of small industry employment was more significant in the 1990s than in the 1980s. Small industry employment (which included partly unorganised manufacturing sector employment as well) was equivalent to about 31 per cent of the total organised sector employment in 1980-81. It went up to nearly 48 per cent of the organised sector employment in 1990-91. By 2000-01, small industry employment increased to two-thirds of the organised sector employment. That is, though the growth rate of small industry employment has come down in the 1990s, it has increased more than proportionately in the period of globalisation compared with the protection period, with respect to other sectors of the Indian economy. As a result, its size relative to organised sector employment has gone up.

TABLE – 18.3

SMALL INDUSTRY IN NATIONAL INCOME, EXPORTS AND EMPLOYMENT

(Per cent)

Year	*National Income*	*Exports*	*Employment*
1980-81	9.2	24.5	31.0
1990-91	11.0	29.7	47.6
2000-01	7.8*	30.9	66.4

Note: * For the year 1997-98.

Source : GoI (1998, 2002), RBI (2001); EPW Research Foundation (2002). Bala Subrahmanya (2009).

Problems/Constraints faced by Small Industry

On the whole, small industry performance does indicate that the sector faces a tough challenge for its survival and growth in the period of globalisation.

Infrastructural Bottlenecks

The pertinent issue is, why should liberalisation and globalisation affect Indian small industry to such an extent? The reasons are not far to seek. A substantial majority of Indian small industry does not have access to reliable and efficient infrastructure even today, which in turn impedes small industry competitiveness. According to Kulkarni and Parishwad (2001), about 40 per cent of the 2.6 lakh small industry units in Karnataka have been closed due to infrastructural bottlenecks and lack of orders from PSUs, among others. In Peenya Industrial Estate, Bangalore, which is considered to be the largest in south and south-east Asia, only about 2,000 units function out of the total 3,500 units, and lack of infrastructure and competition are considered to be the major causal factors (Menon and Raghunandan, 2003).

The infrastructural constraints confronted by small industry can be broadly classified as economic, technological, marketing and financial. Stable and reliable economic infrastructure such as power, water, transport and communications are a prerequisite for the efficient functioning of any economic activity, including small industry. Inadequate economic infrastructure is a major factor that affects the performance and competitiveness of small industry.

Technological Obsolescence

Technological obsolescence has been a characteristic of small industry in India across a wide variety of sectors. In the early 1990s, two survey-based studies showed that technological obsolescence in the small industry affects quality and productivity adversely.

However, the need for improving the competitive strength of small industry through technology improvement and modernisation was recognised as early as in the 1950s, with the setting up of the Small Industries Development Organisation (SIDO) and a network of small industries service institutes (SISIs), National Small Industries Corporation (NSIC) and National Research Development Corporation (NRDC). Since then, over a period of time, particularly in the 1990s, exclusive technology infrastructure has come up for small industry to facilitate technology transfer (Bala Subrahmanya *et al.,* 2002). Thus, policy makers in India have considered technology development in small industry only from a single dimension, that is, through institutional technology transfer. This implies that small industry in India is perennially external-technology dependant.

Finance

Timely availability of adequate finance is another issue that crucially determines the survival and growth of small firms. Small firms are largely dependent on bank credit to meet their financing requirements, while large firms have alternative sources of finance (RBI, 2003). To ensure better financial infrastructure, SIDBI was set up in 1990. Today, SIDBI operates through the head office, five regional offices and 36 branch offices across the country (SIDBI, 2002). In addition, based on the recommendations of the Nayak committee, set up by RBI (1992), 370 exclusive bank branches for small industry were set up by public sector banks by 1998 (DCSSI, 1999). Further, as per the Nayak committee recommendations, the Reserve Bank of India has directed banks to meet the working capital needs of small industry at the rate of 20 per cent of annual output subject to an individual upper limit of Rs. 20 million (DCSSI, 1999). However, despite the development of exclusive financial infrastructure for small industry, growth in the amount of bank credit extended to small industry declined in the 1990s from that in the 1980s. In fact, the decline in growth rate was more pronounced relative to total priority sector, medium- and large-scale industry sector and total non-food bank credit. As a result, credit to small industry as a percentage of non-food gross bank credit increased marginally from about 14 per cent in 1980-81 to 15.14 per cent in 1990-91 but declined to 13 per cent in 2000-01. Further, the total bank credit extended to small industry as a percentage of small industry output declined marginally from about 9.4 per cent in 1993-94 to 8.7 per cent in 2000-01. This shows that despite policy support, credit flow to small industry has actually declined relatively in the 1990s (Bala Subrahmanya, 2009).

Lending to micro enterprises, which is stipulated at 60 per cent of the total credit to MSE sector, has fallen from 51.2 per cent in 2002–2003 to 45.1 per cent at the end of 2005-06. Moreover, difficulty in arranging collaterals or third-party guarantees continues to be a problem. Though the RBI had issued instructions to advance collateral free loans up to Rs. 5 lakh, at the end of 2005-06, only 24 per cent of the total outstanding loans under Rs. 5 lakh were without collaterals. The high cost of credit to MSEs also impacts the competitiveness of their products.

Non-availability of Quality Raw Materials and Packaging Facilities on a Timely Basis

Non-availability of quality raw materials such as dyes and yarn (especially for handlooms and powerlooms); vital inputs such as power (for powerlooms, handicrafts, other industrial MSEs); and proper packaging facilities continue to be a major bottleneck. Lack of credit combined with inadequate raw materials often forces weavers, artisans and entrepreneurs into the clutches of loan sharks and middlemen. The modern manufacturing MSE units are also constrained due to non availability of quality raw materials in adequate quantity. Though the National Small Industries Corporation (NSIC) and State Small Scale Industries Development Corporations are providing some raw materials, their efforts are not in consonance with the requirements.

Insufficient Market Research, Linkages and Design Inputs

Most MSEs do not have money to invest in market research and are unable to carry out design and technical improvements to keep up with market demands. Unlike big businesses, they cannot invest in advertising and packaging. This limits their ability to tap markets and attract consumers.

Many segments of MSE, especially the traditional sectors, find it difficult to compete against aggressive marketing by the big domestic and multinational players. Street vendors, petty traders, handloom and powerloom weavers, home-based food processing units, *khadi* institutions, *attar* (perfumers), *zari* workers and rural artisans, many of whom have even lost livelihoods and places of work due to developmental works, are the worst affected. There is a need to evolve a constructive response to this situation. As these sectors employ the most marginalised, our indigenous/traditional industries should be given opportunities to tap both the domestic and international markets.

Technology Upgradation and Achieving 'Economies of Scale'

The investment ceiling on plant and machinery used for defining the small-scale units create problems. Efforts such as raising investment ceiling to Rs. 5 crore for micro and small-scale units will help these units to graduate to medium-scale enterprises. The Tenth Plan schemes such as TUFS and SITP, which have helped some units to modernise, will be continued in the Eleventh Plan as well. There is an urgent need to devise measures to tackle the problem of loss of fiscal benefits when the micro and small-scale units graduate into larger units. The general excise duty exemption, which was traditionally available to the SSIs, is now restricted to Rs. 1.5 crore of the transactions, a figure which is largely insignificant for many of the larger SSEs. As has been demonstrated by units such as Hero Cycles, Nirma detergents, Videocon and Onida electronics, and vertical expansion and upward movement of MSEs to the medium and large sector enables them to achieve economies of scale. But today, MSEs are encouraged to go for horizontal expansion and deliberate fragmentation, mainly to stay within the limits of excise exemptions.

Owing to liberalisation and opening up of the economy, the MSEs are facing stiff competition from imports and need technological upgradation to produce better quality products at cheap rates. They should be able to access production supply units around the world through the Internet. Information dissemination about availability of recent technologies, literature on modern machinery, contact details of suppliers, etc., is essential. A Technology Bank could be set up for this purpose. There is a need to intensify implementation of the Credit Linked Capital Subsidy Scheme (CLCSS) along with ready availability of model modernisation projects for manufacturing industries (11th Five Year Plan 2007-2012).

Rehabilitation of Sick Units

The major causes of sickness in the SSI sector, as per the Third Census of SSI (2001-02), were lack of demand, shortage of working capital, non-availability of raw material, power shortage, marketing problems, etc. Combining the three yardsticks used to measure sickness, *viz.*, (i) delay in repayment of loan over one year, (ii) decline in net worth by 50 per cent, and (iii) decline in output in last three years, 13.98 per cent of the units in the registered SSI sector and 6.89 per cent in the unregistered sector were either sick or incipiently sick. In the total SSI sector, this percentage was 7.82 per cent. The five states of Kerala, Tamil Nadu, Andhra Pradesh, Karnataka and Maharashtra together accounted for 54.28 per cent of the sick/incipiently sick SSI units in the country.

Future Prospects of Small Industry

The central issue of concern for the growth of small industry is how to strengthen its competitiveness. First of all, if small industry has to thrive steadily, infrastructural bottlenecks must be overcome to enable it to compete on its own based on inherent potential. And it is the responsibility of the government to remove any structural bottleneck in small industry performance especially when market forces are given prominence through the removal of 'protective elements'. It is essential to provide the much-needed 'level playing field' to small enterprises through infrastructure development. But overcoming infrastructural bottlenecks for small enterprises is easier said than done.

Small enterprises in India have come up in an unplanned, uncontrolled and haphazard manner. They have emerged anywhere and everywhere—closer to the location of resources as well as markets—in clusters as well as in a dispersed manner, in industrial, commercial and residential areas. Of these, the 2000-odd small industry clusters vary in size with a population ranging from 100 to 1,000 units. Approximately, these clusters would account for 1/3 to 1/2 of the total small industry units in the country. A considerable majority of these clusters are based on natural and traditional skills. By and large, these clusters lack reliable and efficient infrastructural facilities such as power, road, water, transportation and communications, information and technical inputs. But the infrastructural problem is more acute in case of units that are located in a dispersed manner. How does one promote infrastructure to support small industry development?

To enable efficient monitoring and provision of infrastructural facilities, small enterprises should be permitted to come up only in designated industrial areas or estates. Each state should be asked to develop a database of small enterprises, which should be updated at least once in three years with the help of district industries centres (DICs). There is an urgent need to introduce a system of delisting closed registered small industry units (Planning Commission, 2002). This will facilitate 'policy corrections' from time to time. DICs must be revitalised and made the nodal centres for the provision of all infrastructural facilities for small industries at the district level. DICs should have information about the sources of technology and material inputs, opportunities for subcontracting/outsourcing. The ongoing process of 'networking of DICs' is welcome as it will enable effective information dissemination across the country (Bala Subrahmanya, 2009).

In addition, the state governments along with industry associations should involve the private sector in the development of infrastructure in existing industrial estates and clusters and permit provision of infrastructural services on payment. Similarly, private sector investment should be encouraged for the development and management of existing as well as new industrial parks/clusters/estates (Hussain, 1997). Development of industrial parks/estates/clusters should be treated on par with infrastructure development and state governments should prepare guidelines for private investments. These steps would go a long way in strengthening the infrastructure for small industry development in India.

Further, subsequent to the recommendation of the Planning Commission's expert committee on small scale enterprises (Planning Commission, 2001), the government has now decided to cover the entire country by integrated infrastructure development (IID) schemes. This is a welcome development. But the government has not set up any time frame for its completion.

There is a need to explicitly recognise and exploit the 'innovation potential' of small enterprises. In developed countries, small enterprises are promoted, among others, as the 'seed bed' of innovation (Bala Subrahmanya *et al.*, 2002). Small enterprises have the specific advantages of flexibility, concentration and internal communications for carrying out technological innovations. Technological innovations contribute to competitiveness. Even in the Indian context, a significant number of small firms do carry out technological innovations and thereby, enhance their competitiveness (Bala Subrahmanya *et al.*, 2002). Therefore, it is appropriate to incorporate schemes in the existing policy and institutional network to provide technological and financial assistance to in-house technological innovations at the district level and make it easily accessible to small enterprises.

There is a need to create R&D fund at the state level for disbursement as margin money through DICs to small industry units to encourage them to undertake formal an R&D and technological innovations. In addition, the Department of Science and Technology (DST) may allocate funds to universities and engineering institutions, which could provide institutional infrastructure for R&D or conduct R&D for small industry units at the regional level (Bala Subrahmanya *et al.*, 2002).

These schemes are not to undermine the significance of the present strategy of 'technology transfer'. It is essential to pursue with more intensity the existing strategy of technological upgradation and modernisation by involving local governments and small industry associations, particularly with a focus on small industry clusters. However, it needs to be emphasised that the technological transformation of Indian small industry is a gigantic task and that government alone cannot achieve this objective, however extensive its infrastructure may be. Therefore, the major initiative has to come from small industry itself, particularly through their associations. The importance of 'achieving and sustaining competitiveness in the long run' and investing 'self-efforts and resources' needs to be realised and spread among small industry units through its associations at the regional level. This will have a crucial role to play in its long-term development.

The increase in the competitiveness of small industry will also be determined by the availability and quantum of finance. The demand for finance, implicit as well as explicit, from small industry will be substantial considering its size, structure, growth pattern, need for restructuring and technology development (Bala Subrahmanya, 2002a). Particularly, the investment demand for finance from small industry will increase considerably due to technology upgradation and modernisation, expansion (of efficient ones), quality improvement, R&D and technological innovations, and environment-related investments (industry-specific). In South Korea, expansion and modernisation together accounted for more than 50 per cent of the total investment demand for finance of small and medium enterprises (SMEs) in the 1980s, that is, when the Korean economy was undergoing industrial restructuring. R&D demand formed a meagre 0.2 per cent of the total investment demand of SMEs in 1982, but went up to 1 per cent by 1986 (ADB, 1997). To meet the growing and diversified investment demand requirements, it is essential to broaden financial infrastructure, specifically to take care of the technological transformation of small industry and lay more thrust on adequate flow of finance to the sector (Bala Subrahmanya, 2002a).

Globalisation and liberalisation need not affect Indian small industry only adversely. It would have created beneficial opportunities as well. The removal of quantitative restrictions and the reduction of import duties, particularly after the setting up of WTO in 1995, have opened up foreign markets to Indian small industry as much as the Indian market has opened up to foreign goods. Many efficient and export-oriented small firms would have gained out of this development. Such opportunities should act as an incentive to many a small firm in India to enhance their competitiveness to penetrate the global market. This could also be achieved by small firms becoming vendors or subcontractors to foreign large-scale industries. The trend is outsourcing of supplies by TNCs and they are always on the lookout for firms that could supply reliable and quality products (Sabade, 2001).

As in other countries, globalisation can also act as a tool for development of the MSE sector. MSEs engaged in the manufacturing of engineering and automobile products have shown excellent growth in the past decade due to their expertise in supplying OEM assemblies and sub-assemblies, components, etc. What is needed is a rational policy which offers adequate support and protection to this sector, enabling it to reach Indian markets. MSEs have many inherent advantages such as exclusivity, ability to produce small order quantities, etc. In a globalised world, they can tap new markets, especially in the West where there is a big demand for handcrafted products. Information technology can be used as a tool to provide online information on indigenous products and producers, while the GI Act and patents can be used to prevent cheap imitations of our designs and products by other countries.

In fact, outsourcing is the major factor contributing to the growth of the Indian software industry (MoF, 2001) and business process outsourcing (BPO) (*EPW*, 2003). After software and BPO, auto parts is being mentioned as the site of the next big outsourcing wave likely to bring in a clutch of investors looking for a low-cost, high quality production base. A number of the world's largest automobile and equipment-makers have already announced plans to source parts from Indian companies or expand their own production operations in the country, especially for export. This trend is likely to gain further momentum as a recession-hit global automotive industry struggles to cut production costs (*EPW*, 2003). Such opportunities should be exploited with concerted efforts in other industries as well by the government, small industries and their associations working together.

Finally, irrespective of the degree of support extended by the government and irrespective of the amount of effort put in by small industries and their associations, India is going to experience the emergence of the small industry sector, which is qualitatively superior, technologically vibrant and internationally competitive, in the next 5-10 years because the 'inefficient ones' are likely to vanish gradually. The objective of the policy makers as well as small industry associations should be to enable the sector to be vibrant and competitive without a considerable reduction in its size and thereby, enable it to make a sustainable contribution to national income, output and exports (Bala Subrahmanya, 2009).

Eleventh Plan Strategies for Promotion of MSEs

The Eleventh Plan approach to the MSE sector marks a shift from the welfare approach to that of empowerment. The Plan looks at this sector as an engine for sustained and inclusive economic growth and employment. The strategy is two-pronged—it focuses on livelihood and social security. This is not just a rights issue but also makes economic common sense—artisans and entrepreneurs can be most productive only when they are physically and mentally fit.

The Eleventh Plan considers the MSE sector as an important segment of industry which is unorganised and hence, needs support and access to all schemes of industry with special enabling provisions.

Thus, providing enabling provisions for artisans, weavers and small entrepreneurs within industrial policies and schemes will automatically fulfil the constitutional requirement and the commitments made by various Plans. While planning infrastructure development for industries, the needs of the micro and small sector would be kept in mind. There is need to move from adversarial to complementary relationships between various segments of industry and MSE. For instance, handlooms can target hi-end exclusive products—stoles, shawls, *sarees*, and furnishings—while powerloom mills do bulk production for *gamcha*s, *dhoti*s, towels, bed and table linen, etc. Big brands can continue to develop products such as suitings, shirtings, t-shirts, etc.

The MSE sector, including handlooms and handicrafts, presents an opportunity for exports. Exclusivity, which stems from the dispersed nature of this sector, is its biggest strength. And yet, the dispersed nature of the sector makes it difficult to meet bulk orders, raises quality control issues, robs the workers of bargaining power, limits access to credit and markets, results in absence of social security, and prevents enterprises from benefiting from economies of scale. The effort during the Plan period will therefore be to organise this sector, to create clusters and SHGs of weavers/artisans to improve their bargaining power and to enable them to pool resources. These groups, comprising weavers, artisans and entrepreneurs, will be given full control over cluster decisions and will be provided support in the form of credit, inputs, expertise and marketing links.

The Working Group on MSMEs for the Eleventh Plan had projected the need for Rs. 2,96,400 crore as the working capital and term loans for MSEs during the Eleventh Plan. At present, there is no subsector target for the MSE sector within the overall stipulated 40 per cent ceiling for the priority sector lending.

For micro and small entrepreneurs who cannot bring in sufficient equity/promoter's contribution, a flexible debt–equity ratio may need to be adopted while sanctioning export credit. Banks will be encouraged to ensure that all loans upto Rs. 5 lakh to MSEs (excluding credit from MFIs) are given free of collateral at the interest rate of 8 per cent. Coverage under the Credit Guarantee Trust Fund will be increased. As international experience indicates cluster-based financing is the most effective way of providing credit to MSEs, 100 MSE clusters based on the PPP model will be adopted on a pilot basis.

During the Eleventh Plan period, an aggressive marketing campaign using the media and icons will be launched. Handlooms, handicrafts, food processing and other cultural industries will be linked to tourism. In the West, the cultural industries have become the most rapidly growing sector in the world, contributing over 7 per cent of the world's GDP. Giving an 'industry' status to craftspersons is important because it entitles them to tax benefits and export promotion schemes, makes them eligible for banking and credit support, and helps them lobby for protection of intellectual property.

An effective preference policy for procurement of goods and services produced by MSEs both at Central and state levels will be developed. A policy for women in the micro and small sector, particularly in the unorganised segments, will also be formulated to ensure that women get their rights and that their special needs are catered to.

New Initiatives

The Small Industries Development Organisation now called Micro, Small and Medium Enterprises Development Organisation has a network of more than 3000 technically qualified personnel working through its small industries service institutes (and branch SISIs), testing centres and autonomous organisations such as the tool room, product and process development centres, etc. In the Eleventh Plan, the Ministry of MSME will establish a Technology Mission to promote new and emerging technologies, assess present levels of technology and their upgrdation, set up technology information centres/data banks and an IT portal for information dissemination to carry out detailed technology audits.

In 2006, the government launched the National Manufacturing Competitiveness Programme. The NMCC and the Ministry of MSME chalked out a five-year programme with a projected expenditure of Rs. 850 crore. The programmes include: setting up of design clinics, application of lean manufacturing technologies for increasing competitiveness of firms by systematically identifying and eliminating waste throughout the business cycle. These programmes will be demand driven and will be implemented in the PPP mode in selected industrial clusters.

Infrastructural constraints, notably the power outages, affect the MSEs much more than the larger enterprises. Although some states do offer differential power tariffs in favour of the MSEs, the real deficiency is the quality and quantity of power supply. During the Eleventh Plan, group/associations of the MSEs will be incentivised to establish captive power plants as enjoined in the Electricity Act, 2003 or to set up common large-scale generation facilities with dedicated feeder lines. Roads, transport, water and other infrastructure problems, or their total absence, push up operating costs of MSEs as against goods produced in more favourable conditions in other countries and it is, therefore, imperative for the government to develop adequate infrastructure.

Labour laws and factory laws have created problems for MSE units in terms of number of inspections. The committee set up under Member (Industry) Planning Commission recommended a system of third-party inspection to give enterprises an option to get their regulatory compliance certified by accredited agencies. Once such certification has been obtained, the unit would be exempted from routine inspection. Special inspections would be authorised only on receipt of credible complaints. Early implementation of this recommendation during the Eleventh Plan will provide relief to the MSMEs.

A proper database is critical for formulation of appropriate schemes for the MSE sector. The recently announced 'Package for Promotion of Micro and Small Enterprises (SMEs)' contains a proposal for providing financial support to the MSE Associations for their capacity building and for strengthening the database and contacts with the grassroots. This initiative would be carried forward during the Eleventh Five Year Plan.

An outlay of Rs. 11500 crore has been allocated to Ministry of MSME, out of which Rs. 4000 crore is for DC (MSME) and Rs. 7500 crore is for agro and rural industries.[3]

Summary and Conclusions

Small industry in India has found itself in an intensely competitive environment since 1991, thanks to globalisation, domestic economic liberalisation and dilution of sector-specific protective measures. As a result, its growth in terms of units, employment, output and exports has come down. This has resulted in a less impressive growth in its contribution to national income and exports, though not in terms of employment, in the 1990s. Lack of reliable and stable economic infrastructure, reduced growth of credit inflow and technological obsolescence, which together would have led to inferior quality and low productivity are the major bane of small industry in India.

But at the same time, international and national policy changes have thrown open new opportunities and markets for the Indian small industry. Concerted effort is needed from the government and small industry to imbibe technological dynamism. Technological upgradation and in-house technological innovations and promotion of inter-firm linkages need to be encouraged consciously and consistently. The benefits and need to go for technology development, through either technology transfer or technological innovations or inter-firm linkages should be emphasised in the light of the dimensions of global competition and its negative fallouts as well as opportunities, to small industry entrepreneurs through seminars and workshops at the local level. Financial infrastructure needs to be broadened and adequate inflow of credit to the sector be ensured taking into consideration the growing investment demand, including the requirements of technological transformation. Small industry should be allowed to come up only in designated industrial areas for better monitoring and periodic surveys through DICs which should enable policy corrections from time to time. A technologically vibrant, internationally competitive small industry should be encouraged to emerge, to make a sustainable contribution to national income, employment and exports. It is essential to take care of the sector to enable it to take care of the economy.[4]

---

3. Planning Commission (2008). *op.cit.*
4. Subrahmanya (2009). *op.cit.*

Questions

1. Write a short note on Problems of small scale industries. *[B.A. (P) 2009]*
2. What is the difference between small scale and cottage industries in India? What role they have played in our economic development. *[B.Com. 2008]*
3. What are the problems faced by small and cottage industries in India. How far have these problems been redressed by the New Small Enterprises Policy? *[B.A. 2007]*
4. Write a brief note on: Problems of the cottage and small-scale industries in India. *[B.Com. 2007, 2008]*
5. What role can cottage and small-scale sectors play in modern India? Briefly outline measures adopted byt he government ot promote the growth of this sector. *[B.Com. 2006]*
6. Why should cottage and small-scale industries be encouraged in India? Give reasons for your answer. *[B.A. 2005]*
7. Examine the case of small-scale industries in a market-oriented economy. Suggest measures to promote these industries. *[B.Com. 2005]*
8. What do you understand by small-scale industries? Examine their role in the economic development of a country like India. In this context, what policy changes would you advocate. *[B.A. 2004]*
9. Discuss the importance of small scale and cottage industries in India. What steps are being taken by the government to solve their problems. *[B.Com. 2004]*
10. Discuss the importance of small scale and cottage industries in India. What steps are have been suggested in the industrial policy of 1991 to improve their position? *[B.A. 2003]*
11. What is the difference between cottage and small scale industries. What are the difficulties faced by these industries in India. *[B.A. 2002]*
12. What are the various problems faced by small scale industries? Comment on their relevance in the present Indian context. *[B.A. 2001]*
13. Discuss the role of small-scale and cottage industreis in India. What are the problems faced by it and what solution would you recommend. *[B.Com. 2001]*

19

Foreign Capital and Multinational Corporations

The Debate on the Role of Foreign Capital

THEORETICAL and empirical research on the role of foreign capital in the growth process have generally yielded conflicting results. Conventionally, the two-gap approach justifies the role of foreign capital for relaxing the two major constraints to growth—the saving constraint or gap and the foreign-exchange constraint or gap. Saving-investment gap i.e., resource gap between targeted or desired investment and locally mobilised savings.

The second contribution, analogous to the first, is its contribution to filling the gap between targeted foreign-exchange requirements and those derived from net export earnings plus net public foreign aid. This is the so-called foreign-exchange or trade gap (Todaro, 2004: 639).

With the growing influence of the new growth theories in the second half of the 1980s that recognised the effects of positive externalities associated with capital accumulation on growth, the role of foreign capital in the growth process assumed renewed importance. In the endogenous growth framework, the sources of growth attributed to capital flows comprise:

- the spillovers associated with foreign capital in the form of technology, skills and introduction of new products;
- the positive externalities in terms of higher efficiency of domestic financial markets;
- improved resource allocation and efficient financial intermediation by domestic financial institutions.

In brief, foreign capital supplements domestic savings and thus provides larger capital resources for development, facilitates developmental imports and thus reduces balance of payments difficulties, brings in modern technology and managerial skills, ensure better use of capital and save the country from problems related to repayment of foreign loans.

FORMS OF FOREIGN CAPITAL

Foreign Direct Investment

Capital flows in the form of FDI have been widely believed to be an important source of growth in recent years. FDI is the best means of transferring business knowledge from the developed countries. This consists not only of technology defined in the conventional sense of production processes for existing and new products, but also organisational, managerial, marketing, distribution, procurement and logistics knowledge and systems.[1] Favourable tax treatment, protected domestic market and low labour costs represent the primary pull factors for FDI. Sound policies, strong and resilient financial systems and liberal exchange control norms also help in creating the congenial environment for augmented inflows under FDI.

Growth impulses originating from FDI are primarily ascribed to superior technology and greater competition that generally accompany FDI. Local firms of many developing host countries also do not invest enough on R&D to offer and sustain competition with Transnational Corporations (TNCs). Investment on R&D by TNCs in foreign affiliates is, however, found to be low, accounting for as little as 1 per cent of the total R&D investment even though TNCs are generally viewed as R&D intensive (UNCTAD, 1999). Despite the usual concerns that inappropriate technology is generally transferred to the foreign affiliates, empirical assessments suggest that technology—both public and private—that accompany FDI are complementary and inter-firm collaboration helps in augmenting growth. In such cases also, FDI may augment growth in a country if its initial technology gap is higher and openness to FDI is significant.

Whether FDI promotes competition or facilitates development of oligopolistic structures depends upon whether FDI crowds-out or crowds-in domestic investment. FDI can potentially displace domestic

1. Virmani, Arvind (2004). *Accelerating Growth and Poverty Reduction: A Policy Framework for India's Development*. New Delhi: Academic Foundation.

producers by preempting their investment opportunities. It is possible, however, that the adverse growth effect emanating from crowding-out could be more than offset by the increase in productivity resulting from advanced technology that often accompanies FDI.

Since trade is an important vehicle for growth, FDI could also contribute to growth by promoting exports. For sustaining an export-led growth strategy, it becomes important to attain dynamic shifts in comparative advantage and FDI can play a major role in imparting the desired dynamism on account of its global marketing network.

Portfolio Capital

Portfolio capital has emerged as the key channel for integrating capital markets worldwide. For developing countries, the growth process in the initial phase is often characterised by self-financed capital investment, which is replaced gradually by bank-intermediated debt finance and supplemented over time by both debt and equity from the capital market. Portfolio capital flows can ease the constraint on growth imposed by illiquid and small sized capital markets in the early and intermediate stages of the growth process. Countries that reduced barriers to portfolio flows exhibit significant improvements in the functioning of their stock markets. Greater liquidity in the capital market makes it possible to take up investment projects in developing countries that require lumpy and long-term capital. Equity, unlike debt, allows a permanent access to capital.

Surges in portfolio flows can, however, adversely affect growth. Greater liquidity and opportunities for risk diversification may reduce household saving and excess volatility in the stock market may hinder investment. Unlike FDI, for the portfolio flows there is no one-to-one relationship with real investment. When portfolio activities are entirely concentrated in the secondary market, there is no direct link with real investment in the economy. At the macro level, portfolio flows finance the current account gap when alternative forms of foreign capital prove inadequate. Otherwise, it is only by enhancing the efficiency and liquidity of capital markets that portfolio flows can propel growth.

External Aid

The role of external aid in enhancing growth has waned in recent years. In several developing countries, including India, public and publicly guaranteed capital flows have been supplanted by a growing recourse to private capital flows. Except for the poorest countries and those with very limited access to commercial capital, a general sense of aid fatigue has set in. Donors have also gradually de-emphasised the role of aid in international economic relations resulting in a significant decline in aid flows as percentage of GDP of the donors since the 1960s.

Commercial Debt Capital

Commercial debt capital includes a whole range of sources of foreign capital where the overriding consideration is commercial, i.e., risk adjusted rate of return. External commercial loans could include bank loans, buyer's credit, supplier's credit, securitised instruments such as Floating Rate Notes and Fixed Rate Bonds, and commercial borrowings from the private sector window of multilateral financial institutions.

Capital Flows and Growth in India: The Recent Experience

Capital flows into India have been predominantly influenced by the policy environment. Recognising the availability constraint and reflecting the emphasis on self-reliance, planned levels of dependence on foreign capital in successive Plans were deliberately held at modest levels. Economy in the recourse to foreign capital was achieved through import-substitution industrialisation in the initial years of planned development. The possibility of exports replacing foreign capital was generally not explored until the 1980s. It is only in the 1990s that elements of an export-led growth strategy became clearly evident alongside compositional shifts in the capital flows in favour of commercial debt capital in the 1980s and in favour of non-debt flows in the 1990s.

A large part of the net capital flows to India in the capital account is being offset by the debt servicing burden. As a consequence, net resource transfers have fluctuated quite significantly in the 1990s, turning negative in 1995-96.

Till the early 1980s, the capital account of the balance of payments had essentially a financing function (Rangarajan, 1996). Nearly 80 per cent of the financing requirement was met through external assistance. Aid financed imports were both largely ineffectual in increasing the rate of growth and were responsible for bloating the inefficient public sector. Due to the tied nature of bilateral aid, India had to pay 20 to 30 per cent higher prices in relation to what it could have got through international bidding. The real resource transfer associated with aid to

India, therefore, was much lower. There were occasions "when India accepted bilateral aid almost reluctantly and without enthusiasm because of the combination of low priority of the project and the inflated price of the goods".

In the 1980s, India increased its reliance on commercial loans as external assistance increasingly fell short of the growing financing needs. The significant pressures on the balance of payments as the international oil prices more than doubled in 1979-80 and the world trade volume growth decelerated sharply during 1980-1982, triggered an expansion in India's portfolio of capital inflows to include IMF facilities, greater reliance on the two deposit schemes for non-resident Indians—the Non-Resident External Rupee Accounts (NRERA) (that started in 1970) and Foreign Currency Non-Resident Account (FCNRA) (that started in 1975)—and commercial borrowings on a modest scale. A few select banks, all-India financial institutions, leading public sector undertakings and certain private corporates were allowed to raise commercial capital from the international market in the form of loans, bonds and Euro notes.

The policy approach to ECB has undergone fundamental shifts since then with the institution of reforms and external sector consolidation in the 1990s. Ceilings are operated on commitment of ECB with subceilings for short-term debt. The ceiling on annual approvals has been raised gradually. The focus of ECB policy continues to place emphasis on low borrowing cost, lengthened maturity profile (liberal norms for above eight years of maturity), and end-use restrictions.

NRI deposits represent an important avenue to access foreign capital. The policy framework for NRI deposits during 1990s has offered increased options to the NRIs through different deposit schemes and by modulation of rate of return, maturities and the application of Cash Reserve Ratio (CRR). Capital flows from NRIs have occasionally taken the form of large investments in specific bonds, i.e., the India Development Bond (IDB) in 1991, the Resurgent India Bond (RIB) in 1998 and India Millennium Deposits (IMD) in 2000.

Foreign investment responded favourably to the liberalised policy environment and the generalised improvement in macroeconomic conditions. By 1993-94, FDI and portfolio flows taken together emerged as the most important source of external finance and non-debt flows exceeded net debt flows in the form of NRI deposits, external commercial borrowings and external assistance. Since then, foreign investment has remained as the most important form of external financing for India.

It is difficult to assess the direct contribution of these flows, particularly FDI, to the growth process. Anecdotal evidence suggests that foreign-controlled firms often use third-party exports to meet their export obligations. Another factor that contributes to widening the technology gap in FDI in India is the inappropriate Intellectual Property (IP) regime of India. Survey results for 100 US multinationals indicate that about 44 per cent of the firms highlighted the weak IP protection in India as a constraining factor for transfer of new technology to Indian subsidiaries. For investment in sectors like chemicals and pharmaceuticals, almost 80 per cent of the firms viewed Indian IP regime as the key constraining factor for technology transfer. It appears that the lure of the large size of the domestic market continues to be one of the primary factors causing FDI flows into India.

FDI Policy: A Historical Perspective

Over the last five decades, there have been significant changes in approaches and policies relating to FDI in India in tune with the developments in the industrial policies and also foreign exchange situation, from time to time. There is a view in the literature that the attitude and approach to FDI reflected the under current of balance of payments crisis in the respective periods. Depending upon the thrust and direction of the policies at different time period, one can identify four distinct phases in the evolution of the policies:

i) first phase from 1950 to 1967—characterised by receptive attitude or cautious welcome;

ii) second phase from 1967 to 1980—marked by restrictive and selective policies;

iii) third phase from 1980 to 1990—gradual liberalisation; and

iv) fourth phase from 1991 till date—paradigm shift to open door policy. Major features of FDI policies during the above four phases are reviewed below. Exhibit 19.1 provides the major features of FDI policies during the four phases.

First Phase 1950-1967

After Independence, especially with the Second Five Year Plan, India's development strategy focused on import substituting industrialisation. At that point of time, the availability of capital, technology, skills, entrepreneurship, etc., was very limited. Hence, the attitude towards FDI was increasingly receptive (Kumar, 1998). During this period, FDI was sought on mutually advantageous terms, though the majority local ownership was preferred. As foreign investment was considered necessary, foreign investors were assured of non-discriminatory treatment on par with domestic enterprises. There were no restrictions on the remittances of profits and dividends. Foreign investors were assured of fair compensation in the event of acquisition. However, it was provided that, as a rule, the major interest in ownership and effective control would always be in Indian hands. With the foreign exchange crisis in 1957-58, FDI policies were further liberalised and offered a host of incentives and concessions. Thus, during this phase, the country had given cautious welcome to the foreign capital.

Second Phase 1967-1980

By the middle of sixties, there was considerable investment in various industries. Besides, India's scientific and technological knowledge and infrastructure were developing and manpower was getting more skilled and constraints on local supply of capital and entrepreneurship have begun to ease somewhat. On the other hand, outflow on account of servicing of FDI and technology imports from the earlier period has begun to rise in the form of dividends, profits, royalties and technical fees, etc. These factors forced the government to adopt a more restrictive attitude towards FDI (Kumar, 1998). Major features of the policies followed during the phase are:

i) restrictions were imposed on proposals of FDIs without technology transfer and those seeking more than 40 per cent foreign ownership;

ii) the government listed industries in which FDI was not considered desirable in view of local capabilities;

iii) foreign collaborations required exclusive use of Indian consultancy services wherever available;

iv) the renewals of foreign collaboration agreements were restricted;

v) from 1973 onwards, the further activities of foreign companies along with those of local large industrial houses were restricted to a select group of core or high priority industries. The enactment of Foreign Exchange Regulation Act (FERA), 1973 became the key to guiding and controlling FDI inflows. The phase of tight regulation and selective policy was implemented by an administrative system based on discretionary power.

Third Phase 1980-1990

There was a gradual liberalisation of FDI policies in the eighties due to the deterioration of foreign exchange position in the wake of second oil crisis and India's failure to boost her manufactured exports. During this phase, policies were specially designed to encourage higher foreign equity holding in export-oriented units and investments from oil exporting developing countries. Approval systems were streamlined. A degree of flexibility was introduced in the policy concerning foreign ownership, and exceptions from the general ceiling of 40 per cent on foreign equity were allowed on the merit of individual investment proposals. The rules and procedures concerning payments of royalties and lump sum technical fees were relaxed and withholding taxes were reduced. A fast channel was set up in 1988 for expediting clearances of FDI proposals from major investing countries, *viz*., Japan, Germany, the US and the UK. Thus, the third phase witnessed a concrete move towards liberalisation of FDI policies.

Fourth Phase-1991 Onwards

There has been a paradigm shift in the policies on FDI right from the early nineties with the adoption of the Industrial Policy Statement of July 1991. One of the objectives of Industrial Policy Statement was that "foreign investment and technology collaboration will be welcomed to obtain higher technology, to increase exports and to expand the production base". The Industrial Policy Statement of 1991 has followed an 'open-door' policy on foreign investment and technology transfer. The policy since then has been aimed at encouraging foreign investment particularly in the core and infrastructure sectors. During the fourth phase, favourable policy environment consisting of the liberalisation policies on foreign investment, foreign technology collaboration, foreign trade and foreign exchange, have been exerting positive influence on foreign firms' decisions on investment and business operations in the country.

During this period, the FERA, 1973 has been amended and restrictions placed on foreign companies by the FERA have been lifted. In 1999, FERA has been replaced with Foreign Exchange Management Act. Government has permitted, except for a small negative list, access to the automatic route for FDI. Hence, foreign investors only need to inform the RBI within 30 days of bringing in their investment. Companies with more than 40 per cent of foreign equity are now treated on par with fully Indian owned companies. New sectors such as mining, banking, telecommunications, highways, construction, airports, hotel and tourism, courier service and management have been thrown open for FDI. Even the defence industry sector is opened upto 100 per cent for Indian private sector participation with 26 per cent FDI, subject to licensing. (FDI is not permitted in the following industrial sectors: i) arms and ammunition, ii) atomic energy, iii) railway transport, iv) coal and lignite, and v) mining of iron, manganese, chrome, gypsum, sulphur, gold, diamonds, copper and zinc). The liberal policies have been accompanied by active courting of foreign investors at the highest level. The international trade policy regime has been considerably liberalised too with removal of quantitative restrictions lowering of peak tariffs to 30 per cent and sharp pruning of negative list for imports. The rupee was made convertible on current account and gradually to capital account.

Now FDI is permitted under the following four forms of investments: i) through financial collaboration, ii) through joint ventures and technical collaborations, iii) through capital markets *via* Global Depository Receipts (GDRs) (Euro issues), and iv) through private placements or preferential allotments.

Transparency and openness have been the most significant features of FDI policies in the fourth phase. The degree of openness is reflected in: (i) the sectors open to FDI, (ii) higher level of foreign equity participation, and (iii) transparency in approval procedures. One striking aspect of the present liberalisation policy is that unlike the previous phases, it is not necessary that FDI is accompanied by foreign technology agreements. There is a liberal approach towards investment by non-resident Indian (NRIs): NRIs and overseas corporate bodies can invest up to 100 per cent in high priority industries. Another distinctive feature of the policy is the simplification of procedures.

Thus, the ongoing measures taken since 1991 are focused towards a virtual elimination of both the direct and indirect barriers to foreign direct investment (indirect barriers in the form of investor protection, differences in accounting standards, legal and regulatory structure). In short, the evolution of FDI policies in India are characterised by receptive attitude till the mid-sixties to a policy of restrictions and controls till 1980 and then to gradual liberalisation till 1990 and finally to a policy of full-fledged liberalisation since 1991.

EXHIBIT – 19.1

MAJOR FEATURES OF FDI POLICIES DURING THE FOUR PHASES

Phase I *1950-1967*	*Phase II* *1967-1980*	*Phase III* *1980-1990*	*Phase IV* *1991 Onwards*
Receptive Attitude or Cautious Welcome	*Restrictive Attitude*	*Gradual Liberalisation*	*Open Door Policy*
• Non-discriminatory treatment to FDI.	• Restriction on FDI without technology.	• Higher foreign equity in export-oriented units allowed.	• Liberal policies relating to technology collaboration, foreign trade and foreign exchange.
• No restrictions on remittance of profits and dividends.	• Above 40% stake not allowed.	• Procedure for remittance of royalty and technical fees liberalised.	• Encouraging FDI in core and infrastructure industries.
	• Allowed only in priority area.		• FERA replaced with FEMA.
• Ownership and control with Indians.	• FDI controlled by FERA.	• Fast channel for FDI clearance.	• Procedures transparent.
			• Liberal approach for NRI investments.
	• Discretionary power in sanctioning the projects.		• FDI need not be accompanied by technology.
			• FDI through Mergers and Acquistions.
			• FDI in services and financial sector—banks, NBFCs, insurance.

FDI Inflows in India in a Comparative East Asian Perspective

According to Nagesh Kumar, although FDI inflows into Indian economy have increased considerably during the 1990s following the reforms, India's share would appear too small, especially if it is compared with that of other countries in the region such as China. In 2001, India's reported inflows of about $ 3.4 billion represent a mere 1.7 per cent of total inflows attracted by developing countries. In contrast, China received an estimated $ 46.8 billion of inflows in the same year representing nearly 23 per cent total developing country FDI inflows.

Magnitudes of FDI Inflows

The comparison of about US $ 3.4 billion in annual inflows of FDI by India with US $ 45 billion of FDI inflows by China is often made. It has been pointed out however, that the figures of FDI inflows in India and China are not comparable because of several differences.[2] Firstly, the Indian figures of inflows do not follow the IMF's BOP Manual that is followed internationally. The principle difference is that Indian figures only count the fresh inflows of equity and do not take into consideration the reinvested earnings by foreign affiliates in the country nor the inter-corporate debt flows that are generally included while computing the FDI figures as per the IMF Guidelines. Therefore, the Indian figures tend to underreport the inflows. Secondly, FDI inflows in China are believed to be overestimating the real FDI inflows in view of round-tripping of Chinese capital to take advantage of more favourable tax treatment of FDI. Therefore, the figures of India and China are not strictly comparable and tend to overplay the difference between the intensity of inflows between the two countries. Finally, the size of the Chinese economy is much larger than the Indian economy and hence, the figures should be normalised.

Quality of FDI Inflows in Indian and China: Sectoral Composition and Other Differences

India's post-reform experience suggests that a substantial proportion of FDI has gone to services, infrastructure and relatively low technology-intensive consumer goods manufacturing industries compared to high concentration in technology-intensive manufacturing industries in the pre-reform period. In China and other South-East Asian countries, the bulk of FDI is concentrated in manufacturing. In the pre-reform period, FDI was consciously channelled into technology-intensive manufacturing through a selective policy. In the post-reform period, however, opening up of new industries such as services and infrastructure to FDI has led to a lot of FDI going to them, thus bringing down the share of manufacturing. Within the manufacturing too, now that there is no policy to direct the FDI to certain branches, consumer goods industries that did not have so much exposure to FDI have risen in importance. On the other hand, while following in general a liberal

2. Government of India, *Eleventh Five Year Plan 2007-2012*, Vol. I, Planning Commission.

policy towards FDI, China and other South-East Asian countries have directed FDI to manufacturing with export-obligations, FDI also accounts for a relatively very high share of manufactured exports in these countries. It suggests while according to a liberal treatment, a broad direction needs to be given to improve quality of FDI and make it contribute more to the industrialisation and building export capability. Specific promotion of export-oriented FDI may also be fruitful.

Impact of FDI Inflows

Given their intangible assets, MNE affiliates can contribute to their host country's development with generation of output, employment, balanced regional development, technological capability and export-expansion, among other parameters.

Foreign direct investment (FDI) directly impacts on output growth in India by augmenting the available investible capital. However, a far more important impact of FDI is through externalities leading to higher efficiency and productivity. FDI typically serves to increase competition in markets, bring new technology into India, and foster skill acquisition amongst domestic labour. FDI by international corporations is also central to the process of India being utilised as a platform for global production chains, which would pave the way for strong exports growth.

FDI, Growth and Domestic Investment

FDI inflows could contribute to growth rate of the host economy by augmenting the capital stock as well as with infusion of new technology. However, high growth rates may also lead to more FDI inflows by enhancing the investment climate in the country. Therefore, the FDI-growth relationship is subject to causality bias given the possibility of two-way relationship.

Shares in Sales, Capital Formation and GDP

The growing importance of FDI inflows in the Indian economy can also be judged from the rising ratios of FDI inflows as a proportion of gross fixed capital formation from 0.3 per cent in 1990 to 4 per cent and of inward FDI stock as a percentage of GDP rising from 0.5 to 5.4 per cent over the same period.

FDI Policy Review 2006

Government has put in place a liberal, transparent and investor-friendly FDI policy, wherein FDI up to 100 per cent is allowed under automatic route for most of the sectors/activities, where the investor does not require any prior approval. Only notification to the Reserve Bank of India within 30 days of inward remittance or issue of shares to non-residents is required. Cases requiring prior Government approval are considered by the Foreign Investment Promotion Board (FIPB) in a time-bound and transparent manner.

A comprehensive review of the FDI policy was undertaken in 2006 with a view to consolidate the liberalisation already effected and further rationalise the FDI policy governing various activities. New sectors/activities *viz.*, single brand product retailing, power trading, coffee and rubber processing and warehousing were opened for FDI.

As a result of the comprehensive review of the FDI policy, wide-ranging policy changes were notified in 2006, extending automatic routes, increasing equity caps, removing restrictions, simplifying procedures and extending the horizon of FDI to vistas like single brand product retailing and agriculture. Of late, several steps have been initiated to facilitate FDI inflows which, among other things, include: raising the equity cap in civil aviation; organising Destination India events in association with CII and FICCI with a view to attract investments; activating the Foreign Investment Implementation Authority (FIIA) towards speedy resolution of investment-related problems; setting up of National Manufacturing Competitiveness Council (NMCC) to provide a continuing forum for policy dialogue to energise the growth of manufacturing; regular interactions with foreign investors through bilateral/regional/international meets and meetings with individual investors; and making the website of the Department of Industrial Policy & Promotion (*www.dipp.nic.in*) more user-friendly with online chat facility.

Investors are showing their growing confidence in the immediate and medium term prospects of the Indian economy. A recent confidence survey by global consultancy AT Kearney rated India as the third most favoured FDI destination, next only to China and United States. Moreover, for the first time, manufacturing investors surveyed by AT Kearney considered India as a superior manufacturing location than even the US.

FDI Outlook

AT Kearney FDI Confidence Index 2006 based on a seven-year survey of top 1000 firms, covering 68 countries receiving 90 per cent of the FDI has rated India ahead of the US in terms of business confidence index. The top honours go to China. US is the fourth in the list. Forty-five per cent of global investors are upbeat about India compared to last year. The report predicts India to be on the cusp of FDI take off, in view of the government focus on reforms, overcoming narrow business interests, de-bottlenecking infrastructure, logistics and regulatory barriers.

India has improved its position by two places in the World Economic Forum's Global Competitive Index (GCI) rankings for 2006-07, coming in 43rd, well ahead of Brazil (66), China (54) and Russia (62).

Strategy for FDI During the Eleventh Five Year Plan

Given the current scenario, FDI could increase significantly during the Eleventh Plan. During the Eleventh Plan, steps would need to be taken to consolidate the gains from FDI by reducing the delays in state-level clearances required by investors to establish enterprises. Progress towards elimination of FDI limits in key sectors also need to continue in order to increase FDI flows and stimulate transfer of technology, which is critical for improving competitiveness.

MULTINATIONAL CORPORATION (MNCs)

Multinational Corporation (MNCs) also known as Transnational Corporations (TNCs) are huge industrial organisations which extend their industrial and marketing operations through a network of their branches or their Majority Owned Foreign Affiliates (MOFAs). Instead of aiming for maximisation of their profits from one or two products, the MNCs operate in a number of fields and from this point of view, their business strategy extends over a number of products and over a number of countries. There are now 40,000 TNCs with over 2,50,000 overseas affiliates. The 200 top MNCs control over a one-fourth of the world's economic activity. Their sales were equivalent to 28.3 per cent of world GDP in 1998. In fact, because of their huge capital resources, latest technology and worldwide goodwill, MNCs are in a position to sell whatever product they choose to manufacture in different countries.

The main reason why MNCs have been encouraged by the underdeveloped countries to participate in their industrial development is on account of the technological superiorities which these firms possess as compared to national companies. The underdeveloped countries regard transfer of technology from MNCs useful on account of the following reasons: (a) the resources of these countries are insufficient to sustain the industrial progress on their own; (b) local manpower, materials, local capital equipment etc., have to be optimally exploited and these countries are unable to accomplish this; (c) depending totally on local companies would require heavy imports of raw materials, capital equipment, machinery and technical knowledge whereas MNCs bring these on their own; and (d) the underdeveloped countries have to face stiff competition for selling their products in international markets. Unless their goods meet international standards and quality specifications, they cannot sell. MNCs help them in producing such goods.

MNCs in Indian Economy

A common form of MNC participation in Indian industry is through entering into collaboration with Indian industrialists. Foreign collaboration agreements are made between Indian companies and foreign parties, involving sale of technology, as well as use of foreign brand names for the final products. As a result of liberalised foreign investment policy announced in July-August 1991, there has been a further spurt of foreign collaborations. For instance, over the period August 1991 to August 2002, the government approved 7,464 foreign technology collaborations and 15,998 foreign direct investment proposals. The total amount of foreign direct investment approved over the period August 1991 to November 2005, amounted to a mammoth Rs. 2,57,952 crore (equivalent to $ 69,001 million). However, actual inflows were only a little more than half of the approvals.

The policy of the government in the field of foreign collaboration has been criticised on the following counts:

(i) A large number of agreements were concluded for the manufacture of products which are non-essential or which could be produced with the help of local technology. These items included vacuum flasks, lipstick, toothpaste, cosmetics, ice-cream, biscuits, dry batteries, readymade garments, etc. Clearly such collaborations were directed to serve the needs of high income groups and to take advantage of a foreign brand name;

(ii) The government permitted multiple collaborations, i.e., repetitive import of the same or similar technology. This resulted in repetitive payments without adding to the stock of technical knowledge in the country;

(iii) The terms of payment were also drawn up so as to squeeze out the maximum payment under one head or other. Generally 5 per cent of the annual turnover for 10 years as royalty plus 5 per cent of the imported plant cost as technical fees in the case of royalty-cum-technical fees, or 10 per cent of the issued capital as lumpsum payment for technical fees alone, were the limits of official policy. However, these tended to become routine;

(iv) The most important part related to the presence of various restrictive clauses in the agreements;

(v) Foreign collaborations have helped the growth of monopolies and concentration. They joined hands with the big business houses and the latter were only too eager to enter into understanding with them since the presence of foreign links often conferred certain strategic advantages (patent, resources, foreign exchange, etc.) enabling the big business houses to diversify and expand;

(vi) As far as transfer of technology to underdeveloped countries is concerned, the behaviour pattern of MNCs reveals that they do not engage in R&D activities within the underdeveloped countries. Their R&D efforts are concentrated in laboratories in the home country or in other industrialised countries. Though R&D activities continue to be centralised in the parent country, the host countries have to bear the bulk of their costs since the affiliates of the MNCs in these countries remit payments on this account generally in relation to their sales volume. The satisfaction expressed on technology transfer is partly misconceived also on account of the fact that MNCs which generally command a semi-monopolistic position in their product lines do not transfer their first-line or most advanced technology until foreign firms compel them to do so. In many cases, the technology transferred is of a capital-intensive nature which is not useful from the point of view of a labour surplus economy.

Control Over Multinational Corporations

The responsibility of controlling the activities of multinational corporations in India rests on different government agencies. These agencies are:

(i) the Ministry of Company Affairs;

(ii) the Reserve Bank of India;

(iii) the Ministry of Industrial Development; and

(iv) the Ministry of Finance.

However, these agencies do not work in close cooperation with each other. As a result, there is no coordination in their functioning. Each case is discussed on its own merits by the authorities. There are no objective criteria for approving applications and the procedure resorted to by the various ministries is lengthy and cumbersome. The most effective curb on the activities of foreign companies, especially MNCs, was supposed to come with the passing of the Foreign Exchange Regulation Act (FERA) in 1973.

Foreign Exchange Regulation Act (FERA), 1973

Foreign Exchange Regulation Act (FERA) was promulgated in 1973 and it came into force on January 1, 1974. Section 29 of this Act referred directly to the operations of MNCs in India. According to the Section, all non-banking foreign branches and subsidiaries with foreign equity exceeding 40 per cent had to obtain permission to establish new undertakings, to purchase shares in existing companies, or to acquire wholly or partly any other company.

In line with the liberalisation measures announced in the new industrial and trade policy in 1991 and the subsequent period, the government announced major concessions to FERA companies.

As a result of long list of concessions, FERA was made redundant and efforts were made to place FERA companies at par with Indian companies. In fact, the Union Budget, 1998-99, advocated repealing FERA and replacing it with FEMA (Foreign Exchange Management Act). Consequently, the government adopted FEMA in 1999. Under FEMA, the emphasis is on ‘management’ rather than ‘regulation’.

FEMA: A Major Departure from FERA

As is clear from the name of the Act itself, the emphasis under FEMA is on ‘exchange management’ whereas under FERA the emphasis was on ‘exchange regulation’ or ‘exchange control’. The purpose of FEMA is to ‘facilitate external trade and payments’ and ‘promote the orderly development and maintenance of foreign exchange market in India’. The contravention will now be treated as a civil offence as against criminal offence under FERA.

According to Biswajit Dhar and Mritunjay Mohanty, FEMA represents major departures from the past policies in two other important respects: “First, it can be seen as an initial step towards capital account convertibility. Secondly, by removing the FERA from the statute book and replacing it with the FEMA, the government seems to have finally decided to give up even the bare intention of regulating foreign capital in the country."

Concluding Remarks and Policy Lessons

Although the magnitude of FDI inflows has increased, the bulk of them have gone into services and soft technology consumer goods industries bringing the share of manufacturing and technology intensive among them down in sharp contrast to the east Asian countries. Although the importance of FDI as a source of capital and output generation has risen, its impact on direct investment and growth is mixed as some FDI inflows possibly crowd-in domestic investments while some others crowd it out (Kumar, 2009).

Liberalisation of FDI policy may be necessary but not sufficient for expanding FDI inflows. The overall macroeconomic performance continues to exercise a major influence on the magnitude of FDI inflows by acting as a signalling device for foreign investors about the growth prospects for the potential host economy. Hence, paying attention to macroeconomic performance indicators such as growth rates of industry through public investments in socio-economic infrastructure and other supportive policies and creating a stable and enabling environment would crowd-in FDI inflows. Studies have shown that policies that facilitate domestic investments also pull in FDI inflows. While investment incentives may not be efficient, active promotion of FDI by developing certain viable projects and getting key MNEs interested in them could be useful in attracting investments in desirable directions.

Questions

1. Write short note on : Role of multinational corporations in India. *[B.A. (P) 2009]*
2. What are the multinational corporations? What has been their role in the industrial development of India? *[B.A. (P) 2005, B. Com 2008]*
3. Describe briefly the policy of the government towards foreign capital. What changes have been made in its policy since 1991 to liberalise it? *[B.Com. (P) 2006]*
4. Write short note on 'Role of multinational corporations in Indian economy'. *[B.A. (P) 2006, 2000, 1999; B.Com. (P) 2000]*
5. Examine the merits and demerits of foreign capital in a developing economy like India. *[B.A. (P) 2005]*
6. Discuss the role of foreign capital in the development of Indian economy. *[B.A. (P) 2004]*
7. Write brief note on 'Role of foreign capital in India'. *[B.Com. (P) 2004]*
8. Examine critically the role of foreign capital in India's economic development. What role would you like to assign to multinational corporations in future? *[B.Com. (P) 2003]*
9. Explain the role of foreign capital in economic development. Examine the policy of Government of India towards foreign capital. *[B.Com. (P) 2001]*
10. Define multinational corporations. What are the advantages and disadvantages of multinational corporations for industrial development in a country like India? *[B.Com. (P) 1995, 1999]*
11. What role has foreign capital played in India's economic development? In this context would you advocate a policy of encouraging investment by multinational corporations in India? *[B.Com. (P) 1990]*

20

Foreign Trade

Role and Importance of Foreign Trade

According to the standard theory, international trade leads to allocation of resources that is consistent with comparative advantage. This results in specialisation which enhances productivity. While the classical theory of comparative advantage was based on assumptions of perfect competition, constant returns to scale and fixed technology, the "new trade theory" which takes into account imperfect competition, increasing returns to scale and changing technology also comes to the conclusion that openness leads to improved rates of growth (Frankel, 2000). The new trade theory talks of dynamic gains from international trade. It is accepted that international trade, in general, is beneficial and that restrictive trade practices impede growth. That is the reason why many of the emerging economies which originally depended on a growth model of import substitution have moved over to a policy of outward orientation.

Foreign trade contributes to economic development in a number of ways:

(i) Foreign trade makes available imports of capital goods essential for economic development.

(ii) It provides technology which increases total factor productivity.

(iii) It generates pressure for dynamic change through: (a) competitive pressure from imports (b) pressure of computing for exports markets and (c) a better allocation of resources.

(iv) Exports help in fuller utilisation of capacity and in reaping economies of scale.

Foreign trade has served as an engine of growth for today's developed countries like Great Britain and Japan. In recent times, the Newly Industrialising Countries (NICs) called *Miracle Economies* have been able to achieve high growth rates through foreign trade by adopting outward oriented growth stategy.

TABLE – 20.1

FOREIGN TRADE AS PERCENTAGE OF GDP

Country	*1970*	*1999*
US	11	24
Canada	43	84
Japan	20	19
UK	44	53
France	30	50
Germany	**	57
Italy	32	49
EU	3.6	2.7
Hong Kong	181.0	261.0
Singapore	232	**
Korea	37	77
India	8	27

Note : Foreign trade refers to exports and imports of goods and services.
Source : World Development Indicators, 2001, World Bank.

India's Economic Policy towards Foreign Trade

India's economic policy towards foreign trade and foreign investment in the first four decades after India's Independence was restrictive. Import substitution constituted a major element of country's foreign trade and industrial policies. India's share in world exports which stood at 1.85 per cent in 1950 fell to 0.58 per cent in 1992. In the wake of the economic crisis that overtook the country in 1991, the approach to and content of economic policy underwent a far reaching change. This change was reflected in trade and investment policies. An outward orientation began to emerge. Tariff rates have been steadily brought down while quantitative controls have been dismantled.

While recognising the fact that the Indian economy in the last decade has become more open, it is also necessary to note that the Indian economy is much less open than many other economies. Taking the most commonly used indicator of openness which is the proportion of import and export of goods and services to GDP, it is seen that this ratio has increased from 15 per cent in 1980 to 25 per cent in 1998. However, this ratio of 25 per cent is much smaller than many other countries. For small countries like Malaysia and Singapore with a high outward orientation, this ratio exceeds 200 per cent. Among the industrially advanced countries, the United States is the only country which has a ratio similar to that of India (Table 20.1). Tariff levels are another indicator of openness. Here again, while India's weighted mean tariff rate has come down from 49.8 per cent in 1989-90 to 29.5 per cent in 1999, it is still high compared with many other countries. While the weighted average tariff rate is nil for Hong Kong and Singapore, it is as low as 2.7 per cent in European Union countries and 2.8 per cent in the US. However, it is of significance to note that the standard deviation of the tariff rates in US is high at 11.4 per cent which means that the rates on certain products are very high (World Bank, 2001).

Growth of India's Foreign Trade

Since Indepedence, there has been a tremendous increase in value and volume of India's foreign trade. With the continued increase in tempo of economic development, imports of capital goods, machinery, transport equipment, petroleum products, etc., have grown manifold. And since payment for imports has to be made in foreign currency which can be earned through export of goods, sustained efforts have been made to expand and diversify exports. Consequently, there has been a sharp increase in value of imports as well as exports that have tremendously increased India's trade turnover or value of foreign trade.

Far from viewing foreign trade as an engine of growth, Indian planners sought to minimise import demand and viewed exports more or less as a necessary evil mainly to generate the foreign exchange earnings to meet that part of the import bill not covered by external assistance. They created an elaborate administrative regulatory machinery in an attempt to control investment and resource allocation in the economy and ensure their consistency with five year plan targets. Controls over imports and exports were also part of this regulatory system.

Broad Trends: Exports and Imports

Exports

1. **1950 to early 70s** - Import substitution became the keystone of development strategy in the late 1950s. Consequently, exports were neglected by the Government. The value of exports as a percentage of GDP at market prices declined from an average of over 6 per cent (1950-51 to 1955-56) to less than 4 per cent in the period following. This declining trend in the value of exports continues till 1971-72. The decline is in spite of the introduction of many incentive scheme for the exporters in the sixties. The sixties can be seen as the period of induction of export orientation through incentive schemes for exports along with import substitution. With the decision to devalue the rupee in 1966, changes in tariffs and export subsidy policy, it was evident that the policy makers were trying to use fiscal measures to step up exports and curb imports. But the incentives given to exporters could not offset thc bias against exports which was implicit in the over valued exchange rate (except for 1966 devaluation) and the prevalent level of import restrictions.

2. **Early 70s to late 80s** - The value of exports as a percentage of GDP at market prices picked up after 1971-72 and increased till end of seventies. Eighties again shows a declining trend in value of exports with a recovery to over 6 per cent level only in the last couple of years in eighties (Table 20.2). It was realised after the first oil shock of 1973 that India had to step up exports simply to finance the rising import bill on account of an increase in oil prices.

   Eighties can be viewed as a period of growing uneasiness with the policies of excessive protectionism. The Abid Hussain Committee on import and export policies (1985-1988) recommended more liberal access to imports by exporters. The second major recommendations of the Committee was that the real exchange rate of the rupee should not be allowed to appreciate and it should be maintained at a level considered appropriate for ensuring the competitiveness of exports.

3. **1990s** - The 1990s have witnessed an increase in the value of exports as a percentage of GDP at market price to over 8 per cent from over 6 per cent level (Table 20.3). After the payment crisis of 1990-91, when the foreign exchange reserves had

TABLE – 20.2

VALUE OF EXPORTS AND IMPORTS—1950-51 TO 2008-09

(US $ Million)

Year	*Exports*	*Imports*	*Trade Balance*	*Rate of Change*	
				Exports	*Imports*
1950-51	1269	1273	-4	24.9	-1.5
1960-61	1346	2353	-1007	0.3	16.7
1970-71	2031	2162	-131	8.8	3.5
1980-81	8486	15869	-7383	6.8	40.2
1990-91	18143	24075	-5932	9.2	13.5
1993-94	22238	23306	-1068	20.0	6.5
1994-95	26330	28654	-2324	18.4	22.9
1995-96	31797	36678	-4881	20.8	28.0
1996-97	33470	39133	-5663	5.3	6.7
1997-98	35006	41484	-6478	4.6	6.0
1998-99	33218	42389	-9171	-5.1	2.2
1999-2000	36822	49671	-12849	10.8	17.2
2000-01	44560	50536	-5976	21.0	1.7
2001-02	43827	51413	-7586	-1.6	1.7
2002-03	52719	61412	-8693	20.3	19.4
2003-04	63843	78150	-14307	21.1	27.3
2004-05	83535	111516	-27982	30.8	42.7
2005-06	103092	149167	-46076	23.4	33.8
2006-07	126360	185747	-59387	22.6	24.5
2007-08	162904	251439	-88535	28.9	35.4
2008-09(P)[a]	**168704**	**287759**	**-119055**	**3.6**	**14.4**

Note: P: Provisional; a: Growth rate on provisional over revised basis.

Source: Government of India, Economic Survey, 1998-99, Statement 7.1 (B) p. S-81 and *Economic Survey*, 2000-01, 2001-02, 2003-04, 2004-05, 2005-06, 2007-08, 2008 2009, A 81.

fallen drastically and were enough to pay for two weeks of imports, the process of economic reforms was started in 1991. The chief elements of reforms are devaluation of the rupee, liberalisation of import licensing, reduction in tariffs, abolition of cash subsidies for exports, introduction of partial convertibility of the rupee on the current account and later full convertibility of the rupee on the current account.

TABLE – 20.3

CURRENT ACCOUNT TRANSACTIONS AS A PERCENTAGE OF GDP AT CURRENT MARKET PRICES 90S

	Exports X	*Imports M*	*Trade Balance*	*X* M(%)*	*Current Account Balance*	*X+M*
1990-91	5.8	8.8	-3.0	66.2	-3.1	14.6
1991-92	6.7	7.7	-1.0	86.7	-0.3	14.4
1992-93	7.1	9.4	-2.2	77.6	-1.7	16.5
1993-94	8.3	9.8	-1.5	84.8	-0.4	18.1
1994-95	8.3	11.1	-2.8	74.8	-1.0	19.4
1995-96	9.1	12.3	-3.2	74.8	-1.7	21.4
1996-97	8.9	12.7	-3.8	69.7	-1.2	21.6
1997-98	8.7	12.5	-3.8	69.7	-1.4	21.2
1998-99	8.3	11.5	-3.2	72.1	-1.0	19.8
1999-2000	8.4	12.4	-4.0	67.8	-1.1	20.8
2000-01	9.8	13.0	-3.1	75.8	-0.5	22.8
2001-02	9.4	12.0	-2.6	85.2	0.2	21.4
2002-03	10.6	12.7	-2.1	85.8	1.2	23.3
2003-04	11.1	13.3	-2.5	81.6	2.3	24.1
2004-05	12.2	17.1	-4.8		-0.4	29.3
2005-06	13.0	19.4	-6.4		-1.2	32.4
2006-07	14.0	20.9	-6.9		-1.1	34.9
2007-08	14.1	21.9	-7.8		-1.5	36.0
2008-09 (Apr.-Dec.)	**15.2**	**27.1**	**-12.0**		**-4.1**	**42.3**

Note : * Export-import ratio is not given as a percentage of GDP at current market prices.

Source : *Economic Surveys* including 2007-08 and 2008-09.

After three successive years of robust growth at an annual average of 19.7 per cent (in US dollars) during 1993-94 to 1995-96, export momentum slowed down since 1996-97, with exports registering a modest growth of 5.3 per cent and decelerating further to 1.5 per cent in 1997-98. Both global and domestic factors have contributed to the slowdown in export growth in India since 1996-97. The share of east Asian countries in India's exports was around one-sixth before the crisis. India could not escape the fallout from the import compression in these countries. The slump in global trade and continued recessionary phase has caused not only import contraction, but has also triggered protectionist measures.

Amongst the domestic factors that continue to hamper exports infrastructure constraints, high transaction costs, SSI reservations, labour inflexibility, quality problems and quantitative ceilings on agricultural exports remain problematic. The growth of exports picked up in 1999-2000 and 2000-2001.

India's merchandise exports (in dollar terms and customs basis), by continuing to grow at over 20 per cent per year in the last three years since 2002-03, have surpassed targets. In 2004-05, export growth was a record of 28.5 per cent, the highest since 1975-76 and the second highest since 1950-51, supported by a buoyant world economy (5.1 per cent). The good performance of exports (growth of 23.49 per cent and 22.6 per cent) continued in 2005-06 and 2006-07 and culminating in a new record of 28.9 per cent in 2007-08.

Composition of India's Exports

The composition of India's exports has, as expected, shifted moderately away from primary products to manufactured goods, whose share rose from about 45 per cent in 1950-51 to 71 per cent in 1990-1991. In recent years, however, primary exports have been virtually stagnant, and manufactured products have accounted for almost the entire growth in total exports. Among manufactured products, just four items—leather, gems, garments and textiles—account for most of the growth in recent years. In contrast, the export of engineering goods, which rose by over 20 per cent per year in value terms between 1950-1951 and 1975-76 and between 1970-71 and 1978-79, declined between 1980-81 and 1985-86. The value of engineering goods exports grew at an average annual rate of 20.5 per cent during the period 1985-1990. Chemical exports show a similar pattern.

Diversification of exports constitutes an important element of India's export promotion strategy. Reflecting the policy thrust as also the evolving pattern of industrial development, India has gradually transformed from a predominantly primary products exporting country into an exporter of manufactured goods. However, it may be noted that this was more prominent in the 1970s. The progress has, however, stalled thereafter. Aided by various export promotion measures, the share of 'manufactured goods' in India's total exports increased from 70.7 per cent during 1987-1990 to 75.3 per cent during 1992-1997 and further to 77.4 per cent during 1997-2002.

TABLE – 20.4

AVERAGE SHARE OF EXPORTS OF SELECTED COMMODITIES

(Per cent)

Category	*1987-1990*	*1990-91*	*1992-1997*	*1997-2002*
	1	*2*	*3*	*4*
Primary Products	24.2	23.8	21.9	18.5
Manufactured Goods	70.7	71.6	75.3	77.4
of which:				
Leather and Manufactures	7.5	8.0	5.8	4.6
Chemicals and Allied Products	5.9	7.2	7.2	9.1
Engineering Goods	11.0	12.4	13.8	14.7
Readymade Garments	11.2	12.3	12.0	12.2
Textile Yarn, Fabrics, Made-ups	8.0	8.5	10.9	11.2
Handicrafts including Gems and Jewellery	22.6	18.9	19.7	20.1
Petroleum Products	3.1	2.9	1.8	2.1

Source : Directorate General of Commercial Intelligence and Statistics.

Destination-wise analysis of the Indian exports indicates an unchanged position in respect of the Organisation for Economic Cooperation and Development (OECD) group being the largest market, increasing prominence of the Organisation of Petroleum Exporting Countries (OPEC) and the developing countries (Asia, Africa and Latin America), and a steep erosion in the relative position of the Eastern Europe. With the break-up of the Soviet Union, the share of the East European countries fell dramatically from 17.9 per cent in 1990-91 to just 2.9 per cent in 2001-02, primarily on account of the termination of Rupee trade and its adverse impact on exports of agricultural products such as tea, tobacco and spices to this region. The loss of this market share was, however, made up by increasing the shares in developing countries and the OPEC region, both of which doubled between the years 1987-88 and 2001-02 (Table 20.5).

India's export share in world trade has increased perceptibly during the recent period. India's exports as a percentage of world exports improved to 0.56 per cent during 1991-1996 and further to 0.65 per cent during 1996-2002 from 0.48 per cent in the 1980s. The ratio was 0.71 per cent in 2000-01. Nonetheless, India's share in world exports was still very low and appears unimpressive when compared with the other major trading Asian countries, such as, China and other East Asian economies like Malaysia, Thailand, Singapore, Korea and Indonesia. China demonstrated the most dramatic change as its share in world exports more than doubled in a decade from 2.0 per cent in 1991 to 4.4 per cent in 2001. Group-wise, India's share in the imports of industrialised countries in the 1990s declined as compared to that in 1986. In respect of the developing countries as a group, however, it has increased from 0.5 per cent in 1986 to 1.1 per cent during 1996-2000.

TABLE – 20.5

DIRECTION OF INDIA'S FOREIGN TRADE—SHARE IN TOTAL EXPORTS

(Per cent)

Group/Country	*1987-88*	*1990-91*	*1995-96*	*1999-2000*	*2000-01*	*2001-02*
	1	*2*	*3*	*4*	*5*	*6*
I. OECD Countries	58.9	56.5	55.7	57.3	52.7	49.3
of which:						
a. EU	25.1	27.5	27.4	25.5	23.4	22.5
b. North America	19.7	15.6	18.3	24.4	22.4	20.8
of which: USA	18.6	14.7	17.4	22.8	20.9	19.4
c. Asia and Oceania	11.6	10.4	8.3	5.8	5.1	4.5
d. Other OECD Countries	2.5	3.0	1.6	1.6	1.9	1.6
II. OPEC	6.1	5.6	9.7	10.6	10.9	11.9
III. Eastern Europe	16.5	17.9	4.2	3.5	3.0	2.9
IV. Developing Countries	14.2	17.1	28.9	28.4	29.2	30.9
a. Asia	11.9	14.4	23.0	22.3	22.5	23.6
b. Africa	2.0	2.2	4.8	4.2	4.4	5.2
c. Latin American Countries	0.3	0.5	1.2	1.9	2.3	2.1

Source: Directorate General of Commercial Intelligence and Statistics.

Imports

1. **1950 to early 1970s** - The value of imports as a proportion of GDP at market prices, fluctuated through the 1950s (around 6 to 9.8 per cent) and thereafter declined slowly till the early 1970s (from 6.8 per cent in 1960-61 to 4.2 per cent in 1972-1973).

   The severe foreign exchange crisis of 1956-57 led to the adoption of strict measures for import controls. The import licensing system was intensified in the late fifties and early sixties. After a brief attempt at using fiscal measures instead of physical controls in mid-sixties, the import licensing was intensified. Import policy became increasingly restrictive and complex. The quantitative restrictions were used to provide protection to any domestic activity that substituted for imports. The decline in public investment and industrial growth after the mid-1960s also contributed to reducing the pressure on imports.

2. **Early 1970s to late 1980s** - After 1972-73, the value of imports as a proportion of GDP showed a distinct increase. The import needs became stronger as the industrial growth recovered in mid-seventies and showed an accelerating trend in the 1980s. The eighties is marked with a clear shift in the trade strategy towards reduction of quantitative restrictions on imports. The number of items in the category of OGL—that is, a licence to import but with no quantitative restrictions—increased substantially in this period. The rise in the value of imports as a proportion of GDP at market prices is in spite of the sharp increase in tariffs in eighties. The value of imports as a proportion of GDP increased from a level of 4.6 per cent (1973-74) to over 6 per cent in the remaining years of seventies. It was around 8 to 9 per cent in the decade of eighties.
3. **1990s** - The value of imports as a proportion of GDP at market prices show a distinct increase in the 1990s except for 1991-1992. The decline in 1991-92 was due to severe import curbs introduced after the payment crisis of 1990-91. The value of imports as a proportion of GDP increased from 8.8 per cent in 1990-91 to 12.5 per cent in 1997-98 and 13 per cent in 2000-2001 (Table 20.3).

The commodity-structure of India's imports has also shown marked changes, reflecting, *inter alia*, the impact of trade policy, the movements in international prices and the pattern of domestic demand. The share of oil imports in India's total imports increased from 17.1 per cent during 1987-1990 to 23.9 per cent during 1992-1997 and further to 27.2 per cent in 2001-02. While the share and absolute value of these imports showed sharp fluctuations over the years mainly on account of the large movements in international crude prices, the volume of such imports has grown significantly on account of increase in domestic consumption and the stagnation in domestic crude oil production. Given the large swings in international crude prices, as also a trend rise in the oil import bill, there is a need for a comprehensive review of energy policy of the country covering the demand-supply aspects, as well as the price policy. Renewed efforts to improve energy supply from domestic sources by encouraging explorations, and stepping up of production and refining capacities are necessary to bring about a structural change in this area.

Imports of capital goods registered sharp increases in the initial reform years from US $ 4.5 billion in 1992-93 to US $ 10.3 billion in 1995-96 but exhibited a declining trend thereafter. The share of these imports, which had declined from 29.5 per cent in 1987-88 to 24.2 per cent in 1990-91, rose in the post-reform period to 28.2 per cent in 1995-1996 but dropped to 18.1 per cent in 2001-02, reflecting the lack of investment demand associated with the sluggish pace of domestic industrial activity. Among other import items, the relative shares of fertilisers, non-ferrous metals, 'metalliferous ores and metal scrap' and 'iron and steel' generally showed a declining trend.

There are noticeable changes in the sources of India's imports and in country shares. The share of the OECD countries and the Eastern Europe in India's imports declined between the years 1987-88 and 1999-2000 while that of the developing countries and the OPEC group increased during the same period. The share of India's imports from the OPEC region rose significantly to 25.9 per cent in 1999-2000 from 16.3 per cent in 1990-91, mainly on account of the increase in the oil imports.

India's Merchandise Trade 2001-02 to 2008-09

The Foreign Trade Policy (2004-2009), announced by the Government in August 2004, had visualised a doubling of India's merchandise trade in five years. With an enabling policy framework and concerted efforts by the Government for facilitating a favourable environment for international trade, exports have nearly tripled between 2001-02 and 2006-07. India's merchandise exports (in US dollar terms and on customs basis), which have grown continuously at more than 20 per cent since 2002-03, posted 22.6 per cent growth in 2006-07. The average annual growth rate of exports during 2005-06 to 2007-08 was 25.0 per cent. Imports, however, grew even faster at an annual average rate of 29.5 per cent during 2005-06 to 2007-08.

As a proportion of GDP, imports were 22.0 per cent of GDP in 2007-08 while exports were at 14.2 per cent. Thus, trade deficit widened to 7.8 per cent of GDP in 2007-08. The higher trade deficit could be attributed to a rise in imports of petroleum, oil and lubricants (POL) as well as non-POL imports (Economic Survey, 2008-09).

India's share in world merchandise exports, after remaining unchanged at 0.8 per cent between 2003 and 2004, reached 1.0 per cent in 2005, and remained there in 2006 and 2007. This increase was due to India's exports growing at more than double the rate of growth of world exports since 2005. China has been a stellar export performer for years; for the first time, in 2005 and the first eight months of 2006, India's export growth surpassed that of China.

India's significant export growth in recent years was on account of a host of favourable external developments and domestic policy initiatives. Improved global growth and recovery in world trade aided the growth of Indian exports. The opening up of the economy and corporate restructuring has enhanced the competitiveness of Indian industry. There is a far greater export-orientation of domestic manufacturers, and corporate sector has been pursuing new growth strategies in response to economic reforms. Firming up of domestic economic activity, especially resurgence of the manufacturing sector, provided a supporting base for strong sector-specific exports. Trade policy reforms, continued trade promotion, market diversification and trade facilitation efforts seem to have paid good dividends.

India's Merchandise Imports

Merchandise imports grew by 24.5 per cent to US$ 185.7 billion in 2006-07 due to the high growth of 30 per cent of POL and 22.2 per cent of non-POL. POL import growth was due to both volume growth by 13.8 per cent and increase in import price of the Indian crude oil import basket by 12.1 per cent.

Imports at US$ 238.9 billion recorded a growth of 30.6 per cent during April-December 2008 (28.2 per cent during April-December 2007). The higher growth rate was mainly due to a sharp rise of 43.3 per cent in oil imports during April-December 2008, as against 24 per cent growth in oil imports in April-December 2007.

Reflecting the impact of higher growth in imports coupled with the slowdown in export growth, merchandise trade deficit (exports minus imports) widened significantly to US$ 105.3 billion during April-December 2008 from US$ 69.3 billion in April-December 2007 (52.1 per cent increase). As per cent of GDP, exports were 15.2 per cent and imports 27.1 per cent in 2008-09 (April-December) *vis-à-vis* 13.5 per cent and 21.8 per cent respectively during the corresponding period of

2007-08. Trade deficit increased from 8.2 per cent of GDP in 2007-08 (up to Q3) to 12.0 per cent in 2008-09 (up to Q3).

TABLE – 20.6

PERFORMANCE OF THE FOREIGN TRADE SECTOR
(ANNUAL PERCENTAGE CHANGE)

Year	*Export Growth*			*Import Growth*			*Terms of Trade*	
	Value (in US dollar terms)	*Volume*	*Unit Value*	*Value (in US dollar terms)*	*Volume*	*Unit Value*	*Net*	*Income*
1990-2000	7.7	10.6	8.4	8.3	12.4	7.2	1.5	11.7
1990-1995	8.1	10.9	12.6	4.6	12.9	7.6	5.0	16.5
1995-2000	7.3	10.2	4.3	12.0	11.9	6.9	-2.0	7.0
2000-01	21.0	23.9	3.3	1.7	-1.0	8.2	-4.5	18.3
2001-02	-1.6	3.7	-1.0	1.7	5.0	1.1	-2.1	1.5
2002-03	20.3	21.7	0.3	19.4	9.5	10.7	-9.4	10.3
2003-04	21.1	6.0	8.5	27.3	20.9	-0.1	8.6	15.1
2004-05	30.8	17.6	8.9	42.7	14.7	21.6	-10.9	5.0
2005-06	23.4	11.8	9.0	33.8	48.2	-10.7	22.7	36.9
2006-07	22.6	15.8	8.1	24.5	24.1	2.7	5.2	21.8
2007-08*	21.6	-	-	25.9	-	-	-	-

Note: * April-December 2007.
Source : DGCI&S, Kolkata, *Economic Survey, 2007-08.*

During 2008-09, import growth was subdued at 14.4 per cent with growth in both POL and non-POL imports moderating to 16.9 per cent and 13.2 per cent respectively. Gold and silver imports registered a negative growth of (-)7 per cent and non-POL non-bullion imports grew by 15 per cent. This was due to the global recession resulting in lower fuel prices, slowdown in industrial activity and lower demand for exports resulting in lower demand for imports needed for exports and industrial activity. In fact, import growth started declining from October 2008, with a one month lag from export growth and even turned negative from January to March 2009. The negative trend continued in April 2009 with import growth at (-)36.6 per cent. While oil import growth was lower at 58.5 per cent, non-oil import growth was lower at 24.6 per cent over April 2008.

Trade deficit increased to US$ 88.5 billion (as per customs data) in 2007-08 and US$ 119.1 billion in 2008-09 but fell in April 2009 by 42.8 per cent.

APPENDIX – 20.1

BALANCE OF TRADE

Balance of trade, simply defined is, the difference between the value of export of goods and the value of import of goods or more generally between exports and imports or (X - M) where X denotes value of exports and M, value of imports.

When value of exports is more than value of imports (i.e., X > M), balance of trade (BoT) is said to be favourable or positive. On the other hand, when exports are less than imports (X < M) or imports more than exports (M > X), the balance of trade (BoT) is said to be unfavourable or negative, or there is said to be a deficit in the balance of trade.

Since goods are also called merchandise, the balance of trade or trade balance is also called balance of merchandise account.

India's Balance of Trade

Ever since the beginning of planning era in 1951, India has continued to suffer from an unfavourable balance of trade. The only exceptions to this trend have been the years 1972-73 and 1976-77 when the country had a positive trade balance of Rs. 104 crore and Rs. 68 crore, respectively.

In the early years after Independence, the value of India's exports as well as imports were low and the difference between them was small. This resulted in comparatively lower magnitude of deficit in trade balance. From Rs. 163 crore, average annual deficit rose to an annual average of Rs. 36,363 crore during 1997 and 2002 and Rs. 6,06,253 crore during 2002-2007. The year 2007-08 and 2008-09 witnessed negative balance of trade to the tune of -88535 and -119055 respectively (Table 20.2). Thus, the trade deficit has not only persisted since 1951 but has increased widely over the years.

Causes of Unfavourable Balance of Trade

Continued excess of imports over exports has perpetuated the unfavourable balance of trade since 1950-51. To begin with, the trade deficit was small, but it widened over time, more particularly from the Sixth Plan onwards, it rose sharply to assume serious dimensions during and after the Eighth Five Year Plan. This has happened because exports from India have not been able to keep pace with the high growth rate of imports.

APPENDIX TABLE – A-20.1

INDIA'S BALANCE OF TRADE

(Rs. Crore)

Plans		*Average Annual*		*Trade Balance*
		Exports	*Imports*	
First Plan	(1951-1956)	605	735	-130
Second Plan	(1956-1961)	606	973	-367
Third Plan	(1961-1966)	753	1,240	-487
Annual Plans	(1966-1969)	1,238	1,998	-760
Fourth Plan	(1969-1974)	1,810	1,973	-163
Fifth Plan	(1974-1979)	4,728	5,538	-810
Annual Plans	(1979-1980)	6,418	9,143	-2,725
Sixth Plan	(1980-1985)	8,967	14,683	-5,716
Seventh Plan	(1985-1990)	17,382	25,112	-7,730
Annual Plans	(1991-1992)	38,297	45,525	-7,278
Eighth Plan	(1992-1997)	86,557	97,609	-11,352
Ninth Plan	(1997-2002)	1,68,400	2,04,763	-36,363
Tenth Plan	(2002-2007)	20,52,041	26,58,294	-6,06,253
Eleventh	**(2007-08)**	**6,55,864**	**10,12,312**	**-3,56,448**
Plan	**(2008-09)(P)[a]**	**7,66,935**	**13,05,503**	**-5,38,568**

Note: P : Provisional

a : Growth rate on provisional over revised basis and based on Department of Commerce methodology.

Source : Compiled from *Economic Survey*, 2003-2004, 2005-06, 2007-08 and 2008-09.

Large Increase in Imports

In terms of value, India's imports have increased sharply between 1950-51 and 2007-08 from a level of Rs. 608 crore to estimated Rs. 1305503 crore in 2008-09. Some of the factors that have contributed to this massive import growth are as below:

(i) Large Increase in Developmental and Other Imports: Under planned economic development of the country starting with the First Plan, there has been a continuous expansion in imports of capital goods, machinery equipment, etc. Also with globalisation and liberalisation, imports of all kinds have increased.

(ii) Large Increase in Import of Petroleum: Petroleum, oils and lubricants (POL) have registered more than 500-fold increase between 1960-61 and 1991 as the value of POL imports increased from Rs. 69 crore to Rs. 10,816 crore, which further rose to Rs. 3,20,655 crore in

2007-08. Petroleum is a major source of energy used in industry and in surface as well as air transport.

(iii) Fertiliser Imports: In spite of increased domestic production, fertilisers are imported to meet their fast growing consumption requirements. Thus, between 1960-61 and 2000-01, import of fertilisers has gone up from Rs. 13 crore to Rs. 3,034 crore in 2000-01 and Rs. 20,308 crore in 2007-08.

(iv) Import of Pearls and Precious Stones: The import of unfinished and finished/worked precious and semi-precious stones has increased from Rs. 1 crore in 1960-61 to Rs. 32,114 crore in 2007-08.

Modest Growth in Exports

Growth of exports was quite low and insignificant till the Third Five Year Plan. The total value of exports increased from Rs. 606 crore in 1950-51 to Rs. 642 crore in 1960-61 and Rs. 810 crore in 1965-66. However, the growth of exports picked up after the 3rd Plan to reach the level of Rs. 36,711 crore in 1980-81 and Rs. 32,553 crore in 1991. The policy of liberalisation following the economic reforms resulted in marked improvement in export performance. In the year 2000-01, the total value of exports was Rs. 2,03,571 crore which jumped to Rs. 6,55,864 crore in 2007-08 and Rs. 7,66,935 crore in 2008-09 (P).

Inspite of this large increase in exports, the gap between the value of imports and value of exports not only persisted but also widened particularly during the last decade. Both external and the internal factors are responsibles for this.

Some of the external factors are: low world demand for our products due to continuing recession and downturn in many countries; low income and price elasticity of demand for some of our exports; import restriction on our goods entering foreign countries and disintegration of the Soviet Union—our largest trading partners providing a big market for Indian goods.

Among the internal factors, the important ones are: increasing domestic demand, not leaving large surplus for export and low quality and high cost of production.

Measures to Correct Deficit in Balance of Trade

The Government of India has been adopting and implementing various policies for restricting imports and promoting exports to reduce trade deficit.

Restrictions on Imports

Following measures have been taken to regulate imports:

(i) Licensing of Imports: For quite a long time, the import of non-essential consumer goods was not permitted while the importers of capital goods essential for country's development were given import licences. However, now under the liberalised trade policy, licensing requirements for most of the goods have been abolished; only a small negative list of import items remains under licensing system.

(ii) Tariff Restrictions: For the goods that are permitted to be imported under licence from the government, further restrictions are imposed by way of custom duties or import duties also called import tariffs. This means a tax is imposed on the goods which arrive at the Indian ports and thus, the price of such goods becomes higher for the Indian buyers. The higher the rate of custom duty, the greater is the price that Indian buyers need to pay for imported goods. These high prices of imported goods are expected to reduce their demand in the domestic market and thereby to restrict imports.

(iii) Quantitative Restrictions: The government may determine the total import quota of goods, i.e., the total amount of goods that can be imported and allot this quota to various importers. Nothing beyond the quota is allowed to be imported. This naturally limits the quantity of imports. However, under an agreement with the World Trade Organization (WTO), such quantitative restrictions have been removed on many goods, while for others they are to be removed in near future.

Export Promotion

With the continuing large deficits in India's balance of trade and limited scope for imports reduction, the only long-term solution to the problem lies in promotion of exports to earn sufficient foreign exchange to pay for our growing imports. Export promotion measures opening up wider international market for our entrepreneurs will stimulate industrial development in the country under the incentive of larger world demand for our goods.

Export Promotion Measures

The export promotion measures adopted by the Government of India include monetary and non-monetary incentives, fiscal reliefs, credit facilities, establishment of institutions to help exporters as well as strict quality controls and inspection of goods meant from export. Some of the major steps in this direction are as below:

(i) Devaluation: In July 1991, the rupee was devalued by about 20 per cent in terms of major world currencies. This was expected to cheapen our goods to foreign buyers, thereby encouraging our exports.

(ii) Cash Assistance: Under this scheme, cash assistance is given to exporters to compensate them for indirect taxes (e.g., custom duties) levied on the imported inputs that are used in production of goods for exports.

(iii) Income Tax Concessions: Income from exports is given several concessions under the income tax laws. For example, profits from exports are totally exempted from income tax.

(iv) Import Concessions: Several concessions in imports of machinery, equipment and technology are given to export production units. Export-oriented units are allowed duty-free imports of machines, raw materials and technology. Exporters are also allocated foreign exchange for import of raw materials used in production of export goods.

(v) Concessional Bank Credit to Exporters: For financing production meant for exports and also for financing exports themselves, banks give credit to exporters at concessional terms.

(vi) Import Licences to Exporters: Since imported goods fetched very high prices in the domestic market as their imports were highly restricted, the exporters were granted licences for import of goods up to a certain percentage of value of goods exported by them. This was expected to provide added incentive for exports.

(vii) Issue of Exim Scrips: The system of granting import licences to exporters was later replaced by exim scrips. The exporters were given exim scrips equivalent to 30 per cent of value of their exports. These exim scrips could be used to import a large variety of items. The exim scrips could also be sold in the market. Since these enjoyed a premium, the exporters could make additional profits from their sale. This could act as a great incentive to exporters.

(viii) Convertibility of the Rupee: The system of exim scrips was also replaced by partial convertibility of rupee in March 1992. Under this scheme, exporters, who earlier had to surrender their entire foreign exchange earnings to the Reserve Bank of India (RBI) at a rate fixed by it, were now obliged to sell only 40 per cent of their exchange earnings at the official rate to the RBI. The rest, they were free to sell in the market at the market determined rate, which was obviously higher

than the official rate. This indeed was a great liberalisation measure and a bigger incentive. In March 1997, even this was replaced by a system of full convertibility of rupee on the trade account.

(ix) System of Advanced Licensing: Exporters are given advance licences for duty-free import of goods used in production of export items.

(x) Relaxation of Controls on Exports and Simplification of Procedures: Controls on exports have been relaxed. Exports of many items have been decontrolled while export procedures and formalities have been simplified.

(xi) Export Processing Zones: Many export processing zones have been set up. The units operating there are allowed free trade with other countries. They also enjoy various concessions like five-year tax holiday.

(xii) Export Promotion Organisations: Some such organisations are Export Advisory Council, Export Promotion Councils, Directorate of Export Promotion, etc.

(xiii) Export-Import Bank: The EXIM Bank provides financial services to exporters and importers and coordinates the work of other institutions engaged in financing export trade. It pays special attention to export of capital goods.

Questions

1. Distinguish between Balance of trade and Balance of payments. Point out the reasons for adverse balance of payments situation in India. *[B.Com. (P) 2008]*
2. Explain the significant changes in India's foreign trade since 1991. *[B.A. (P) 2007]*
3. Discuss the various export promotion measures taken by the Government of India in the last decade. How far is the export oriented strategy superior to import substitution. *[B.A. (P) 2006]*
4. Examine the composition and direction of India's foreign trade in the post 2000 period. *[B.Com. (P) 2006]*
5. Describe the trends in the composition and direction of India's foreign trade since 1980's *[B.A. (P) 2004]*
6. Write brief note on 'Export Promotion'. *[B.Com. (P) 2004]*

21

Balance of Payments and Trade Policy

Concepts

BALANCE of payments (BoP) is a systematic record of all economic transactions between the residents of a country and the rest of the world. Like all double-entry book keeping accounts, it always balances i.e., Sum of credit entries = Sum of debit entries.

There are two types of accounts in BoP, namely: (i) Current Account and (ii) Capital Account.

Current account records transfers of goods and services i.e., merchandise trade and net invisibles which includes services like travel, transportation, insurance, etc., and transfer payments.

Capital account shows transfers of claims to money or titles to investment between a country and the rest of the world. It includes foreign investment inflow minus the foreign investment outflow, loans including external assistance and external commercial borrowings (inflow – outflow) and other capital which includes rupee debt service, IMF transactions and SDR allocation.

A current account deficit is financed through net inflow of capital on the capital account and the change in the Government's foreign exchange reserve position.

Trade Policy: An Overview

Import Substitution Based Strategy

As we embarked on a period of planning, during the fifties, import substitution came to constitute a major element of India's trade and industrial policies. Planners, more or less chose to ignore the option of foreign trade as an engine of India's economic growth. This was primarily due to the highly pessimistic view taken on the potential for export earnings. A further impetus to the inward orientation was provided by the existence of a vast domestic market. In retrospect, it is now abundantly clear that the policy makers not only underestimated the export possibilities but also the import intensity of the import substitution process itself. As a consequence, India's share of total world exports declined from 1.91 per cent in 1950 to about 0.53 per cent in 1992.

India's participation in world markets declined steadily during the second half of the twentieth century, with only a marginal improvement following the reforms of the 1990s. Its share of world merchandise exports was 2.2 per cent in 1948, higher than China's 0.9 per cent or Japan's 0.4 per cent. It fell to one-fifth its initial level, 0.5 per cent in 1983 and recovered only marginally to 0.7 per cent in 2000. Japan, in contrast, progressively increased its share from 0.4 per cent in 1948 to a peak of 10.0 per cent in 1993. China's share first increased to a high of 1.3 per cent in 1963, then fell to a low of 1.0 per cent in 1973, later recovering dramatically after its opening to the world economy in 1978 to 4.0 per cent in 2000.

There is no widely accepted single quantitative indicator that captures the depths and degree of integration of a given country with the world economy, but the ratio of exports plus imports to GDP is a commonly used measure. India's ratio was a mere 16.6 per cent in 1980, compared with China's 22.3 per cent, South Korea's 75.5 per cent and Thailand's 54.4 per cent. India has become more integrated with the world economy since then, but not as much as its neighbouring countries. India's trade ratio increased to 24.2 per cent in 1999, while China's trade ratio more than doubled during the same period, increasing to as high as 49.2 per cent (Srinivasan, 2003).[1]

India's inward orientation has had significant economic costs in lower overall growth and stagnating living standards. Japan's rapid export growth was associated with very rapid GDP growth and improvements in living standards. Its export sector became more efficient over time. Its image as a producer of low-cost, low-quality imitative products shifted to that of a world leader in producing high quality high-technology goods. Though China's internal market is large, international trade has played a powerful instrumental role in its growth

1. Srinivasan, T.N. and S.D. Tendulkar (2003). *Reintegrating India with the World Economy*. New Delhi: Oxford University Press.

process. The country achieved an average annual growth rate of more than 10 per cent during the period 1980-2000 (World Bank, 2002) and its real GDP and exports have grown even more rapidly since 1980.

India's GDP growth rate, in contrast, averaged 3.75 per cent a year from 1950 to 1980, putting it in the category of a low-income, slow growing economy among the 41 "Third World" countries examined by Reynolds (1985).

The origins of economic nationalism in India can be traced to the beliefs held by those fighting for independence from British rule. They perceived the British colonial policy of *laissez faire* and free trade to be the major causes of India's economic underdevelopment. Their thoughts about economic development strategies and vision of a state-guided closed economy were heavily influenced by Soviet planning. They viewed international trade as a "whirlpool of economic imperialism".

India's international trade policy had the direct effect of limiting its participation in world trade. It sought to minimise imports by supporting indigenous production and according priority to domestic use in the disposition of production. Import tariffs, based on the recommendations of the Tariff Commission, were initially used to provide infant-industry protection to selected industries. The ambitious investment in heavy industries at the start of the Second Five Year Plan (1956-1961) led to a significant spurt in import demand and a rapid depletion of foreign exchange reserves, and it precipitated a balance of payments crisis in 1957.

Quantitative restrictions (QRs) on imports were initially imposed to meet the crisis but continued until early 2001 in varying intensities. Graded import tariffs (highest on "least essential" consumer goods, lower on industrial intermediate inputs, and the lowest on capital goods deemed "essential" for development) were also introduced in the 1960s in an effort to contain balance of payments deficits.

Persistent deficits in the balance of payments were mitigated by increases in tariff levels and in the severity of QRs rather than by devaluation of the rupee.

India became increasingly insulated from the world economy under this development strategy. The volume of world exports expanded at an average rate of 7.9 per cent annually from 1950 to 1973, but India's exports grew by only 2.7 per cent annually. Thus, widening the gap between world and Indian exports. The ratio of exports to GDP also showed a declining trend from a high of 7.3 per cent in 1951 to the lowest level of 3 per cent in 1965 and remained below 4 per cent until 1973. A similar trend is also visible in the figure with regard to the ratio of exports plus imports to GDP (Srinivasan, 2003).

The inward looking industrialisation process did result in high rates of industrial growth between 1956 and 1966. However, several weaknesses of such a process of industrialisation soon became evident, as inefficiencies crept into the system and the economy turned into an increasingly 'high-cost' one. Over a period of time, this led to a 'technological lag' and also resulted in poor export performance.

In the meantime, some change in the attitude towards exports became perceptible. Several export promotion measures were put in place from the early 1960s. The 1966 devaluation, while not resulting in the expected improvement in trade deficit due to a combination of circumstances, brought out the problems stemming from an overvalued exchange rate. Nevertheless, it will be correct to say that until the end of the 1970s, exports were primarily regarded as a source of foreign exchange rather than as an efficient means of allocating resources. Import substitution over a wide area remained the basic premise of the development strategy.

Towards Efficient Import Substitution

Foreign trade policy issues became the subject of intensive discussion in early eighties. It came to be realised that a scheme of import licensing under which imports were permitted only to the extent that domestic production fell short of domestic demand irrespective of difference in cost and prices, could only lead to inefficiency. The view gained ground that a more liberal policy of imports of capital goods and technology would enable India to reap the benefits of international division of labour. *The attempt therefore was to move away from import substitution per se towards efficient import substitution,* so that considerations relating to cost and efficiency were incorporated in the overall policy framework. It also became increasingly clear that production for export could not be isolated from production for the home market and that trade policy had to be integrated with the policy for domestic industrialisation.

With the realisation of the drawbacks of the excessively inward looking trade strategy on the one hand and the need for modernisation and technology upgradation of the Indian industry on the other, certain policy measures in the direction of trade liberalisation were initiated in the late seventies. The strategy towards a greater integration of the Indian economy with the rest of the world has been pursued since then. The liberalisation process remained somewhat slow during the first half of the eighties and it gathered momentum during the second half of the decade.

The policy changes have been influenced, *inter alia*, by the recommendations of a number of Committees, which were set up during the seventies and the eighties. In this context, mention may be made about two prominent Committee Reports—the Report of the Committee on Import Export Policies and Procedures (Chairman: P.C. Alexander, 1978) and the Report of the Committee on Trade Policies (Chairman: Abid Hussain, 1984). The Alexander Committee recommended simplification of the import licensing procedure and provided a framework involving a shift in the emphasis from 'controls' to 'development'. Following the recommendations of the Alexander Committee, selective import liberalisation measures were initiated in the late seventies primarily aiming at making the import of capital goods easier. Imports of certain raw materials that were not available indigenously were also placed under the Open General Licence (OGL) List. The emphasis of the policy efforts was also to simplify the procedures governing India's foreign trade. During this period, special measures were initiated to boost the export of project goods.

The Abid Hussain Committee envisaged "growth-led exports" rather than "export-led growth" and stressed upon the need for harmonisation of foreign trade policies with other economic policies arguing for a phased reduction of effective protection. The Committee also favoured announcement of trade policies for longer periods in order to impart a degree of continuity and facilitate long-term planning of export business. In line with these recommendations, long-term trade policy was introduced with the announcement of an import export policy covering the period 1985-1988. The policy was formulated with the aim of boosting exports and encouraging efficient import substitution.

While the signs of liberalised trade policy became visible in the latter half of eighties, it was only in 1991 that the country embarked on a truly liberalised trade policy with a short negative list of exports and imports and with quantitative controls over imports withdrawn for all, except consumer goods. It was recognised that trade, exchange rate and industrial policies must form part of an integrated policy framework if the aim was to improve the productivity and efficiency of the economic system.

Trade Policy since 1991

Outward Orientation Focusing on Export Promotion

The trade policy changes in the post-1991 period sought to minimise the role of quantitative restrictions and substantially reduce the tariff rates on the lines suggested by the Tax Reforms Committee (Chairman: Raja J. Chelliah). The developments in India's trade policy during this period needs to be viewed in conjunction with policy reforms initiated in other spheres of the economy. The devaluation of the Rupee in July 1991 and the transition to the market-based exchange rate regime deserve mention in this regard. These measures were aimed at enhancing the price competitiveness of exports. The policies governing foreign investment and foreign collaboration also have undergone significant change, which have a bearing on trade performance. Apart from unilateral measures, the liberalisation of India's trade policies also reflects the multilateral commitments of the country to the World Trade Organization (WTO).

The focus of these reforms has been on liberalisation, openness, transparency and globalisation with a basic thrust on outward orientation focusing on export promotion activity and improving competitiveness of Indian industry to meet global market requirements. In early 2002, the Government presented a Medium-Term Export Strategy (MTES) for 2002-2007 providing a vision for creating a stable policy environment with indicative sector-wise targets, with a mission to achieve one per cent of global trade by 2007. The Export and Import (EXIM) Policy framed for the period 2002-2007 and unveiled on 31 March 2002 also sought to usher in an environment free of restrictions and controls.

Trade policy reforms in the recent past, have provided an export-friendly environment with simplified procedures for trade facilitation. Such continued trade promotion and trade facilitation efforts of the Government have also aided the current strengthening of export growth. On August 31, 2004, a new Foreign Trade Policy for the period 2004-2009, replacing the hitherto nomenclature of EXIM Policy by Foreign Trade Policy (FTP) was announced with the following two objectives: (i) to double the percentage of global merchandize trade within 5 years and (ii) use trade expansion as an effective instrument of economic growth and employment generation. A vigorous export-led growth strategy of doubling India's share in global merchandise trade in the next five years, with a focus on the sectors having prospects for export expansion and potential for employment generation, constitute the main plank of the Policy. These measures are expected to enhance international competitiveness and aid in further increasing the acceptability of Indian exports.

In the last five years, our exports witnessed robust growth to reach a level of US$ 168 billion in 2008-09 from US$ 63 billion in 2003-04. Our share of global merchandise trade was 0.83 per cent in the year 2003 which rose to 1.45 per cent in the year 2008 as per WTO estimates. our share of global commercial services export was 1.4 per cent in 2003 which rose to 2.8 per cent in 2008. India's total share in goods and services was 0.92 per cent in 2003; it increased to 1.64 per cent in 2008. On the employment front, studies have suggested that nearly 14 million jobs were created directly or indirectly as a result of augmented exports in the last five years.

However, the year 2008-09 was marked by adverse developments in the external sector of the economy, particularly during the second half of the year, reflecting the impact of global financial crisis on emerging market economies including India. Emerging economies were affected in varying degrees depending upon the extent of openness and the dependence on capital flows as the external environment deteriorated on account of slowdown in global demand, reversal of capital flows and reduced access to external sources of finance in the face of adverse global credit market conditions.[2]

The global financial meltdown and consequent economic recession in developed economies have clearly been major factor in India's economic slowdown. Given the origin and dimension of the crisis in the advanced countries, which some have called the worst since the Great Depression, every developing country has suffered to a varying degree. No country, including India, remained immune to the global economic shock.

The current account, which had recorded an annual average surplus of 1.4 per cent of GDP, during 2001-02 to 2003-04 returned to an annual average deficit of 1.1 per cent during 2004-05 to 2007-08. The current account deficit widened to 4.1 per cent of GDP during April-December 2008, following the slowdown in external demand and deceleration in capital flows (Economic Survey 2008-09).

---

2. Government of India, Ministry of Finance (2009). *Economic Survey 2008-09*.

India's Balance of Payment Trends 1950-51–2008-09[3]

The Decades of Fifties and Sixties

Prior to 1956-57, for most years in the fifties, India had a current account surplus. But the position changed in 1956-57 when India faced BoP crisis. The trade deficit increased from 3.8 per cent of GDP at market prices to 4.5 per cent. The BoP crisis of 1956-57 precipitated the imposition of exchange controls which then became endemic to the import substitution regime.

The BoP position deteriorated once again in 1966-67. In 1965, the United States suspended its aid in response to the Indo-Pakistan war and later refused to renew the PL 480 agreement on a long-term basis. There was a concerted effort by the United States, the World Bank and the IMF to use external assistance as an instrument to induce India: (a) to adopt a new agricultural strategy, and (b) to devalue the rupee. The rupee was devalued by 36.5 per cent in June 1966, and tariffs and export subsidies were simultaneously rationalised, on the understanding that the inflow of aid would be substantially increased.

The BoP improved after 1966-67 but largely because of the decline in imports. Exports performed indifferently despite the devaluation.

Balance of Payments in the Seventies

A Decade of Comfort

India's balance of payments remained comfortable during the seventies. The adjustment to the first oil shock of 1973-74 was rendered smooth by a happy combination of buoyant exports, spurt in private transfer receipts and increased inflow of aid. Exports, benefited by the expansion in global trade, rose at an annual rate of 6.8 per cent in volume terms and by 15.6 per cent in US dollar terms during the decade. An effective depreciation of the rupee occurred due to the link with Pound Sterling until 1973 and later, because of the lower growth in prices in India relative to other countries. Private transfers rose seven-fold from $ 296 million in 1974-75 to $ 2175 million in 1979-80 and in fact, in the post-first oil shock period, financed roughly 80 per cent of the trade deficit. Within two years of the shock, the current account balance turned into surplus and it was only in 1978-79 that a deficit of about 0.2 per cent of GDP appeared. The utilisation of aid was significant and was substantially higher than the financing requirement

3. This section draws from C. Rangarajan's paper, *India's Balance of Payments: The Emerging Dimensions*, in Uma Kapila (ed.), *Indian Economy Since Independence* 2004-05 edition, *op.cit.*

for the decade, allowing for a build-up of reserves. At the close of the decade, the foreign exchange reserves stood at $ 7361 million providing cover for over seven months of imports.

Balance of Payments in Eighties

The Period of Difficulties upto 1981-82

During the eighties, issues relating to the balance of payments came to occupy the centre stage in terms of India's macroeconomic management. The impact of the second oil shock of 1979, the full effects of which spilled over into the eighties, was more severe than of the 1973-74. Between 1978-79 and 1981-82, imports almost doubled. The increase in POL imports accounted for a little over half the increase in the overall imports. This was followed by the second-round effects on non-POL imports. Export performance was depressed by the severe international recession of 1980-1983 and recorded a volume growth of just a little over 3 per cent. Net invisible receipts continued to provide support to the balance of payments, largely in the form of earnings from tourism and the sustained buoyancy of private transfers. However, the sharp widening in the merchandise trade deficit resulted in a turnaround in the current account balance from a surplus in 1977-78 to a deficit in 1981-82 of the order of US $ 3,166 million or 1.8 per cent of GDP. Adjustment efforts consisted essentially of an Extended Fund Facility (EFF) negotiated with the IMF, although there were also intensified efforts to improve domestic production of crude petroleum.

Easing of Pressure during 1982-83 to 1984-85

A reprieve came during the period 1982-83 to 1984-85, with the easing of pressure on the balance of payments mainly due to a decline in the volume growth of imports from an average rate of 11.0 per cent during 1978-1982 to a little over 2 per cent. Net oil imports (net of crude oil exports which commenced in 1981-82 after the discovery of crude oil in Bombay High), declined substantially as domestic production spurted to 29.0 million tonnes by 1984-85. This indeed was the main cause of the easing of the balance of payments. Non-POL imports rose at an average rate of 3.6 per cent in dollar terms. Exports, however, grew only at an average rate of 3.2 per cent, in volume terms, due to a combination of adverse internal and external conditions. The invisibles account deteriorated as the interest payments to service external borrowing acquired a steady rising trend. Private transfers stagnated with the arrest in the labour migration boom. As a result, invisibles including private transfers and other surpluses, which had financed 89 per cent of the trade deficit in 1978-79 could meet only 57 per cent of the trade deficit in 1984-85. The current account deficit fell to US $ 2,416 million or 1.2 per cent of GDP in 1984-85 and reserves, which were US $5,952 million at the end of the year, stood to cover a little over 4 months of imports. Twenty-nine per cent of the financing requirement of the first half of the eighties was met by the EFF. Commercial borrowings and non-resident deposits emerged as important sources of finance, meeting 21 per cent and 15 per cent respectively of the financing need. However, external assistance remained the major source of foreign capital inflows, accounting for 39 per cent of the financing requirement.

The Build-up to the Crisis during 1985-1990

The second half of the eighties witnessed the building up of strains on the balance of payments. Current account deficits acquired a structural character, remaining at high levels throughout. Large trade deficits occurred year after year despite a robust growth in exports. Recovering from the stagnation in 1985-86, the volume growth of exports in the succeeding four years ranged between 10 to 12 per cent per annum on an average. The share of manufactured exports rose from 56 per cent in 1980-81 to 75 per cent in 1989-90. Imports in US dollar terms rose in every year of the period. The volume of net POL imports increased from 12.4 million tonnes in 1984-85 to 23.5 million tonnes in 1989-90. However, the fall in crude oil prices during the period helped to contain the oil import bill. On the other hand, non-oil imports rose sharply by an average of 13.4 per cent in US dollar terms partly due to large imports of food grains in 1988-89. Imports of capital goods rose by an average of 16.2 per cent during the period. Export-related imports as well as other miscellaneous imports also rose significantly. The support from invisible receipts fell in the face of steadily growing interest payments and the outgo on account of profits, dividends, royalty, technical fees and professional fees. The current account deficit averaged $ 5.8 billion or 2.4 per cent of GDP during the period as against the Planning Commission's estimate of 1.6 per cent. The period also marked a deterioration in fiscal imbalances as the ratio of gross fiscal deficit to GDP rose from 6.3 per cent in the first half of the eighties to 8.2 per cent during 1985-1990. Repurchases from the IMF under the EFF exacerbated the deterioration in the balance of payments. External assistance, commercial borrowing and non-resident deposits shared equiproportionally in the financing need. The result was a doubling of external debt and a rise in the debt service ratio from 13.6 per cent in 1984-85 to 30.9 per cent in 1989-90.

The Crisis: 1990-1992

In 1991, India found itself in its worst balance of payments crisis since 1947. That there was a crisis in the making during the second half of 1980s had been evident for a long time. The inflow of foreign borrowing had increased at a rapid rate during the late 1980s. This was due to the excess domestic expenditure over income—the fiscal deficit of the Centre and the states soared to over 11 per cent in 1991. During this period, total public debt as a proportion of GNP doubled reaching the level of 60 per cent and foreign currency reserves were depleted rapidly.

Matters were made worse by an accompanying double-digit inflation in 1990-91. The oil price increase resulting from Iraq's invasion of Kuwait in August 1990 reinforced the crisis-like situation in India.

India's credit rating got downgraded as, for the first time in its history, India was on the verge of defaulting on its international commitments and was denied access to external commercial credit markets. A net outflow of Non-Resident Indian (NRI) deposits commenced in October 1990 and continued during 1991. The only way left for India was to borrow against the security of its gold reserves transported abroad.

But something good emerged out of the BoP crisis of 1991—the long overdue economic reforms. Apart from an immediate programme of macroeconomic stabilisation, structural reforms were also introduced in the industrial and trade policy regimes with a view to improving the efficiency, productivity and international competitiveness of India's economy.

The overvalued exchange rate was corrected by devaluation in 1991, followed by partial convertibility of rupee in 1992-93 and then making the rupee fully convertible on trade account in 1993-94. Tariffs were also cut steeply to open Indian industry to foreign competition. The focus of import liberalisation has primarily been on intermediate and capital goods industries with the imports of consumer goods remaining, by and large, regulated.

Balance of Payments during 1993-94 to 2005-06

The initial response of the economy, especially exports, was very good. The years 1993-94 to 1995-96 were years of excellent economic performance with GDP having grown at 6.2 per cent in 1993-94 and by more than 7.5 per cent during 1994-95 and 1996-97. Exports grew by 19.7 per cent during 1993-94 to 1995-96.

The major reasons for such a high growth rate in exports were:[4]

- World GDP grew by an average rate of 4.1 per cent per annum during 1994-1997 compared with 2.4 per cent during 1990-1993.
- World trade (dollar terms) grew by an average rate of 9.8 per cent per annum during 1994-1997 compared with 6.0 per cent during 1990-1993.
- Imports of advanced countries (dollar terms) grew by an average rate of 11.5 per cent during 1994-1997 compared with 2.1 per cent during 1990-1993.
- Increase in India's share in world exports of its three major commodity groups, *viz.*, textiles, yarn and fabrics; pearls, precious and semi-precious stones; and clothing and accessories during 1994-1996.
- Increase in the Index of Comparative Advantage (ICA) of the above.
- Other export commodity groups in which India gained in terms of ICA during 1994-1996 include fish and fish preparations; rice; coffee and substitutes; organic chemicals; footwear; and gold and silver jewellery.

However, the boom was short-lived. Since 1996, India's export performance has been poor.

There could be several explanations for this. Firstly, there has been a major downturn in world trade since 1996, which has affected India's trade as well. Export growth has been further hampered by an appreciation of the real effective exchange rate in 1996-97 and 1997-1998. This trend has, however, been reversed since 1998-99. There has also been an adverse movement in terms of trade, which appears to have affected exports. Finally, there are the host of domestic factors—both policy related and administrative—which continue to hamper imports. These include infrastructure constraints, high transaction costs, SSI reservations, labour inflexibility, quality problems and quantitative restrictions on export of agricultural commodities.

However, the surplus on invisibles has helped to reduce the deficit on the current account. Earnings from invisibles have helped particularly during the critical years of 1996-97 and 1997-98 when the deficit on the trade account touched alarming levels close to $ 1.5 to 1.6 billion.

4. Chadha, Rajesh (1999). "Balance of Payments and Trade Policy", paper presented at ADB-NCAER Seminar on *Economic and Policy Reforms in India* (Dec. 9), India International Centre, New Delhi.

A current account surplus for the third successive year, coupled with an expanding capital account, further strengthened India's balance of payments in 2003-04. The year witnessed accumulation of reserves of US$ 31.4 billion (excluding valuation changes, gold, Special Drawing Rights and Reserve Tranche at the IMF). Almost one-third of the reserves were contributed by the surplus in the current account. Rising surpluses in the current account have been one of the distinguishing features of India's balance of payments in the current decade, as it has been for most other major Asian economies (e.g. China, Hong Kong, Japan, Korea, Malaysia, the Philippines, Singapore, Taiwan and Thailand). While for the predominantly export-oriented South East Asian economies (e.g. Korea, Malaysia, the Philippines, Singapore, Taiwan and Thailand), strong growth in merchandise exports has been the main driver behind the current account surpluses, buoyant invisible inflows, particularly private transfers comprising remittances, along with software services exports, have been instrumental in creating and sustaining current account surpluses for India.

The strength provided by the surplus in the current account was reinforced by robust capital inflows in 2003-04. During the year, capital account surplus was almost double its previous year's level. While major components of loans (e.g. external assistance and commercial borrowings) recorded net outflows, foreign investment flows increased more than three-fold. Heavy portfolio inflows, comprising essentially FII investment, shored up total foreign investment and the overall capital account surplus. Banking capital inflows, particularly expatriate deposits, also contributed to the expanding surplus.

Balance of Payment during 2006-07 to 2008-09

The current account, which had recorded an annual average surplus of 1.4 per cent of GDP during 2001-02 to 2003-04, returned to an annual average deficit of 1.1 per cent during 2004-05 to 2007-08. The current account deficit widened to 4.1 per cent of GDP during April-December 2008, following the slowdown in external demand and deceleration in capital flows (Economic Survey, 2008-09).

A comparison of current account position across country groups during 2001-2008 reveals that advanced economies and central and eastern Europe recorded current account deficits, while developing Asia and Middle East showed current account surpluses. The current account surplus of China improved steadily from 1.3 per cent of GDP in 2001 to 11.0 per cent in 2007 and was 10.0 per cent in the year 2008, characterised by an adverse external environment. India's current account deficit moved in a narrow range of 1.0-1.3 per cent and was 2.8 per cent in 2008.[5]

Current Account

Under current account of the BoP, transactions are classified into merchandise (exports and imports) and invisibles. Invisible transactions are further classified into three categories, *viz*.: (a) Group of Services–Travel, Transportation, Insurance, Government Not Included Elsewhere (GNIE) and Miscellaneous Services, which encompass communication services, construction services, financial services, software services, news agency services, royalties, management services and business services, (b) Income, and (c) Transfers (grants, gifts, remittances, etc.) which do not have any *quid pro quo.*

The current account, after being in surplus during 2001-02 to 2003-2004, reverted to a deficit from the year 2004-05. This was despite a robust growth in net invisibles account fuelled by software exports and private transfers. Thus, large merchandise trade deficit coexisted with a lower deficit on the goods and services account because of the surplus on non-factor services. The current account, therefore, has been characterised by persistence of high trade deficit and buoyant invisibles surplus, which have provided support to current account position.

Invisibles

The surplus on the invisible account has played a key role in balancing the high trade deficit and lowering the current account deficit. The net invisibles (services, transfers and investment income) surplus was US$ 74.6 billion in 2007-08 and US$ 68.9 billion during April-December 2008.

Despite higher invisibles surplus, the trade deficit widened mainly on account of higher growth in imports coupled with slowdown in export growth in the third quarter of 2008-09. The current account deficit (CAD) therefore, was higher at US$ 36.5 billion in April-December 2008 (135.1 per cent increase, over US$ 15.5 billion during April-December 2007). The ratio of CAD to GDP also increased from 1.8 per cent in 2007-08 (up to Q3) to 4.1 per cent in 2008-09 (up to Q3).

During the third quarter of the year 2008-09 (October-December), there was a nominal negative growth for both invisible receipts and payments reflecting the adverse impact of global economic slowdown.

5. Government of India, (2009). *Economic Survey 2008-09*, ch. 6.

Invisible receipts declined on account of fall in travel, transportation and insurance receipts in the services category and private transfers and investment income receipts. Net invisibles surplus financed 59.7 per cent of trade deficit in Q3 of 2008-09 (82.6 per cent in Q3 of 2007-2008). Accordingly, the current account deficit rose sharply to US$ 14.6 billion (5.1 per cent of GDP) during Q3 of 2008-09, as compared to US$ 4.5 billion (1.5 per cent of GDP) in Q3 of 2007-08.[6]

Sustainability of Current Account

One of the factors underlying the external payments crisis of 1991 was the high levels of current account deficit (CAD) maintained during the 1980s which at the time of the crisis had reached 3.1 per cent of GDP, well above the sustainable level for India. Concerted efforts directed at imparting strength and stability to the external sector emphasised a policy of maintaining the CAD within a sustainable level of about 2 per cent. This is broadly in line with the recommendations of the High Level Committee on Balance of Payments (RBI, 1993), which recommended that CAD-GDP ratio could be sustainable at 1.6 per cent. The current account deficit averaged only about 1.0 per cent of GDP during the last decade (1992-2002), as compared with 1.8 per cent in the 1980s, and recorded a surplus in 2001-2002 after a period of 23 years. Among the components of current account, while the trade deficit (BoP basis) declined marginally from 3.2 per cent of GDP during the 1980s to 3.0 per cent during 1992-2002, the invisibles surplus increased significantly from 1.4 per cent of GDP to 2.1 per cent over the same period . With the narrowing of the current account deficit in the recent years, there is a need for revisiting the issue of sustainability of current account in the Indian context.

It has been noted that developing countries typically run CAD in their early stages of development to supplement their domestic saving to achieve higher level of investment and growth. This process enables recipient countries to achieve higher growth without cutting their current consumption; at the same time, higher productivity of capital in developing countries benefits foreign lenders by earning higher returns on their capital. This raises the question of an optimal CAD level for a country which, however, needs to be circumscribed by a sustainable level of capital flows. The external payments problems faced by India in 1991 and the East Asian crisis in 1997 have highlighted, *inter alia*, the role of large current account deficits and the consequent build-up of external debt, in precipitating the crisis.

6. Ibid.

Capital Account

Capital inflows can be classified by instrument (debt or equity) and maturity (short-term or long-term). The main components of capital account include foreign investment, loans and banking capital. Foreign investment comprising foreign direct investment and portfolio investment represents non-debt liabilities, while loans (external assistance, external commercial borrowings and trade credit) and banking capital including non-resident Indian deposits are debt liabilities.[7]

Capital inflows, as a proportion of GDP, were on an uptrend during 2003-04 to 2007-08. They reached a high of 9.3 per cent of GDP in 2007-08 after a modest growth of 3.1 per cent in 2005-06 and 5.1 per cent in 2006-07. Capital inflows were lower at 1.8 per cent of GDP during 2008-09 (April-December) due to the global financial crisis.[8]

Net capital flows rose from a level of US$ 45.2 billion in 2006-07 to US$ 108.0 billion in 2007-08, indicating a growth of 139 per cent, attributable to a significant rise in foreign investment in term of direct and portfolio investment, large inflow of banking capital and a quantum jump in loans, particularly short-term credit and external commercial borrowings (net). However, the net capital inflow during 2008-09 (April-December) was only US$ 15.3 billion.[9]

Capital Account Balance

The capital account surplus has increased over the years from US$ 24.9 billion (3.1 per cent of GDP) in 2005-06 to US$ 46.1 billion (5.1 per cent of GDP) in 2006-07 and further to US$ 109.1 billion (9.3 per cent of GDP) in 2007-08. Capital account balance of US$ 16.1 billion (1.8 per cent of GDP) during 2008-09 (up to Q3) represented a decline of 80.5 per cent from US$ 82.7 billion during the corresponding period in 2007-08.[10]

During Q3 of 2008-09, the capital account balance turned negative indicating a net outflow of US$ 3.7 billion, as against an inflow of US$ 31.0 billion in Q3 of 2007-08 attributable to net outflow under portfolio investment, banking capital and short-term trade credit.

---

7. Ibid.
8. Ibid.
9. Ibid.
10. Ibid.

External Debt

India's external debt stock at US$ 224.77 billion (Rs. 8,98,750 crore) at end-March 2008 recorded an increase of US$ 53.44 billion over end-March 2007. Of the total increase, long-term debt accounted for US$ 34.6 billion and short-term debt was higher by US$ 18.9 billion.

During 2008-09 up to December 2008, total external debt increased further by US$ 6.1 billion (2.7 per cent) to US$ 230.8 billion (Rs. 11,18,565 crore). Long-term debt at US$ 183.4 billion at end-December 2008 posted an increase of US$ 5.6 billion and accounted for 79.4 per cent of the total external debt (79.1 per cent at end-March 2008). Short-term debt increased marginally to US$ 47.5 billion at the end of December 2008 and constituted 20.6 per cent of the total external debt (20.9 per cent at end-March 2008).

Commercial borrowings emerged as the largest component of external debt, with its share increasing from 27.8 per cent at end-March 2008 to 28.7 per cent at end-December 2008. Non-resident Indian deposits accounted for 17.5 per cent of the total external debt, followed by multilateral debt (17.3 per cent), bilateral debt (9.3 per cent), export credit (6.0 per cent) and rupee debt (0.7 per cent). Under the short-term debt, trade related credits at US$ 43.8 billion constituted 92.1 per cent of total short-term debt and 18.9 per cent of total external debt at the end of December 2008.

Government (sovereign) external debt at US$ 56.9 billion at end-March 2008 registered an increase of 17.8 per cent over end-March 2007 and increased marginally to US$ 57.4 billion at the end of December 2008. However, sovereign debt as per cent of GDP declined from 5.1 per cent in 2006-07 to 4.8 per cent in 2007-08 and its share in total external debt fell from 28.2 per cent at end-March 2007 to 25.3 per cent at end-March 2008 and further to 24.8 per cent at end-December 2008.[11]

India ranked sixth in terms of total external debt stock (at end-December 2008) among select developing countries. The ratio of short-term debt to total external debt stood at 20.6 per cent and it accounted for 18.5 per cent of total foreign exchange reserves at the end of December 2008. The ratio of external debt stock to gross national income as of 2007, as per World Development Indicators Database was 18.9 per cent and was the fourth lowest after that of China, Mexico and Brazil.[12]

11. Ibid.
12. Ibid.

Global Crisis

The world economy is going through an unprecedented crisis which started in the financial sector in the US but has now spread globally. What started off as a subprime crisis in the US housing mortgage sector has turned successively into a global banking crisis, global financial crisis and now a global economic crisis. It is the first financial crisis since the Great Depression that originated in the advanced economies and rapidly engulfed the whole world (Subbarao, 2009).[13] It is a crisis that started in the financial sector of what was thought of as the country with the most sophisticated financial system, and that has spread almost universally and with startling rapidity by virtue of either financial or trade interdependence or both (Subramanian and Williamson, 2009).[14]

Global Economic Outlook

Many economists are now predicting that this 'Great Recession' of 2008-09 will be the worst global recession since the 1930s.

Major world economies are in recession. In the last quarter of 2008, the US economy declined by more than 6 per cent a year, the Euro zone contracted by 1.5 per cent and Japan contracted at an unprecedented 12 per cent a year. Britain, Russia and Canada are in recession while the Chinese, Brazilian, South Korean and Indian economies have slowed down rapidly. Smaller economies like Spain, Mexico, Ireland, Iceland, Singapore, Greece, Ecuador, Hungary, Latvia, Pakistan and Ukraine are in deep trouble. This is in spite of massive bailout packages put together by various governments. The US alone, according to one estimate, has put together a package of more than $8.8 trillion and already spent $2 trillion (*New York Times,* 2009). The total commitment (not all spent) by all governments is in excess of $11 trillion (Kumar, 2009).[15]

The WTO estimates project a grim forecast that the global trade this year is likely to decline by 9 per cent in volume terms while the IMF has projected a decline of over 11 per cent. This recessionary trend has huge social implications. World Bank estimate suggests that 53 million more people would fall into the poverty net this year and over a billion people would go chronically hungry. Fortunately India has not been affected to the same extent as other economies of the world, but

13. Subbarao, D. (2008). "The Global Financial Turmoil and Challenges for the Indian Economy", *Economic Developments in India,* Vol. 132. New Delhi: Academic Foundation.
14. Subramanian, Arvind and John Williamson (2009). "The World Crisis: Reforms to Prevent a Recurrence", *Economic and Political Weekly* 13: 55-58, March 28.
15. Kumar, Arun (2009). "Tackling the Current Global Economic and Financial Crisis: Beyond Demand Management", *Economic and Political Weekly* 13: 151-157, March 28.

our exports have suffered a decline in the last 10 months due to contraction in demand in the traditional export markets. In this economic climate, some countries have resorted to protectionist measures posing barrier to free trade, which has aggravated the problem.

India's Response to World Economic Crisis

The Finance Minister has announced a series of measures which aim at stimulating economic growth through stimulus packages of 3.5 per cent of GDP. The Cash Reserve Ratio was reduced to 5 per cent and the Statutory Liquidity Ratio to 24 per cent and the Reverse Repo Rates and the Repo Rate were also slashed. Liquidity has also been infused in the market through SIDBI, NHB and EXIM Bank, and State Governments have been permitted to borrow an additional 0.5 per cent of their gross domestic product. These measures have had a salutary effect on our economy and we have seen some signs of recovery. The index of industrial production for the month of July has shown a growth of 7 per cent and the core sectors have also demonstrated a positive upward trend.

The New Foreign Trade Policy 2009-2014

Outlining the contours of the new Foreign Trade Policy (August 27, 2009), the Commerce Minister states[16], "Given the current economic climate, policy measures being outlined by me are for a two-year period, and thereafter we shall take stock for making mid course corrections. The immediate objective of this policy is to arrest and reverse the declining trend of exports and to provide additional support, especially to those sectors which have been hit badly by recession in the developed world. We would like to achieve an annual export growth of 15 per cent over 2010-11 with an annual export target of US$ 200 billion by March 2011. In the remaining three years of this Foreign Trade Policy, the country should be able to come back on the high export growth path of around 25 per cent per annum. By 2014, we expect to double India's exports of goods and services. The long term policy objective for the Government is to double India's share in global trade by 2020."

"In order to meet these objectives, the Government would provide a policy environment through a mix of measures including fiscal incentives, institutional changes, procedural rationalisation, and efforts for enhanced market access across the world and diversification of export markets. The three pillars which would support us to achieve

16. Speech by the Minister of Commerce & Industry on Foreign Trade Policy, August 27, 2009.

the targets are improvement in export related infrastructure, lowering of transaction costs and providing full refund of all indirect taxes and levies."

"In this policy we have given a special thrust to the employment oriented sectors which have witnessed job losses in the wake of recession especially in the field of textiles, leather, handicrafts, etc."

In the present economic climate, as the developed countries have shown a negative growth trend, it is intended to expand and diversify our export markets especially in the emerging markets of Africa, Latin America, Oceania and CIS countries. For this, we will have to offset the inherent disadvantages which our exporters face in these markets, such as credit risks and higher trade costs, through appropriate policy instruments.

In the era of global competitiveness, there is an imperative need for Indian exporters to upgrade their technology and reduce their costs. Accordingly, an important element of the Foreign Trade Policy is to help exporters for technological upgradation. Technological upgradation of exports is sought to be achieved by promoting imports of capital goods for certain sectors under EPCG at zero per cent duty.

Concluding Remarks

The external sector reform programme initiated in the wake of the balance of payments crisis of 1991 was all encompassing. Even though the reforms were largely crisis-led, the policy initiatives were unique in terms of their gradual, cautious and country-specific approach. As against balance of payments problems of varying intensities experienced during 1956-1991, India's balance of payments position strengthened over the 1990s even as the period coincided with the liberalisation of external account, external currency crises and domestic political uncertainties.

Prudent exchange rate management, low current account deficit, steady flow of non-debt creating capital flows, particularly in the form of FDI, a significant reduction in the external debt to GDP ratio and containment of short-term debt to manageable and prudent limits have been some of the positive outcomes of policy reform in the external sector. Resilience of the external sector has helped India successfully avert the contagion effects of the East Asian crisis.

The year 2008-09 was marked by adverse developments in the external sector of the economy, particularly during the second half of the year, reflecting the impact of global financial crisis on emerging market economies including India. Emerging economies were affected in varying degrees depending upon the extent of openness and the dependence on capital flows as the external environment deteriorated on account of slowdown in global demand, reversal of capital flows and reduced access to external sources of finance in the face of adverse global credit market conditions.

The external sector of the Indian economy exhibited resilience despite sharp deceleration in net capital flows during 2008-09 (April-December), which turned negative during October-December 2008. The impact of slowdown in export demand was partly offset by lower oil imports bill during October-December 2008 due to decline in the prices of crude oil in the international markets. The non-oil imports also moderated, following decline in commodity prices. The invisible receipts, particularly remittances and software services remained higher during April-December 2008 than the corresponding period last year. India remained an attractive investment destination as FDI flows on net basis (inward FDI-outward FDI) more than doubled to US $ 15.4 billion during April-December 2008 (US $ 6.9 billion during April-December 2007). The comfortable foreign exchange reserves position also alleviated the impact of global crisis on the external sector of the economy (Economic Survey, 2008-09).

Questions

1. Write short note on: Balance of Payments Problems in India. *[B.A .2001; B.Com 2008]*

2. Distinguish between 'balance of trade' and 'balance of payments'. Point out the reasons for adverse balance of payments situation in India. *[B.Com 2008]*

3. Discuss the balance of payments position of India since 1980s. Examine the new export-import policy in this respect. *[B.Com. (P) 2007]*

4. Explain the causes of deficit in our Balance of Payments. How far can export promotion help in solving this problem? *[B.A. (P) 2006]*

5. Write short note on 'limitations of import substitution'. *[B.Com. (P) 2006]*

6. Distinguish between 'balance of trade' and 'balance of payments'. Briefly point out the main reasons for India's adverse balance of payments situation. What remedial measures have been undertaken by the Government in this regard?
[B.A. (P) External+Correspondence, 2006]

7. What are the causes of adverse balance of payments in India? Will effective export promotion measures be able to solve the problem? Explain. *[B.A. (P) 2005]*

8. Write short note on 'Tariff or Import duty'. *[B.Com. (P) 2005]*

9. Examine the different methods adopted in India to solve the problem of balance of payments disequilibrium in India.
[B.Com. (P) 2005]

10. Explain the relevance of export promotion and import substitution as measures to control the deficit in the balance of payment of India in recent years. *[B.A. (P) 2004]*

11. What are the causes of adverse balance of payments in India? Suggest measures for reducing it. *[B.Com. (P) 2004]*

12. Explain the relevance of export promotion and import substitution as measures to control the deficit in the balance of payment of India in recent years. *[B.Com. (P) Correspondence, 2004]*

13. How will you differentiate between balance of trade and balance of payments? What remedial measures have been undertaken by the Government of India to correct adverse balance of payment problem in the country? *[B.Com. (P) 2003]*

14. Do you think that the solution to India's balance of payments problem lies more in export promotion than in import substitution? Analyse your answer in the light of India joining WTO (World Trade Organisation). *[B.A. (P) 2003]*

15. Write a short note on Import Substitution vs. Export Promotion.
[B.A. (P) 2003]

16. Explain the concept of balance of payments. What measures have been adopted by the government to solve the persistent balance of payments problem in India? *[B.Com. (P) 2000]*

22

India and the WTO

World Trade Organization

THE World Trade Organization (WTO) is an international organisation that oversees the operation of the rules-based multilateral trading system. The WTO is based on a series of trade agreements negotiated during the Uruguay Round (1986-1994), the eighth and final trade round conducted under the General Agreement on Tarriffs and Trade (GATT). The Treaty of Marrakesh established the WTO at the close of the Uruguay Round in 1994. The WTO began operations on January 1, 1995, it was comprised of 148 members. The WTO is one of the big three international organisations that oversee economic relations among nations, joining the International Monetary Fund (IMF) and the World Bank. The WTO's headqurters is located in Geneva, Switzerland.

The WTO's main function is to monitor and enforce trade rules in the global economy. The WTO administers the complex trade agreements listed in the WTO agreement. Article 1 of the WTO agreement, the General Agreement on Tariffs and Trade, deals with rules of merchandise trade. The General Agreement on Tariffs and Trade in Article 1 is often called GATT 1994 to distinguish it from the orginal GATT agreement of 1947. Article 2, the General Agreement on Trade in Services (GATS), pertains to the trade of commercial services. Article 4, the Agreement on Trade-Related Aspect of Intellectual Property (TRIPS), provides uniform legal protections for scientific, technological and artistic achievements. In addition, the WTO is a forum for trade negotiations, a dispute settlement mechanism, a source of technical expertise on trade and development for the world's poorer countries and a sister organisation to the World Bank and IMF. Unlike the World Bank and IMF, the WTO does not make loans to countries.

The WTO inherited many of GATT's guiding principles. These fundamental principles are incorporated in the numerous agreements that comprise the Agreement Establishing the World Trade Organization. In its *Understanding the WTO* (2003), the World Trade Organization identified five core principles.

The first principle is "trade without discrimination," which involves most-favoured-nation (MFN) status and national treatment. MFN states that a trade concession granted to one WTO member automatically applies to all members. National treatment guarantees equal treatment of imported goods with domestically produced output in nations' markets.

The second principle is freer trade through the progressive liberalisation of trade regimes.

The third principle is the predictability of trade rules. Predictability, in this context, prevents governments from arbitrarily raising existing tariffs or non-tarriff trade barriers.

The fourth principle is fair competition. Fair competition attempts to level the playing field in international trade and minimise the market distortions caused by export subsidy, dumping and other disruptive trade practices.

The fifth principle is economic development through trade. Economic development for the world's poorer countries should be enhanced by trade assistance and increased market access through preferential trade arrangements.

The WTO's dispute settlement process is the enforcement arm of the organisation. The WTO's apparatus for dispute settlement is stronger and more defined than GATT's dispute settlement procedures. The WTO's dispute settlement process is the essence of multilateralism. That is, a country or group of countries can air trade grievances in a global forum. A trade complaint is made to the WTO's Dispute Settlement Body (DSB), which consists of the entire WTO membership. The DSB, in turn, establishes a panel of three to five experts to hear the evidence and render a ruling. The panel's ruling can only be reversed by a unanimous vote of the DSB. Under normal conditions, the entire process takes one year or less to complete. One or both sides in the dispute can appeal the panel's decision. A seven-member Appellate Body considers an appeal and renders a decision. Again, only a unanimous vote of the DSB can reverse the Appellate Body's ruling. The appellate process could add as much as three months to the dispute settlement process. A member country found guilty breaking WTO trade rules is required to correct the violation with due speed. The DSB is empowered to initiate retaliatory tariffs or other trade sanctions for non-compliance with a WTO ruling.

India and the WTO

India was one of the 23 founding contracting parties to the General Agreement on Tariffs and Trade (GATT) that was concluded in October 1947. India has often led groups of less developed countries in subsequent rounds of multilateral trade negotiations (MTNs) under the auspices of the GATT.

In the last round (8th) of the multinational trade negotiation under the auspices of the GATT, the World Trade Organization was created to subsume the GATT in 1995. Even after the inception of WTO in 1995, till the Doha Ministerial (2001), the developing countries were not very active at the negotiating table. It is indeed ironic, as free trade is much more favourable for a developing country than its developed counterparts. However, a new trend emerged from Cancun (2003) onwards and since then, the former group has become much more vocal at the multilateral trade forums on the protectionist policies of the latter.

Despite being a founder member of GATT, India was never very active in various negotiating rounds until late eighties. Since the Indian economy followed the import substitution-led growth strategy during sixties and seventies, gaining from the import liberalisation at principal export markets (the EU and US) was never a prime objective. In addition, a considerable proportion of India's trade was directed to the Soviet bloc countries, and the presence of this assured market weakened the incentive to search for newer outlets. On the other hand, opening the domestic market to foreign competition through progressive tariff cuts was perceived harmful for the local industries. Instead, the country was more willing to discuss trade and development related issues at UNCTAD forums in collaboration with other developing countries like Brazil (primarily through the G-77 network). Despite adoption of a proactive approach at WTO, India still feels comfortable to discuss trade-related issues at UNCTAD forums for coalition building among developing countries on areas pertaining to mutual interest.

India's Participation in WTO Meetings

Table 22.1 illustrates India's participation in WTO meetings (Sengupta *et al.*, 2006).[1]

1. Sengupta, Dipankar, Debashis Chakraborty and Pritam Banerjee (eds.) (2006). "India at the WTO: The Story so Far", in *Beyond the Transition Phase of WTO: An Indian Perspective on Emerging Issues*. New Delhi: Academic Foundation in association with Centre de Sciences Humaines.

TABLE – 22.1

INDIA AT THE WTO MEETINGS

No. of Ministerial	Place of Occurrence	Year	Outcome	India's Role
1.	Singapore	1996	Information Technology Agreement was signed. In addition, four new issues were discussed, Trade and Investment, Competition Policy, Transparency in Government Procurement, and Trade Facilitation.	Mere presence.
2.	Geneva	1998	Global E-commerce Agreement was signed. Also, the implementation issues were discussed.	Mere presence.
3.	Seattle	1999	The negotiations failed as several developed countries wanted to incorporate environmental and labour-standard related issues under the wings of WTO. The move was strongly opposed by developing countries.	Was vocal against introduction of environmental and labour-standard related issues under WTO.
4.	Doha	2001	A new round was launched and the concerns for developing countries like India (e.g. TRIPS and Public Health) were attended. The market access and implementation issues were also given due notice.	Mostly singled out in its protest. However, made its presence and position felt for the first time.
5.	Cancun	2003	The members could not arrive at a common viewpoint even on the last date of the conference. The ministerial decided to take stock of progress in negotiations and other work under the Doha Development Agenda. The developing country solidarity at the ministerial was formed for the first time.	Actively protested against EU-US draft on agriculture jointly with other developing countries.
6.	Geneva	2004	Five member countries came forward to create an atmosphere for initiating multilateral negotiations once again.	Played a constructive role in the process while protecting developing countries' interests.
7.	Hong Kong	2005	Resulted in a much more acceptable Ministerial Declaration as compared to one circulated at Cancun but yet to reach their goal—reduction in agriucltural subsidisation level in developed countries. Witnessed a North-South divide, with G20 and G90 coming together as G110 to push the development agenda of Doha Work Programme.	Played an active role in the deliberations for protecting developed countries interest.

Source: Compiled from WTO Ministerial Declarations and other documents.

The most important factor responsible for enhancing India's participation in WTO negotiations was the outcome of the dispute settlement cases involving her. In general, the period between 1995 and 1998 witnessed a substantial rise in the number of cases in WTO's dispute settlement mechanism. India was among one of the victims of this provision as a number of developed countries moved to the dispute settlement body complaining about the WTO-compatibility of Indian policies.

In the Seattle Ministerial (1999), India was vocal at the multilateral forum for the first time, protesting against a developed country initiative to incorporate labour and environmental standards under the aegis of the WTO. Due to the protests of the developing countries, the developed countries were not successful in incorporating this element in the agenda. The Ministerial meeting ultimately ended in failure as the members could not arrive at a mutually agreeable solution. The then Commerce Minister Mr. Maran viewed the Seattle outcome as a success for India as for the first time, developing and poorer countries were united in mutual interest.

During the Seattle-Doha period, India, for the first time, started communicating its dissatisfaction over several issues and sharing its position with other countries at various appropriate forums of WTO and other international bodies. Broadly speaking, a clearly distinguishable and proactive stand emerged before the Doha ministerial, and India became particularly concerned with: (i) non-realisation of anticipated benefits (e.g., Agreement on Textiles and Clothing and Agreement on Agriculture), (ii) inequities and imbalances in WTO (TRIPSs, Subsidies, Anti-dumping, etc.), and (iii) non-binding nature of special and differential provisions (market access, DSB, etc.). In short, India strongly objected to the inclusion of any new issue in the negotiating agenda before realisation of Uruguay round promises, the non-implementation of which was costly to developing countries.

Buoyed by the success achieved at Doha, India tried to utilise the two-year period before Cancun in a much productive manner and coalition-formation experience with other developing countries were fruitful not only for general agreements that affected merchandise and services trade, but also in case of institutional arrangements like dispute settlement. The movement towards a proactive strategy at the WTO was accompanied towards implementing an increasingly WTO compatible regime at home and frustration mounted at not obtaining the desired level of market access in principal export destinations. In Cancun, India principally negotiated over liberalisation of agricultural trade and trade in services.

If we are to measure the trajectory of India's learning curve by a sector-by-sector basis, two areas stand out immediately. The first is anti-dumping, where India has transformed itself from the major affected country to an aggressor becoming quick to intiate investigations. While in the mid-nineties, it was one of the major affected countries, during the last two years, it has topped the list by being the initiator of the maximum number of anti-dumping investigations.

The second area where India has evolved is with regards to its outlook towards regional trading arrangements. Not too long back, India was unhappy with the growth of regional trade agreements, which was constraining its market access. However, from 2003 onwards, i.e., from Cancun days, it has initiated negotiations on preferential access with a number of developing countries, which would clearly help it in guaranteeing an assured export market on one hand, and an ally in future negotiations on the other.

It is pertinent to point out what the WTO does for India—by supplementing India's internal market with global market it offers India the opportunity to utilise its most abundant factor labour, both skilled as well as not so skilled. It also:

- offers India the opportunity to supplement its meagre capital with investment from the rest of the world to enhance growth, and
- allows Indian entrepreneurs to plan for global markets given the fact that their export destinations have to be governed by laws that are WTO compatible and thus, are rule based and not run by administrative fiat.

However, the Doha round of free-trade talks collapsed on July 24, 2006 after nearly five years of haggling. It has been reported, "The suspension of WTO's Doha round came after a 14-hour marathon meeting of the group of 6 failed in a last-ditch attempt to overcome differences on farm trade". The G-6 comprises the US, the EU, Japan, Brazil, India and Australia. The EU and India accused US of "Stone-walling" by demanding too high a price for cutting the $20-billion it spends on farm subsidies. EU trade commissioner Peter Mandelson said, "Surely, the richest and strongest nation in the world, with the highest standards of living, can afford to give as well as take." But the US was adamant and neither the EU nor India were prepared to offer the sort of access to their markets that Washington needed to make a deal on subsidies worthwhile. The commerce minister (Kamal Nath) remarked, "Developing countries could not permit their farmers to lose their livelihoods and food security to provide market access to subsidised agriculture products from developed countries."[2]

After the suspension in negotiations during July 2006 due to the wide gaps in the positions of WTO members, especially on agricultural domestic support and market access, there was a soft resumption of negotiations on November 16, 2006. Subsequently there was full-scale resumption of negotiations on February 7, 2007, on the principles that it preserves the architecture of the negotiations, inclusiveness and the progress made so far, and leads to an outcome that is balanced, ambitious and pro-development.

While safeguarding the interests of India's low income and resource poor agricultural producers (which cannot be traded off against any gains elsewhere in the negotiations) remains paramount for India, making real gains in services negotiations where it is a demander is no less important. In the case of industrial tariffs, India's growth and development concerns need to be addressed where India has taken a stand along with NAMA-11 coalition.

WTO Negotiations and India[3]

The year 2008-09 saw an intensive process of negotiation following the resumption of the Doha Round of talks in February 2007. A mini-ministerial meeting was held from July 21-29, 2008 in the WTO to discuss the modalities in agriculture and non-agricultural market access (NAMA). In agriculture, the issues discussed included reductions in overall trade distorting domestic support by developed countries, tariff cuts, designation of sensitive products, special products, the special safeguard mechanism (SSM) for developing countries, etc. While in the end, discussion focused almost exclusively on the SSM which could not be resolved, this was not the only contentious issue. Several issues in agriculture and NAMA were not discussed at all and remained unresolved.

The Doha Round of WTO negotiation is a development round and development concerns are at the core of the round. The major issues for negotiations are related to agricultural negotiations, NAMA, services negotiations and rules negotiations. In the context of recent

---

2. *The Financial Express*, July 25, 2006.
3. Government of India (2009). *Economic Survey* 2008-09.

developments, self-designation of an appropriate number of special products (SPs) to take care of India's food security, livelihood security and rural development needs were considered in the revised draft text of December 6, 2008. It proposes an average tariff cut of 11 per cent for a 12 per cent of total tariff lines to be designated as SPs with 5 per cent of tariff lines taking zero or no tariff cuts. Although the issue was discussed during the mini-ministerial meeting, there are a number of elements yet to be resolved to the full satisfaction of India and its coalition partners in the G-33.

G-20

The leaders of G-20 met in London on April 2, 2009 at the backdrop of the worst economic and financial crisis, a crisis which has deepened further since the Washington Summit held on November 15, 2008.

India has strongly emphasised the need to continue with coordinated contracyclical policies within an overall framework of fiscal sustainability and restoration of the banking system in the industrialised countries to full functionality; to avoid protectionist sentiments in the trade of both goods and services emerging in the industrialised economies in the backdrop of global financial crisis; and to take concrete steps to ensure adequate credit flows, including trade finance, to developing countries for which it is imperative to raise resources of the international financial institutions (IMF, World Bank, ADB), and to bring forward the quota review in the IMF.

Further, India has stressed upon the need for longer term reform of the global financial architecture including increasing the representation of developing and emerging market economies; reform of the global financial system through stronger regulation and improved supervision.

For *resisting protectionism and promoting global trade and investment,* members have committed to refrain from raising new barriers to investment or to trade in goods and services, imposing new export restrictions, or implementing World Trade Organization (WTO) inconsistent measures to stimulate exports and will not retreat into financial protectionism, particularly measures that constrain worldwide capital flows, especially to developing countries.

To conclude, while India, so far, may not have been able to gain a lot from the negotiations, it certainly came out of seclusion during the Doha Ministerial (2001) and is currently leading the developing country coalitions at WTO. Furthermore, expansion of the negotiating agenda (e.g., environmental services) in recent years depicts an evolving learnig curve, which is no less important. A similar 'learning through trading' is observed in the case of several other developing countries as well. On the other hand, the aversion of several developed countries towards ensuring free trade is becoming quite obvious in recent years.

Questions

1. Write short note on India and the WTO.
2. What is WTO? Comment on India's participation in WTO meetings.

23

Prices
Monetary and Fiscal Policies

Measurement of General Price Level

THE variation in the price level in India can be measured in terms of the Wholesale Price Index (WPI), or the implicit National Income Deflator (NID) or the Consumer Price Index (CPI). The WPI is the main measure of the rate of inflation often used in India. The WPI is available for all commodities, and for major groups, sub-groups and individual commodities. The basic advantage of this measure of inflation is its availability at high frequency, i.e., on weekly basis with a gap of about two weeks, thereby enabling continuous monitoring of the price situation for policy purposes. This index does not cover non-commodity producing sectors *viz.*, services and non-tradable commodities.

The national income deflator, on the other hand, is a comprehensive measure but statistically derived from national accounts data released by the Central Statistical Organisation (CSO) as a ratio of GDP at current prices to GDP at constant prices. Since it encompasses the entire spectrum of economic activities including services, the scope and coverage of national income deflator is wider than any other measure. At present, the GDP deflator is available only annually with a long lag of over one year and hence, has very limited use for the conduct of policy.[1]

The important measure at the point of consumption is the Consumer Price Index for Industrial Workers (CPI-IW) which is meant to reflect the cost of living conditions and is computed on the basis of the changes in the level of retail prices of selected goods and services on which a

1. Reddy, Y.V. (1999). "Inflation in India: Status and Issues", *RBI Bulletin*, October.

homogeneous group of consumers spend the major part of their income. Its coverage is broader than the other indices of CPI for Agricultural Labourers (AL) and the CPI for Urban Non-Manual Employees (UNME). Besides, CPI-AL and CPI-UNME are not considered as robust national inflation measures because they are designed for specific groups of population with the main purpose of measuring the impact of price rise on rural and urban poverty.

Of these three, the urban industrial workers price index is generally used for determination of dearness allowance of urban salaried workers—government as well as private. This price index, however, measures cost of living of lowest category of wage earners.

While each of the measures has its advantages as well as weaknesses, the selected measure of inflation should broadly capture the interplay of effective demand and supply forces in the economy at frequent intervals. This will be facilitated if the price indices have a high periodicity of release, and it is in this sense that WPI is superior to CPI. WPI's coverage of commodities is also high. While services do not come under the ambit of WPI, the coverage of non-agricultural products is better in WPI than CPI, making WPI less volatile to relative price changes as against the CPI. The coverage of tradable items, essentially manufactured products (weight = 57.06 per cent) is higher in the case of WPI whereas the coverage of non-tradables like services pertaining to education, medical care and recreation are more in the case of CPI-IW.

The choice of WPI as a headline measure appears justifiable on grounds of convenience as well as analytical reasoning. First, the WPI with a weekly frequency has just a two weeks lag as against the monthly frequency of CPI-IW with a lag of two months. Secondly, the commodity coverage in WPI is wider than that in CPI. Thirdly, WPI is computed on all-India basis whereas CPI is just constructed for specific centres and then aggregated to get the all-India index. Because of this feature WPI is more easily understood.

Review of Inflationary Trends in India

During the fifties, the average decadal rate of inflation was very low at 1.7 per cent, with the rate varying in a wide range from a negative value of 12.5 per cent to a positive value of 13.8 per cent. The minimum inflation at a negative rate in 1952-53 was in response to the bumper agricultural production in that year while the maximum inflation rate in 1956-57 was mainly attributed to demand pressures, especially investment demand, both public and private.

During the sixties, the average decadal inflation edged up to 6.4 per cent. The inflationary pressures started mounting from 1962-63, on account of the Chinese War in 1962 and unsatisfactory supply position. The Pakistan War in 1965, and the famine conditions during 1965-66 aggravated the situation further. The maximum inflation at 13.9 per cent was recorded for the year 1966-67, but the minimum inflation rate of (-) 1.1 per cent was in 1968-69 attributed primarily to the bumper agricultural production in the preceding year.

The average inflation rate during the seventies was still higher at 9.0 per cent. The maximum inflation recorded in the year 1974-75 at 25.2 per cent was mainly attributed to the failure of *kharif* crops in 1972-73 as also to the hike in crude oil prices in 1973. The minimum inflation rate for the decade at (-) 1.1 per cent was recorded in the following year, i.e. 1975-76, in response to the substantive anti-inflationary measures taken by the government. The year 1979-80, however, witnessed a strong resurgence of inflationary tendencies mainly due to poor agricultural output and the second hike in international oil prices. The decade was the most tumultuous as far as the price situation was concerned.

During the eighties, the decadal average inflation moved down somewhat to 8.0 per cent. What is more significant is that variation in prices was small as compared to any of the preceding decades. The highest inflation rate for the decade was at 18.2 per cent in 1980-81 and the minimum inflation rate was at 4.4 per cent for 1985-86.

The Period of 90s

The first half of the 1990s saw a sharp increase in inflation. The decade began with double digit inflation attributable to the large-scale monetisation of fiscal deficits. This was intensified by hikes in procurement prices as well as supply-demand imbalances in essential commodities like pulses, oilseeds and edible oils. The severe foreign exchange shortage that the country faced at the time constrained the ability of the authorities to augment the supply position through imports and also contributed to inflationary pressures. Increases in fuel prices and other administered items also fed higher inflation. The inflationary pressures continued during 1993-94 and 1994-95 in the wake of unprecedented capital inflows and the consequent higher monetary expansion. The focus of monetary policy, therefore, shifted to the moderation of money supply with the objective of containing inflation to create an enabling environment for the process of structural adjustment.

The second half of the 1990s was marked by a significant turnaround in the inflation outcome. The inflation rate declined from an average of 11.0 per cent during 1990-1995 to 5.3 per cent during the second half of the 1990s.

Box 23.1 highlights the trends in inflation rate since the mid-1950s.

BOX – 23.1

FIVE-YEAR AVERAGE INFLATION RATE

Though on an average, inflation based on the WPI remained below the 7 per cent level through the 1950s and 1960s, it accelerated during the first half of the 1970s to touch double digit figures but decelerated in the second half of 1970s as also through the 1980s. Four out of the first five years of the 1990s registered double digit inflation, with a 13.7 per cent peak reached in 1992-93.

5-year Average Annual Inflation Rate

(Per cent)

Period	52-week Annual Average
1956-57 to 1960-61	5.3
1961-62 to 1965-66	5.8
1966-67 to 1970-71	6.7
1971-72 to 1975-76	12.0
1976-77 to 1980-81	8.5
1981-82 to 1985-86	6.5
1986-87 to 1990-91	7.8
1991-92 to 1995-96	10.6
1996-97 to 2000-01	5.1

During the post-reforms period, inflation has had a distinct decelerating trend as liberalisation of both internal and external trade and continual reduction and rationalisation of taxes has led to greater competition and cost-efficiency. Average annual WPI inflation decelerated from 10.6 per cent in the first half of 1990s to 5.1 per cent during the second half 1996-2001 by far the lowest (Box 23.1).

In recent years, supply side factors have been more instrumental in determining the direction and magnitude of price rise. The occurrence of drought, decline in agricultural production, increase in global crude oil prices, supply shortages and increased international prices of imported commodities like crude oil, steel and edible oils are some of the factors that have played a crucial role in fueling inflation in the recent past. Imported inflation has therefore, a crucial role to play in setting the direction of domestic inflation.

Recent Trends 2000-01 to 2008-09

The inflation trends by broad commodity groups for each of the years beginning from 2000-01 to 2008-09 are given in Table 23.1. The 52-week averages show that inflation in 2000-01, 2004-05 and 2008-2009 had been above the 6 per cent threshold with 2008-09 recording the highest average in the current decade. In contrast, annual inflation as on end-March 2009 recorded the lowest rate of 0.8 per cent overall and negative inflation of 6.1 per cent in the fuel and power group. Similarly, 2006-07 and 2007-08 stand out with inflation (at end March) in primary articles in the band of 10-11 per cent, though the 52-week average was only in the range of 5 (+)/(-) 0.5 per cent.

TABLE – 23.1

ANNUAL WPI INFLATION RATE (%) (BASE: 1993-94 = 100)

Year	*March end Annual Inflation Rate (Per cent)*				*52-week Avg. (All Items)*	*Range of Inflation during 52 Weeks*
	Primary Articles	*Fuel, Power, Light & Lubri.*	*Manu-factured Products*	*All Commodities*		
Weights (Per cent)	22.02	14.23	63.75	100.00	100.00	100.00
2000-01	1.5	15.1	4.0	5.5	7.2	4.9 - 8.8
2001-02	3.9	3.9	0.0	1.6	3.6	1.1 - 5.6
2002-03	6.1	10.8	5.1	6.5	3.4	1.4 - 6.5
2003-04	1.6	2.5	6.7	4.6	5.5	3.8 - 6.9
2004-05	1.3	10.5	4.6	5.1	6.5	4.3 - 8.7
2005-06	5.4	8.9	1.7	4.1	4.4	3.3 - 6.0
2006-07	10.7	1.0	6.1	5.9	5.4	3.7 - 6.7
2007-08	9.7	6.8	7.3	7.8	4.7	3.1 - 8.0
2008-09	5.2	-6.1	1.7	0.8	8.4	0.7 - 12.9

Source : D/o Indl Policy & Promotion
Economic Survey 2008-09.

WPI inflation declined gradually from 6.3 per cent in April 2007 to 3.1 per cent in October 2007 and began to climb upwards thereafter to end at 7.5 per cent at the close of the fiscal year 2007-08. The year 2008-09 saw the uptrend continuing from 8.0 per cent in April 2008 to a peak of 12.8 per cent in August 2008, followed by a reduction to 11.0 per cent in October 2008, 4.9 per cent in January 2009 and 1.2 per cent in March 2009.

The high domestic inflation in the first half of the year 2008-09 mirrored the inflation that prevailed in the global economy, driven by progressively rising prices of crude, which touched a record US$ 147 in July 2008, as well as of metal prices.

From August 2008, inflation decelerated in the global economy, triggered by the financial crisis which surfaced in September 2008 in the United States and which spread rapidly across the globe. The corresponding fall in the domestic WPI inflation began from September 2008, with the downward impetus gathering momentum with the passage of time and reaching a level of 1 per cent in March 2009.

Consequences of Inflation

Economists often argue that a mild dose of inflation is good for an economy. When prices steadily rise at a rate of 2-3 per cent per annum, favourable climate is created for investment which eventually results in larger income and fuller employment. But the way prices had risen in India over a period of more than four decades, has done more harm than good to the economy and the people. This not only inflicted sufferings on the masses, but also disrupted the developmental efforts time and again.

Increase in Economic Inequalities: When prices rise continuously over a long period, inequalities of income and wealth increase. People with fixed income find that inflation results in erosion of their purchasing power. Producers and traders, on the contrary, earn huge profits. This process if not immediately arrested, wipes out even the lifetime savings of the people whose money incomes are more or less fixed, and the wealth of the country gets concentrated in the hands of traders and producers. The worst sufferer in the whole process have been the agricultural workers who are least organised in this country. With no alternative opportunities, their bargaining power is very little. Big farmers, industrialists and traders have benefited the most from this inflationary price rise.

Hampers Development: The continuous price rise during the planning period has turned out to be an obstacle to development. This is particularly due to the rigidity about plan outlays. When a plan is finalised and outlay determined, it is generally not revised even if it becomes necessary due to upward movement of prices. This approach invariably leads to non-completion of projects in the required period. Continuously rising prices in India in the past have discouraged savings.

According to C. Rangarajan[2], an important issue that arises in the context of development is "whether there is a trade-off between economic growth and inflation. In the short run perhaps there is such a trade-off. Some of the econometric models for India indicate the existence of a trade-off but at a heavy cost. A higher growth rate can be achieved only at the cost of a fairly high inflation rate. Over a long period, growth cannot be bought with the aid of higher prices. On the other hand, it is price stability which provides a better environment in which growth can occur and social justice can be ensured."

Adverse Effects on the Balance of Payments: Although since the World War II, inflation has been a worldwide phenomenon, prices in India have risen more sharply than in most of the other countries. This created two problems in this country from the point of view of balance of payments. First, the demand for India's products declined in foreign markets and the task of increasing exports became more difficult. Moreover, in the home market the profitability increased and as such even the producers had little interest in stepping up exports. Secondly, Indian importers, finding that foreign goods were cheaper, tried to increase imports. The government, however, introduced various control measures to restrict non-essential imports. Recently, the government has adopted the policy of import liberalisation making the task of reducing trade deficit difficult.

Inflation and Output Growth Rate

It is often conjectured that a mild inflation is conducive to growth. International evidence on inflation (p) and growth (g) across countries suggest that there is a trade-off between p and g; the countries with relatively faster growth rate also have relatively higher inflation rate and vice versa. Bhattacharya's study, however, shows a very weak relationship between inflation rate (p) and real GDP growth rate (g) in India. The correlation between annual g and annual p also turns out to be very poor (R^2 is –0.03).

Anti-inflationary Measures

Containment of inflation remains high on the agenda of the Government, as inflation hurts everybody, particularly the poor whose

2. Rangarajan, C. (2009). *India: Monetary Policy, Financial Stability and Other Essays*. New Delhi: Academic Foundation.

incomes are not indexed to prices. High inflation puts pressure on interest rates leading to a rise in project costs and investment. It also tends to reduce real interest rates, thereby adversely affecting the savings rate. Anti-inflationary policies of the Government include:

(i) strict fiscal and monetary discipline,

(ii) rationalisation of excise and import duties of essential commodities so that there is no undue burden on the poor,

(iii) effective supply-demand management of sensitive items through liberal tariff and trade policies, and

(iv) strengthening the public distribution system.

Monetary Policy

According to Rangarajan, "The broad objectives of monetary policy in India have been: (i) to maintain a reasonable degree of price stability and (ii) to help accelerate the rate of economic growth. The emphasis as between the two objectives has changed from year to year, depending upon the conditions prevailing in that year and in the previous year."[3]

The case of price stability as the objective of monetary policy rests on the assumption that volatility in prices creates uncertainty in decision-making. Rising prices adversely affect savings while they make speculative investments more attractive. The most important contribution of the financial system to an economy is its ability to augment savings and allocate resources more efficiently. A regime of rising prices vitiates the atmosphere for promotion of savings and allocation of investment. Apart from all these, there is a social dimension particularly in developing countries. Inflation adversely affects those who have no hedges against it and that includes all the poorer sections of the community. The fiscal consolidation also becomes easier in an environment of reasonable degree of price stability. In a period of rising prices, the gap between revenues and expenditures widens (Rangarajan and Arif (1990)). Expenditures tend to grow at a faster rate than revenues because many components of expenditures such as employees' compensation are closely linked to variations in prices.

Another way of reconciling the conflicting objectives of price stability and economic growth in the short run is through estimating the "threshold level of inflation". It is this inflation threshold which will provide some guidance to the policy makers. Below and around this

---

3. Rangarajan, C. *op cit*.

threshold level of inflation, there is greater maneuverability for the policy makers to take into account other considerations. Interestingly, the Chakravarty Committee regarded the acceptable rise in prices as 4 per cent. This, according to the Committee, will reflect changes in relative prices necessary to attract resources to growth sectors. According to Rangarajan, in the Indian context, inflation rate around 6 per cent may be acceptable.

The Reserve Bank has been using various quantitative and qualitative controls to control inflation. The various instruments that are used by the RBI are:

- Controlling money supply (M3)
- Increasing the bank rate
- Offering Government securities for sale in the open market
- Increasing CRR and SLR
- Rationing of consumer's credit
- Raising the margin requirements.

However, under the present circumstances, the monetary policy is subject to a number of institutional and other limitations. They are:

(a) The proportion of total credit provided by non-banking institutions and agencies is much higher and the linkages between banks and these other institutions are not so well-developed.

(b) There are inhibitions regarding frequent and sharp changes in the bank rate as these are supposed to conflict with development or equity objectives.

(c) With prolonged period of inflation, margin requirements against most of the commodities are so high that the scope for further increases is exremely limited.

(d) Credit restraints whenever they are imposed sometime hit most adversely the priority sectors of the economy.

Monetary Developments in 2008-09

Practitioners of monetary policy in India, as in other countries of the world, have faced an extraordinary economic situation in the recent past, calling for innovative solutions not only backed by economic theory and sophisticated mathematical models but also by initiatives to respond in time and even ahead of the time curve. While the task of monetary management by the RBI in India has centred around managing a judicious balance between price stability and sustaining the growth momentum, the global financial turmoil reinforced the importance of preserving financial stability through prudent regulatory surveillance and effective supervision. The current policy challenge, accordingly, was perceived as the need to strike an optimal balance between preserving financial stability, maintaining price stability, anchoring inflationary expectations, and at the same time sustaining the growth momentum.[4]

During financial year 2007-08 in the backdrop of increased capital inflows, changes in the policy rates mainly involved the cash reserve ratio (CRR) (which was increased by 150 basis points from 6.0 per cent as it prevailed on April 1, 2007 to 7.5 per cent w.e.f. November 10, 2007); the repo rate (RR) at 7.75 per cent and the reverse-repo rate (R-RR) at 6.0 per cent were left unchanged.[5]

Other Measures

Government had taken a number of measures covering a wide range of articles of mass consumption to enhance supply and availability. To augment availability of cereals, minimum support prices (MSP) have been systematically increased, leading to increased acreage, production, productivity and central procurement.

To avoid depletion of domestic food grains stock, the exports of wheat and non-*basmati* rice had been banned. Exports of pulses and edible oils had been banned, but branded consumer packs of 5 kgs or less can be exported up to 10,000 tonnes, while public sector undertakings were allowed to import pulses to enhance domestic availability, with reimbursement of losses up to 15 per cent. Customs duty on butter and *ghee* had been reduced to 30 per cent and 20 per cent import duty imposed on crude degummed soyabean oil from November 2008.

To maintain price stability, the central issue price for rice and wheat had not been revised since July 2002. The offtake by states for TPDS increased to 84.77 per cent in 2008-09. Further, with a view to augment domestic availability, import duties of rice, wheat, pulses, edible oils (crude) and maize, butter and *ghee* had been kept at zero; while those on refined and hydrogenated oils and vegetable oils had been reduced to 7.5 per cent. Vegetable oils imports increased in 2008-09 due to

4. Government of India. (2009). *Economic Survey* 2008-09.
5. Ibid.

reduced customs and import duties and a scheme was launched to distribute 1 MT of imported edible oils at a subsidised Rs. 15 per kg under PDS, with 1 kg per ration card per month. To check rising sugar prices, the Government allowed higher free-sale releases and additional allocations, stipulated monthly sale of fixed quantity of dismantled buffer stock, monitored open market sale with the central excise authorities, initiated proceedings against delinquent mills under Essential Commodities Act, 1955 and discontinued reimbursement of expenses earlier available for exports from October 2008.

Concluding Remarks

The domestic economy is currently witnessing the contagion effects of the global economic slowdown. It is necessary to ensure the continued sound health of the economy and the productive sectors through adequate liquidity and credit from the financial sector. The objective is to restore the economy to a high growth path consistent with price and financial stability.

In the first half of the fiscal year 2008-09, the inflationary pressure was on account of the momentum in the international commodity prices and the domestic prices of food items like cereals and pulses. The Government has been alert and responsive to situation as it unfolded and took the required administrative and fiscal measures in tandem with the monetary policy initiatives of the RBI, which bore fruit. Though agricultural imports by India are limited, the constraints in the global agricultural production might exacerbate the supply side concerns in India. There is need to address these concerns, particularly in the medium term through productivity gains and efficient supply management. The continued food inflation, could undermine inclusive growth, in particular, the efforts to combat poverty.

While risks from the uncertainties in the global financial markets continue to persist, there are some concerns on the domestic front as well. In respect of the monetary policy, the effort to maintain ample liquidity in the system, as some would argue, might be sowing the seeds of the next inflationary cycle. It would be important, therefore, to ensure that once economic growth picks up sufficient momentum, the excess liquidity is rolled back in an orderly manner. There is also the concern related to transmission channels, the lags and the impact of monetary policy changes on the financial and real sectors of the economy.

Questions

1. What are the causes of rise in price level in the last five years? What steps have been taken by the government to control prices? *[B.A. (P) 2009]*

2. What are the causes of rise in prices since 1980? Give suggestions to curb the price rise. *[B.Com. (P) Correspondence, 2006]*

3. Write short note on 'Consequences of Rising Prices in India'. *[B.A. (P) 2005]*

4. Write brief note on 'Causes of price rise in India'. *[B.Com. (P) 1999, 2004]*

5. Discuss the reasons for rise in prices in India in recent times. Suggest suitable measures to contain them. *[B.Com. (P) 2001]*